Foundations of SQL Server 2005 Business Intelligence

Lynn Langit

Apress®

Foundations of SQL Server 2005 Business Intelligence

Copyright © 2007 by Lynn Langit

ISBN-13 (pbk): 978-1-59059-834-4

ISBN-13 (electronic): 978-1-4302-0248-6

Printed and bound in the United States of America (POD)

Trademarked names may appear in this book. Rather than use a trademark symbol with every occurrence of a trademarked name, we use the names only in an editorial fashion and to the benefit of the trademark owner, with no intention of infringement of the trademark.

Lead Editor: James Huddleston
Technical Reviewer: Matthew Roche
Editorial Board: Steve Anglin, Ewan Buckingham, Gary Cornell, Jason Gilmore, Jonathan Gennick, Jonathan Hassell, James Huddleston, Chris Mills, Matthew Moodie, Jeff Pepper, Paul Sarknas, Dominic Shakeshaft, Jim Sumser, Matt Wade
Project Manager: Beth Christmas
Copy Edit Manager: Nicole Flores
Copy Editor: Julie McNamee
Assistant Production Director: Kari Brooks-Copony
Production Editor: Kelly Gunther
Compositor: Patrick Cunningham
Proofreader: Nancy Sixsmith
Indexer: Carol Burbo
Artist: April Milne
Cover Designer: Kurt Krames
Manufacturing Director: Tom Debolski

Distributed to the book trade worldwide by Springer-Verlag New York, Inc., 233 Spring Street, 6th Floor, New York, NY 10013. Phone 1-800-SPRINGER, fax 201-348-4505, e-mail orders-ny@springer-sbm.com, or visit http://www.springeronline.com.

For information on translations, please contact Apress directly at 2855 Telegraph Avenue, Suite 600, Berkeley, CA 94705. Phone 510-549-5930, fax 510-549-5939, e-mail info@apress.com, or visit http://www.apress.com.

Contents at a Glance

Contents

About the Author

LYNN LANGIT is the founder and lead architect of WebFluent, which for the past six years has trained users and developers in building BI solutions. A holder of numerous Microsoft certifications, including MCT, MCITP, MCDBA, MCSD.NET, MCSE, and MSF, she also has ten years of experience in business management. This unique background makes her particularly qualified to share her expertise in developing successful real-world BI solutions using SQL Server 2005. Lynn has recently joined Microsoft, working as a Developer Evangelist. She is based in the Southern California territory. For more information, read her blog at http://blogs.msdn.com/SoCalDevGal.

About the Technical Reviewer

MATTHEW ROCHE is the chief software architect of Integral Thought & Memory LLC, a training and consulting firm specializing in Microsoft business intelligence and software development technologies. Matthew has been delivering training on and implementing solutions with Microsoft SQL Server since version 6.5 and has been using SQL Server 2005 since its early beta releases. Matthew is a Microsoft Certified Trainer, Microsoft Certified Database Administrator, and a Microsoft Certified IT Professional Database Developer, Business Intelligence Developer, and Database Administrator. He also holds numerous other Microsoft and Oracle certifications. Matthew is currently involved in several consulting projects utilizing the full SQL Server 2005 BI toolset, Microsoft Office SharePoint Server 2007, and Office 2007.

Acknowledgments

Life is about people—my sincere thanks to the people who supported my efforts:

My technical editor, Matthew Roche. Your dedication and tenacity are much appreciated.

Sybil Earl, who gave me the freedom to make this possible and who introduced me to the world of SQL Server.

Chrys Thorsen, who gave me the last little "you can do it" push that I needed to get started with this project.

The "lab team" (otherwise known as the best trainers on earth): Karen Henderson, Beth Quinlan, Bob Tichelman, Cheryl Boelter, Barry Martin, Al Alper, Kim (Cheers!) Frank, and Anton Delsink. You all inspire me. I feel privileged to know and work with each one of you.

My two best friends, Lynn and Teri, what fun we have!

My daughter—no greater joy is possible. Thanks for the "writing schedule"—it worked! Mom, you are ALWAYS there for me. Dad, I wish you could've stuck around to see this one.

CHAPTER 1

■ ■ ■

What Is Business Intelligence?

This chapter presents a blueprint for understanding the exciting potential of SQL Server 2005's BI technologies to meet your company's crucial business needs. It describes tools, techniques, and high-level implementation concepts for BI.

This chapter covers:

- Defining Business Intelligence

- Understanding BI from an end-user perspective

- Understanding the business problems BI addresses

Just What Is BI?

Business Intelligence (BI) is defined in many ways. Often particular vendors "craft" the definition to show their tools in the best possible light. For the purposes of this book, Microsoft's vision of BI using SQL Server 2005 is defined as

> *Business Intelligence is a method of storing and presenting key enterprise data so that anyone in your company can quickly and easily ask questions of accurate and timely data. Effective BI allows end users to use data to understand why your business got the particular results that it did, to decide on courses of action based on past data, and to accurately forecast future results.*

> *BI data is displayed in a fashion that is appropriate to each type of user, i.e. analysts will be able to drill into detailed data, executives will see timely summaries, and middle managers will see data presented at the level of detail that they need to make good business decisions. Microsoft's BI uses cubes, rather than tables, to store information and presents information via reports. The reports can be presented to end users in a variety of formats: Windows applications, Web Applications, and Microsoft BI client tools, such as Excel or SQL Reporting Services.*

Figure 1-1 shows a sample of a typical BI physical configuration. You'll note that Figure 1-1 shows a Staging Database Server and a separate BI server. Although it is possible to place all components of BI on a single physical server, the configuration shown in the figure is the most typical for the small-to-medium BI projects that I've worked on. You may also need to include more servers in your project, depending on scalability and availability requirements. You'll learn more about these concepts in Chapter 13.

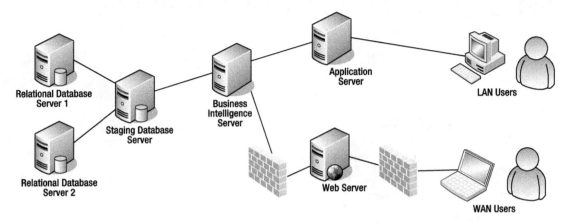

Figure 1-1. *An enterprise BI configuration*

In addition to the term *business intelligence*, there are several other terms commonly used in discussing the technologies depicted in Figure 1-1:

Data warehouse: A single structure that usually, but not always, consists of one or more cubes. Data warehouses are used to hold an aggregated, or rolled-up and read-only view, of the majority of an organization's data; sometimes this structure includes client query tools.

Tip Data warehousing is not new. The most often quoted spokespeople from the world of data warehousing theory are Bill Inmon and Ralph Kimball. Both have written many articles and books and have very popular Web sites talking about their experience with data warehousing solutions using products from many vendors.

To read more about Ralph Kimball's ideas on Data Warehouse design modeling, go to http:// www.ralphkimball.com. I prefer the Kimball approach to modeling (rather than the Inmon approach) and have had good success implementing Kimball's methods in production BI projects.

Data mart: A defined subset of a data warehouse, often a single cube from a group (see Figure 1-2). The single cube represents one business unit (for example, marketing) from a greater whole (that is, the entire company). Data marts were the basic unit of organization in Analysis Services 2000 due to limitations in the product; this is no longer the case for SSAS 2005 (Sequel Server Analysis Services). Now data warehouses consist of usually just one cube.

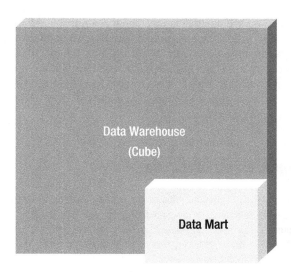

Figure 1-2. *Data marts are subsets of enterprise data (warehouses) and are often defined by time, location, or department.*

Cube: A storage structure used by classic data warehousing products in place of many (often normalized) tables. Rather than using tables with rows and columns, cubes use dimensions and measures (or facts). Also, cubes will usually present data that is aggregated (usually summed), rather than each individual item (or row). This is often stated this way: cubes present a summarized, aggregated view of enterprise data, as opposed to normalized table sources that present detailed data. Cubes are populated with a read-only copy of source data (or production data). In some cases, cubes contain a complete copy of production data; in other cases, cubes contain subsets of source data. The data is moved from source systems to the destination cubes via ETL (Extract, Transform, and Load) processes. We will discuss cube dimensions and facts in greater detail in Chapter 2.

Note Another name for a cube or set of cubes is an *online analytical processing* (OLAP) system. Some writers actually use the terms *data warehouse*, *cube*, *OLAP*, and *DSS* interchangeably. Another group of terms you'll hear associated with OLAP are MOLAP, HOLAP, and ROLAP. These terms refer to the method of storing the data and metadata associated with a SSAS cube. The acronyms stand for multidimensional OLAP, hybrid OLAP, or relational OLAP. Storage methods are covered in detail in Chapter 7.

Decision Support System (DSS): This term's broad definition can mean anything from a read-only copy of an online transaction processing (OLTP) database to a group of OLAP cubes or even a mixture of both. If the data source consists only of an OLTP database, this store is usually highly normalized. One of the challenges of using an OLTP store as a source for a DSS is the difficulty in writing queries that execute quickly and with little overhead on the source system.

This challenge is due to the level of database normalization. The more normalized the OLTP source, the more joins that must be performed on the query. Executing queries that use many joins places significant overhead on the OLTP store. Also, the locking behavior of OLTP databases is such that large read queries can cause significant contention (or waiting) for resources by end users. Yet another complexity is the need to properly index the tables in each query. This book is focused on using the more efficient BI store (or OLAP cube) as a source for a DSS system.

NORMALIZATION VS. DENORMALIZATION

What's the difference between normalization and denormalization? Although entire books have been written on the topic, the definitions are really quite simple. *Normalization* means reducing duplicate data by using keys or IDs to relate rows of information from one table to another, for example, customers and their orders. *Denormalization* means the opposite, which is deliberately duplicating data in one or more structures. Normalization improves the efficiency of inserting, updating, or deleting data. The fewer places the data has to be updated, the more efficient the update and the greater the data integrity. Denormalization improves the efficiency of reading or selecting data and reduces the number of tables the data engine has to access or the number of calculations it has to perform to provide information.

Defining BI Using Microsoft's Tools

Microsoft entered the BI market when it released OLAP Services with SQL Server 7.0. It was a quiet entry, and Microsoft didn't gain much traction until its second BI product release, SQL Server 2000 Analysis Services.

Since its first market entry, Microsoft has taken the approach that BI should not be for the few (business analysts and possibly executives) but for *everyone* in the organization. This is a key differentiator from the competitor's BI product suites. One implementation of this differentiation is Microsoft's focus on integrating support for SSAS into its Office products— specifically Excel. Excel 2003 can be used as a SSAS client at a much lower cost than third-party client tools. Microsoft has expanded the support for SSAS features in Excel 2007. The tools and products Microsoft has designed to support BI (from the 2000 release onward) have been targeted very broadly. In typical Microsoft fashion, they've attempted to broaden the BI usage base with each release.

The Microsoft vision for BI is ambitious and seems to be correctly positioned to meet market demand. In the first year of release, the market penetration of Microsoft's 2005 toolset for BI grew at double the average BI toolset rate, approximately 26% as compared to the overall BI market rate of growth, which was around 12%.

If you're completely new to BI, it's important for you to consider the possibilities of BI in the widest possible manner when beginning your project. This means planning for the largest possible set of end-user types, that is, analysts, executive managers, middle managers, *and* all other types of end users in your organization. You must consider (and ask your project supporters and subject matter experts [SMEs]) which types of end-user groups need to see what type of information and in what formats (tabular, chart, and so on).

If you have experience with another vendor's BI product (for example, Cognos, Informatica, or Essbase), you may find yourself rethinking some assumptions based on use of those products because Microsoft's BI tools are not copies of anything already on the market. Although some common functionality exists between Microsoft and non-Microsoft BI tools, there is also a large set of functionality that is either completely new or implemented differently than non-Microsoft BI products. This is a particularly important consideration if you are migrating to Microsoft's BI from a non-Microsoft BI vendor. I've seen several Microsoft BI production solutions that were needlessly delayed due to lack of understanding of this issue. Whether you are migrating or entirely new to BI, you'll need to start by considering the products and technologies that can be used in a Microsoft BI solution.

What Microsoft Products Are Involved?

As of this writing, the most current Microsoft products that support BI are the following:

SQL Server 2005: This is the preferred staging and, possibly, source location for BI solutions. Data can actually be retrieved from a variety of data stores (Oracle, DB2, and so on), so a SQL Server installation is not strictly required to build a Microsoft BI solution. However, due to the integration of some key toolsets that are part of nearly all BI solutions—for example, SSIS or SQL Server Integration Services, which is usually used to perform the ETL of source data into the data warehouse—most BI solutions will include at least one SQL Server 2005 installation. Another key component in many BI solutions is SQL Server Reporting Services (SSRS). When working with SQL Server to perform OLAP administrative tasks, you will use the management interface, which is called SQL Server Management Studio (SSMS).

Sequel Server Analysis Services 2005 (SSAS): This is the core server in Microsoft's BI solution. SSAS provides storage for the data used in cubes for your data warehouse. This product may or may not run on the same physical server as SQL Server 2005. I will detail how to set up cubes in Chapters 4, 5, 6, 7, 10, and 13. Figure 1-3 shows the primary tool—Business Intelligence Development Studio (BIDS) —that you'll use to develop cubes for Analysis Services. You'll note that BIDS opens in a Visual Studio (VS) environment. A full VS installation is *not* required to develop cubes for SSAS. If you do not have VS on your development machine, when you install SSAS, BIDS will install as a stand-alone component. If you do have VS on your development machine, then BIDS will install as a component (really a set of templates) into your existing VS instance.

Figure 1-3. *You use the Business Intelligence Development Studio (BIDS) to implement BI solutions.*

Data Mining Using SSAS: This is an optional component included with SSAS that allows you to create data mining structures. These structures include data mining models. *Data mining models* are objects that contain source data (either relational or multidimensional) that have been processed using a particular type of data mining algorithm. These algorithms either classify (group) only or classify and predict one or more column values. Although data mining was available in Analysis Services 2000, Microsoft has significantly enhanced the capabilities of this tool in the 2005 release, for example in the 2000 release there were only two data mining algorithms available, in the 2005 release there are nine algorithms. I will provide an overview of data mining in general, and the capabilities available in SSAS for implementing data mining in Chapter 11.

SQL Server 2005 Integration Services (SSIS): This toolset is a key component in most BI solutions that is used to import, cleanse, and validate data prior to making the data available to the Analysis Services for reporting purposes. It is typical to use data from many disparate sources (relational, flat file, XML, and so on) as source data to a data warehouse. For this reason, a sophisticated toolset, such as SSIS is used to facilitate the complex data loads that are often common to BI solutions. As stated earlier, this functionality is often called ETL (Extract, Transform, and Load) in a BI solution. In SQL Server 2000, the available ETL toolset was named Data Transformation Services (DTS). SSIS has been completed re-architected in this release of SQL Server. Although there is some overlap in functionality, SSIS really is a new release, as compared to DTS, for Microsoft. I will discuss the use of SSIS in Chapters 3, 8, and 9.

SQL Server 2005 Reporting Services (SSRS): This is an optional component for your BI solution. Microsoft has made many significant enhancements in the most current version that makes using SSRS an attractive part of a BI solution. The most important of which is the inclusion of a visual query designer for SSAS cubes, which facilitates rapid report creation by reducing the need to write manual queries against cube data. I will discuss reporting clients, including SSRS, in Chapter 12.

Excel 2003 or 2007: This is another optional component for your BI solution. Many companies already own Office 2003, so use of Excel as a BI client is often attractive for its low cost and (relatively) low training curve. I will compare various client solutions in Chapter 12. Office 2007 is released as of the writing of this book; I will provide a "first look" at new features for Excel 12 (or 2007) in Chapter 14.

Tip Connecting to an OLAP data source from Excel also requires that MS-Query be installed. MS-Query is listed under optional components on the Office installation DVD.

SharePoint Portal Server 2003 or Microsoft Office SharePoint Server 2007 (MOSS): This is yet another optional component to your BI solution. Most easily used in conjunction with SSRS, using the freely available SSRS Web parts, SharePoint can expand the reach of your BI solution. As mentioned previously, I will detail options using different BI clients in Chapter 12. Office 2007 has a planned release of early spring 2007. SharePoint Services will have many significant enhancements related to BI solutions, which are discussed in Chapter 14.

Note A Web part is a pluggable UI showing some bit of content. It is installed globally in the SharePoint Portal Server Web site and can be added to a portal page by any user with appropriate permissions.

Visio 2003 or 2007: This is my favorite modeling tool for BI projects. It is optional as well; you can use any tool that you are comfortable using. Sections in Chapter 2 that concern modeling for OLAP include sample Visio diagrams. As with other products in the Office suite, Microsoft has increased the BI integration capabilities with Visio 2007.

ProClarity (acquired by Microsoft in 2006): This is a high-end client tool. Prior to its acquisition, ProClarity was my recommended business analyst tool of choice. ProClarity, as you might imagine, is currently undergoing quite a transition as it becomes part of Microsoft. Microsoft has announced that all ProClarity functionality will be integrated into a new product. This product is called Performance Point Server (PPS). PPS is currently in CTP (Community Technology Preview) release (and set for final release in late 2007). I'll provide an update in Chapter 14.

> **Note** Microsoft has added significant BI integration into Office 2007—particularly for Excel 2007, SharePoint 2007 (now called Microsoft Office SharePoint Server, or MOSS), and for the renamed Business Scorecards Manager Server (which will be called Performance Point Server). Microsoft has further announced that PPS will include the next release of ProClarity, which means that ProClarity will no longer be available as a stand-alone product.

The capability and feature differences between SSAS editions (standard, enterprise, and so on) for the products in the BI suite are highlighted in Chapter 2, and key feature differences are discussed throughout the entire book. These differences are significant and affect many aspects of your BI solution design, such as the number of servers, number and type of software licenses, and server configuration.

You may be thinking at this point, "Wow, that's a big list. Am I required to buy (or upgrade to) all of those Microsoft products to implement a BI solution for my company?" The answer is no, the only server that is *required* is the SSAS. Many companies also provide tools that can be used in a Microsoft BI solution. Although I will occasionally refer to some third-party products, I will primarily focus on using Microsoft's products and tools to build a BI solution in this book.

BI Languages

An additional consideration is that you will use at least three languages when working with SSAS. The first, which is the primary query language for cubes, is *not* the same language used to work with SQL Server data (T-SQL). The query language for SSAS is called MDX. SSAS also includes the capability to build data mining structures. To query the data in these structures, you'll use yet another language—DMX. Finally, Microsoft introduces an administrative scripting language in SSAS 2005—XMLA. Here's a brief description of each language.

MDX (Multidimensional Expressions): This is the language used to query OLAP cubes. Although this language is officially an open standard, and some vendors outside of Microsoft have chosen to adopt parts of it into their BI products, the reality is that very few developers are proficient in MDX. A mitigating factor is that the need for you to manually write MDX in a BI solution can be relatively small—not nearly as much T-SQL as you would manually write for a typical OLTP database. However, retaining developers who have at least a basic knowledge of MDX is an important consideration in planning a BI project. MDX is introduced in Chapter 10.

Figure 1-4 shows a simple example of an MDX query in SQL Server Management Studio (SSMS).

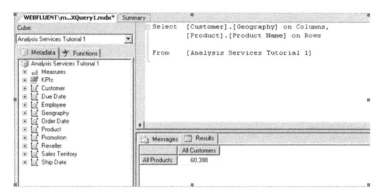

Figure 1-4. *The MDX query language is used to retrieve data from SSAS cubes. Although MDX has a SQL-like structure, MDX is far more difficult to master. This is due to the complexity of the SSAS source data structures—cubes.*

DMX (Data Mining Extensions): This is the language used to query data mining structures (which contain data mining models). Although this language is officially an open standard, and some vendors outside of Microsoft have chosen to adopt parts of it into their BI products, the reality is that very few developers are proficient in DMX. A mitigating factor is that the need for DMX in a BI solution is relatively small (again, not nearly as much T-SQL as you would manually write for a typical OLTP database). Also, Microsoft's data mining interface is heavily wizard driven, more than creating cubes (which is saying something!). However, retaining developers who have at least a basic knowledge of DMX is an important consideration in planning a BI project that will include a large amount of data mining. DMX is introduced briefly in Chapter 11.

XMLA (XML for Analysis): This is the language used to perform administrative tasks in SSAS. Here are some examples of XMLA tasks: viewing metadata, copying, backing up databases, and so on. Although this language is officially an open standard, and some vendors outside of Microsoft have chosen to adopt parts of it into their BI products, the reality is that very few developers are proficient in XMLA. A mitigating factor is that Microsoft has made generating XMLA scripts simple. In SSMS, when connected to SSAS, you can right-click any SSAS object and generate XMLA scripts using the GUI interface. XMLA is introduced in Chapter 13.

Because I've covered so many acronyms is this section, and I'll be referring to these products by their acronym going forward in this book, a quick list is provided in Figure 1-5.

Acronym	Name
BI	Business Intelligence
BIDS	Business Intelligence Development Studio
BSM	Business Scorecards Manager Server
DMX	Data Mining Extensions
DSS	Decision Support System
HOLAP	Hybrid OLAP
MDX	MultiDimensional Expressions
MOLAP	Multidimensional OLAP
MOSS	Microsoft Office SharePoint Server
OLAP	Online Analytical Processing
OLTP	Online Transaction Processing
PPS	Performance Point Server
ROLAP	Relational OLAP
SPS	SharePoint Portal Server
SSAS	SQL Server Analysis Services
SSIS	SQL Server Integration Services
SSMS	SQL Server Management Studio
SSRS	SQL Server Reporting Services
VS	Visual Studio
XMLA	XML for Analysis Services

Figure 1-5. *For your convenience, the various BI acronyms used in this book are listed here.*

Understanding BI from an End User's Perspective

You may be wondering where to start at this point. Your starting point depends on the extent of involvement you and your company have had with BI technologies. Usually you will either (a) be completely new to BI; (b) be new to SSAS 2005, that is, you are using SSAS 2000; or (c) be new to Microsoft's BI, that is, you are using another vendor's products to support BI. If BI is new to you and your company, then a great place to start is with the end user's perspective of a BI solution. To do this, you will use the simplest possible client tool for SSAS—an Excel pivot table. This is a great way to familiarize not only yourself, but also other members of your team and your executive sponsors about basic BI concepts.

■**Note** If you have experience with basic BI end-user tools (particularly pivot tables), you may want to skip to the next chapter.

Demonstrating the Power of BI Using Excel 2003 Pivot Tables

Although this may seem like a strange way to showcase a suite of products that is as powerful as Microsoft's BI toolset, my experience has shown over and over that this simple approach is quite powerful.

There are two ways to implement the initial setup. Which you choose will depend on the amount of time you have to prepare and the sophistication level of your audience. The first approach is to create a cube using the sample database (AdventureWorksDW) that Microsoft provides with SSAS. Detailed steps for using the first approach are provided later in this chapter. The second approach is to take a very small subset of data from your company and to use it for a demonstration or personal study. If you want to use your own data, you'll probably have to read a bit more of this book to be able to set up a basic cube using your own data.

The rest of this chapter will get you up and running with the included sample. At this point, we are going to focus simply on clicks, that is "click here to do this." We are not yet focusing on the "why" at this point. The rest of the chapters will explain in detail just what all this clicking actually does and why you click where you're clicking.

Building the First Sample—Using AdventureWorksDW

To use the SQL Server 2005 AdventureWorksDW sample database as the basis for building a SSAS cube, you'll need to have at least one machine with SQL Server 2005 and SSAS installed on it. While installing, make note of the edition of SQL Server that you are using (you can use the Developer, Standard, or Enterprise editions) because you'll need to know the particular edition when you install the sample cube files.

If you're installing SQL Server, remember to choose the option to install the sample databases. This option is *not* selected by default. If SQL Server is already installed, you can download (and install) the sample database AdventureWorksDW. You will use AdventureWorksDW rather than AdventureWorks as the source database for your first SSAS OLAP cube because the former is modeled in a way that is most conducive to easy cube creation. Chapter 2 details what modeling for SSAS cubes consists of and how you can apply these modeling techniques to your own data.

Tip The AdventureWorksDW database comes on the source media for SQL Server 2005. To install it, you can either rerun setup, or, if you don't have access to the source media, you can download the sample database from `http://www.microsoft.com/downloads/details.aspx?FamilyID=E719ECF7-9F46-4312-AF89-6AD8702E4E6E&displaylang=en`. This URL includes detailed instructions for installing this sample database after you have downloaded it.

To create the sample cube, you will use the sample AdventureWorks Analysis Services project. The sample consists of a set of physical files that contains metadata that SSAS uses to structure the sample Adventure Works cube. As mentioned earlier, you'll work with these sample files in BIDS. The sample is available in the Standard Edition and the Enterprise Edition. You will select the sample file from the directory that matches the edition that you have installed. There are significant feature differences between the two editions, which you will learn about in detail as you work through the available features in this book.

Note The Developer Edition has an identical feature set to the Enterprise Edition (for the purposes of your development, demonstration, or personal review). If you have installed the Developer Edition, then select the sample from the Enterprise Edition folder.

How to Deploy the Standard Edition Version of the Sample Cube

To deploy the standard edition of the sample cube:

1. Open the SQL Server Business Intelligence Development Studio (BIDS) from the Start menu.

2. From the BIDS Menu, click File ➤ Open ➤ Project/Solution.

3. Browse to `C:\Program Files\Microsoft SQL Server\90\Tools\Samples\ AventureWorks Analysis Services Project\Standard`, select the file `Adventure Works DW Standard Edition.sln`, and click Open. This dialog box is shown in Figure 1-6.

Figure 1-6. *To install the SSAS sample cube, select the folder with the edition name that matches the edition of SSAS that you have installed and then double-click Adventure-Works.sln to open the solution in BIDS.*

4. Set the connection string to the server name where you deployed AdventureWorksDW by right-clicking on the Adventure Works.ds data source in Solution Explorer. Click the Edit button on the General tab in the Data Source Designer dialog box to change the connection string. This setting is shown in Figure 1-7.

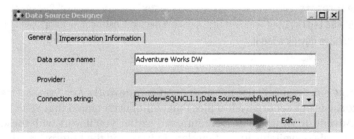

Figure 1-7. *When deploying the sample, be sure to verify that the connection string information is correct for your particular installation.*

Note If you are using the Enterprise Edition, you can follow these steps as well. Simply select the files from the sample Enterprise folder from the path listed next.

Be sure to test the connection as well. You do this by clicking on the Test Connection button on the bottom of the Connection Manager dialog box as shown in Figure 1-8.

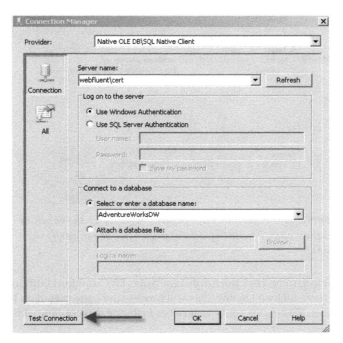

Figure 1-8. *You'll want to test the connection to the sample database, AdventureWorksDW, as you work through setting up the sample SSAS database.*

5. Right-click the name of the project (Adventure Works DW Standard Edition) in Solution Explorer, and then click on Properties from the context menu. You must verify the name of the Analysis Services instance that you intend to deploy the sample project to. The default is localhost. If you are using localhost, then you do not need to change this setting.

You can also use a named server instance, as shown in Figure 1-9. In that case, in the project's Properties Pages dialog box, click on Deployment, and set the target sever name to the computer name and instance name separated by a backslash character where you have deployed SSAS (see Figure 1-9).

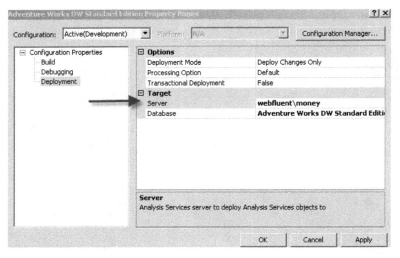

Figure 1-9. *Before deploying the sample SSAS project, right-click the solution name in BIDS, and then click Properties. In the properties sheet, verify the SSAS instance name.*

6. From Solution Explorer, right-click the Adventure Works DW Standard Edition project name, and then click on Deploy. This will process the cube metadata locally and then deploy those files to the Analysis Services instance you configured in the previous step.

After clicking deploy, wait for the "deployment succeeded" message to appear at the bottom right of the BIDS window. This can take up to 5 minutes or more depending on the resources available to complete the processing. If the deployment fails (which will be indicated with a large red X in the interface, read the messages in the Process Database dialog box to help you to determine the cause or causes of the failure. The most common error is incorrectly configured connection strings.

Now you are ready to take a look at the sample cube using the built-in browser in BIDS. This browser looks much like a pivot table so that you, as a cube developer, can review your work prior to allowing end users to connect to the cube using client BI tools. Most client tools contain some type of pivot table component, so the included browser in BIDS is a useful tool for you. To view the sample cube using the built-in cube browser in BIDS, perform the following steps:

1. In Solution Explorer, expand the Cubes folder, and then double-click the Adventure Works cube to open the BIDS cube designer work area (see Figure 1-10).

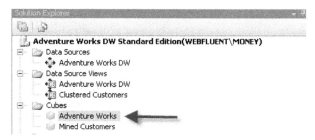

Figure 1-10. *To view the sample cube in BIDS, double-click the cube name in Solution Explorer.*

2. In the cube designer work area (which appears in the center section) of BIDS, on the AdventureWorks main tab, click on the Browser subtab as shown in Figure 1-11.

Figure 1-11. *The cube designer interface has nine tabs. To browse a cube, you click on the Browser tab. The cube must have been successfully deployed to the server to browse it.*

3. Now you can drag and drop items from the cube (dimensions and facts) onto the viewing area. This is very similar to using a pivot table client to view a cube. The functionality is similar, by design, to BI client tools such as Excel pivot tables; however, there are some built-in limitations (for example, on the number of levels of depth you may browse in a dimension), and the Browser tab, like all of BIDS, is designed for cube designers and *not* for end users.

■ **Note** You may be wondering what the dimensions and facts (or measures) are that you see onscreen? We will review these concepts in more detail in Chapter 2, however, as an introduction, you can think of *facts* as important business values (for example daily sales amount or daily sales quantity), and you can think of *dimensions* as attributes (or detailed information) related to the facts (for example, which customers made which purchases, which employees made which sales, and so on).

Spend some time in the BIDS browser interface exploring; drag and drop different items onto the display surface and around the display surface. Also, try right-clicking on the design surface to find many interesting built-in options to display the information differently.

You can use Figure 1-12 as a starting point. The Order Count measure is displayed in the data area, the Calendar Year hierarchy from the Date dimensions is displayed on the columns axis, the Country hierarchy from the Geography dimension is displayed on rows, the Employee Department attribute from the Employees dimension is displayed as a filter, and the Product Model Categories hierarchy from the Product dimension is set to filter the browser results to include only measure values where the Product Model Category is equal to Bikes.

Tip To remove any measures or dimensions from the browse area, click on the item you want to remove and drag it back over the tree listing of available objects.

Figure 1-12 is a view of the sample Adventure Works cube. Note that you can place dimension members and hierarchies on the rows, columns, or filter axis and that you can view measures in the area labeled Drop Total or Detail Fields Here.

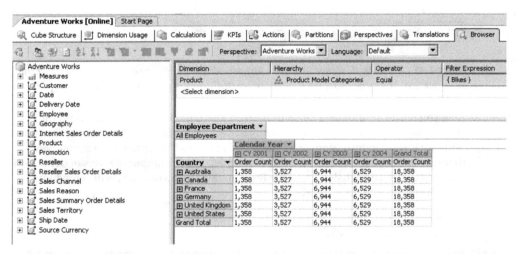

Figure 1-12. *The BIDS cube browser uses a pivot table interface to allow you to view the cube that you have built (or, in this case, simply deployed) using the BIDS cube designer.*

Note If you are wondering whether you can view sample data mining models in BIDS, the answer is yes. The AdventureWorks samples include data mining structures. Each structure contains one or more data mining models. Each mining model has one or more viewers available in BIDS. Data mining is a deep topic, so I'll spend all of Chapter 11 discussing the mining model types and BIDS interfaces. Also, Excel 2003 does *not* support the display of SSAS mining structures. Excel 2007, however, does, so I'll discuss these features in Chapter 14.

How to Connect to the Sample Cube Using Excel 2003

Now that you've set up and deployed the sample cubes, you will probably want to experience an end user's perspective. An easy way to do this is with a pivot table in Excel 2003:

1. Open Excel 2003.

2. Select Data ➤ Pivot Table.

3. On the PivotTable Wizard Step 1, select Connect to External Data Source.

4. On the PivotTable Wizard Step 2, click the Get Data button as shown in Figure 1-13.

Figure 1-13. *When connecting to a SSAS cube in Excel, you must configure the connection to the SSAS server by clicking on the Get Data button on Step 2 of the PivotTable wizard.*

5. In the Choose Data dialog box, select the OLAP Cubes tab, and then select <new>.

6. In the Create New Data Source dialog box, name your connection, select Microsoft OLE DB Provider for Analysis Services 9.0 in the Select an OLAP provider for the database you want to access box, and then click the Connect button (see Figure 1-14).

Figure 1-14. *When you are configuring your connection to the SSAS cube, be sure to select the OLE DB Provider for Analysis Services 9.0.*

7. In the first Multidimensional Connection 9.0 dialog box, enter the instance name of the Analysis Services where you deployed the sample project, and then click Next.

8. In the second Multidimensional Connection 9.0 dialog box, click on the name of your sample project (Adventure Works DW Standard [or Enterprise] Edition) in the list of databases to select it. Click Finish. You are returned from the MS Query dialog boxes back to the Create New Data Source dialog box (shown in the previous figure).

9. In this dialog box, click on the 4. Select the Cube that contains the data you want drop-down list box, select AdventureWorks, and click OK. This will return you to the Choose Data Source dialog box. Click OK.

10. You are now returned to the PivotTable Wizard Step 2. Click Next to advance to Step 3. On the Step 3 dialog box, click the Layout button as shown in Figure 1-15.

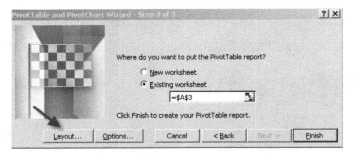

Figure 1-15. *In Step 3 of the PivotTable wizard, you'll click on the Layout button to display the area to drag and drop your dimensions or measures onto the pivot table layout surface.*

11. On the PivotTable Wizard layout, drag the items that you want to show on the rows, columns, and center area. Figure 1-16 shows a sample. The dimensions are listed first in the list of items, and the measures are listed at the end. It is a bit difficult to read the dimension and measure names in this page of the wizard because the fixed button size truncates the dimension and measure names. If you try to drag an item to a layout area where it cannot be displayed (for example, drag a measure to the column area), then the Layout wizard will not allow you to drop that item. The dialog box provides visual hints to help you lay out your pivot table correctly.

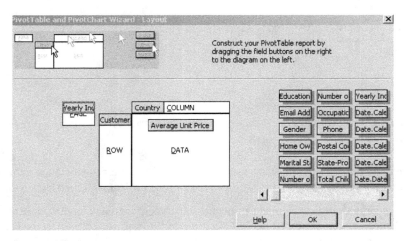

Figure 1-16. *Using the Layout dialog box, you drag and drop dimensions and measures onto the layout area. Drag only measures to the DATA area.*

12. Click OK and Finish. Your pivot table will look somewhat similar to Figure 1-17. If you want to remove items, simply drag the (grey) headers out of the pivot table area. The cursor will change to a red X when the item can be removed from the pivot table. If you want to add items, display the pivot table toolbar (View ➤ Toolbars), and click the last button to show the pivot table field list on the screen. When that list is visible, you can drag items to the pivot table to make their values visible.

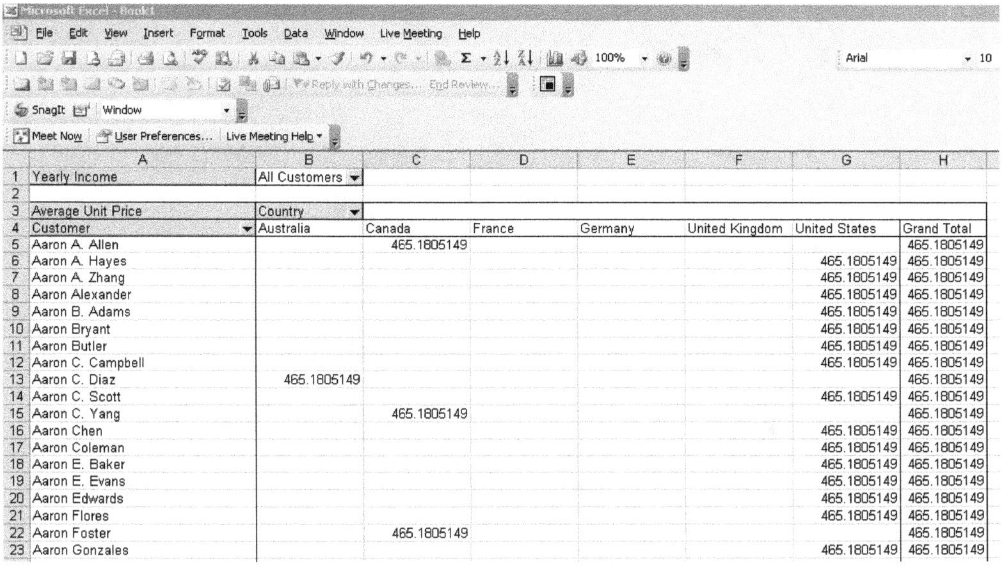

	A	B	C	D	E	F	G	H
1	Yearly Income	All Customers						
2								
3	Average Unit Price	Country						
4	Customer	Australia	Canada	France	Germany	United Kingdom	United States	Grand Total
5	Aaron A. Allen		465.1805149					465.1805149
6	Aaron A. Hayes						465.1805149	465.1805149
7	Aaron A. Zhang						465.1805149	465.1805149
8	Aaron Alexander						465.1805149	465.1805149
9	Aaron B. Adams						465.1805149	465.1805149
10	Aaron Bryant						465.1805149	465.1805149
11	Aaron Butler						465.1805149	465.1805149
12	Aaron C. Campbell						465.1805149	465.1805149
13	Aaron C. Diaz	465.1805149						465.1805149
14	Aaron C. Scott						465.1805149	465.1805149
15	Aaron C. Yang		465.1805149					465.1805149
16	Aaron Chen						465.1805149	465.1805149
17	Aaron Coleman						465.1805149	465.1805149
18	Aaron E. Baker						465.1805149	465.1805149
19	Aaron E. Evans						465.1805149	465.1805149
20	Aaron Edwards						465.1805149	465.1805149
21	Aaron Flores						465.1805149	465.1805149
22	Aaron Foster		465.1805149					465.1805149
23	Aaron Gonzales						465.1805149	465.1805149

Figure 1-17. *After you've completed configuring the connection to your SSAS sample cube using the PivotTable wizard in Excel, the result appears to the end user as a regular pivot table.*

Tip Would you like to practice a bit more with pivot tables? Microsoft has a site where you can download and work with 25 different sample pivot tables: `http://office.microsoft.com/en-us/assistance/HA010346331033.aspx`.

You may also want to create a pivot chart. Some people simply prefer to get information via graphs or charts rather than rows and columns of numbers. As you begin to design your BI solution, it is very important to consider the needs of all the different types of users of your solution. To create a pivot chart, simply display the pivot table toolbar and click on the Chart Wizard button. Figure 1-18 is a sample of a pivot chart.

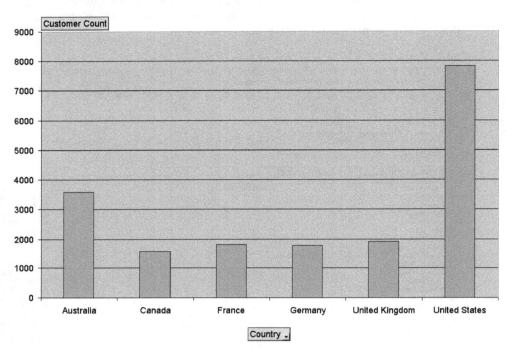

Figure 1-18. *The method used to create a pivot chart using SSAS cube data is similar to that used when creating a pivot table.*

Understanding BI Through the Sample

Now that your pivot table is set up, what exactly are you trying to understand by working with it? How is a pivot table that gets its data from a SSAS cube different from any other Excel pivot table? Here is a list of some of the most important BI (or OLAP) concepts:

- BI is *comprehensive* and flexible. A single, correctly designed cube can actually contain all of an organization's data, and importantly, this cube will present that data to end users consistently. To better understand this concept, you should try working with the AdventureWorksDW sample cube as displayed using the Excel pivot table to see that multiple types of measures (both Internet and Retail Sales) have been combined into one structure.

    Most dimensions apply to both groups of measures, but not all do. For example, there is no relationship between the Employee dimensions and any of the measures in the Internet Sales group because there are no employees involved in these types of sales. Cube modeling is now flexible enough to allow you to reflect business reality in a single cube.

In previous versions of SSAS and in other vendor's products, you would've been forced to make compromises such as creating multiple cubes or being limited by structural requirements. This lack of flexibility in the past often translated into limitation and complexity in the client tools as well.

- BI is *accessible* (intuitive for all end users to view and manipulate). To better understand this aspect of BI, try demonstrating the pivot table based on the SSAS sample cube to others in your organization. They will usually quickly understand and be impressed (some will even get excited!) as they begin to see the potential reach for BI solutions in your company.

  Pivot table interfaces reflect the way many users think about data, which is "what are the measures (or numbers) and what attributes (or factors) created these numbers?"

  Some users may request a simpler interface than a pivot table (that is, a type of "canned report"). Microsoft provides client tools, such as SSRS, which facilitate that type of implementation. It is important for you to balance this type of request, which entails manual report writing by you, versus the benefits available to end users who can use pivot tables. In my experience, most BI solutions include a pivot table training component for those end users who haven't worked much with pivot tables before.

- BI is *fast to query*. After the initial setup is done, queries can easily run 1000% faster in an OLAP database than in an OLTP database. Your sample won't necessarily demonstrate the speed of query in and of itself. However, it is helpful to understand that the SSAS server is highly optimized to provide a far superior query experience (than to provide a typical relational database) because the SSAS engine itself is actually designed to quickly fetch or calculate aggregated values. We will dive into the details on this topic in Chapter 7 of this book.

- BI is *simple to query*. End users simply drag items into and around the pivot area; developers write very little query code manually. It is important to understand that SSAS clients (like Excel) automatically generate MDX queries when users drag and drop dimensions and measures onto the design surfaces. This is a tremendous advantage as compared to traditional OLTP reporting solutions where T-SQL developers must manually write all of the queries.

- BI provides accurate, near real-time, *summarized* information. This will improve the quality of business decisions. Also with some of the new features available in SSAS, most particularly Proactive Caching, cubes can have latency that is only a number of minutes or even seconds. We'll discuss configuring real-time cubes in Chapter 7.

  Also, using drilldown, users who need to see the detail (that is, the numbers behind the numbers) can do so. *Drilldown* is, of course, implemented in pivot tables via the simple "+" interface that is available for all (summed) aggregations in the AdventureWorksDW sample cube.

- BI *improves ROI* by allowing more end users to make more efficient use of enterprise information so many companies have all the information they need. The problem is that the information is not accessible in formats that are useful for the people in the company to use as a basis for decision making in a timely way.

It's really just that simple; OLAP (or BI) solutions simply give businesses a significant competitive advantage by making more data available to more end users so that those users can make better decisions in a more timely way. What's so exciting about BI is that Microsoft has made it possible for many companies who couldn't previously afford to implement any type of BI solution to be able to "play" in this space by including all of the core BI tools and technologies needed to implement cubes in the box with SQL Server. As previously stated, it is important to understand which features require the Enterprise Edition of SQL Server or Analysis Services. We will review feature difference by edition in detail throughout this book.

In addition to broadening BI's reach by including some BI features in both the Standard and Enterprise Editions of SQL Server, Microsoft is also providing some much needed competition at the enterprise level by including some extremely powerful BI features in the Enterprise Editions of SQL Server and SSAS. I'll talk more about that at the end of this chapter.

Understanding the Business Problems that BI Addresses

As you learn more about SSAS capabilities, you can begin to match some of the strengths of the BI toolset available in SQL Server 2005 (and companion BI Microsoft products) to current challenges you and your company may be facing when working with your enterprise data. I call these challenges "pain points" and list some OLAP (or BI) solutions to commonly seen challenges in Table 1-1.

Table 1-1. *List of Business Pain Points and OLAP Solutions*

Pain Point	OLAP Solutions
Slow-to-execute queries	Use cubes that are optimized for read-only queries and can be 1000% faster to return query results than OLTP systems due to the efficiency of the SSAS engine to aggregate data.
General system slowdowns	Greatly reduce locking overhead from OLTP source systems. (OLAP systems do not use locks, except during processing.)
Manual query writing	Allow end users to click to query (click and drag on pivot table), which eliminates the wait time associated with traditional T-SQL, where end users must usually request reports, which results in developers manually writing queries against OLTP systems.
Disparate data sources	Combine data into central repositories or cubes using ETL packages that can be automated to run on a regular basis.
Invalid/inconsistent report data	Based on data that has been cleaned and validated (prior to cube load) using the ETL toolset available in SSIS. Cubes provide a consistent and unified view of enterprise data all across the enterprise.
Data is not available to all users	Designed to be accessed by all business users.
Too much data	Can use data mining (along with the other tools, that is, cubes, available in SSAS) to find patterns in large amounts of data automatically. SSAS now contains nine different types of data mining (called algorithms) to help you group, correlate, and predict data values.

Reasons to Switch to Microsoft's BI Tools

In addition to providing a great suite of tools for companies that are just getting started with BI, Microsoft's 2005 release of the BI tools has also targeted companies that are using other vendor's BI products. Microsoft has done this by providing a raft of enterprise features in its data warehousing products. Many of these features are available only in the Enterprise edition of the various BI products, that is, Analysis Services, SQL Server Integration Services, and SQL Reporting Services.

■**Tip** The comprehensive feature comparison list for each edition of SQL Server 2005 is available at
`http://www.microsoft.com/sql/prodinfo/features/compare-features.mspx`.

Here's a list of BI-specific features that require the Enterprise edition of Analysis Services 2005:

- Advanced Business Analytics

- Proactive Caching

- Advanced Data Management

- Writeback

- Advanced Data Mining Tuning

- Advanced SSIS Transforms

- Text Mining Support

These features will be reviewed in more detail in the subsequent chapters of this book.

Also, Microsoft has built its BI tools so that they will integrate with other vendor's products. It is quite common, for example, to use SSAS to create cubes from Oracle or DB2 data sources. Another example is to use SSRS with a mainframe or an Informix source data. Microsoft is aggressively adding support for interoperability across the entire suite of BI tools. Interestingly, the number one BI vendor for Oracle is no longer Oracle, even though Oracle does provides a rich set of BI tools. Due to lower cost, ease of implementation, and a comparable feature set, SSAS now takes first place as an Oracle-sourced BI solution provider.

Another compelling aspect of Microsoft's BI offering is the inclusion of intelligent wizards and GUI tools that allow you to get up and running quickly and easily. The catch, however, is that the use of these tools and wizards is heavily dependent on your understanding and implementation of basic OLAP modeling concepts. We will look at that topic in the next chapter.

Summary

This chapter covered basic data warehousing terms and concepts, including OLAP, BI, dimension, and fact. We then reviewed the process and procedures you use to quickly set up a sample SSAS cube using BIDS. You worked with the AdventureWorksDW sample, connecting to it with an Excel 2003 pivot table, to give you a quick view of an OLAP solution from an end user's perspective.

In the next chapter, we'll dig deeper into OLAP concepts and learn about basic modeling for cubes.

CHAPTER 2

■■■

OLAP Modeling

You've got executive support and a great BI team assembled. You've diligently set up standards and practices. The development environment is set up (and secured!), and your team is ready to start designing your solution. What is the next step? It all starts with a star—a star schema, that is.

Properly designed OLAP schemas are the foundation of all successful BI projects built using SSAS 2005. With star schemas as a starting point, you or your ETL gurus can begin the data mapping process, and you or your report writers can begin to create report prototypes. This chapter will explain design models for OLAP schemas—stars, snowflakes, and more—all of which are the basis for OLAP cubes. Modeling for data mining is *not* covered here because it is discussed in Chapter 11.

This chapter covers the following topics:

- Modeling OLAP source schemas: stars, snowflakes, and other types

- Understanding dimensional modeling, including modeling for changing dimensions

- Understanding fact (or measure) and cube modeling

- A quick introduction to other types of modeling, such as KPIs, Actions, and Translations

Modeling OLAP Source Schemas—Stars

Learning about OLAP modeling always starts with a thorough review of the "classic" OLAP source model: the star schema. The next section reviews the concepts behind star schema modeling in detail.

Before we start however, let's take a minute to discuss an even more fundamental idea for your BI project. Is a star schema strictly required? The technical answer to this question is "no" because Microsoft purposely does *not* require you to base OLAP cubes off of only data that is in a star schema format. In other words, you can create cubes based off of OLTP (or relational and normalized data). SSAS 2005 is designed with more flexibility than SSAS 2000 (which really did require you to use strict star schemas as sources); this change is based on customer requests.

However, and this is a *big* however, it is critical for you to understand star schema modeling and to attempt to provide SSAS with data that is as close to this format as possible. The reason for this is that although Microsoft *has* included flexibility in SSAS, that flexibility is really designed for those of you who intend to create cubes manually. Particularly if you are new to BI (using OLAP cubes), you'll probably want to build your first project by taking advantage of the included wizards and tools in BIDS. These time savers are designed to work using traditional star schema source data. When you become more experienced, you will probably find yourself enjoying the flexibility to go "outside the star" and then will build some parts of your BI solution manually.

Understanding the Star Schema

A *star schema* consists of at least one fact table and a number of dimension tables. These tables are relational database tables, often stored in SQL Server. The star schema source tables are not required to be stored in SQL Server. In fact, many OLAP solutions use other RDMS systems, including Oracle, DB2, and others, to hold source star data.

A star schema fact table consists of at least two types of columns: keys and measures. The *keys* are foreign-key (FK) values that relate rows in the dimension tables to rows in the fact table. The *measures* are numeric values—usually, but not always, additive—that express the business metrics. An example of this is a sales amount for a particular product, sold on a particular day, by a particular employee.

Fact tables can also contain columns that are neither keys nor facts (which are also called measures). These columns are the basis for a special type of dimension called a *degenerate dimension*. For example, in the fact table in Figure 2-1, the SalesOrderNumber column provides information about each row (or fact), but it is neither a key nor a fact.

Figure 2-1 also shows a typical fact table structure: the first columns are all named xxxKey and of datatype int. These columns are the FK values. They provide the relationship to the dimension tables and are said to "give meaning" to the facts. In Figure 2-1, the columns that will be translated into measures in the cube start with the OrderQuantity column. Note the datatypes for the fact columns. You may be surprised to see the use of the money datatype. If a fact column represents a monetary value, then it is preferred to use the money datatype in the fact table because some MDX functions are dependent on this datatype.

■ **Note** Facts or measures, what's the difference? Technically, *facts* are individual values stored in rows in the fact table, and *measures* are those values as stored and displayed in an OLAP cube. The terms are commonly used interchangeably in OLAP literature.

Another important consideration when modeling your fact tables is to keep the tables as narrow as possible. The reason for this is that a star schema fact table generally contains a much larger number of rows than any one-dimension table. So fact tables represent your most significant storage space concern in an OLAP solution. It is especially important for you to justify every column added to any fact table in your star schemas against your project's business requirements.

Column Name	Data Type	Allow Nulls
ProductKey	int	☐
OrderDateKey	int	☐
DueDateKey	int	☐
ShipDateKey	int	☐
CustomerKey	int	☐
PromotionKey	int	☐
CurrencyKey	int	☐
SalesTerritoryKey	int	☐
SalesOrderNumber	nvarchar(20)	☐
SalesOrderLineNumber	tinyint	☐
RevisionNumber	tinyint	☑
OrderQuantity	smallint	☑
UnitPrice	money	☑
ExtendedAmount	money	☑
UnitPriceDiscountPct	float	☑
DiscountAmount	float	☑
ProductStandardCost	money	☑
TotalProductCost	money	☑
SalesAmount	money	☑
TaxAmt	money	☑
Freight	money	☑
CarrierTrackingNumber	nvarchar(25)	☑
CustomerPONumber	nvarchar(25)	☑
		☐

Table - dbo.FactInternetSales | Summary

Figure 2-1. *Fact tables consist of keys and facts (or measures) and, sometimes, additional columns, like* SalesOrderNumber, *which provide additional information. The keys are FKs to the dimension table rows. Measures are usually, but not always, numeric and additive values.*

Understanding a Dimension Table

As mentioned previously, the dimension table rows provide meaning to the rows in the fact table. Each *dimension table* describes a particular business entity or aspect of the facts (rows) in the fact table. Typical dimension tables are time, customers, and products. Dimension tables should consist of three types of columns. The first is a newly generated primary key (PK) for each row in the dimension table. The second is the original PK, and the third is any number of additional columns that further describe the business entity.

Keys

Dimension tables are not strictly required to contain two types of keys. You could actually create dimension tables using only the original PK; however, this practice is *not* recommended. One reason to generate a new unique dimension key is that it is common to load data into dimensions from disparate data sources (for example, a SQL Server table and an Excel spreadsheet). Without generating new keys, you would have no guarantee of having a unique identifier for each row.

As mentioned previously, you should model for two types of keys (or identifiers) in dimensional source data. The first is the original PK, which is the key from the OLTP source system. This is also sometimes called the *business key*. In addition to this key, it is a best practice to generate a new, unique key during the ETL load process of the dimension table. This is often called a *surrogate key*.

Even if you are retrieving source data from a single source database initially, it is an important best practice to add this new surrogate key on loading the dimension table. The reason is that business conditions can quickly change—you may find yourself having to modify a production cube to add data from another source for many reasons (business merger, acquisition, competitor data, and so on). You should always use surrogate keys when building dimension tables.

You'll note that the DimCustomer dimension table shown in Figure 2-2 contains both the original identifier, called CustomerAlternateKey, and a new unique identifier called CustomerKey.

Table - dbo.DimCustomer	Summary	
Column Name	Data Type	Allow Nulls
CustomerKey	int	☐
GeographyKey	int	☑
CustomerAlternateKey	nvarchar(15)	☐
Title	nvarchar(8)	☑
FirstName	nvarchar(50)	☑
MiddleName	nvarchar(50)	☑
LastName	nvarchar(50)	☑
NameStyle	bit	☑
BirthDate	datetime	☑
MaritalStatus	nchar(1)	☑
Suffix	nvarchar(10)	☑
Gender	nvarchar(1)	☑
EmailAddress	nvarchar(50)	☑
YearlyIncome	money	☑
TotalChildren	tinyint	☑
NumberChildrenAtHome	tinyint	☑
EnglishEducation	nvarchar(40)	☑
SpanishEducation	nvarchar(40)	☑
FrenchEducation	nvarchar(40)	☑
EnglishOccupation	nvarchar(100)	☑
SpanishOccupation	nvarchar(100)	☑
FrenchOccupation	nvarchar(100)	☑
HouseOwnerFlag	nchar(1)	☑
NumberCarsOwned	tinyint	☑
AddressLine1	nvarchar(120)	☑
AddressLine2	nvarchar(120)	☑
Phone	nvarchar(20)	☑
DateFirstPurchase	datetime	☑
CommuteDistance	nvarchar(15)	☑
		☐

Figure 2-2. *Dimension tables contain denormalized source data. The rows give meaning to the facts. It is typical for dimension tables to contain columns for many types of attributes.*

Attributes

You may be surprised to see the large number of columns in the DimCustomer table. The denormalized-style of modeling is completely opposite of that which you were probably taught when learning database modeling for OLTP systems. That's actually the point—OLAP modeling is quite different from modeling for OLTP!

Your SSAS cube can contain tens, hundreds, or even thousands of attributes to describe the business entities. The attributes are built from the source columns in the dimension source table or tables. Although most limits to the quantity of dimensional attributes that you can associate to a particular business entity have been removed in SSAS 2005, you do want to base the inclusion of columns in your dimension tables on business needs. In my real-world experience, this value is usually between 10 and 50 attributes per dimension.

Unlike erring on the conservative side (as I recommend you do when modeling the fact table)—that is, if in doubt, leave it out—when you are modeling dimensions, I recommend the opposite approach. If there is a possibility that a particular attribute will be of interest to a set of your end users, then add it to the star schema model. It is trivial to include, rename, or even exclude attributes when building your cube. Unless you anticipate that your dimension will be huge, having for example, more than a million members (which sometimes can be found in a dimension for customers, for example), then being "inclusive" in dimensional modeling is preferred.

There are additional options to OLAP modeling (that is, using table types other than fact tables and star dimension tables), which I will discuss later in this chapter, but the basic concept is simply a fact table and some related dimension tables. Figure 2-3 shows a conceptual star schema; note that I've modeled the dimensions keys in the preferred way in this diagram, that is, using original and new (or surrogate) keys.

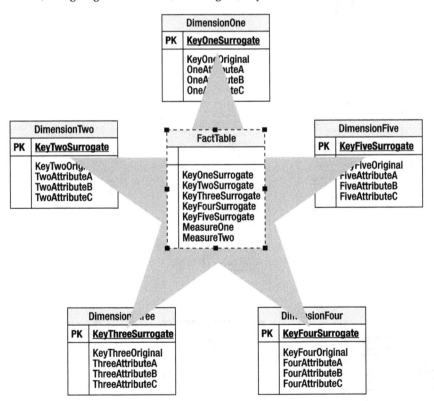

Figure 2-3. *A star schema consists of at least one fact table and many dimension tables. The dimension table rows are related to the fact table rows by keys.*

Why Create Star Schemas?

As discussed earlier, the simplest answer is that star schemas work best in the BIDS development environment for SSAS. Although it is possible to create a cube from OLTP (or normalized) source data, the results will be not optimal without a large amount of manual work on your part, and I do not recommend this practice. Also, flawed data in source systems is commonly discovered during the lifecycle of a BI project. Usually at least some source data needs to be part of a data cleansing and validation process. This is performed during the ETL phase of your project. Again, I've seen many a BI project "go astray" because source data was assumed to be "perfect" and found, upon investigation, to be far from that.

With the 2005 release of SSAS, Microsoft has improved the flexibility of source structures for cubes. This means you start with a series of star schemas and then make adjustments to your model to allow for business situations that fall outside of a strict star schema model. One example of this is the ability to base a single cube on multiple fact tables. Figure 2-4 shows an example of using two fact tables in an OLAP schema. This type of modeling is usually done because some, but not all, dimensions relate to some, but not all, facts. You'll see an example of this shortly.

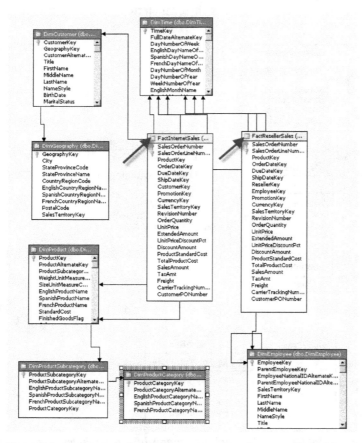

Figure 2-4. *SSAS 2005 cubes can now use more than one fact table as part of the source data, which results in greater flexibility in cube building.*

As will be discussed later in this chapter, there is additional flexibility in SSAS 2005 that allows you to model and implement in your OLAP cube which reflect many common business scenarios and which are not part of star schemas. Just one example of this is the need to allow null values to be loaded into a dimension or fact table and to define a translation of those nulls into a value that was understandable by end users, for example, "unknown." Scenarios such as this had been very difficult to model in SSAS 2000 using the strict star schema constraints. Remember, however, that this flexibility is not so broad as to eliminate the need to do standard OLAP modeling entirely.

In SSAS 2000, you had to create one cube per each fact table and then "union" those cubes together by using Virtual Cubes (which were in essence just views against multiple cubes). In SSAS 2005, the SSAS Data Matrix tab in the cube designer in BIDS allows you to define the grain of each relationship between the rows in the various fact tables to the rows in the dimension tables. This improved flexibility now results in most BI solutions being based on a single, large (or even huge) cube (or view of Enterprise Data). This type of modeling reflects the business need to have a single, unified version of relevant business data. This cube presents the data in whatever level of detail that is meaningful for the particular end user; that is, it can be summarized, or detailed, or any combination of both. This ability to create "one view of the (business) truth" is one of the most compelling features of SSAS 2005.

To drill into the Data Matrix, look at Figure 2-5. Here the employee dimension has no relationship with the rows (or facts) in the Fact Internet Sales table (because no employees are involved in Internet sales) but does have a relationship with the Fact Reseller Sales table (because employees are involved in reseller sales). Also, the customer dimension has no relationship with the rows in the Fact Reseller Sales table because customers are not resellers, but the customer dimension does have a relationship with the data in the Fact Internet Sales group (because customers do make Internet purchases). Dimensions common to both fact tables are products and time (due date, order date, and ship date). Note that the time dimension has three aliases. Aliasing the same dimension multiple times is called a *role-playing dimension*. We'll discuss this type of dimension in more detail in Chapter 6.

Dimensions	Fact Internet Sales	Fact Reseller Sales
Dim Product	Dim Product	Dim Product
Dim Time (Due Date)	Dim Time	Dim Time
Dim Time (Order D...)	Dim Time	Dim Time
Dim Customer	Dim Customer	
Dim Time (Ship Date)	Dim Time	Dim Time
Dim Employee		Dim Employee

Figure 2-5. *The Data Matrix in SSAS 2005 allows you to associate more than one fact table with a single cube, to set the level of granularity for each dimension, and to choose not to associate specific dimensions with specific fact tables.*

When creating a cube, the SSAS New Cube wizard attempts to detect the relationships between dimension and fact table rows and populates the Data Matrix using its "best guess" by examining the source column names. You can review (and update if needed) the results to exactly match your particular business scenarios.

Effectively Creating Star Schema Models Using Grain Statements

So, if the star schema is all-important, what's the best way for you to quickly and accurately create this model? In my experience, if you begin with "The End" in mind, you'll arrive at the best result in the quickest fashion. "The End" is a series of grain statements. So what exactly does this mean? To determine (or validate) grain statements, you can ask the following questions:

- What are the *key metrics* for your business? Some examples for a company that sells products include sales amount, sales quantity, gross profit, net profit, expenses, and so on.

- By what *factors* do you evaluate those key metrics? For example, do you evaluate sales amount by customer, by employee, by store, by date, by "what"?

- By what *level of granularity* do you evaluate each factor? For example, do you evaluate sales amount by day or by hour? Do you evaluate customers by store or by region?

Effective OLAP modelers use the grain statements gathered during the requirements phase of the project. It is critical that both subject matter experts (SMEs) and business decision makers validate each of the grain statements prior to beginning the modeling phase. I use a sign-off procedure to ensure that appropriate validation of grain statements has taken place.

Here are some examples of simple grain statements:

- We want to see sales amount and sales quantity by day, by product, by employee, and by store location.

- We want to see average score and quantity of courses taken, by course, by day, by student, by manager, by curriculum, and by curriculum type.

- We want to see a count of offenders by location, by offense type, by month, and by arresting officer.

Caution You might be tempted to skip entirely or to move too quickly through the requirements gathering/modeling phases of your BI project to get to the "real work" of actually building the cube in BIDS. I've seen this mistake repeated many, many times in the real world. The results are, at best, longer-than-needed development cycles, particularly in cases where people try to build cubes directly off of relational source (or slightly modified) data, or, at worst, projects have to be restarted from scratch. Don't make this costly mistake!

As you can see by my examples, BI solutions can be used by a broad variety of organizations. In my experience, although the "show me sales by day..." model is the most typical, it's not the only situation in which BI can prove useful. Some other interesting projects I've worked on included using OLAP cubes to improve decision support for the following business scenarios:

- Improve detection of foster care families not meeting all state requirements (SSAS data mining was also used in this scenario)

- Provide a flexible, fast query system to look up university course credits that are transferable to other universities

- Improve food cost and labor costs for a restaurant by viewing and acting on both trends and exception conditions

- Track the use and effectiveness of a set of online training programs by improving the timeliness and flexibility of available reports

When considering why and where you might implement SSAS in your enterprise, it is important to think broadly across the organization; that is, you should consider which groups would benefit from an aggregated view of their (and possibly other groups) data. It is Microsoft's position, and I agree, that any organization with stored data can benefit from using BI implemented on SSAS OLAP cubes.

Tools for Creating Your OLAP Model

My modeling tool of choice for designing star schemas is Visio 2003 Enterprise Edition. It's easy to use, readily available, and can be used to quickly generate the T-SQL DDL (Data Definition Language) source statements so that your design for star schemas can be rapidly materialized on your development server.

OLAP MODELING METHODS

You can also use the BIDS to create a star schema model. There are two ways to do this. You can use the New Cube wizard with the option of creating a new cube *without* using a data source. In this first method, you design all parts of the cube using the SSAS wizards.

The second method you can use is to build a dimension or a cube *without* using a data source and *with* one or more template files. You can use the included sample template files to explore this method. The default cube template files are located at `C:\Program Files\Microsoft SQL Server\90\Tools\Templates\olap\1033\Cube Templates`. The default dimension template files are located at `C:\Program Files\Microsoft SQL Server\90\Tools\Templates\olap\1033\Dimension Templates`. Later in this book, you will learn how to generate metadata files for cubes and dimensions you design. You could also use files that you have generated from cubes or dimensions that you have already designed as templates to design new cubes or dimensions.

For both of these methods, after you complete your design, in BIDS, you choose Database ➤ Generate Relational Schema. This will generate the T-SQL DDL code to create the empty star schema in the database that you configure in the dialog box for this wizard.

Although these methods are interesting and practical for some (simple) design projects, I still prefer to use Visio for most projects because it is more flexible than using SSAS. However, that flexibility comes with the tradeoff that you must design the entire model from scratch in Visio. Using BIDS, you may choose to use wizards to generate an iteration of your model, and then you manually modify that model. I can see how this would lend itself to rapid prototyping. The key decision factor is your depth of knowledge with OLAP concepts—the BIDS method assumes you understand OLAP modeling, Visio, of course, does not.

You'll usually start your design with dimension tables because much of the dimension data will be common to multiple grain statements. In the example I've provided in Figure 2-6, you can see that the relatively few tables are highly denormalized (meaning they contain many columns with redundant data; for example in StudentDim, the region, area, and bigArea columns).

StudentDim	
PK	**newStuID**
	oldID
	LName
	FName
	Alias
	standardTitle
	jobTitle
	jobTitleSummary
	specialistRole
	StartDateInRole
	HRMgrLName
	HRMgrFName
	HRMgrAlias
	salesLocation
	subRegion
	region
	area
	areaManager
	bigArea
	bigAreaManager
	Role
	clothingCut
	shirtSize
	pictureUrl
	bioText
	birthDate
	expertAreas
	majorAccounts
	numYearsInIndust
	specAwardsRcvd
	awardNameAndTime
	topChallenges

InstructorDim	
PK	**newInstID**
	oldID
	LName
	FName
	Alias
	AcademyMgrID
	Role
	HRMgrLName
	HRMgrFName
	HRMgrAlias
	salesLocation
	subRegion
	region
	area
	areaManager
	bigArea
	bigAreaManager
	isTopGun
	isSpecialContributor
	isInstructor
	isPresenter
	clothingCut
	shirtSize
	pictureUrl
	bioText
	birthDate
	expertAreas
	majorAccounts
	numYearsInIndust
	specAwardsRcvd
	awardNameAndTime
	topChallenges
	isOneOnOneConv
	prefClassOne
	prefClassTwo
	prefClassThree
	instNominee
	instStatus
	instNotes

StaffDim	
PK	**newStaffID**
	oldID
	LName
	FName
	Alias
	Role
	isVisitor
	salesLocation
	subRegion
	region
	area
	bigArea
	clothingCut
	shirtSize
	pictureUrl
	bioText
	birthDate

TimeDim	
PK	**newTimeID**
	Year
	HalfYear
	Quarter
	Month
	Day
	Hour
	Notes

OfferingDim	
PK	**newOfferingID**
	oldID
	offeringStatus
	offeringDescription
	offeringShortTitle
	offeringFullTitle
	offeringLevel
	offeringType
	academyType
	curriculumShortTitle
	curriculumFullTitle
	offeringCategory
	offeringCategoryType
	productGroupCategory
	busGroupCategory

SurveyDim	
PK	**newSurveyQuestionTypeID**
	oldID
	surveyType
	newQuestionID
	questionTextGeneric
	questionTextOriginal
	questionResponseID
	isSpecialReportQuestion
	reportNameForQuestion
	newOfferingID

Figure 2-6. *This model shows mostly star-type (or single table) dimensions. There is one snowflake-type (or multitable) dimension:* SurveyDim *and* OfferingDim.

Contrast this type of design with OLTP source systems, and you'll begin to understand the importance of the modeling phase in an OLAP project. In Figure 2-6, each dimension source table, except two (OfferingDim and SurveyDim), is the basis of a single cube dimension; for example, StudentDim is the basis of the Student dimension, InstructorDim is the basis of the Instructor dimension, and so on. These are all examples of star dimensions. OfferingDim and SurveyDim have a PK/FK relationship between the rows. They are the basis for a snowflake (or multitable sourced) dimension. You'll learn more about snowflake dimensions later in this chapter.

Also notice in Figure 2-6 that each table has two identity (or key) fields: a NewID and an OldID. This is modeled in the preferred method discussed earlier in this chapter.

Figure 2-7 shows the fact tables for the same project. You can see that there are nearly as many fact tables as dimension tables in this particular model example. This isn't necessarily common in OLAP model design; more commonly, you'll use 1 to 5 fact tables with 5 to 15 dimension tables, or more of both types. This model is used to illustrate reasons for using multiple fact tables; for example, some Session types have facts by day, whereas other Session types have facts by hour.

DailySessionFact	
PK	newID
	newOfferingID
	newStuID
	newInstID
	newStaffID
	studentStatus
	studentStatusDateID
	activity
	activityDateID
	outcome
	outcomeScore
	outcomeDateID

ConsensusSurveyValueFact	
PK	newID
	newSurveyQuestionTypeID
	consensusSurveyID
	newStuID
	newInstID
	newStaffID
	newTimeID
	consensusQuestionID
	responseValue
	isNonSession

ConsensusSurveyFreeTextFact	
PK	newID
	newSurveyQuestionTypeID
	consensusSurveyID
	newStuID
	newInstID
	newStaffID
	newTimeID
	consensusQuestionID
	responseFreeText
	isNonSession

ConsensusSurveyCountTextFact	
PK	newID
	newSurveyQuestionTypeID
	consensusSurveyID
	newStuID
	newInstID
	newStaffID
	newTimeID
	consensusQuestionID
	responseSelectedText
	isNonSession

HourlySessionFact	
PK	newID
	newOfferingID
	newStuID
	newInstID
	newStaffID
	studentStatus
	studentStatusDateID
	studentStatusTimeID
	accessType
	outcome
	outcomeScore
	outcomeDateID

Figure 2-7. *This model shows five fact tables that will be used in a single cube.*

Tip Because your project is now in the developing phase, any and all documents, including your .vsd models, must be under source control if multiple people will be working on the OLAP models.

As mentioned previously, although I've used Visio for modeling in all of my projects, if you are comfortable with a different database modeling tool, such as ERWIN, by all means, use it. The primary requirements for your modeling tool is that it generates a visual representation along with DDL code; so anything you are comfortable using for OLTP can be used for OLAP modeling as well.

As in relational modeling, OLAP modeling is an iterative process. When you start, you'll simply create the skeleton tables for your star schema by providing table names, keys, and a couple of essential column names (such as first name, last name for customer). As you continue to work on your design, you will refine the model by adding detail.

Because it is so critical, look back at the conceptual diagram of an OLAP star schema, shown earlier in Figure 2-3, one more time. Remember that this is the structure that you are trying to emulate. The closer you can get your models to true stars, the more quickly and smoothly the rest of the entire BI project will run.

Also remember the importance of using the customer's business terminology when naming objects in your model. The more frequently that you can name tables and columns per the captured taxonomy, the more quickly and easily your model will be understood, validated, and translated into cubes by everyone working on your project.

Modeling Source Schemas—Snowflakes and Other Variations

As mentioned previously, SSAS has increased the flexibility of source schemas to more easily accommodate the most common business needs that weren't easily modeled using star schemas. This section discusses some of those new or improved options.

Understanding the Snowflake Schema

A *snowflake* is a type of source schema used for dimensional modeling. Simply put, it means basing a dimension on more than one source relational table. The most common case is to use two source tables. However, if more than two tables are used as the basis of a snowflake dimension, there must be a key relationship between the each of the tables containing the dimension information.

Note in the example in Figure 2-8 that the DimCustomer table has a GeographyKey in it. This allows for the snowflake relationship between the rows in the DimGeography and the DimCustomer table to be detected by the New Cube wizard in BIDS.

The Data Matrix section of SSAS usually reflects the snowflake relationship, which you have modeled when you initially create the cube using the New Cube wizard (as long as the key columns have the same names across all related tables). If necessary, you can manually adjust any relationships after the cube has been created using tools provided in BIDS.

As shown previously in this chapter, Figure 2-9 again shows the Data Matrix. This time, we are going to drill down a bit deeper into using it. To adjust, or verify any relationship, click the Build button (the small grey square with the three dots on it) on the dimension name at the intersection of the dimension and fact tables. We'll start by looking at a "Regular" or star dimension by clicking the Build button at the intersection of DimProduct and Fact Internet Sales.

Figure 2-8. *The customer dimension uses two tables as its sources:* DimCustomer *and* DimGeography. *The rows in the tables are related by the* GeographyKey *field.*

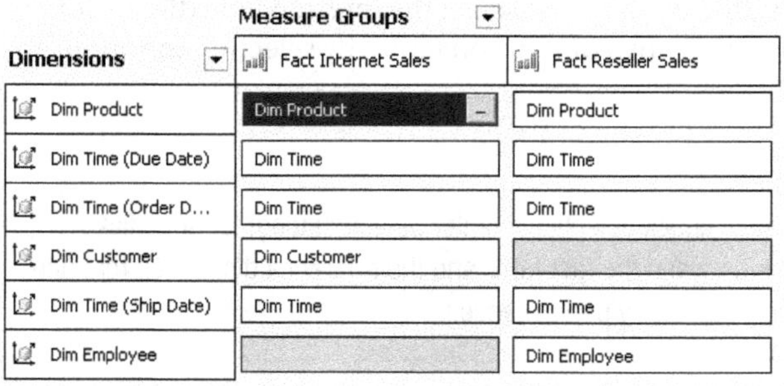

Dimensions ▾	Measure Groups ▾	
	[ᵢₗᵢ] Fact Internet Sales	[ᵢₗᵢ] Fact Reseller Sales
🗹 Dim Product	Dim Product —	Dim Product
🗹 Dim Time (Due Date)	Dim Time	Dim Time
🗹 Dim Time (Order D…)	Dim Time	Dim Time
🗹 Dim Customer	Dim Customer	
🗹 Dim Time (Ship Date)	Dim Time	Dim Time
🗹 Dim Employee		Dim Employee

Figure 2-9. *The Data Matrix is the starting point for defining the nature of the relationships between the dimension and fact tables. This includes defining the level of granularity of each relationship.*

Clicking the Build button opens the Define Relationship dialog box in which you can confirm that the relationship that BIDS detected during cube build is correct. If the relationship has been incorrectly defined, you can adjust it as well. In Figure 2-10, you can see that a Regular (or star) relationship has been correctly detected in the Select Relationship Type drop-down list—you validate this by verifying that the correct identifying key columns have been detected by BIDS when the cube was initially created. In this example, using the ProductKey from Dim Product (as PK) and Fact Internet Sales (as FK) tables reflects the intent of the OLAP design.

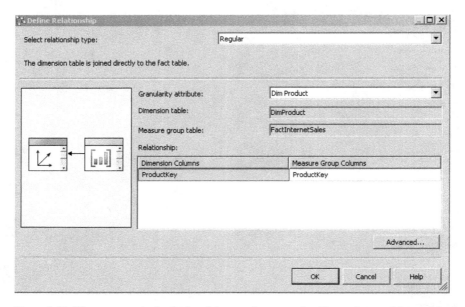

Figure 2-10. *The most typical relationship type between the dimension and fact tables in the Data Matrix is the Regular (or star) type. This means there is a one-to-many relationship between the rows in the fact table and the dimension table, based on the listed key.*

For a snowflake, you review or refine the relationship between the related dimension tables in the Define Relationship dialog box as shown in Figure 2-11. Note that the dialog box changes to reflect the modeling needs; that is, you must select the intermediate dimension table and define the relationship between the two dimension tables by selecting the appropriate key columns.

Note You will generally leave the Materialize check box checked (the default setting) for snowflake dimensions. This causes the value of the link between the fact table and the reference dimension for each row to be stored in SSAS and improves dimension query performance.

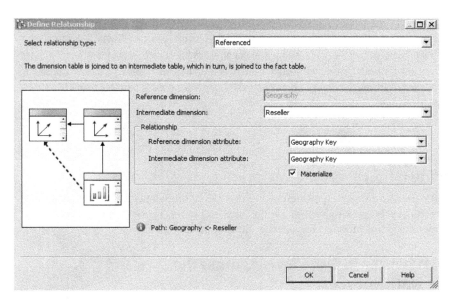

Figure 2-11. *Another possible relationship type between the dimension and fact tables in the Data Matrix is the Referenced type. This means that there is a one-to-many relationship between the rows in the fact table and the dimension table and includes an additional table, still based on the listed key. This is also called a snowflake dimension.*

Knowing When to Use Snowflakes

Because snowflakes add overhead to cube processing time and to query processing time, you should only use them when the business needs justify their use. They add overhead because the data must be joined at the time of process or query, rather than simply retrieved.

The most typical business situation that warrants the use of a snowflake dimension design is one that would reduce the size of the dimension table by removing one or more attributes that are not commonly used to a separate dimension table. An example of this would be a customer dimension with an attribute (or some attributes that are used for less than 20% of the customer records).

An example of this could be the URL of a customer's Web site in a business scenario where very few of your customers actually have their own Web sites. By creating a separate but related table, you significantly reduce the size of the customer dimension table.

Another situation that may warrant the use of a snowflake design is one in which the update behavior of particular dimensional attributes varies; that is a certain set of dimensional attributes should have their values overwritten if updated values become part of the source data, whereas a different set should have new records written for each update (maintaining change history). Although it is possible to combine different types of update behavior depending on the complexity of the dimension, it may be preferred to separate these attributes into different source tables so that the update mechanisms can be simpler.

> **Tip** In the real world, I've often seen inexperienced OLAP modelers overuse snowflakes. It is important to remember that the primary goal of the star schema is to denormalize the source data for efficiency. Any normalization, such as a snowflakes dimension, should relate directly to business needs. As this is opposite of OLTP modeling, it's often difficult to fight the urge to normalize. My experience is that less than 15% of dimensions need to be presented as snowflakes.

Considering Other Possible Variations

With SSAS 2005, there are several new techniques that OLAP modelers can use. These include Many-to-Many dimensions, Data Mining dimensions, and more. These (and other) more advanced modeling techniques are discussed in Chapters 8 and 11.

Choosing Whether to Use Views Against the Relational Data Sources

At this point you may be thinking that this OLAP modeling seems like a great deal of work, so why not just create views against the OLTP source (or sources) to get the same result? Although you technically could do this, as previously mentioned, my experience has been that seldom are the relational source or sources "clean" enough to directly model against.

The most typical situation is that first the OLAP model is created and validated, and then cleaned and validated data is loaded into the newly created OLAP model via ETL processes. Most organizations' data simply isn't prepared to allow for direct OLAP query against OLTP source data.

One area where relational views are sometimes used in OLAP projects is as data sources for the ETL. That is, in environments where OLAP models and ETL engineers are not allowed direct access to data sources, it is common for them to access the various data sources via views created by DBAs.

Also the time involved to write the queries to be used in (and possibly to index) the relational views may be substantial.

Understanding Dimensional Modeling (UDM)

The Unified Dimensional Model (UDM) is one of the key enhancements to Analysis Services 2005. In addition to removing the requirement that each dimension's hierarchies (or rollups) must be defined only at time of creation, Microsoft has further simplified the dimensional modeling system by basing all dimensions on attributes, rather than on groupings of attributes (called *hierarchies*), which was required in SSAS 2000.

Simply put, each column from the source dimension table is (by default) an attribute for that dimensional item.

Hierarchies serve two purposes in SSAS 2005. The first is largely a convenience for end users. This type of hierarchy is called a *browse* (or *navigational*) *hierarchy*. The second type is called a *natural hierarchy* and will be discussed in greater detail in Chapter 4. Natural hierarchies can change how aggregations (or precalculated intersections of facts) are created.

Also, all dimensional information is now public or sharable across all cubes. This differs from previous versions of SSAS, where dimensions could be defined as public or private.

Using the UDM

Understanding the "how" of modeling dimensional data, including understanding dimensions, levels, members, and hierarchies, it's best to start with some definitions (see Table 2-1) and a couple of examples. Figure 2-12 shows the Dimension Structure work area in BIDS.

Table 2-1. *List of OLAP Terms*

Term	Definition	Example
Dimension	Entity and all attributes related to that entity	Customers
Hierarchy	Grouping of attribute values for an entity	Customers by Geography
Member	Instance of entity, including attributes	ID=50, Name = Langit…
Level	Name of rollup position in hierarchy	State Level
Key	Primary identifier, two types: surrogate (or new) and original	NewID = 1, OldID = 101

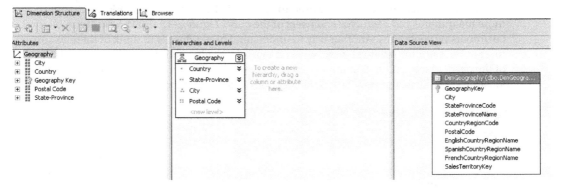

Figure 2-12. *The Dimension Structure work area in BIDS 2005 allows you to view and edit dimension information.*

The most important initial OLAP modeling consideration is to make every attempt to denormalize all source data related to a particular entity. As previously stated, the preferred source design for OLAP is the star schema, which means that each dimension's source data is put into a single table. Typically these tables are very wide, that is, having a large number of columns, and not especially deep, that is not having a large number of rows.

An example of this might be a product dimension. Your company may sell only a couple hundred different types of products, however, you may retain many, many attributes about each product. Some examples could include package size, package color, introduction date, and so on.

There can be exceptions to the general "wide, but not deep" modeling rule. The most common is for the customer's dimension. If it is a business requirement to capture all customers for all time, and if your organization services a very large customer base, then it could be the case that your customer dimension source table could have millions of rows.

One significant architectural enhancement in Analysis Services 2005 is that in this version, only dimension members being viewed by whatever client tool are loaded into memory. This is very different from SSAS 2000, where upon startup, all members of all dimensions were loaded into memory. This enhancement allows you to be inclusive in the design of dimensions, that is, more (attributes) is usually better.

After you've created the appropriate source dimension table or tables and populated them with data, SSAS will retrieve information out of these tables during cube and dimension processing. SSAS then uses a `SELECT DISTINCT` command to retrieve members from each column. If you use the Cube wizard to build your cube, Analysis Services will attempt to locate natural hierarchies in the data. A *dimensional hierarchy* is data that has a one-to-many relationship between data in different columns. A typical example of this is a customer's table with attributes relating to the customer's address. City, State, and Country are detected during cube creation by the wizard and associated into a hierarchy with three levels. If SSAS detects natural hierarchies during the running of the New Cube wizard, then it will name each level in the hierarchy using the column names from the dimension source tables. You can easily update these names during subsequent cube development.

When end users browse cube data, they can look at the facts or measures by any attribute value in any dimension by default. This could result in hundreds, thousands, or even millions of data members at each level in a dimension. Without rollups (or hierarchies), this information could be overwhelming in volume and not especially meaningful when end users try to view the data. These hierarchies are used to aggregate the view of information so that it is more meaningful and useful for end users of the cube. Figure 2-13 shows a common hierarchy, customers by geography. Another way to understand hierarchies is to think of them as summaries. For this particular example, you can look at the information in your cube at the level of the particular location or summarized to the level of all locations in a particular city, all locations in a particular province, or all locations in a particular country.

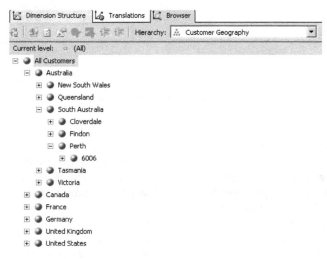

Figure 2-13. *The Dimension Structure work area in Analysis Services 2005 includes a Browser feature so that you can review the structure of the dimension by hierarchy (if hierarchies exist) prior to building your cube. If there are no hierarchies, you'll simply be shown all of the data members in the dimension.*

In addition to the hierarchies that are detected during cube build, you can manually create hierarchies in the cube very quickly and easily. The manual building of both navigations and natural dimensional hierarchies is covered in Chapter 4.

There are a couple of other new features in SSAS dimensions that you should consider when you are in the modeling phase of your BI project. These features include the ability to set the default displayed member for each attribute in a dimension, the ability to convert nulls to a value (usually unknown or 0), and the ability to allow duplicate names to be displayed. You should model for these features based on business requirements, so you should capture the business requirements for defaults, unknowns, and duplicates for each dimension and all of its attributes during the modeling phase of your project.

This ability to create hierarchies easily and with a great deal of flexibility is new to this version of SSAS. In SSAS 2000, you had to create both the dimension and any hierarchies associated with it at the time the cube was built. Changes to those hierarchies required a cube or dimension reprocess. This is no longer the case with SSAS 2005. Cube or dimension reprocessing can make the cube unavailable for end users, so the ability to restructure a dimension in SSAS 2005 provides better availability of the cube and more flexibility during the design process.

The Slowly Changing Dimension (SCD)

The next consideration for you when modeling dimensional data is to review business requirements for the dimension information. You are looking for the desired outcome when dimension member information is updated or deleted.

In OLAP modeling, inserting new dimension members is *not* considered a change. The only two cases you must be concerned with here are updates and deletes. This type of modeling is called slowly changing dimensional (SCD) modeling.

The first question to ask of your SMEs is "What do you want to happen when dimension members no longer have fact data associated with them?" In my experience, most clients prefer to have dimension members marked as "not active" at this point, rather than deleted. In some cases, it has been a business requirement to add the date of deactivation as well.

The next case to consider is the business requirements for dimension member value updates. The most common scenario is names of people, that is, customers, employees, and so on. The question to ask here is "What do you want to happen when an employee changes his or her name, (for example, women getting married)?"

Table 2-2 shows the four different possibilities in modeling, depending on the answer to the preceding question.

Table 2-2. *Possible SCD Modeling Options*

Requirement	Description
No changes	Any change is an error; retain original information.
Last change wins	Overwrite with any change; do not retain original value.
Retain some history	Retain a fixed number of previous values.
Retain all history	Retain all previous values.

Type 1, 2, 3 SCD Solutions

The table of requirements for dimension member changes (Table 2-2) is the basis for you to model the source tables using standard slowly changing dimension type behavior modeling. This standard is implemented across a broad variety of OLAP products, including SSIS packages for the ETL. In this case, we are thinking about SSIS packages that implement updates and deletes to dimension values.

Review the requirements and note that some dimension members will allow changes. You will need to translate those requirements to one of these standard solutions.

- *Type 1*: Means *overwriting* previous dimension member values, which is sometimes also called *last change wins*. This type is called a Changing Attribute in the SSIS Slowly Changing Dimension wizard.

- *Type 2*: Means adding a *new record* (or row value) when the dimension member value changes. This type is called a Historical Attribute in the SSIS Slowly Changing Dimension wizard.

- *Type 3*: Means adding additional *attributes* (or column values) when the dimension member value changes. This type is not supported in the SSIS Slowly Changing Dimension wizard.

Another important reason to use this standard modeling approach is that SSIS (and several other OLAP products) supports these terms and concepts in the new SCD data flow transformation task object. This is important because, although you'll probably manually process updates or deletes to dimensional attribute member values during development, after you move to production, you'll want to automate this process. Using the new SSIS transformation (with its associated configuration wizard) is a quick and easy way to move this type of process to a SSIS package. The key configuration wizard page for this SSIS transformation is shown in Figure 2-14. SSIS packages are designed to automate ETL processes across your BI project.

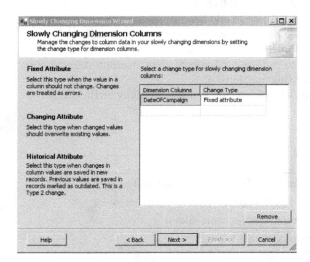

Figure 2-14. *The Slowly Changing Dimension Wizard in SSIS helps you manage the data in this type of dimension.*

The Rapidly Changing Dimension (RCD)

The Rapidly Changing Dimension (RCD) is a dimension whose member values change constantly. *Constantly* is the operative word here. This should be a very small subset of your dimensional data. To work with this type of dimension, you will probably vary the storage location, rather than implementing any particular design in the OLAP model itself.

RCD data storage models are covered in more detail in Chapter 7 (with the rest of the discussion about overall cube data storage). An example of this type of dimension is in a fast food restaurant chain, where the employee dimension may need to reflect very high staff turnover. The employee dimension is modeled as an RCD.

Writeback Dimension

Another advanced capability of dimensions is writeback. *Writeback* is the ability for authorized end users to update the data members in a dimension: insert, update, or delete. In my experience, only a very small number of business scenarios warrant enabling writeback for particular cube dimensions.

If you are considering enabling writeback, verify that it is acceptable given any regulatory requirements, such as SOX, HIPAA, and so on, in your particular business environment.

There are some restrictions if you want to enable writeback. The first restriction is that the dimension must be based on a single table, meaning it must use a star schema modeling format. The second restriction is that writeback dimensions are only supported in the Enterprise Edition of Analysis Services. Finally, writeback security must be specifically enabled at the user level. This is covered in more detail in Chapter 13.

Tip To review features available by edition for SSAS 2005 go to http://www.microsoft.com/sql/prodinfo/features/compare-features.mspx.

Note As mentioned earlier, SSAS 2005 allows for new (and more advanced) dimension modeling types, including Many-to-Many dimensions, and more. These are discussed in more detail in Chapter 6.

Understanding Fact (Measure) Modeling

One key and core part of your BI solution is the business facts that you choose to include. As mentioned previously, facts are also called measures. Measures are the key metrics by which you measure the success of your business. Some examples include daily sales amount, product sales quantity, net profit, and so on. Clearly selecting the appropriate facts is a critical consideration in your model.

If you have been thorough in the business requirements gathering phase of your BI project, then modeling facts should be simple.

In most cases, facts are numeric and are aggregated by summing the facts across all levels of all dimensions. There are, however, exceptions to this rule. An example of the most typical case is a cube that captures sales activity as shown in Figure 2-15 from the AdventureWorks sample.

Name	Measure Group	Data Type	Aggregation
Order Quantity	Fact Internet Sales	Integer	Sum
Unit Price	Fact Internet Sales	Double	Sum
Extended Amount	Fact Internet Sales	Double	Sum
Unit Price Discount Pct	Fact Internet Sales	Double	Sum
Discount Amount	Fact Internet Sales	Double	Sum
Product Standard Cost	Fact Internet Sales	Double	Sum
Total Product Cost	Fact Internet Sales	Double	Sum
Sales Amount	Fact Internet Sales	Double	Sum
Tax Amt	Fact Internet Sales	Double	Sum
Freight	Fact Internet Sales	Double	Sum
Fact Internet Sales Count	Fact Internet Sales	Integer	Count
Order Quantity - Fact Reseller...	Fact Reseller Sales	Integer	Sum
Unit Price - Fact Reseller Sales	Fact Reseller Sales	Double	Sum
Extended Amount - Fact Rese...	Fact Reseller Sales	Double	Sum
Unit Price Discount Pct - Fact ...	Fact Reseller Sales	Double	Sum
Discount Amount - Fact Resell...	Fact Reseller Sales	Double	Sum
Product Standard Cost - Fact ...	Fact Reseller Sales	Double	Sum
Total Product Cost - Fact Res...	Fact Reseller Sales	Double	Sum
Sales Amount - Fact Reseller ...	Fact Reseller Sales	Double	Sum
Tax Amt - Fact Reseller Sales	Fact Reseller Sales	Double	Sum
Freight - Fact Reseller Sales	Fact Reseller Sales	Double	Sum
Fact Reseller Sales Count	Fact Reseller Sales	Integer	Count

Figure 2-15. *The Measures window in BIDS allows you to view and alter properties of measures (or facts) used in your cube.*

Figure 2-15 shows all of the facts (or measures), the measure group (which is simply a folder that has the same name as the source fact table), the data type, and the aggregation type from the cube design tab in BIDS. You may notice that all but two measures use Sum as their aggregation type. There are two count measures shown in the figure. Sum is the default type of aggregation in SSAS.

The built-in aggregation types available for use in SSAS are listed in Table 2-3. Note that the table lists the "Type" of measure. This is a descriptor of the aggregation behavior. Additive means "rolls up the one ultimate total." Semiadditive means "rolls up to a total for each level, but not cumulative, and is applicable only over a time dimension." Nonadditive means "does NOT roll up," that is, only shows that particular value. Also Semiadditive measures require the Enterprise Edition of SSAS.

Table 2-3. *Aggregation Functions Available in SSAS*

Aggregation	Type
Sum	Additive
Count, Min, Max	Semiadditive
FirstChild, LastChild	Semiadditive
AverageOfChildren	Semiadditive
FirstNonEmpty, LastNonEmpty	Semiadditive
ByAccount	Semiadditive
DistinctCount, None	Nonadditive

Note ByAccount aggregation means an aggregation that calculates according to the aggregation function assigned to the account type for a member in an account dimension. An *account dimension* is simply a dimension that is derived from a single, relational table with an account column. The data value in this column is used by SSAS to map the types of accounts to well-known account types (for example, Assets, Balances, and so on) so that you replicate the functionality of a balance sheet in your cube. SSAS uses these mappings to apply the appropriate aggregation functions to the accounts. If no account type dimension exists in the measure group, then ByAccount is treated as the None aggregation function.

Calculated Measure vs. Derived Measure

A final consideration for measures is that you can elect to derive measure values on load of data into the cube. This type of measure is called a *derived measure* because it is "derived" or created when the cube is loaded, rather than simply retrieved using a SELECT statement from the source fact table(s). Creating derived measures is done via a statement (T-SQL for SQL Server) that is understood by the source database. I do not advocate using derived measures because the overhead of creating them slows cube processing times.

Rather than incurring the overhead of deriving measures during cube loads, an alternative way to create the measure value is to calculate and store the measure value during the ETL process, which is used to load the (relational) fact table, rather than the SSAS cube. That way, the value can simply be retrieved (rather than calculated) during the cube load process.

In addition to derived measures, SSAS supports calculated measures. *Calculated measure* values are calculated at query time by SSAS. Calculated measures execute based on queries that you write against the OLAP cube data. These queries are written in the language required for querying SSAS cubes, which is MDX. I will review the process for creating calculated measures in Chapter 10.

Other Types of Modeling

SSAS 2005 supports additional capabilities that may affect the final modeling of your cube source schemas. In my experience, most clients start with the concepts presented in this chapter, load some sample data to validate both the data and the modeling concepts, and then add the more advanced capabilities.

Data Mining

Data mining capabilities are greatly enhanced in SSAS 2005 as compared to SSAS 2000 due to the larger number of more sophisticated algorithms. *Data mining* is the ability to use included algorithms to detect patterns in the data. Interestingly, SSAS's data mining capabilities can be used with either OLTP or OLAP source data. Data mining is covered in more detail in Chapter 11.

KPIs (Key Performance Indicators)

The ability to create key performance indicators (KPI) from inside a SSAS 2005 cube is a much-requested feature. A *KPI* is a method (usually displayed in an end-user tool visually) of showing one or more key business metrics: the current state, comparison to goal, trend over time, and other information. KPIs are usually shown via graphics, such as, red, yellow, or green traffic lights; up arrows or down arrows; and so on. You'll learn about the planning and implementation of SSAS KPIs in Chapter 5.

Actions, Perspectives, Translations

SSAS *actions* give the end users the ability to right-click a cell of the cube and to perform some type of defined action, such as passing the value of the selected cell into an external application as a parameter value and then launching that application. They are not new to this release, but new types of actions are available.

Perspectives are similar conceptually to relational views. They allow you to create named subsets of your cube data for the convenience of your end users. They require the Enterprise Edition of SSAS 2005.

Translations give OLAP modelers a quick and easy way to present localized cube metadata to end users.

All of these capabilities are covered in more detail in Chapter 5.

Source Control and Other Documentation Standards

Already in the OLAP modeling phase, your BI project will contain many files of many different types. While you are in the modeling phase, the files will probably mostly consist of Visio diagrams, Excel spreadsheets, and Word documents. It is very important to establish a methodology for versioning and source control early in your project. When you move to the prototyping and developing phase, the number and types of files will increase exponentially.

You can use any tool that works for you and your team: Visual Source Safe, Visual Studio Team System, SharePoint Document Libraries, or versioning via Office. The important point is that you must establish a system that all of your BI team members are committed to using early in your BI project lifecycle. Also it's important to use the right tool for the right job; for example, SharePoint Document Libraries are designed to support versioning of requirements documents (which are typically written using Word, Excel, and so on), whereas VSS is designed to support source control for OLAP code files, which you'll create later in your project's lifecycle.

Another important consideration is naming conventions. Unlike OLTP (or relational) database design, there are very few common naming standards in the world of OLAP design. I suggest that you author, publish, and distribute written naming guidelines to all members of your BI team during the requirements gathering phase of your project. These naming guidelines should include suggested formats for the following items at minimum: cubes, dimensions, levels, attributes, star schema fact and dimension tables, SSIS packages, SSRS reports, SPS or MOSS pages, and dashboards.

Summary

This chapter covered the basic modeling concepts and techniques for cubes in a BI project. You saw how grain statements can be used for a high-level validation of your modeling work. You learned how best to determine what types of dimensions (fixed, SCD, or RCD) and facts (stored, calculated, or derived) will be the basis for your cubes. I also discussed the concept of hierarchies of dimensional information.

If you are new to BI, you've got some "unlearning" to do. OLAP modeling is very dissimilar to OLTP modeling, mostly because of the all prevalent concept in OLAP of deliberate denormalization. As your design evolves, the next step in the BI project process is to begin to match your source data to your intended destination schemas. This is the world of data mapping and ETL using SSIS, and that's the focus of the next chapter.

CHAPTER 3

■■■

Introducing SSIS

You've captured business requirements and are working on creating a basic OLAP design. The next task in creating your BI solution is to map the data from the source system(s) to your OLAP model. In larger BI projects, it is common for different people (or teams) to be working on an OLAP design and an ETL design concurrently.

Data maps are used as a basis for beginning your ETL design. As mentioned in Chapter 1, ETL stands for Extract, Transform, and Load. It is important that you don't underestimate the amount of work involved in this portion of your project. In fact, 75% of the initial project work in a BI solution commonly consists of ETL process design, execution, and debugging. The SQL Server 2005 ETL toolset is called SQL Server Integration Services (SSIS).

Note The toolset available in SQL Server 2000 to perform ETL tasks was called Data Transformation Services (DTS). Although SSIS bears some resemblance to DTS in that both toolsets include features to perform the ETL of data, SSIS has been redesigned from scratch and is, in reality, quite a different from DTS.

This chapter covers the following topics:

- Methods, processes, and tools for ETL

- Using the Import/Export Wizard

- An example of a simple SSIS package

- Adding transformations to the data flow

Understanding ETL

ETL, in a BI project context, is the process of preparing all source data for use in an OLAP cube. The rich SSIS toolset can be used for other types of data movement, for example, data consolidations and migrations. In this book, we will focus on the BI project use of SSIS, which is extracting, transforming, and loading data from one or more source systems into an OLAP model. This process may also involve the use of an intermediate staging server that contains a staging database with staging tables. The use of a staging server and database is usually driven by the complexity and "messiness" of the source data. For example, in a recent project

I worked on, there were 16 data sources, each with its own unique validation issues. The ETL project consisted of an intermediate staging table for each data source.

Another consideration is whether or not the source data is contained in a relational structure. If a project will be using a large number of nonrelational source files, .csv, .txt, .xml, and so on, then a staging server and database are often used as part of the ETL process.

The first part of the BI ETL process is to create a documented plan for your project's ETL. You will often create a high-level overview diagram like the one shown in Figure 3-1 that shows the data sources you will include in your project. When creating your data diagram (which is just one part of your documented ETL plan; other parts include specific [data] control flows for package design, security credentials to access data sources, and so on), you should first make a list of all possible data sources for your project. A typical mistake is to not include all data sources in this selection. Your source data will most probably include one or more relational databases; however, you should not restrict yourself to relational data only. It is very common to use data from a variety of sources in the organization. These sources can include relational databases, flat-file databases, Excel spreadsheets, XML files, text files, Active Directory, ERP (or Enterprise Resource Planning (or ERP) systems, output from a mainframe, and so on.

You may also add detail to this diagram. Detail can include load window times (between which times you may extract data) and type of access, for example, FTP for files, and so on.

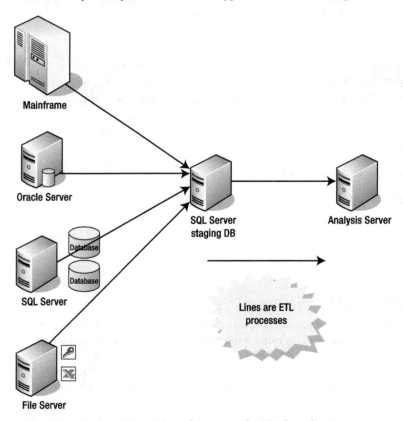

Figure 3-1. *A Visio representation of an example ETL data diagram*

Data Maps

After you've created a complete list of your data sources for extract by creating a high-level diagram and a complementary and more detailed list containing extraction information such as load windows, authentication type, transfer protocol, and so on in something like Excel, then the next step is to design a detailed data map.

To do this, you will begin to map the data sources more specifically to the data destination locations. The destinations are based on the OLAP star schemas that you've already created and may include "map through" staging tables, if you've chosen to use them. As you continue your design documentation, you will add more detail to the information captured in this diagram. The outcome of this process is called a *data map*.

You may remember that the use of an intermediate or staging server was shown in Figure 3-1. Although this is not a requirement for use of Analysis Services, using a separate staging server (from your production OLTP server and separate from your Analysis Services server) is common practice. In addition to choosing to add this dedicated server due to data load complexity, another consideration is that you can offload work from the production OLTP server and consolidate ETL processes onto one physical machine.

You may not have a one-to-one match for some of the tables or the table fields at this point. At this early stage, you are beginning to match source data with destination data. Later you will identify SSIS transformations and map from source to destination all the way to the column level for each table of each data source. An example of a portion of an early data map is shown in Figure 3-2. Within the three meta-sections in this figure—sources, transformations, and destinations—boxes represent items that will need to be mapped; that is, there is an .xls source for customers, and that .xls will need a concatenation transformation and will be sent to the DimCustomer table destination.

You will commonly work with SMEs to make corrections in your OLAP star schema based on new information discovered during the ETL mapping process. You might also need to work with SMEs due to nonintuitive source information, such as obscure column names in source tables, or data that must be translated from a numeric to a text value to be meaningful. Sometimes this will result in your OLAP star schema design changing, and sometimes this will also result in the inclusion of more source data than was originally planned for.

All stakeholders should approve any significant changes to the scope of your BI solution. These changes may also cause budget and resources to be adjusted for your BI project.

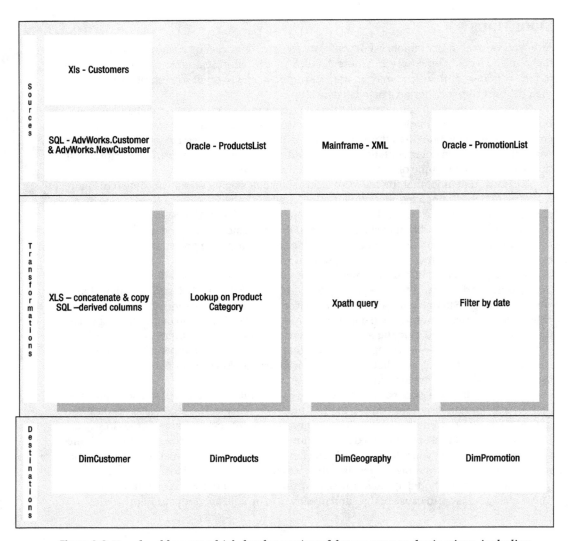

Figure 3-2. *You should create a high-level mapping of data sources to destinations, including partial transformation information during the early stages of creating your BI project data map.*

Refining a Data Map

The next step in your ETL-mapping process is to create a more detailed data map. I've used Excel for this in past BI projects. Your goal here is to add as much detail as possible to your data map prior to starting development of SSIS processes (or packages as they are called in SQL Server 2005).

Figure 3-3 is an example of a more detailed data map. Note the addition of all columns in the destination table and a partial mapping of sources to destinations at the column level.

Strive to be as complete as possible in your data map prior to starting actual SSIS package development.

Dimension Table Name	Dimension Column Name	Constraint Type	Surrogate Key	Exist in OLAP Only	Data Type	Original Data Source FC
StaffDim						
	NewStaffID	PK	Yes	Yes		
	OldID					Academy.Member.MemberID
	LName					Academy.Member.LastName
	FName					Academy.Member.FirstName
	Alias					Academy.Member.Email
	Role					Academy.role.Title
	IsVisitor				bit	if Academy.Role.Title = visitor then true
	SalesLocation					Unknown
	SubRegion					Unknown - EDS
	Region					Unknown - EDS
	Area					Unknown
	BigArea					Unknown
	ClothingCut					Academy.StaffProfile.ProfileStatusXml.ClothingCut
	ShirtSize					Academy.StaffProfile.ProfileStatusXml.ShirtSize
	PictureUrl					Academy.StaffProfile.ProfileStatusXml.PictureUrl
	BioText					Academy.StaffProfile.ProfileStatusXml.BioText
	BirthDate					Academy.StaffProfile.ProfileStatusXml.BirthDay+BirthMonth

Figure 3-3. *More detailed data mapping, showing a single destination table, with source data listed for each column*

Staging Servers

In Figure 3-1, the physical implementation of a BI solution shows a separate physical server as a "staging server." Although this separate physical server is not required for all BI solutions, you should consider the factors that might cause you to add this server to your solution.

Although you can easily install both SQL Server 2005 (which includes SSIS) and SSAS on the same physical server, there are many good reasons for separating these two products. In most production BI solutions that I've implemented, separating SSIS and SSAS has been selected as the final production configuration.

By using two servers for SSIS and SSAS, you are separating two key components of your BI solutions: the ETL processes and the cube processing/hosting environments. In doing this, you are creating a configuration that is easier to maintain, performance tune, and scale, than if you were to use one server for both types of functionality.

Although the "two server" configuration is the one I've most commonly used in production, it is valid to install both SQL Server 2005 and SSAS on the same physical server for development or testing. Of course, it is always preferred to duplicate the production environment in the testing and development areas, but the reality for many of my customers is that their resource constraints necessitate simpler solutions in testing and development.

After you decide the appropriate physical configuration given your particular requirements and constraints (and have a relatively complete data map), then you are ready to begin the actual ETL process development for your BI project. You will usually use SQL Server 2005 SSIS to do this.

If your source data is exceptionally clean, it is theoretically possible to use a simpler method, such as, for example, T-SQL statements (if all source data was contained in SQL Server), rather than SSIS packages to perform the ETL portion of your BI project. This is "theoretical" because although a couple of customers have suggested this simplified approach to me, I've not found the business environment yet that was sufficiently disciplined to provide data that was clean enough to be directly used in a BI project.

ETL Tools for BI/SSIS Packages

SSIS has been completely redesigned in SQL Server 2005. As mentioned previously, in SQL Server 2000, these tools were called *Data Transformation Services* (DTS). The reason for the name change is a dramatic enhancement in functionality. SSIS packages are the basic units of the ETL processes in a BI solution. SSIS packages contain four fundamental parts: control flow, data flow, error handlers, and configurations. Although you can design packages with these four fundamental parts in BIDS, we're not going to start there just yet; rather, you'll use an included wizard to design your first package. There are three reasons for doing this: simple data movement is quicker, wizard-designed packages can serve as templates or starting points for other packages, and the wizard encapsulates quite a bit of functionality.

Creating a Basic SSIS Package with the SQL Server Import/Export Wizard

The most basic functionality in SSIS, however, remains relatively unchanged from the previous version of DTS in SQL Server 2000. For the simplest possible data movement, you can use the SQL Server Import/Export Wizard from inside of SSMS.

■ **Note** You can also access the Import/Export Wizard from inside of BIDS by creating a project of type SQL Server Integration Service and right-clicking the SSIS packages folder in the Solution Explorer window.

To access the wizard, right-click any database in the Object Explorer window in SSMS, and then click on Tasks ➤ Import Data or click on Tasks ➤ Export Data. This will start the wizard as shown in Figure 3-4.

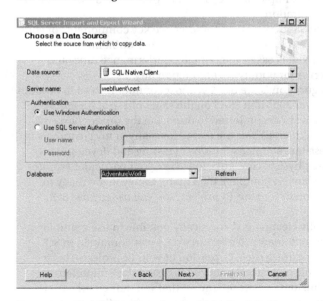

Figure 3-4. *Choosing a Data Source is the first step in using the SQL Server Import/Export Wizard for SSIS.*

The next step is choosing a destination for your data. The wizard can work with SQL Server and non-SQL sources and destinations. After you've selected both source and destination, you'll then need to choose one of two options: (1) Copy data from one or more tables or views or (2) Write a query to specify the data to transfer (which copies some subset of data to your selected destination) as shown in Figure 3-5.

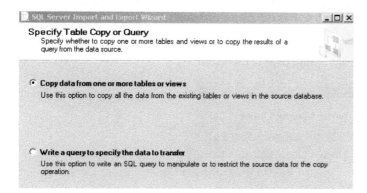

Figure 3-5. *In this step of the Import/Export Wizard, you select from one of the two shown options.*

If you select the first option, the wizard will allow selecting one or more tables or views from the source location. The default is to copy the object metadata (or structure) and data to the destination location in the same format as the source. You can adjust this, however, by clicking the Edit Mappings button in the Select Source Tables and Views option page of the wizard. If you do this, you can skip importing selected columns by setting the Destination column value to <ignore>. This is shown for the column named rowguid in Figure 3-6.

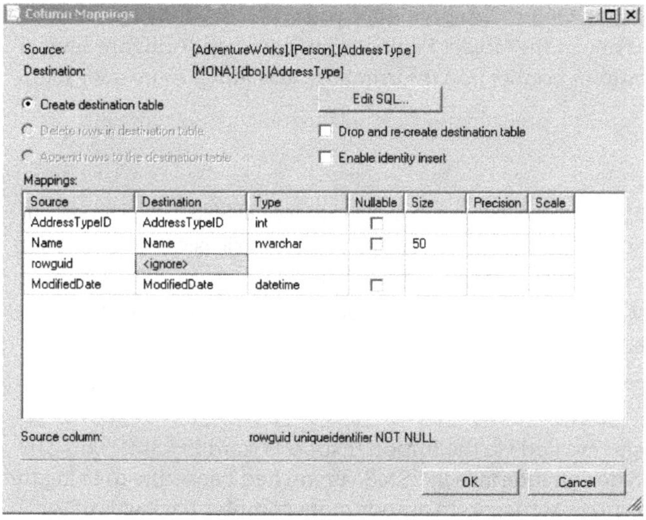

Figure 3-6. *In this step of the wizard, you can set the package to skip or ignore selected columns.*

The next step of the wizard allows you to run the import (or export) process that you've configured immediately, and (optionally) to save it as a SSIS package. You can select from two locations if you want to save your package: SQL server or the file system.

If you store your package on SQL server, you will have to specify a server name and authentication credentials. The package will be stored in the MSDB database on the server you selected. If you select storage on the file system, you must supply a path. The package will be stored at that location as a file with a .dtsx extension. Although not required, the preferred method is to store your packages on a SQL Server instance in MSDB, so that you can more easily attend to administrative tasks, such as performing backups, scheduling execution, and so on. Figure 3-7 shows the storage option page of the wizard.

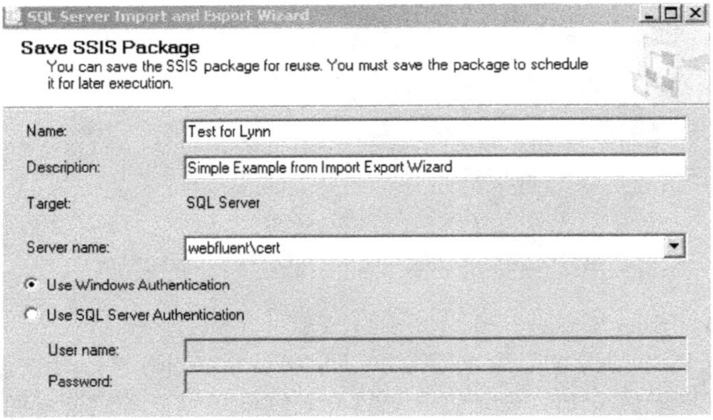

Figure 3-7. *In the final step of the wizard, you can save and store the package on SQL Server.*

If you want to rerun your package, you can view and run it from SSMS. Unlike SQL Server 2000 Enterprise Manager, which included a DTS node, in SQL Server 2005 SSMS, you must click Connect ➤ Integration Services in Object Explorer. After you've successfully connected, you'll see the package in the menu tree in the Object Explorer. You can then configure several runtime properties—error log locations, connection information, and much more—for the package as shown in Figure 3-8.

Note As of this writing, there are bugs when connecting to a named instance of SSIS. First SSIS will not allow you to connect to a named instance using SSMS. If you attempt to do so, you'll receive an error dialog box. Also, changing the <SERVERNAME> element to the name of the named instance where SSIS is installed in the SSIS configuration file (MsDtsSrvr.ini.xml) as directed per the BOL "Configuring the Integration Services Service" does not appear to fix this bug.

Although you can save packages created via the Import/Export Wizard in SSMS, you cannot create packages using the SSIS design interface in SSMS, as you had been able to using the DTS node of SQL Server 2000 Enterprise Manager. To author more complex packages of the type typically used in ETL processes for BI projects, you must use BIDS.

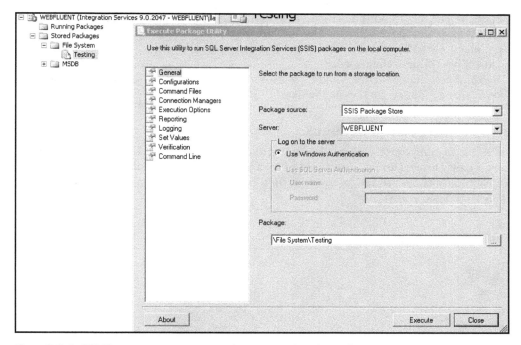

Figure 3-8. *In SSMS, you can set many runtime properties of a package.*

Note You can create SSIS packages in SSMS for SQL Server Maintenance. To do this, you right-click the Maintenance Plan folder (located in the Object Explorer window under the Management folder), and then select New Maintenance Plan. This type of package wouldn't normally be used as part of the ETL for a BI project.

One reason to use the Import/Export Wizard in SSMS rather than using BIDS to create simple packages is to quickly create prototype packages (templates as well) that you can later edit using BIDS.

Basic SSIS Packages Using BIDS

As with other types of BI design, such as cubes, you'll open BIDS to begin creating an SSIS package. BIDS functionality is accessed via a set of included BI template types that are available inside of the Visual Studio 2005 interface. It is not a requirement to install VS 2005 to use BIDS; however, if you do have VS 2005 installed, then BIDS will be completely integrated into the VS 2005 environment.

BI objects are created using the BIDS templates, including templates to create SSAS databases (cubes, dimensions, and data mining structures and models), SSIS projects (SSIS packages), and SSRS reports and report models. Templates consist of starter folders and files that are specific to the project type selected. To start working in BIDS, you open it from the Start menu, click File, click New and then select the appropriate project type from the templates of type Business Intelligence.

VS 2005 contains solutions and projects. *Solutions* are containers for projects, and *projects* are containers for files and folders.

Developing SSIS Packages

As with designing your first cube, developing SSIS packages requires that you use BIDS to create a new project. In this case, you'll select a project from the BI category and of type Integration Services Project. After you do that, you'll see the development environment shown in Figure 3-9.

Figure 3-9. *SSIS packages are authored using BIDS with a project type of Integration Services Project.*

Because BIDS provides a completely new interface for ETL, let's review each section of the development surface. The first section you'll use is the Solution Explorer. This shows the name of the project and is, in essence, a container for multiple .dtsx packages. Projects are used now because they are a natural way to group packages together for doing the ETL processes for a particular BI project (or SSAS database, which will typically contain one or more OLAP cubes). In SQL Server 2000, DTS packages were designed in Enterprise Manager because the concept of projects was not available.

The nodes, or folders, below the project name are provided in Table 3-1.

Table 3-1. *List of Folders in BIDS for SSIS Package Template*

Folder	Purpose
Data Sources	Contains connections used in one or more packages (global connections)
Data Source Views	Contains abstractions against one or more data sources
SSIS Packages	Contains SSIS packages (.dtsx files)
Miscellaneous	Contains other file types, that is, .txt, .xml, and so on

If you wanted to edit a package that you had created in SQL SSMS using the Import/Export Wizard, you could import it into BIDS by right-clicking the SSIS Packages folder in Solution Explorer and choosing Add Existing Package. In the Package location drop-down list in the Add Copy of Existing Package dialog box, you choose SSIS Package Store (see Figure 3-10).

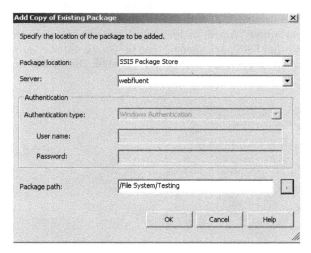

Figure 3-10. *In the Add Copy of Existing Package dialog box in BIDS, you select the import package from whatever SSIS Package Store location you've originally stored your package(s) in to be able to edit packages created in SSMS using the Import/Export Wizard.*

Note What is the difference between storing a SSIS package on the file system or SQL Server versus storing it in the SSIS package store? The SSIS package store is actually a (fixed) file location, found by default in the C:\Program Files\Microsoft SQL Server\90\DTS\Packages folder. If you store a package on a file system location, you can specify any valid path at the time of saving the package. Packages stored in SQL Server are stored in the MSDB database.

Designing SSIS Packages

Now you are ready to design your first SSIS package. Using your detailed data map, you should have information about the source, destination, and potential transformations documented. This will be the basis for your package design. For BI projects, best practice is to design one or more packages per destination table and not design individual packages that load data into multiple tables. By following this simple guideline—and ideally documenting it as a standard for your ETL team—you'll be reducing the effort involved in updating and maintaining your SSIS packages over the lifetime of the BI solution.

For our first example, you'll create a simple package that extracts data from a single source location and loads it into a staging (or intermediate) table in your star schema database. The first thing to consider is how you'll connect to the data sources.

Configuring Connections

Although it is possible to define connections only within each package, as a matter of convenience, you will most often reuse connections across multiple packages within the same project. To create a new connection in this way, right-click the Data Sources folder in the Solution Explorer window to open a Data Source Wizard. In this wizard, you can either reuse a previously defined connection for any other SSIS package designed on your computer, or you can create a new connection. Click New to open the Connection Manager Dialog dialog box shown in Figure 3-11.

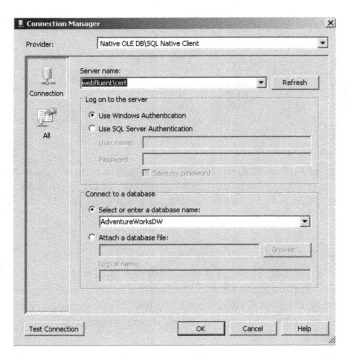

Figure 3-11. *In the Connection Manager dialog box in BIDS, you configure reusable connections. The All button on the left allows you to set advanced connection properties, such as connection timeout values.*

The next step is to associate this global connection with the specific package that you are working on. To do this, right-click the bottom-center area of the package design surface in BIDS titled *Connection Managers,* and a menu of connection types appears, as shown in Figure 3-12. Click New Connection from Data Source, and select the connection name that you previously created. You will now be able to associate this connection with tasks in your particular package.

Figure 3-12. *Data source types to select from*

To add a connection specific to the particular package that you are designing and *not* globally available to all packages in the project that you are working on, right-click in the Connection Manager area, click the context menu item that reflects the provider (that is, OLE DB, ADO.NET, and so on), and then configure the connection as per your requirements. Figure 3-12 shows the complete list of available providers in a default installation of SSIS. You can see and work with this list by selecting New Connection from the context-sensitive menu that is available after you right-click in the Connection Manager design area for SSIS packages in BIDS.

Adding Control Flow Tasks

Your next step in package design is to select one or more control flow items from the Toolbox and drag them to the Control Flow design surface section. Separating control flow from data flow and allowing you to select from different types of tasks or transformations to add to the control flow or data flow is a major enhancement in SSIS 2005. In contrast, in SQL 2000 DTS, control flow and data flow tasks and transformations were combined into one area (with a very large number of nested dialog boxes!).

Figure 3-13 shows the Toolbox for the control flow items. You can see by looking at the names of the items in Figure 3-13 that *control flow* refers to items that perform some sort of action (most all of the task names are self-explanatory). You can also see BOL for a more detailed explanation of the functionality associated with each item. We will review some of the more complex control flow tasks in Chapters 8 and 9.

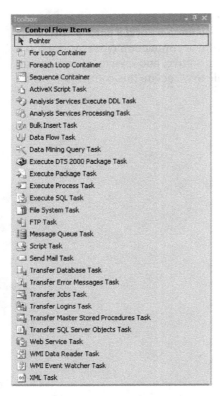

Figure 3-13. *The Control Flow Items section in the BIDS Toolbox displays a variety of tasks to use in your SSIS packages.*

For your first package, you will use just two of the tasks from this Toolbox: Data Flow and Send Mail. Drag each of the items to the center work area in BIDS. Drag the green line from the Data Flow Task to the Send Mail Task until the two tasks are connected. You'll notice that the Send Mail Task has a red warning icon on it. If you pass your mouse over the error icon, a tooltip will tell you that the "SMTP server is not specified," so the task cannot execute. To review the cause of this error, right-click the task and select Edit. You'll then be presented with the Send Mail Task Editor configuration dialog box shown in Figure 3-14.

So far, you've created a package that will complete some kind of data movement or flow and will send an email via SMTP on successful completion of that data flow task (after you added the SMTP server location information). For the purposes of this quick discussion, we aren't going to bother to complete that configuration. The next step in the design of this pseudo-package is to configure the data flow itself.

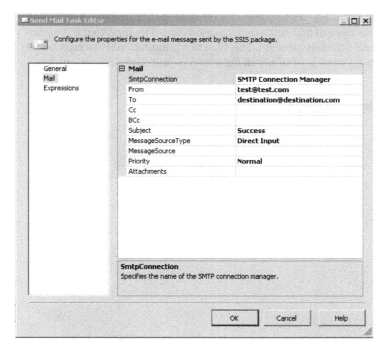

Figure 3-14. *The Send Mail Task Editor dialog box requires you to configure a SMTP connection and to supply from and to information.*

Configuring Data Flow Tasks

As mentioned previously, in SQL Server 2000 DTS, the data flow was shown on the same surface as the control flow items. A black arrow connecting data sources and destinations represented the data flow. Data flow was configured by right-clicking the black arrow and navigating a series of nested dialog boxes. Due to a large amount of negative feedback about this interface design, Microsoft redesigned it in SQL Server 2005 SSIS. Now the data flow interface has been replaced by a separate work area in BIDS, which is shown on the Data Flow tab.

When you double-click the Data Flow Task on the Control Flow design surface, you are taken to the Data Flow design surface for that particular Data Flow Task (see Figure 3-15).

Figure 3-15. *The Data Flow work area in BIDS allows you to visually configure a data flow for a particular Data Flow Task in the control flow area of your SSIS package.*

You will usually select at least one data source, one transformation, and one destination from the Toolbox. You do not need to add any transformations to a data flow; that is, you can simply add a data source and a data destination. This type of configuration is *not* common in production BI SSIS packages. Figure 3-16 shows all data sources and data destinations from the BIDS Toolbox.

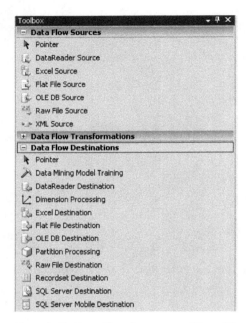

Figure 3-16. *Data Flow Sources and Data Flow Destinations from the Toolbox in BIDS reflect a variety of interoperability between different types of data sources and data destinations in SSIS packages. Note the (new) support for XML sources.*

For this particular example, you'll simply drag on an OLE DB source and an OLE DB destination.

To configure each OLE DB Source, right-click each source and then click Edit. Associate them with the existing AdventureWorks connection. After you've completed this step, drag the green arrow from the Source to the Destination as shown in Figure 3-17. In this case, no transformations were added between the Source and Destination. Although atypical in the real world, it demonstrates the simplest possible data flow.

■**Tip** When should you use a DataReader source (or destination) and when should you use an OLE DB source (or destination)? Use a DataReader when consuming or providing data to any .NET data provider. Use an OLE DB source (or destination) when consuming or providing data to any OLE DB provider.

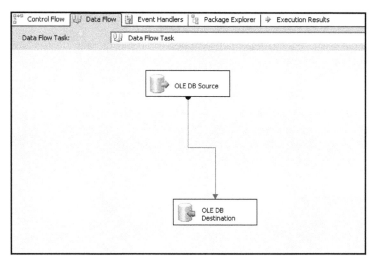

Figure 3-17. *Configure data flows by using data sources and destinations in the DataFlow work area of SSIS.*

To test your first package, click the package name in Solution Explorer and then click Execute Package. BIDS not only allows you to execute packages, but it also shows execution status by changing the color of the source and destination items (as well as any transformations—this item type is not shown in this example): yellow for executing, green for success, and red for failure. Row counts are also shown on the work surface. In addition to this, SSIS contains a variety of debugging techniques. We'll discuss these in detail in Chapter 9. Figure 3-18 shows the result of a successful execution of this sample package.

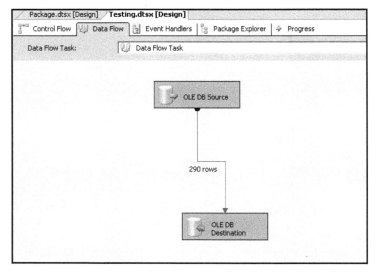

Figure 3-18. *BIDS allows you to execute your SSIS packages, and the design environment indicates data flow status and row count on the design surface.*

Adding Transformations to the Data Flow

Using your data map, you'll want to use 1 or more of 28 supplied data transformations to your package. Figure 3-19 shows the possible options.

■**Note** Some transformation types are only available in the Enterprise Edition of SQL Server 2005, for example, the fuzzy lookup transform. For a complete list see http://www.microsoft.com/sql/ prodinfo/features/compare-features.mspx.

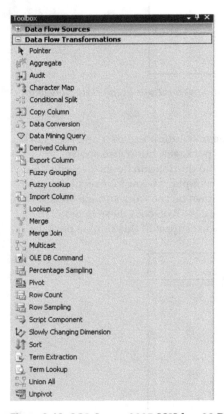

Figure 3-19. *SQL Server 2005 SSIS has 28 Data Flow Transformation types to select from.*

To enhance our basic package, you can add two transformations to the data flow: Derived Column and Sort transformation. Use any source table (such as the Customers table) that has a First Name and Last Name column. Connect the firstName and lastName columns from the source to the Derived Column transformation, and connect the date column to the derived column as shown in Figure 3-20.

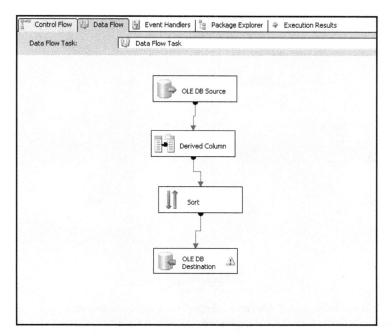

Figure 3-20. *Adding some basic transforms to the data flow. The error icon on the OLE DB Destination is due to possible truncation when mapping the new derived column to an existing database column.*

To configure the Derived Column transformation, right-click the transformation on the design surface, and click Edit. The Derived Column dialog box appears in which you can create the new column using SSIS expression syntax. For more information about the capabilities of SSIS expression syntax, see the BOL topic "*Syntax (SSIS)*." You'll note that all columns and variables available in the data flow are shown in the Derived Column Transformation Editor dialog box. Also, there is a function reference. To create the new column, complete the expression field. I've simply concatenated the firstName and lastName columns for this example as shown in Figure 3-21.

The steps for you to configure the Sort transformation are similar. Right-click the transformation on the design surface, select Edit, and then set the column (or columns) you want to sort by in the dialog box.

There are two other task panes in the SSIS package design area: the Event Handlers area and the Package Explorer area. I'll get into more detail on what these areas are used for in Chapter 9, which covers advanced topics in SSIS.

When you execute the package, the Progress task pane becomes available in the SSIS package design area. The Progress pane shows very detailed information about the execution of each task and step in the package. As shown in Figure 3-22, the level of detail can be very helpful in understanding the overhead involved with package execution.

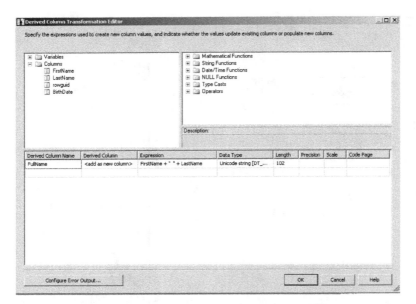

Figure 3-21. *The Derived Column Transformation Editor dialog box allows you to create new columns in data flow using expressions that the data source can understand.*

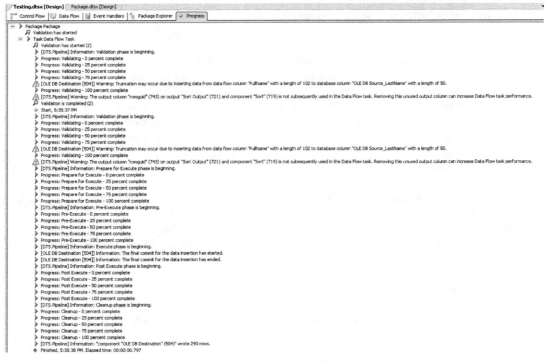

Figure 3-22. *The Progress task pane in the SSIS design area shows you detailed information about the overhead involved with executing each step and task of an SSIS package.*

Summary

Are you beginning to understand the power of SSIS? This component of SQL Server 2005 is incredibly flexible and important to all BI solutions. We've covered only the absolute basics of using the tools available (either in SSMS, with, the SQL Server Import/Export Wizard or in BIDS, with the SSIS Integration Services project type template) to create SSIS packages that will be the workhorses of your ETL processes for BI.

I've really just scratched the surface of what is possible with SSIS. In Chapters 8 and 9, we'll explore the data flow transformations and control flow tasks in greater depth. Also, you'll learn about error handling, debugging, and best practices for SSIS design in BI projects.

CHAPTER 4

■ ■ ■

Using SSAS

Now that you've seen the big picture of BI solutions in Chapter 1, been introduced to OLAP modeling for SSAS in Chapter 2, and been introduced to ETL and SSIS in Chapter 3, it's time to start working with SSAS to build your first cube. It is quite common to prototype cubes built on subsets of enterprise data quickly in a BI project. As with any other type of development, you can expect cube development to be iterative. Generally, ETL development runs somewhat concurrently to these cube iterations, assuming that you have the resources to commit to both of these processes.

This chapter assumes you have a couple of populated star schemas in SQL Server to work with. The data in the samples are, of course, "very clean." This is not to ignore the real-world situation of data cleansing, validation, and transformation; rather, it allows you to focus on cube building using the many features available in SSAS. So, you'll use the handy AdventureWorksDW sample that is part of the SQL Server 2005 sample databases as a source for building your first cube. If you haven't yet installed the sample database, refer to the explanation in "Building the First Sample—Using AdventureWorksDW" in Chapter 1. This chapter will cover the following topics:

- Using SSAS in BIDS, and understanding the development environment

- Creating data sources and Data Source View objects

- Creating cubes using the UDM and the Cube Build Wizard

- Refining dimensions and measures in BIDS

Using BIDS to Build a Cube

As you did for SSIS packages, you'll use BIDS to create SSAS cubes. This environment is also used to create SSAS data mining structures and models (which are covered in Chapter 11) and SQL Server Reporting Services reports and report models (covered in Chapter 12).

To start your work, open BIDS, and select File ➤ New Project. Select the Analysis Services Project template under the Visual Studio installed templates heading as shown in Figure 4-1.

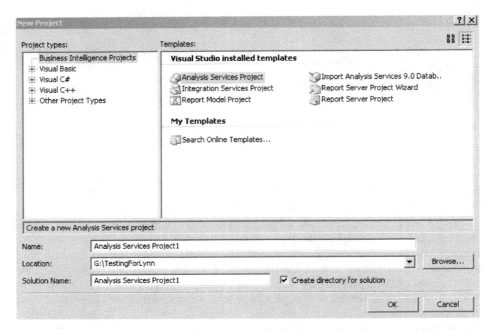

Figure 4-1. *The New Project dialog box in BIDS allows you to select project templates to create a new Analysis Services solution or to import an SSAS database.*

In Solution Explorer, you'll note several new folders or nodes. Each node is designed to hold a different type of item or file. Data sources work similarly to the way they are used in SSIS projects; that is, you can create global data sources or connections and reuse these throughout your entire SSAS project. Data Source View (DSV) objects also work similarly to how they work in SSIS, however, they take on a larger importance here. It is common for SSAS designers to want to make usability improvements against the star schema. In some situations, SSAS designers will not have permissions to create objects (such as views) in source star schema databases.

Some of the enhancements that can be made via DSVs are as follows:

- Rename tables or columns to create more end-user friendly names.

- Add calculated columns, which can include column concatenations, or any other manipulation that the source database understands (in our case, using T-SQL).

- Remove columns that are not needed for the UDM.

- Add derived measures to the fact table, much like calculated columns for the dimension tables (in our case using T-SQL).

To create a DSV, right-click the folder with that name in Solution Explorer, and select the tables shown in Figure 4-2. To make any of these types of changes to the DSV (in the preceding list), right-click the object in the DSV, and select either New named calculation or New relationship.

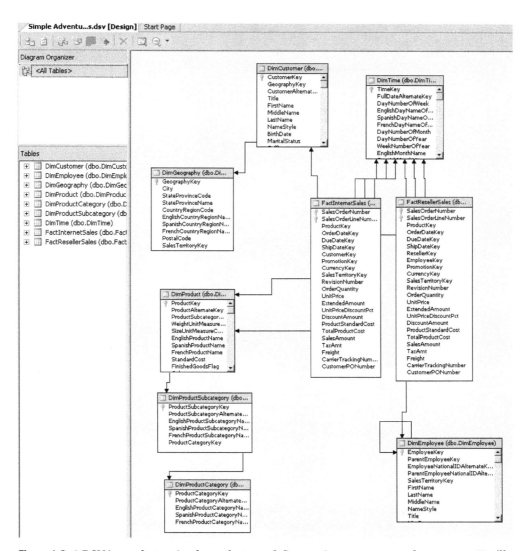

Figure 4-2. *A DSV is an abstraction layer that you define against one or more data sources. You'll use the DSV to build your cube.*

In addition to making changes to your source schema, you can explore the data in the tables and views in your DSV by right-clicking any table in the DSV window and clicking on Explore Data. You'll then be presented with four different ways to look at the source data: via a table, a pivot table, a chart, or a pivot chart. This feature can be helpful in the development of a useful DSV as a basis for your cube because it allows you to easily and quickly explore the data in a variety of output formats. You can quickly validate data values by examining the data in tabular and charted output formats. Figure 4-3 shows the pivot table option for the DimEmployee table.

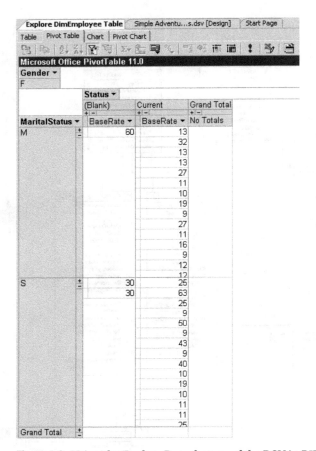

Figure 4-3. *Using the Explore Data feature of the DSV in BIDS can help you make intelligent decisions about refining the DSV for your cube.*

An interesting option available in the DSV is displayed only if foreign-key (FK) relationships do not exist in the underlying data source. This is the `NameMatchingCriteria` property, which allows you to specify whether you prefer to have Analysis Services generate relationships between columns in the source tables of the DSV automatically. The three options to pick from are listed:

- Same name as primary key

- Same name as destination table name

- Destination table name + primary key name

Building Your First Cube

After creating at least one data source (which is, in essence a connection) and at least one DSV, you are ready to build your first cube. One of the major enhancements to SSAS 2005 is the

Cube Wizard. This is really more of a tool than a wizard, but it will help you build cubes quickly and correctly. You can (and usually will) make many refinements to OLAP cubes generated using the wizard after the initial run of the wizard.

Also, this flexible and useful wizard includes the capability to go back at any point, so if you are not happy with the results of a particular page, you can click Back, adjust input parameters, and then proceed again. It is also the only way to create a new cube in BIDS. Unlike in SSAS 2000, you cannot access the cube design surface without first creating a cube using the wizard. To access it, you'll right-click on the cubes folder in Solution Explorer, and then click New Cube.

Note It is technically possible to create a cube without a DSV or data source. This type of activity is done most often during the prototyping phase of your project and was discussed in Chapter 2. If you chose the Build a cube without a data source option, you can ask SSAS to generate a relational schema based on your answers to the wizard's pages in the destination of your choice. For example, if the destination is SQL Server, then the wizard will generate T-SQL DDL code based on the schema you define in BIDS.

Your first decision is whether to create a cube with or without a data source. This means with or without referring to a DSV. The first cube references the data source built earlier. Figure 4-4 shows this option page of the wizard.

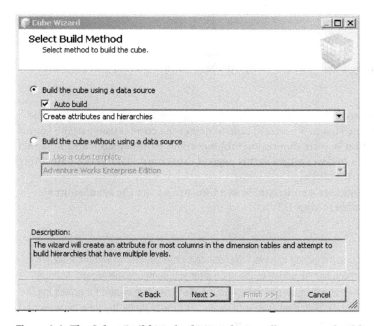

Figure 4-4. *The Select Build Method Wizard page allows you to build a cube based on a data source (and a DSV) or not. If you create a cube using a data source, Analysis Services will generate attributes and will attempt to find natural hierarchies in those attribute groups by default.*

In the next page of the wizard, you are asked to select which DSV you want to use to build the cube, assuming that you've created at least one DSV prior to starting to use the Cube Wizard. If you've not yet created a DSV, the wizard will prompt you to create one at this time. After a bit of processing, you'll see the wizard page that tells you that Analysis Services has analyzed your source schema and has built a cube from it (see Figure 4-5). Subsequently, you are presented with a series of pages to review the choices that Analysis Services has made.

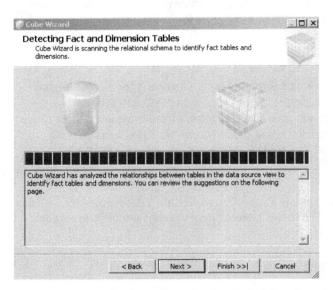

Figure 4-5. *You can let the Analysis Services Cube Wizard analyze your DSV and build a cube based on the source schema. You will be asked to review the schema in subsequent pages in the wizard.*

The first thing you need to review is whether the wizard correctly detected your fact and dimension tables. In other words, was the wizard able to detect the correct usage of the source tables in your star schema, that is, were dimension tables marked as dimension, and were fact tables marked as fact? You can make changes in this page of the wizard, if it did not detect the appropriate usage of your source tables.

Also, you may need to designate a source table as a time table from the set of source tables (if you created a time table in your DSV).

Tip A new feature of SSAS 2005 is the ability to have SSAS create a time dimension without a source time table. This Server Time dimension can be added to the cube after you complete the wizard. Although this method of creating a time dimension is quick and easy, I usually don't use this wizard for producing BI solutions. The reason for this is that by creating my own custom source time table for the time dimensions, I can include additional information, for example, holiday flags, that many customers find useful.

You are then asked to select (and verify those that the wizard has already detected) from the detected dimensions to be included in your cube. Be sure to select at least one fact table in this wizard page as well as any dimensions that you want to include.

If you've selected a source time table, then in the next page of the wizard, you are asked to map columns from the source `TimeDimension` table to the time dimension in your cube. This defines the levels of the time hierarchy, for example, days, months, years, and so on. Note that you can match columns from your source table to several types of time hierarchies, such as fiscal, reporting, manufacturing, and so on. Figure 4-6 shows a mapping of two columns from the source `DimTime` table in AdventureWorks.

Note also that you can map all the way down to the "seconds" level of granularity. Most solutions I've implemented used a time dimension that had the day level at its lowest level of granularity. Business requirements should drive all decisions on granularity, and this is a particularly important consideration when determining the grain for the time dimension. The reason for this is that each level of granularity increases the quantity of rows in the associated fact tables by an order of magnitude; for example, deciding to implement hours rather than days would increase the size of all associated fact tables by a factor of 24.

Another important consideration when implementing the time dimension is whether or not your business requirements include different types of calendars. A common example of this is to include both a regular calendar and a fiscal calendar, or a standard calendar and a manufacturing calendar.

These different types of calendars can be easily accommodated in SSAS by using the included time hierarchy generation wizards. One example of where to find this functionality is by using the Add Business Intelligence Wizard to Add Time Intelligence. This wizard is available in many places in the BIDS interface. For example, you can start it by clicking the Add Business Intelligence icon (the first icon) on the toolbar in the cube design surface (after you've opened a cube in BIDS).

The BI wizard is only available if you are using the Enterprise Edition of SSAS.

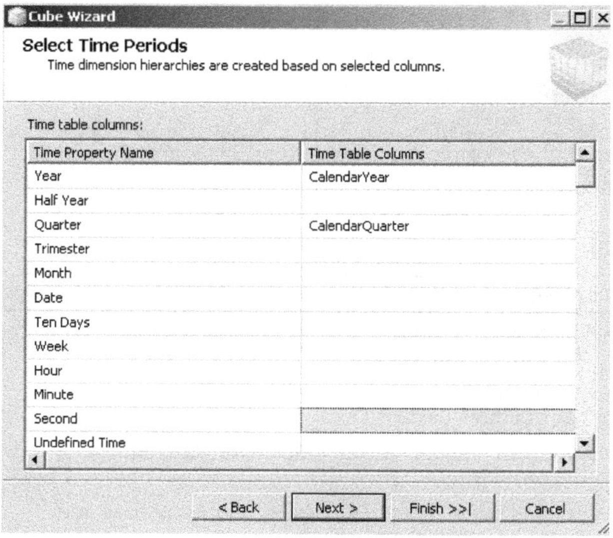

Figure 4-6. *Using the Cube Wizard allows you to associate columns from the source time table to hierarchy levels in the time dimension for your cube.*

In the next page of the wizard, you select which columns you want to include as measures. Most often, you will remove some of the default selections (often all columns with the word "key" in them because these values represent foreign keys rather than measure values), so that the only measures that remain selected are numeric and usually additive values from the fact table(s) only. After you make your selections and click Next, SSAS performs some processing and shows you the work it has completed in the bottom of the next page of the wizard.

On the next page, you are shown the dimensions, attributes, and hierarchies that have been detected by BIDS. You can delete items that you don't want to include in your cube by removing the item's check mark. You can also rename values to better reflect the business taxonomy by right-clicking the item and clicking Rename. This dialog box is shown in Figure 4-7.

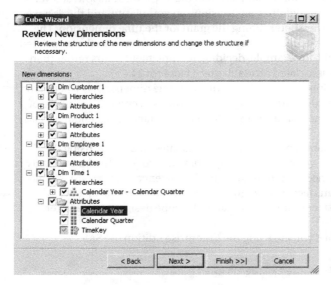

Figure 4-7. *In the Review New Dimensions page of the Cube Wizard, you can remove dimensions, attributes, or hierarchies that you do not want to include in your cube.*

Table 4-1 lists the step in the wizard, the information presented by SSAS, and the action(s) that you are expected to take to continue.

Table 4-1. *Steps of the Cube Wizard in BIDS*

Wizard Step	Actions by SSAS	Actions by You
Build Method with a DSV*	Creates dimensional attributes and natural hierarchies	Select the Auto build check box
Identify Fact and Dimension Tables	Detects and displays source tables as Fact, Dim, or Both	Adjust selections
Identify Fact and Dimension Tables	Detects and displays source tables as Fact, Dim, or Both	Select TimeDim table
Review Shared Dimensions	Displays existing shared dimensions in SSAS database	Select dimensions to add

Wizard Step	Actions by SSAS	Actions by You
Select Time Periods**	Displays time property names	Select matching time table column(s)
Select Measures	Displays all fact table columns; selects all as measures	Deselect columns as needed
Review New Dimensions	Displays new dimensions, hierarchies, and attributes	Deselect columns as needed
Review New Dimensions	Displays new dimensions, hierarchies, and attributes	Rename columns as needed
Completing the Wizard	Displays a suggested name for the cube and its contents	Rename the cube as needed

This step assumes that you've created and selected a DSV; if no DSV is available, the wizard will prompt you to create one.

**This step only appears if you select a new source time table in the Identify Fact and Dimension Tables step. If you selected None for the Select TimeDim table on the Identify Fact and Dimension Tables step, then the Select Time Periods step will not appear.*

Tip You can click BACK at any point in the wizard to make changes or corrections.

Click Next, and you've created the metadata for your first cube. Let's review what you've completed in preparation for understanding how you can further edit and refine your cube in BIDS. To browse your cube, you'll have to build and deploy it first. During the build step, the cube metadata is validated (if there are errors in the metadata, they will be reported to you and the cube will fail to build), and then it is written (called "deployed" in this interface) to the Analysis Services directories so that it can be used by query tools. The location on disk for the metadata is C:\Program File\Microsoft SQL Server\MSSQL.2\OLAP\Data. The instance number, or MSSQL.2, could vary depending on how many instances of SQL Server you have installed on your server and whether or not you've upgraded from a previous version of SQL Server.

The tool in BIDS for querying the cube is called the Cube Browser. Until you build and deploy your cube, you will *not* be able to view the cube results in BIDS. To build the cube you just created (which makes the metadata files that you've generated in BIDS available to SSAS), in the Solution Explorer view, right-click on the cube, and then click Process. The Process Cube dialog box appears as shown in Figure 4-8. The details of processing are covered in Chapter 7, so for now, just click Process.

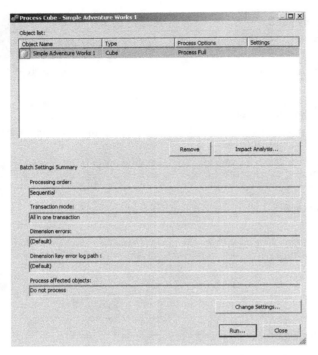

Figure 4-8. *To browse your cube in the BIDS cube browser, you must first process and deploy it.*

After you've clicked Process, BIDS shows a detailed cube-processing dialog box, which shows each step and the progress status. You are looking for a "Process succeeded" message in this dialog box as shown in Figure 4-9.

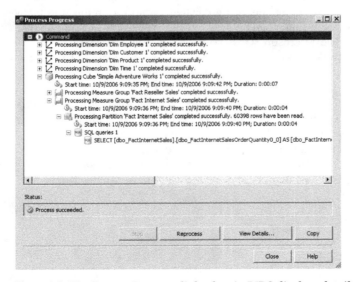

Figure 4-9. *The Process Progress dialog box in BIDS displays detailed information about each step in the cube process task.*

After you see this message, you can click the `Refresh the connection to the cube` link in the cube browser to browse your first cube using a pivot table interface. Figure 4-10 displays the Sales Amount measure with the Calendar Year hierarchy on the rows pivot table axis, the Product Category hierarchy on the columns axis, and the filter set to show only sales results for products whose color is equal to black. Your browse results may look different from Figure 4-10, of course, depending on which values from the metadata browser you've chosen to add to the (cube) Browser area.

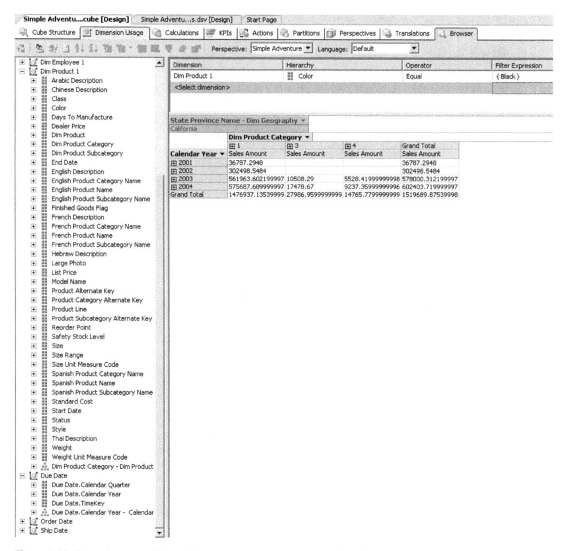

Figure 4-10. *Browsing your first cube using BIDS, you can see the cube from an end-user perspective.*

Refining Your Cube

You can do many, many tasks to refine a cube that you've built using the BIDS wizard. In this preliminary chapter (more on SSAS cube building in Chapters 5 and 6), we'll look at some simple and common cube refinements, including enhancing measures, dimensions, and the cube itself.

You'll learn the BIDS development interface as you proceed with these refinements. Although the environment is a GUI, it is complex; often "half the battle" when working with BIDS is getting to the correct location in the development interface!

Reviewing Measures

A common and simple task when refining your cube is changing the display format of the measures. To do this, you just double-click the cube name (under the cubes folder in Solution Explorer) to open that cube in the BIDS cube design interface. This will load the cube metadata into a series of tabbed interfaces, with the Cube Structure tab open by default.

In the Cube Structure subtab, in the Measures section on the left, right-click the measure that you want to format, and then click Properties. On the bottom right of the BIDS design surface, the property window will be set to that particular measure. Click the selection list for the FormatString property, and select the format type that you need. The property view is shown in Figure 4-11. You can select any of the following values:

- -#

- #,#

- ,#,#.0

- #.#.00

- Standard

- Currency

- Short Date

- Short Time

- Percent

Another interesting use of measure properties in this same interface is to create a derived measure. A *derived measure* is based on a calculation that is "passed through" to the data source for the cube on process. In our case, this would be a T-SQL expression. You enter the expression in the MeasureExpression property in the Properties window for the measure you want to create.

You may choose to do this because the measure may not exist in the source data. Although this is a very flexible option to create additional measures, you should evaluate the overhead that creating a derived measure adds to cube-processing time. You can do this by reviewing the detailed output from the cube-processing window (discussed earlier in this chapter), paying particular attention to the amount of time taken to perform the derivation step.

Figure 4-11. *You can easily format a measure using the Properties windows in BIDS.*

Note As mentioned previously, although it's relatively easy to add derived measures to a cube, I don't often use them in production solutions. I prefer to calculate and store most required measures during the ETL process. If there are measures used by a small number of end users, I prefer to use the resources of SSAS to produce these. This type of measure is called a calculated measure, and it is calculated at query time. We'll talk more about calculated measures in Chapter 10.

Reviewing Dimensions: Attributes

The next step in refining your cube is reviewing the attributes in each dimension that the Cube Wizard created for you. The default is to create an attribute for each non-Key column in each dimension table. Many times, your end users will not need or want to see all of this information, and because the attributes will be visible to end users, removing unnecessary attributes is a good thing to do. It is a common development practice to remove attributes that are not needed.

You might wonder why we load them in the first place. As discussed in Chapter 2, if there is any chance that any set of end users will want to see certain attributes, then include them; however, if those attributes aren't needed in this particular release of your BI project, simply remove them (alternatively, you can include them and mark them as "hidden" in the dimension).

You need to be able to refer back to the business taxonomy and original documentation you created during the planning phase of your project at this time so that you include only required attributes. Your cube needs to be comprehensive but also usable. Reviewing business requirements will help you get the correct balance. Also, removing unneeded attributes will improve cube-processing time and query time. It is also very important to rename attributes to reflect the business language that you captured during the modeling phase. As mentioned previously, your use of business taxonomies dramatically improves cube usability.

To edit the attribute values, names, or properties for a particular dimension, in the lower-left section (Dimensions) of the Cube Structure tab, click the "+" next to the dimension you want to edit, and then click the `edit the dimension` link. You will now be working in the dimension editor area of BIDS with the particular dimension you just selected opened in its own editor. The dimension editor surface contains different sections than the cube editor. The dimensions editor tabs are Dimension Structure, Translations, and Browser as shown in Figure 4-12.

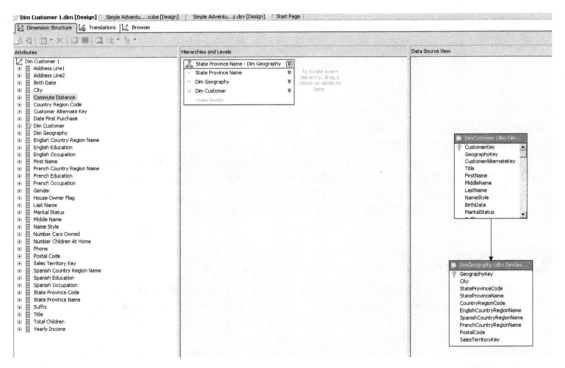

Figure 4-12. *You can use the Dimension Structure tab in BIDS to make structural changes to dimension members. These changes can include renaming, deleting, or adding attributes. Changes also include creating or refining dimensional hierarchies.*

Tip The default value for each dimensional attribute is the first member loaded into the dimension. A simple change you can make to improve dimension usability is to set the default attribute value that will appear in the end-user client tools for key attributes to a more meaningful value. To do this, with the dimension open in the Dimension Structure tab in BIDS, right-click the attribute and then click Properties. In the Properties window, click the text box next to the `DefaultMember` property to activate the Build button (gray icon with three dots), and then click on that Build button to open the Set Default Member - <Attribute Name> dialog box. In this dialog box (see Figure 4-13), you can select a default value or write an MDX expression.

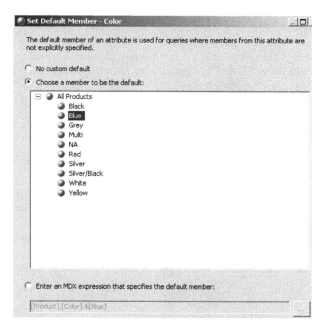

Figure 4-13. *You can use the Set Default Member dialog box to change the default value for individual dimension attributes in BIDS. This can improve dimension (and cube) usability.*

Reviewing Dimensions: Hierarchies

In Chapter 2, we discussed the concept of a dimensional hierarchy as being a rollup of attributes. By default, BIDS creates only one rollup to an `All` member. Sometimes during the initial cube build, BIDS will detect additional hierarchies. During the execution of the Cube Wizard, BIDS will present you with a page in the wizard so that you can review (and make simple changes to) any hierarchies that it has detected.

SSAS uses a couple of types of hierarchies. The first type is called a *natural hierarchy* because the source data reflects a one-to-many relationship between the data in one or more columns from the source table. An example of a natural hierarchy is a geography hierarchy, which is built from a Geography source table with a `State` column and a `City` column, where each state contains many cities. Usually, when you build your cube in BIDS, SSAS will correctly detect natural hierarchies in the source data and will build hierarchies (using the source column names as level names) in the resulting dimension. You can modify (or create) these types of hierarchies manually as well.

An example of a natural hierarchy that I've had to commonly create in production BI solutions is one or more additional time hierarchies. These are used to reflect different business calendars, such as fiscal, 4-5-4 (retail), manufacturing, and so on.

Another type of hierarchy is a *navigational hierarchy*. As the name indicates, these are groupings for one purpose only—navigation. The source data has no particular relationship between the data in the hierarchy levels. An example using the `Customer` dimension shown earlier in Figure 4-12 could be a hierarchy with the `State` attribute listed above the `Gender` attribute. You will have to manually create any navigational hierarchies as part of your cube-refinement process. Navigational hierarchies are a great new feature in SSAS 2005 because they improve cube usability and are easy to add, modify, and delete.

All hierarchies associated with a dimension are displayed in the Hierarchies and Levels section of the Dimension Structure tab in BIDS. BIDS does not distinguish between natural hierarchies and navigational hierarchies in the design interface.

To create a new hierarchy or to modify an existing one, select and drag one or more attributes from the Attributes section of the Dimension Structure tab to the Hierarchies and Levels section. You can also rearrange the levels in a hierarchy by dragging the attributes above or below one another in the hierarchies that you've created.

Another design consideration for natural hierarchies only is whether or not you want to configure attribute relationships that reflect the one-to-many nature of the relationship between the data in the hierarchy levels. BIDS allows you to configure this but does *not* set up these relationships automatically. You may want to add this information to natural hierarchies to improve query-processing performance, to improve dimension-processing performance, and to save disk space. If you create these relationships, then SSAS will build internal indexes to make these three tasks more efficient. If you do not create these relationships, then, for example, a query for all customers in the United States would have to "touch" each fact, rather than traverse a more efficient index.

Caution If you are going to add these relationships, they must be "correct" in the data. That is, the data associated must truly have a one-to-many relationship. If it does not, then your cube may fail to process, or if it does process, your results may be incorrect. Sometimes BIDS marks incorrect created attribute relationships as an error by adding a red line under the error data, but BIDS does NOT catch all possible error conditions.

To add attribute relationships, follow these steps:

1. In the Hierarchies and Levels section of the Dimension Structure tab, click the double carets (^) next to the level name in the hierarchy for which you want to add the attribute relationship (this will be the "many" level in the one-to-many relationship that you want to establish).

2. In the Attributes section of the Dimension Structure tab, click the attribute with "one" level, and drag it and drop on the <new attribute relationship> text underneath the "many" level attribute in the hierarchy that you are working with.

After you've completed this, then delete the existing attribute relationships (by default, all associated with the key column for the particular dimension) by expanding the dimension key column in the Attributes section, right-clicking on the attribute relationships that you added to the hierarchy, and then deleting each one. You'll usually want to repeat this process for each level in the hierarchy. An example using the Geography dimension is shown in Figure 4-14.

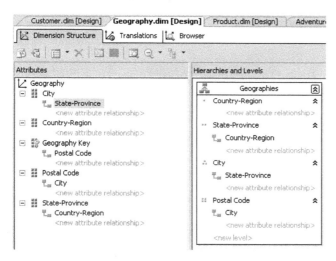

Figure 4-14. *You may want to create attribute relationships in natural hierarchies to improve query-processing time and dimension-processing time.*

Other Parts of the Dimension Structure Tab

The right pane, Data Source View, allows you to explore the data in the source table or tables from the DSV for this dimension using the same techniques discussed previously (that is, Explore Data, and so on). If you want to modify the table data, for example, by adding a calculated column, then you must edit the DSV in the DSV designer, rather than by using the DSV section of the dimension editor. The DSV section of the Dimension Structure tab is read only.

Similar to the cube browser, the dimension work area also has a Browser tab, so that you can view the dimension, its hierarchies, and its attributes for verification purposes. The other tab available in the dimension work area is Translations, which allows you to supply values for the dimension hierarchy, level, or attribute names that are localized for whatever languages your end users prefer.

Dimension Properties

As with measures, you can also set properties for dimensions, attributes, hierarchies, and levels by clicking on the object you want to configure and then setting the property using the Properties window in the lower right of the BIDS work area.

An interesting dimension property new for SSAS 2005 is the UnknownMember. This is set for an entire dimension and allows you to specify whether unknown member values will be visible or not in the cube. Also, you can specify a caption, for example, "unknown" for any unknown members. The Properties window for a dimension is shown in Figure 4-15. One of the reasons this is so interesting is that SSAS provides you with more flexibility in terms of loading nulls. As we'll discuss later, you may now configure dimensions to allow nulls and ask that those values be translated to "unknowns." This welcome change reflects the real-world difficulty of providing "perfectly clean" (that is, no nulls) data to SSAS. We'll talk more about the configuration in Chapter 7 where we'll discuss error handling in more detail.

Figure 4-15. *The Properties window for a dimension allows you to set advanced properties, including the new* UnknownMember *property. This property is set for the entire dimension only.*

It is also common to set properties for attributes or hierarchies using the Properties window. The following are some of the commonly changed settings:

- *Default Member*: This property allows you to set the attribute member value, which will be displayed by default for all end users. The dialog box to configure this was shown earlier in Figure 4-12. You can also set default members for end users in different security groups, for example, the MinnesotaManagers group can see the Minnesota State member of a Geography dimension, and so on. We discussed the procedure to implement this feature earlier in this chapter.

- *Order By*: This property allows you to set the order in which the members will be displayed. The default value is by attribute name.

- *Allow Duplicate Names*: This property allows you to control whether or not duplicate names will be displayed.

- *Member Names Unique*: This property allows you to notify BIDS that all members for a particular level of a particular dimension are unique. The default value of false causes BIDS to issue SELECT DISTINCT to load the dimension data. If this setting is set to true, then BIDS will simply SELECT all members of a dimension at that level. Changing this setting's value to true will reduce dimension-processing times.

Reviewing Dimensions: Member Properties

A *member property* is an alternate representation of an attribute value. In SSAS 2000, member properties were frequently used to overcome various limits in that version of the product. Due to improvements (and removal of most of those restrictions), you'll probably now only use member properties occasionally, preferring to simply create additional attributes, rather than member properties.

Also, member properties are now created by defining attribute relationships. Although you will see the term member property in various places in the BIDS interface (and in MDX), Microsoft's official position (from BOL) is as follows:

> *This feature (member properties) will be removed in the next version of Microsoft SQL Server. Do not use this feature in new development work, and modify applications that currently use this feature as soon as possible.*

Another consideration is whether or not your particular end-user tools support the display of member properties.

If you choose to add member properties to a hierarchy, then you can review them in the dimension Browser tab by clicking the Member Properties button (the fourth button) on the tab's toolbar. From the list of available member properties, select the member properties you want to display and then they will be visible in the BIDS dimension browser (see Figure 4-16).

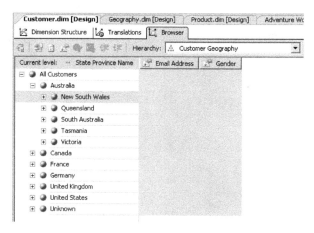

Figure 4-16. *If you associate member properties with attributes in a dimensional hierarchy, you can review the display of those member properties in the BIDS dimension browser.*

The bottom line is that you *should* use attribute relationships, as presented in the previous section ("Reviewing Dimensions: Hierarchies") to improve query performance and processing performance of natural hierarchies, but you should *not* use member properties, rather you should simply create additional dimensional attributes.

After you've finished refining the cube measures and dimensions, you must reprocess the cube before you can browse the results. The procedure for this is described in the "Building Your First Cube" section earlier in this chapter.

Offline vs. Online Mode in BIDS

There are two modes of working with SSAS databases (which contain one or more OLAP cubes) in BIDS. When you initially create a SSAS database, you will always be working in offline mode. This means you are creating cube and dimension metadata by using the wizards and GUI interface in BIDS. This metadata is saved in file formats proprietary to BIDS and SSAS. The metadata you've created while working offline is not yet deployed to SSAS; you must "Process" the particular structure you are working with to deploy those metadata files to SSAS.

One advantage of working in offline mode in BIDS is that you can make changes to SSAS metadata without affecting end users who are currently connected to your production cube(s). Another advantage is that multiple OLAP designers can work on parts of a solution without affecting end users.

After you've successfully deployed your cube, then you may subsequently choose to work offline or online. To work online, you open BIDS, click File ➤ Open ➤ Analysis Services Database, click the SSAS server and database name in the Connect to Database dialog box, and then click OK. If you are working online, any change you make to the metadata is immediately reflected in the production server. There is no Deploy option available on the project, cube, or dimension menus in Solution Explorer. Also the title bar of BIDS shows the name of the SSAS database and then names of the SSAS server, for example, Adventure Works DW Standard Edition(*YourServerName*), to reflect the fact that you are working online. For the majority of this book, we will use online mode in BIDS.

To work offline after you've successfully deployed your cube, open BIDS, click File ➤ Open ➤ Project/Solution, or simply double-click the <Projectname>.sln file. The title bar in BIDS shows only the SSAS database name to reflect that you are working offline. In offline mode, after you save changes, you must still deploy the changes to SSAS.

■**Caution** If you have multiple OLAP developers working offline, you must establish source control procedures outside of BIDS using whatever method works best for you. This could include Visual Source Safe
(VSS), Visual Studio Team System (VSTS), SharePoint Portal Server (SPS), and so on. The product you use
depends of the type of information you want to place under source control. VSS and VSTS are designed to
control code files, and SPS is designed to control specification documents.

The need for external source control when using offline development in BIDS is due to the default
deployment behavior in BIDS. The default deployment gives you only a single, overly generic message if
there are conflicts between the existing metadata on SSAS and new metadata from BIDS. On deployment
BIDS will overwrite anything and everything on SSAS to reflect the entire contents of what is being deployed
from BIDS. In other words, BIDS does not produce a list of changes on deployment; it simply overwrites
everything.

Other Types of Modeling

Analysis Services 2005 supports many additional capabilities that may affect the final modeling of your cube. These include KPIs, Calculations, Actions, Perspectives, and more. These
topics (and more) will be covered in Chapters 5, 6, and 10.

Summary

This chapter covered the processes for creating your first cube. We discussed DSVs in detail,
covering their purpose and the options for refining your schema in BIDS. Next, we walked
through the Cube Wizard, and then we built our first cube quickly and easily. After that, we
refined the measures and dimensions of our cube to make it more efficient and usable.

There's quite a bit more you can do to add features and business value to OLAP cubes. In
Chapters 5 and 6, we'll cover the more advanced cube-modeling techniques. In Chapter 7,
we'll review the processes involved in physical cube storage.

CHAPTER 5

■ ■ ■

Intermediate OLAP Modeling

After you've mastered basic OLAP modeling and the use of SSAS, the next area to investigate is using some of the intermediate and advanced capabilities of SSAS.

This chapter's examples continue to build on the AdventureWorksDW sample. The assumption is that you've built a basic cube using the sample database and now want to further enhance your cube. This chapter will cover the following topics:

- Adding KPIs (Key Performance Indicators)

- Reviewing Perspectives

- Understanding Translations for Currency Localization

- Covering Actions: Regular, Drillthrough, and Reporting Actions

Adding Key Performance Indicators (KPIs)

A key performance indicator (KPI) is an object that helps cube users to quickly check the status of the most important business metrics. Although you will set up KPIs to return results as numbers, that is 1 is good, 0 is ok, and -1 is bad, you'll generally display these results as graphics (such as a traffic light graphics with red, yellow, or green selected, or different colors or types of arrows). The returned number values aren't as compelling and immediate as the graphics to most end users. SSAS has support built in to display several types of graphics instead of the numbers. There is also a built-in KPI designer and browser in SSAS. You can use the KPI browser to view the results as the end users will see them (as long as the user's particular client application supports the display of KPI graphics).

Excel 2007 and Microsoft Office SharePoint Portal Server 2007 support the display of SSAS KPIs using the associated graphics defined in SSAS. The KPI designer is a tab in the cube work area in BIDS (see Figure 5-1).

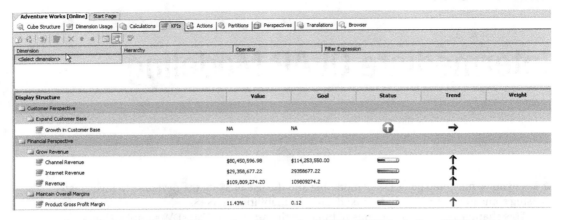

Figure 5-1. *SSAS supports the creation of server-based KPIs; BIDS includes a KPI browser.*

Implementing KPIs in SSAS

KPIs consist of at least four items: Value, Goal, Status, and Trend. These items are defined for a particular measure in a measure group. A *measure group* is, as the name would indicate, a grouping of one or more measures in a cube. The information for these four items is defined using MDX.

■ **Note** MDX (Multidimensional Expressions) is one of the "native" languages used in the SSAS environment (others include XMLA and DMX). MDX is to SSAS as T-SQL is to SQL Server, which means that it is the query language for Microsoft's implementation of OLAP (cubes). Chapter 12 provides a more complete introduction to the MDX language.

Here are definitions for the four most typically used items in KPIs:

- *Value*: MDX statement that returns the *actual* value of the metric.

- *Goal*: MDX statement that returns the *target* value of the metric.

- *Status*: MDX statement that returns Value – Goal as 1 (good), 0 (ok), or -1 (bad).

- *Trend*: MDX statement that returns Value – Goal over time as 1, 0, or -1 (this statement is optional).

You can also nest KPIs, that is, create parent and child KPIs. If you do this, you can then assign a Weight value to the nested KPI, which shows the child's percentage of contribution to the parent KPI value. For example, in a growth ratio percentage for a department of a store, nested (or child) KPIs can be used for each department's growth ratio percentage, rolling up to the parent KPI that can reflect growth ratio percentage for an entire store.

The AdventureWorks sample ships with several sample KPIs, one of which is shown in Figure 5-2. The MDX statement to define the Value and Goal properties is straightforward. You can see in Figure 5-2 that SSAS includes some MDX functions specific to KPIs. These functions are used to create the Status value for the example KPI. The MDX functions KPIValue and KPIGoal are simply aliases for the MDX statements defined earlier for those properties. Note the use of the IIF function and the return values of 0, 1, or -1 for the status expression statement.

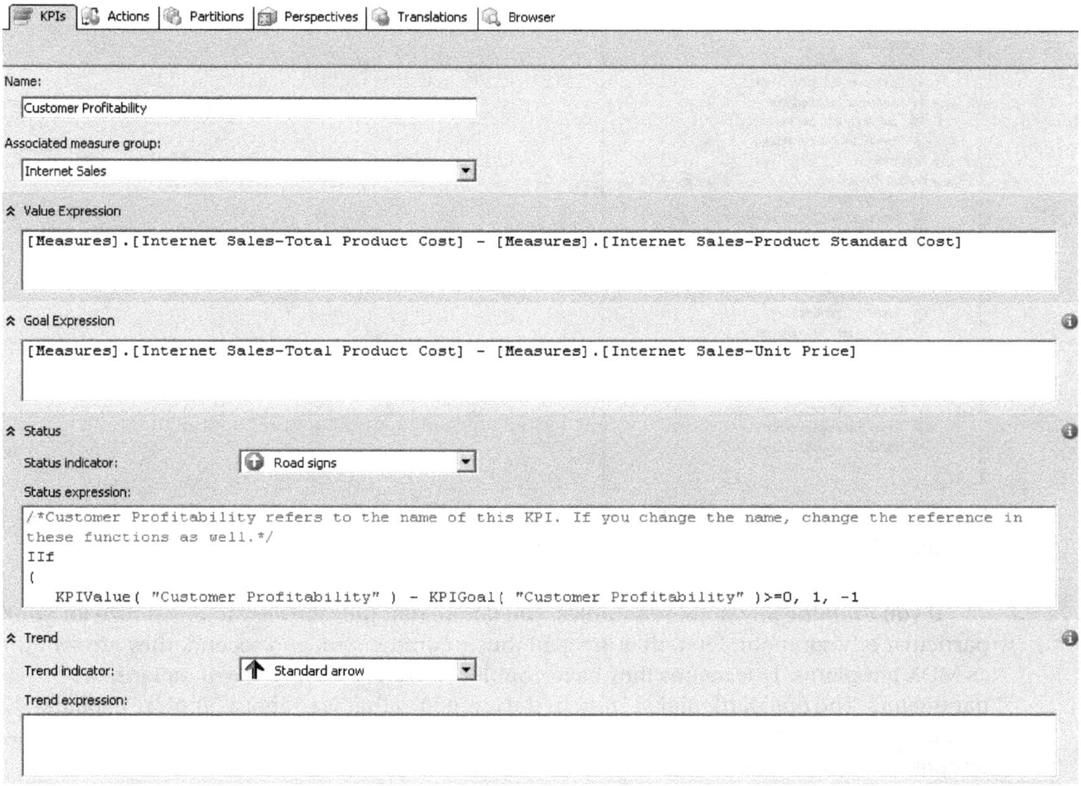

Figure 5-2. *The AdventureWorks sample cube includes a KPI called Customer Profitability. Note the use of MDX to define the key properties of the KPI.*

KPIs are a new feature for SSAS 2005. Because of this, a large number of sample KPIs are included in the AdventureWorks sample cube. These samples represent the most common business scenarios for KPIs. Figure 5-3 shows a partial view of the KPI templates provided.

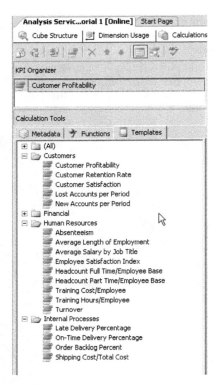

Figure 5-3. *Microsoft provides a large number of templates for KPIs in the AdventureWorks sample cube. These samples represent the most commonly monitored business metrics.*

If you examine any of these samples, you'll note that they are easy to customize for your particular environment. First, they are generously commented, and second, they are set up as MDX templates. This means they have double chevrons (<<) in place of replaceable parameters. The one particular section in the templates that warrants a bit more explanation is the Trend Value. Figure 5-4 shows the template for the Customer Retention Rate KPI template as an example of this.

`Value`, `Goal`, and `Status` expressions are self-explanatory. Trend uses the MDX function `ParallelPeriod` to get a value from the same part of a different time period, such as "this fiscal week last year," to support the trend.

`ParallelPeriod` is one of hundreds of built-in, powerful MDX functions. `CurrentMember` is another built-in function used for the calculation of the `Trend` value.

■ Tip MDX color-codes built-in functions brown in all code windows in SSAS. Also, basic IntelliSense is enabled. So you can type a function followed by an opening parenthesis, and SSAS will display a tooltip with the function arguments.

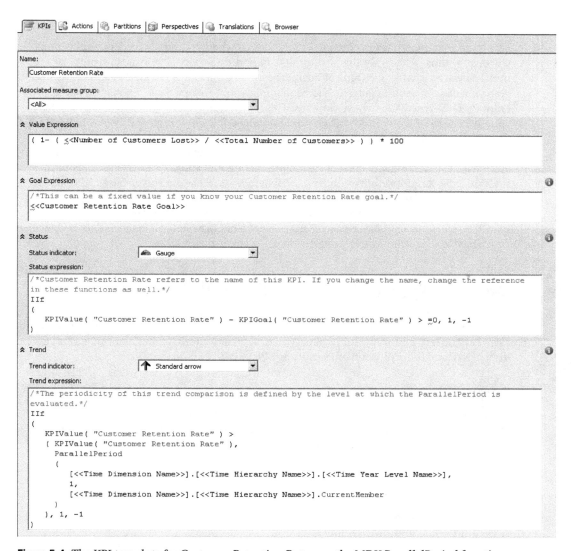

Figure 5-4. *The KPI template for Customer Retention Rate uses the MDX ParallelPeriod function to calculate the* Trend *value.*

The ParallelPeriod function returns a value from a prior period in the same relative position in the time dimensional hierarchy as the specified value. The three arguments are dimension level (for example, DimTime.CalendarTime.Years), a numeric value to say how many periods back the parallel period should be, and a specific value, or member (for example, DimTime.CalendarTime.CurrentMember).

Considering Other KPI Issues

An important concern when creating KPIs in SSAS is whether (and how) client applications will display those KPIs. As of this writing, SQL Reporting Services 2005 displays only the numeric values (that is, the value of the metric, or -1, 0, 1), and does not display the associated graphic icons. Most other current Microsoft applications (for example, Excel 2003 and Share-Point Portal Server 2003) behave similarly. This landscape will change dramatically if/when you upgrade to Office 2007. Microsoft has announced full support for the display of SSAS KPIs throughout the entire Office 2007 suite.

Also of note is the fact that some client applications, such as Business Scorecard Manager 2005, have the capability to create KPIs via the client application. When designing your BI solution KPIs, it is important to understand whether you'll choose server-based KPIs, client-based KPIs, or a combination of both. If your end-user tools support the display of SSAS KPIs, it is most common to use server-based KPIs because they are created once (in the cube) and reused by all end users. Server-based KPIs present a uniform view of business data and metrics, which is a view most often preferred to using client-based KPIs.

Using Perspectives and Translations

Perspectives and Translations are two features that are supported only in the Enterprise Edition of SSAS. They allow you to create custom views of a cube. Perspectives allow you to create view-like subsets, and Translations allow you to associate alternate metadata labels for cube, dimension, and other object names (such as KPIs).

Perspectives

A *Perspective* is a technically saved, named MDX query that appears to the end user as if it were a separate cube. Much like a view in a relational database, Perspectives are simply subsets of a base object. When deciding whether to use Perspectives, consider the following:

- Perspectives are only supported in the Enterprise Edition of SSAS.

- If you chose to use Perspectives, then your client applications must support them.

- Perspectives are best used when the base cube has a complex structure, and simplification would improve usability.

Perspectives are simple to create using BIDS. While working in the cube designer area, you will see a tab devoted to Perspectives. To create a new Perspective, you right-click anywhere on that design surface and then click New Perspective. Figure 5-5 shows that you can choose to include, or not include, the following items from a cube:

- Measure groups or individual measures

- Entire dimensions or individual dimension members (hierarchies and/or attributes)

- KPIs

- Custom MDX calculations defined on areas of the cube (covered in Chapter 12), including calculated members, named sets, and MDX scripts

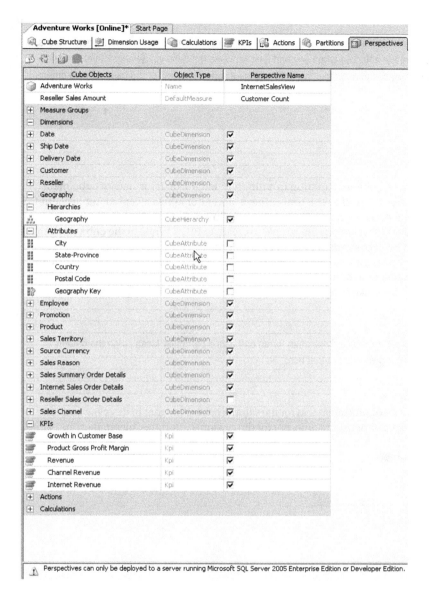

Figure 5-5. *SSAS Perspectives allow you to quickly and easily create simplified views of your base cube.*

The built-in cube browser in BIDS supports browsing cube Perspectives, so you can verify that the Perspective you've created matches the business needs of your particular scenario. If you are familiar with SSAS 2000, Perspectives in 2005 replace Virtual Cubes in 2000. Although an MDX query is being generated in BIDS when you create a Perspective, there is no way for you to directly edit the MDX statement when using BIDS.

Note Unlike relational views, a cube Perspective is not a security mechanism. All security permissions defined on the base cube are enforced when any end user browses the cube via a Perspective. As stated previously, the primary purpose of a Perspective is to provide a simplified view of the base cube to different types of end users.

Translations

A *Translation* is a view of cube information in a different language. It's a view of cube meta-data (which you can also think of as the row, column, and filter labels of a pivot table client for an OLAP cube) in the language that you select when defining the Translation.

As with Perspectives, Translations are simple to create in BIDS. While in the cube work area, you click the Translations tab and then right-click anywhere on the design surface to add a new Translation. After the Translation has been created, client applications that connect to the cube will display the cube metadata in the language that has been defined in the locale settings in the Control Panel. Translations, like Perspectives, require the Enterprise Edition of Analysis Services.

Note If the cube does not contain a Translation for an end user's particular locale, then the default language/translation view is presented to that user.

Figure 5-6 shows a German Translation for the sample cube. Note that in this view, you can only add Translations for a dimension name, not for dimensional attributes, hierarchies, and levels.

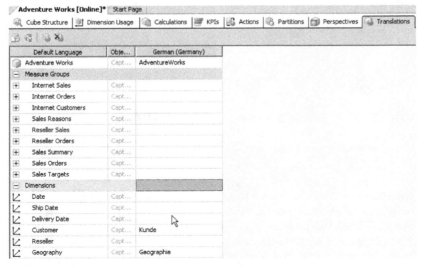

Figure 5-6. *Creating Translations of cube metadata in BIDS allows you to easily localize the metadata for your cube.*

The only complexity with defining Translations is that you define only cube metadata (that is, measure names, dimension names, KPI names, and so on) translations using the preceding process. This can include defining the localized name of the dimensions.

To define localized names for dimensional attribute values (for example, in the Sales Reasons dimension, some of the attribute values are `manufacturer`, `on promotion`, and so on), you first double-click the dimension and then add a Translation for that dimensional hierarchy, level, or attribute (or other value, such as for the `All` member and the `Unknown` member) in the dimension work area. For dimensional attributes, you accomplish this is in the Attribute Data Translation dialog box shown in Figure 5-7.

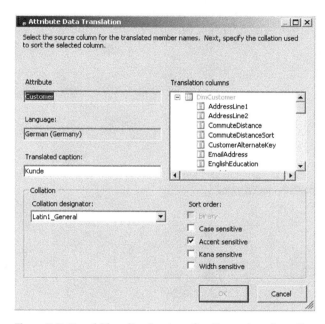

Figure 5-7. *To add localized strings for dimensional attribute values, add a Translation to the dimension in BIDS and then click the Build button next to the localized dimension name value to display the Attribute Data Translation dialog box.*

The BIDS cube and dimension browsers allow you to view your cube and dimension translations. You do this by selecting the particular language from the drop-down list at the top of the browser page.

Localizing Measure Values

Another consideration when localizing a cube is to express the value of measures (usually currency or dates) as localized values. If your business scenario requires this type of localization, you will most generally create custom MDX queries to translate and format these values for a particular user. To localize date values, you still must do this manually; however, SSAS 2005 offers a new Add Business Intelligence feature for currency localization accessed via a wizard in BIDS to make localization via MDX scripts much simpler.

Note Before you run the Add Business Intelligence Wizard to generate a MDX script for implementing currency conversion in BIDS, you must set up three required prerequisites: at least one currency dimension, at least one time dimension, and at least one rate measure group. For more specifics on the required structures of those dimensions, see the SQL BOL topic, "Working with Currency Conversions."

To access the Add Business Intelligence Wizard, you click the Cube menu in BIDS. Clicking Next on Add Business Intelligence launches the first page of the wizard (see Figure 5-8), which lists possible enhancements for the cube. The choices offered vary depending on whether you are working in the cube design or a dimension design window.

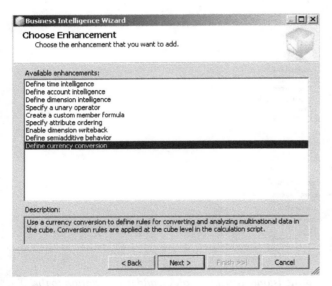

Figure 5-8. *The new Business Intelligence Wizard in BIDS allows you to quickly and easily localize cube currency values by taking you through several steps of a wizard. This will generate a MDX script and make structural changes to your cube to support currency localization.*

In the Set Currency Conversion options page of the wizard (see Figure 5-9), you are asked to make three choices. First, you'll have to select the measure group that contains the exchange rates, then the pivot (or translating) currency, and finally the method you've used to define the exchange rate. You'll define later in the wizard exactly how the translation between source (or sources) currency and destination currency (or currencies) will be performed.

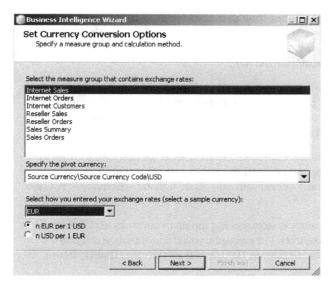

Figure 5-9. *Using the Business Intelligence Wizard allows you to localize currency values in your cube.*

In the Select Members page of the wizard, you select which members of the measures dimension you want to have converted using which measures from the source measure group as shown in Figure 5-10.

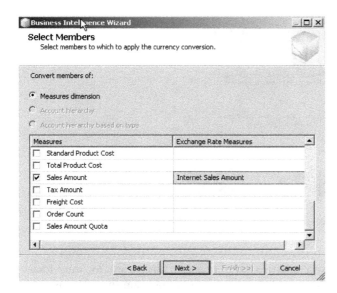

Figure 5-10. *In the Select Members page, you define which measure values you want to convert to localized currency values.*

Click Next, and you are in the most interesting part of this wizard. Here you are presented with three options for performing the currency localization by selecting a cardinality option: many-to-many, many-to-one, or one-to-many. Although there is a description of each option on the wizard page, the options are summarized here:

- *Many-to-many*: The source currencies are stored in their local (or original) formats and then translated using the pivot currency into multiple destinations (or reporting) formats. For example, you could translate currency A, B, C, using the pivot currency, USD, into multiple destination currencies D, E, F.

- *Many-to-one*: The source currencies are stored in their local (or original) formats and then translated using the pivot currency. All sources use the pivot currency value as the destination (or reporting) value. For example, you could translate currency A, B, C all into USD.

- *One-to-many*: The source currency is stored using the pivot currency and then translated into many reporting currencies. For example, you could translate original currencies A, B, C into USD, store values as USD, and then translate that USD into multiple destination currencies.

Figure 5-11 shows the Select Conversion Type Wizard page where you make this selection.

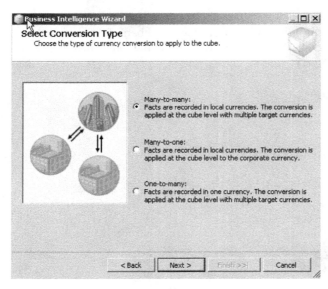

Figure 5-11. *An important step in the Business Intelligence Wizard is selecting the cardinality option.*

After you select the cardinality, you have two more choices in this wizard. You must identify whether a column in the fact table or an attribute value in a dimension should be used to identify localized currency values. The last step is to select your reporting (or destination) currencies. The wizard now has enough information to generate a MDX script to execute your currency calculation. You can see this script in the final step of the wizard (see Figure 5-12).

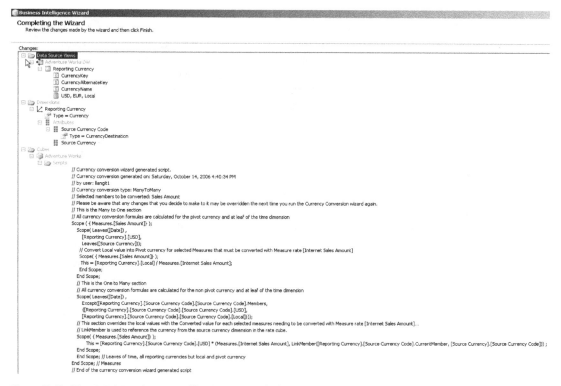

Figure 5-12. *The BIDS Business Intelligence Wizard allows you to generate a sophisticated MDX script by answering a series of questions in the wizard pages.*

The Business Intelligence Wizard is a powerful new tool in SSAS. As we continue to explore advanced cube modeling in Chapter 6, we will review other capabilities built into the wizard.

Using Actions

An *Action* is an activity that an end user can perform by right-clicking either cube metadata (a row or column label) or cube data (a measure value). Actions are added to SSAS cubes and targeted at a particular section, that is, an entire dimension, a particular hierarchy, a particular measure group, and so on.

The ability to use cube Actions is completely dependent on the type of client application your BI solution uses. For example, Excel 2003 does not support SSAS Actions. Actions are created in BIDS using the cube designer work area (Actions tab) by completing the property values and writing MDX scripts. As with many other advanced cube-design techniques, the samples that ship with SSAS include several examples of Actions.

After you've verified that your particular client applications support SSAS cube Actions, then your first decision when considering adding actions to a cube is to select the type of Action you want to add from these Action types:

- *(Regular) Action*: Allows end users to right-click either cube metadata or data and performs an activity by passing the value of the cell clicked to one of the following action types: DataSet, Proprietary, Rowset, Statement, URL. What is returned to the end user depends on which action type has been set up in BIDS. If a URL Action, then a Web page is returned. Rowset Actions return rowsets to the client, DataSet Actions return datasets, and Statement Actions allow the execution of an OLE DB statement. Figure 5-13 shows the syntax for a URL Action.

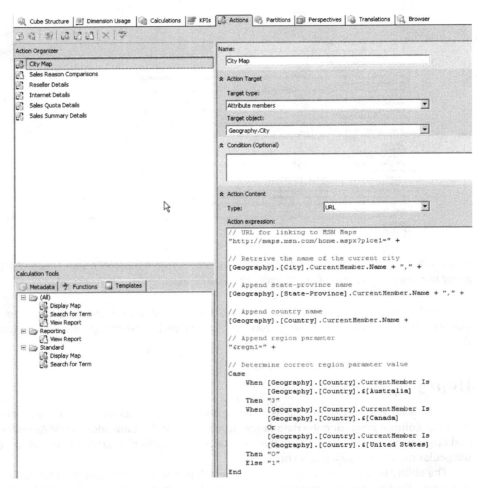

Figure 5-13. *URL Actions allow end users to launch Web pages by right-clicking cube metadata or data in their end-user tool environment.*

Note For (regular) Actions and Reporting Actions, you must determine the value of the target type and target object properties. As their names suggest, these properties determine where in the cube these custom Actions will be available to end users. In Figure 5-13, end users must be viewing the [Geography].[City] attribute to be able to use the CityMap URL Action.

- *Drillthrough Action*: Allows end users to see detailed information "behind" the value of a measure; that is, for this discount amount, what are the values for x, y, z dimensional attributes? This is shown in Figure 5-14 using the cube browser.

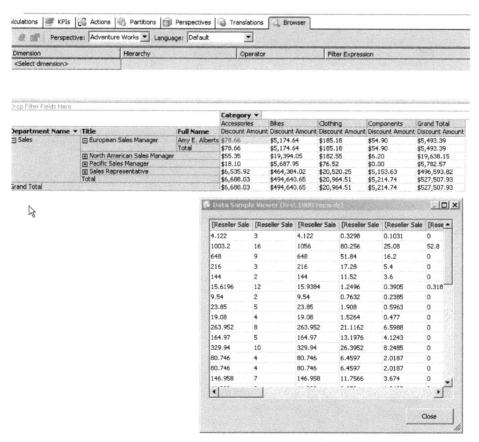

Figure 5-14. *Drillthrough Actions allow end users to see the "detail" behind the measure value for a particular measure.*

Tip Microsoft has changed the drillthrough architecture in SSAS 2005. In this version, unlike in SSAS 2000, all data available for drillthrough must be part of the cube. There is no capability to drill through to the source (relational) database.

Unlike (regular) Actions and Reporting Actions, creating Drillthrough Actions requires that you specify a target measure group (rather than object and level). Figure 5-15 shows an example of the syntax used to create a Drillthrough Action targeted at the Reseller Sales measure group.

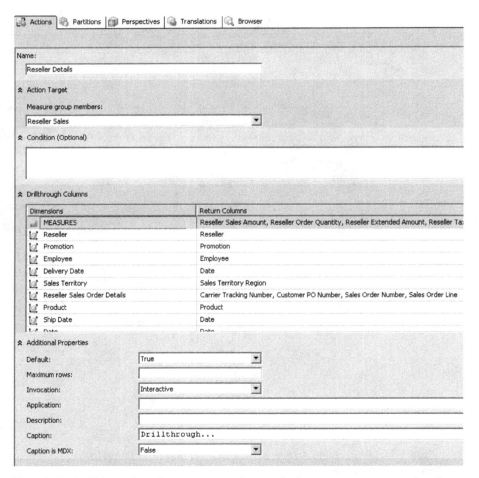

Figure 5-15. *Drillthrough Actions are targeted at particular measure groups rather than attributes or hierarchies.*

- *Reporting Action*: Allows end users to right-click a value and will pass the value of the location clicked as a parameter to SSRS. Activating the Action causes SSRS to launch using the custom URL, which includes the cell value and other properties (for example, the format of the report: HTML, Excel, or PDF). Figure 5-16 shows an example of the syntax used to create a Reporting Action.

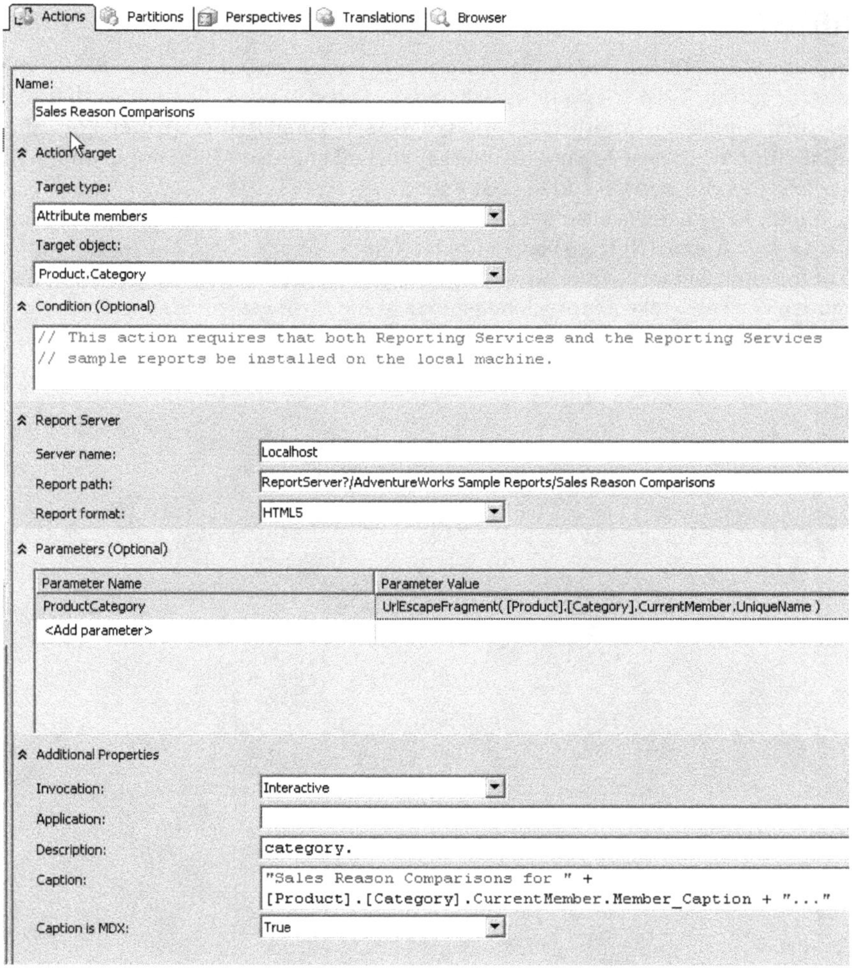

Figure 5-16. *Reporting Actions allow end users to launch SSRS from their SSAS client applications by right-clicking a cell of interest. A custom URL is generated and passed to SSRS.*

In the Invocation drop-down list in the Additional Properties section, you can specify whether the defined action should be started by the end user (the Interactive option) by right-clicking the client interface pivot table cell, or should be implemented automatically (the On Open option) when the end user opens the OLAP client application. The third option, Batch, allows developers to associate a particular command with a SSAS Action.

Other Types of Modeling

SSAS 2005 supports still more capabilities that may affect the final modeling of your cube. These include multiple fact tables, new dimension types, and the ability to add additional types of business intelligence using the wizard. All of these topics will be covered in Chapter 6.

Summary

This chapter covered the processes for adding more power to your cube. I reviewed the processes for adding KPIs, Translations, Perspectives, and Actions. Remember that several of these features require the Enterprise Edition of SSAS as noted in this chapter. The other critical consideration with these features is to verify that all end-user client applications support whatever features you want to add to your cube.

In Chapter 6, we'll delve even deeper into the complexities of SSAS cube modeling. We'll discuss several features that have been added to this version of SSAS. The features include the use of multiple fact tables and advanced dimension types (including many-to-many dimensions). We'll also take a more detailed look at the Business Intelligence Wizard.

CHAPTER 6

■ ■ ■

Advanced OLAP Modeling

SSAS 2005 adds many exciting new capabilities to the modeling toolset for cubes and dimensions. Many of these features were added as a direct result of specific customer requests. The focus for the 2005 release is definitely on giving you much more flexibility to model your complex business scenarios than you had using SSAS 2000.

In this chapter, we'll continue to use the AdventureWorksDW sample to cover the new modeling techniques available to you in SSAS 2005. The chapter will cover the following topics:

- Using multiple fact tables in a single cube

- Modeling nonstar dimension types, including Many-to-Many (using intermediate fact tables), Fact (degenerate), Role-playing, Writeback, and more

- Performing advanced dimension modeling, including modeling for either slowly or rapidly changing dimensions, adding custom error handling, and more

- Using the Business Intelligence Wizard for cubes and dimensions to easily enable write-back, semiadditive measures, account/time/dimension intelligence, unary operators, custom member formulas, attribute ordering, and more

Multiple Fact Tables in a Single Cube

In SSAS 2000, you were limited to basing your cube on a single source fact table (from a star schema). Although you could create unifying views against multiple source cubes in that version (using Virtual Cubes), when you were creating, deploying, and managing multiple cubes, you added a layer of complexity to BI solutions in SSAS 2000 without adding any business value for customers.

SSAS 2005 eliminates this complexity. A single cube can now be based on multiple fact tables. This type of modeling much more closely aligns with the way most customers want to view their enterprise data. Much of the work to incorporate multiple fact tables into one enterprise cube needs to be done during the OLAP modeling phase of your project. Conceptually, you can think of this modeling as multiple star schemas, where multiple fact tables reuse the "points" of the stars (or the dimensions). Figure 6-1 illustrates this concept.

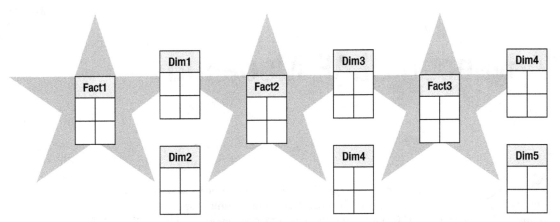

Figure 6-1. *You can visualize using multiple fact tables by thinking of multiple star schemas with shared "points" or dimensions.*

This type of modeling provides your end users with a true enterprise view of as much business data as needs to be added to a single, all-encompassing cube. From a logical modeling perspective, it now makes sense to begin with the single cube model for all BI projects.

A factor that could cause you to implement more than one cube has to do with management and administration, namely physical implementation. If you are working with the Enterprise Edition of SSAS, then you can create physical partitions for your cube to better manage administration. The mechanics of doing this will be covered in Chapter 7. If, however, you are working with the Standard Edition of SSAS, you cannot create any type of cube physical partitions. Cube partitions are used to divide cube-processing times and other management tasks, such as security. This limitation could affect your decision about how many fact tables to include in your cube.

If you choose to include multiple fact tables in your cube, an important consideration is to what level of granularity you plan to load the rows in each fact table. For example, your company might plan to measure both sales facts (such as sales amount, sales quantity, and so on) and marketing facts (such as promotion cost, promotion audience size, and so on). The sales facts may need to be loaded to the day level of the time dimension in one fact table, and the marketing facts may only need to be loaded to the month level from that same dimension in another fact table. Both of these fact tables can be part of the same cube using SSAS 2005.

The Dimension Usage tab of the cube designer work area in BIDS is the place where you adjust the granularity of relationship between the Dimensions and Measure Groups. A *Measure Group* is a container for one of more Measures in a cube. Figure 6-2 shows the AdventureWorks sample cube and whether relationships between various Dimensions and Measure Groups exist for the cube being viewed.

Tabs: Simple Adventu...orks 1 [Online] Customer [Online] **Adventure Works [Online]** Start Page

Cube Structure | Dimension Usage | Calculations | KPIs | Actions | Partitions | Perspectives | Translations | Browser

Measure Groups

Dimensions	Sales Reasons	Reseller Sales	Reseller Orders	Sales Summary
Date		Date	Date	Date
Date (Ship Date)		Date	Date	Date
Date (Delivery Date)		Date	Date	Date
Customer				
Reseller		Reseller	Reseller	
Geography		Reseller	Reseller	
Employee		Employee	Employee	
Promotion		Promotion	Promotion	Promotion
Product		Product	Product	Product
Sales Territory		Sales Territory Region	Sales Territory Region	Sales Territory Region
Source Currency		Source Currency Code	Source Currency Code	Source Currency Code
Sales Reason	Sales Reason			
Sales Summary Order De...				Sales Order
Internet Sales Order Details	Internet Sales Order			
Reseller Sales Order Details		Reseller Sales Order	Reseller Sales Order	
Sales Channel				Sales Channel

Figure 6-2. *The AdventureWorks sample cube Dimension Usage tab shows the relationship between Dimensions and Meaure Groups for the sample AdventureWorks cube. Blank (gray) rectangles indicate that there is no relationship between a particular Dimension and Measure Group.*

To examine the granularity of a particular relationship, you click the white rectangle that forms the intersection between the Measure Group and the Dimension. A small gray Build button (with three dots) becomes available on the intersection rectangle. Click the Build button to open the dialog box that allows you to view (or adjust) the type and level of relationship between the Dimension and Measure Group. You'll note that certain dimensions have no relationship to certain fact tables (the intersection is an empty grey rectangle).

Another modeling option available from the Dimension Usage tab is to add Linked Objects to your cube. Linked objects are either Measure Groups or Dimensions (or both) from a different SSAS database. This option can be used to overcome the SSAS 2005 limit of basing a cube on a single DSV. The ability to use linked objects in SSAS is disabled by default. If you want to use this option, you must enable the property by connecting to SSAS in SSMS, right-clicking the SSAS instance, and then clicking Properties.

You can also enable the ability to link objects in SSAS by clicking the check box for this option in the SQL Server Surface Area Configuration tool as shown in Figure 6-3.

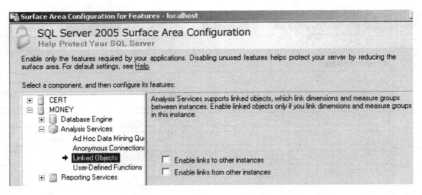

Figure 6-3. *The Surface Area Configuration for Features tool enables you to link objects to your SSAS cube.*

The properties you need to enable are `Feature\LinkToOtherInstanceEnabled` and `Feature\LinkFromOtherInstanceEnabled`. After you've done that, you can use the Linked Object Wizard in BIDS. Figure 6-4 shows the dialog box from the Linked Objects Wizard where you'll select which object from the linked DSV to include in the current cube.

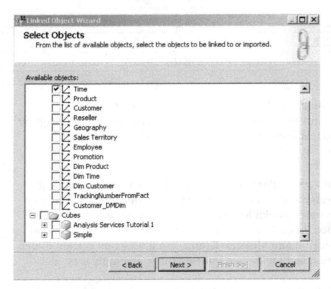

Figure 6-4. *The Linked Object Wizard allows you to include dimensions or cubes defined in DSVs other than the primary data source used by your cube.*

In addition to being able to include multiple fact tables in your cube (whether physically or via links) as the basis for Measure Groups (which contain Measures), there is another reason to include more than one fact table in your cube. Interestingly, this last type of fact table does *not* provide additional measures for the cube; rather, it's used for a new type of dimensional modeling called a many-to-many dimension. This is covered in greater detail in the "Modeling Nonstar Dimensions" section later in this chapter.

Considering Nulls

The OLAP community harbors differing opinions about whether or not it is appropriate to load null data into the fact (or dimension) tables of a cube.

■**Tip** As a general rule of thumb, you should refrain from loading nulls into dimensions and measures because null values are usually not meaningful to end users. It is typical to test for null values (and to either reject data with null values as error data or to convert the null values to either a number, usually zero, or to a string, for example, "unknown") and to convert null values to data values during the ETL process of your BI project. This approach is preferred to loading null values into your SSAS cube because nulls can cause erroneous or unexpected results with MDX aggregate functions.

If you want to load null values into your cube, SSAS 2005 now provides much more flexibility in deciding how to deal with situations during cube load compared to the restrictions in SSAS 2000, which provided you with fewer options.

One of the places you can configure null value handling (for Measure Groups that intersect with Regular [or star] dimensions only) is in the Dimension Usage tab of the cube designer in BIDS (see Figure 6-2). To do so, click the Build button on the white rectangle at the intersection of the dimension and fact table that you want to customize. This opens the Define Relationship dialog box as shown in Figure 6-5.

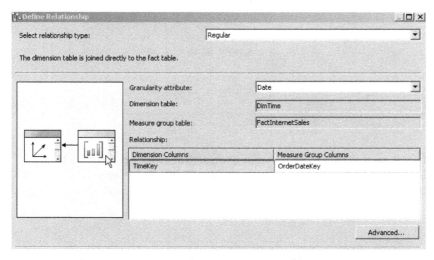

Figure 6-5. *The Define Relationship dialog box Advanced option allows you to customize null processing behavior for a particular dimension and fact table.*

Clicking the Advanced button in the Define Relationship dialog box takes you to the Measure Group Bindings dialog box (see Figure 6-6). Here, you can set the null-processing behavior to one of six possible settings by clicking the Null Processing column value in the Relationship section. Each setting is described here:

- *Automatic*: Converts the null value to zero (for numbers) or a blank string (for strings). This is the default setting.

- *Preserve*: Keeps the null value.

- *Error*: Raises a null key error; the setting of the `NullKeyNotAllowed` property for the measure controls the result. This setting cannot be used with measures.

- *Unknown Member*: Generates an unknown member and raises a null conversion error; the setting of the `NullKeyConvertedToUnknown` property controls the result. This setting cannot be used with columns associated with measures.

- *ZeroOrBlank*: Converts the null value to zero (for numbers) or a blank string (for strings). This setting is primarily available for compatibility with SSAS 2000.

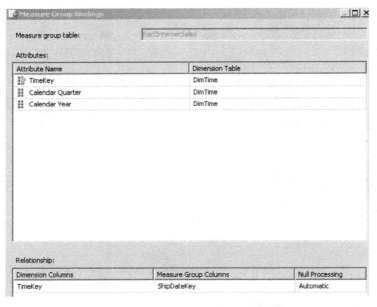

Figure 6-6. *Clicking the Null Processing value in the Relationship section of the Measure Group Bindings dialog box allows you to customize null processing behavior for a particular dimension and fact table.*

Note To set the `NullKeyNotAllowed` and `NullKeyConvertedToUnknown` properties in the BIDS Process Dimension (or cube) dialog box, you click the Change Settings button on the Dimension Key Errors tab. Dimension- and cube-processing options are discussed in more detail in Chapter 7.

Modeling Nonstar Dimensions

You will probably be able to model the majority of your dimensions using the standard star (or single table source type). As SSAS 2005 now gives you the flexibility to model cube measures by basing them on multiple source fact tables, it also gives you the ability to model dimensions in configurations other than simple star schemas. Although it was possible in SSAS 2000 to create a couple of nonstar dimensions, the choices have been greatly expanded in SSAS 2005. The types supported are listed briefly here and explained more fully in the following sections:

- *Snowflake*: This dimension is based on more than one table. This is called a referenced dimension in BIDS.

- *Degenerate*: This dimension is based on a column value from one of the fact tables, rather than using a dimension table. This is called a fact dimension in BIDS.

- *Parent-child*: This dimension is based on a hierarchy derived from a self-referencing relationship within a single dimension table. This is modeled using a regular dimension type in BIDS.

- *Many-to-Many*: This dimension is based on two source tables with an intermediate fact table that establishes the many-to-many relationship between the dimension row values. This is called a many-to-many dimension in BIDS.

- *Role playing*: This dimension relates rows in its table to rows in the fact table multiple times. This is most commonly done for the time dimension. An example would be relating fact rows via an order date, a sales date, and a delivery date. This is modeled as a regular dimension in BIDS.

- *Writeback*: This dimension allows authorized end users to update or make changes to the dimensional attribute values but not the dimensional structure, that is, the dimension name, hierarchy structure, level names, and so on. This option requires the Enterprise Edition of SSAS.

- *Mining Model*: This dimension is based on a SSAS Data Mining model (covered in Chapter 14).

Now that you have an overview of the types of dimensions available, the following sections provide examples of when and how to use each type of dimension.

Snowflake Dimensions

Snowflake dimensions use more than one source table. There must be a key relationship between the rows in each table. For example, a Product dimension might use separate Sub category and Category source tables.

Snowflake dimensions add to cube-processing times, so there should be a business reason to use them. The most compelling of which is when you are modeling an entity for which you have a huge number of rows and discrete attributes by subtype. An example of this could be a products dimension with product category-specific attributes. In other words, product category 1 has a discrete group of attributes, product category 2 has a different group of attributes, product category 3 has yet another group of attributes, and so on.

For example, if your business scenario is to model product sales for a discount chain, then you might need to model these three product categories: makeup, paint, and shoes. The makeup category may have attributes such as "skin type" or "product base type," which are not meaningful to the other product categories. If you used a star design for this example, you could create a needlessly large dimension due to the amount of nulls in the star schema's source dimension table or tables.

Referenced dimensions, like all dimension types, are configured in the BIDS cube designer in the Dimension Usage tab. To configure the relationship between the rows in a particular dimension and fact table, click the gray rectangle that intersects the dimension and fact table. Then, click the Build button (icon with three dots). This opens the Define Relationship dialog box. For a snowflake, you select Referenced dimension from the Select relationship type drop-down list.

The Geography Dimension in the AdventureWorks sample provides an example of a snowflake dimension as shown in Figure 6-7.

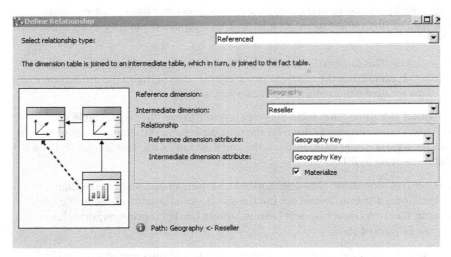

Figure 6-7. *The Define Relationship dialog box in BIDS allows you to set up snowflake (or Referenced) and many other types of dimensions.*

Tip Leaving the default Materialize check box checked is recommended. This speeds up queries by requesting that SSAS store the value of the link between the dimensional tables and fact table as MOLAP metadata (meaning that the metadata is stored on SSAS in a multidimensional format) when the cube or dimension is processed.

Degenerate Dimensions

Degenerate dimensions (called fact dimensions in BIDS) use a column in the fact table as a source. For example, a Sales Order Detail dimension might have an attribute called PO Number.

Defining a dimension-to-fact relationship using BIDS follows the same procedure listed in the previous section, "Snowflake Dimensions." After you've accessed the Define Relationship dialog box, you then select a Fact relationship type. Figure 6-8 shows an example from AdventureWorks.

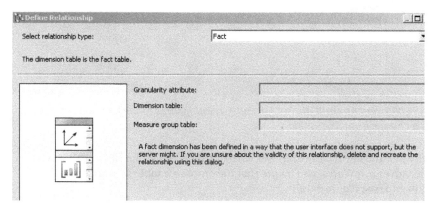

Figure 6-8. *Select the Fact relationship type to create a relationship between a dimension based on a column in the fact table and the fact table itself. This type of dimension is also called a degenerate dimension.*

When you are modeling this type of dimension, you should carefully consider the percentage of end users that will need to browse the attributes included in any fact dimension. These values add significantly to the size of your fact table because each attribute is derived from a new column in the fact table. This, in turn, can add to the cube-processing times and can result in slower queries. For these reasons, in all but the smallest BI solutions, you should avoid using fact dimensions; instead, create a separate dimension source table and a regular dimension for this type of information.

Parent-Child Dimensions

Parent-child dimensions are derived from a single source table. This table must have a primary key and a foreign key that allows a self-join to be performed on this same table. An example from AdventureWorks is the employee table. This type of dimension is used to create a self-referencing, ragged hierarchy. Another way to think of this is a hierarchy that does not necessarily have a larger number of leaf-level members below its parent level, or in the case of the employee table, some employees are managers, or have direct reports, and some are not.

Parent-child dimensions are called *regular* dimensions in the Define Relationship dialog box. This is a change from the previous version of SSAS, where this type of dimensions was called parent-child rather than regular. An example using the employee table is shown in Figure 6-9.

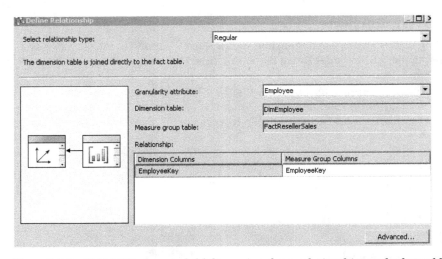

Figure 6-9. *In SSAS 2005, parent-child dimensions have relationships to the fact table of type, regular, which is a change from SSAS 2000.*

You can verify that the key relationship was correctly detected in the DSV for the cube. Using the sample, AdventureWorks, you'll note that the employee table shows this self-referential relationship (see Figure 6-10).

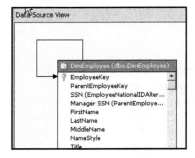

Figure 6-10. *In SSAS 2005, parent-child relationships can be verified in the DSV for the cube.*

Another way to verify that you've set up the parent-child relationship correctly is to browse the dimension in BIDS, where the source columns will be shown as attributes. You'll review the Usage property for the columns listed as attributes. The three possible values are Parent, Key, and Name. In this example, BIDS will generate an attribute named Employee with a Parent Usage, an attribute called EmployeeKey with Key Usage, and other attributes for all other columns in the source table (with the same name as the source columns) with a Name Usage.

Many-to-Many Dimensions

The many-to-many dimension is a new feature introduced in SSAS 2005. This involves two source dimension tables, plus an intermediate table, which makes a total of at least three source tables. At least two of these tables are typical dimension tables.

What is new is the need to use an intermediate fact table to establish the relationship between the rows in the first dimension table and the second dimension table. The relationship between the rows in the second dimension table and the main fact table is established via keys in those two tables.

You can think of the secondary fact table as similar to a relational junction table in OLTP modeling. An example of this is provided in the AdventureWorks sample for the salesReason dimension. The business case is that each Internet sale can have many sales order lines; each order line can have a sales reason. So that each Internet sale can have many sales order lines and each order line has a sales reason, the relationship between order lines and sales reasons is many-to-many. The first step to using many-to-many dimensions is modeling correctly, in other words, creating the appropriate source tables as shown in Figures 6-11 and 6-12.

| Explore DimSalesReason Table | Sales Reason [Online] | Adventure Works [Online] | Internet Sales . |

| Table | Pivot Table | Chart | Pivot Chart | |

	SalesReasonKey	SalesReasonAlternateKey	SalesReasonName	SalesReasonReasonType
▶	1	1	Price	Other
	2	2	On Promotion	Promotion
	3	3	Magazine Advertisem	Marketing
	4	4	Television Advertise	Marketing
	5	5	Manufacturer	Other
	6	6	Review	Other
	7	7	Demo Event	Marketing
	8	8	Sponsorship	Marketing
	9	9	Quality	Other
	10	10	Other	Other

Figure 6-11. *Many-to-many dimensions require two source dimension tables, plus an intermediate fact table (that functions much like a relational junction table). One of the tables lists the dimensional attribute value. In the AdventureWorks example, this is the* SalesReason *table.*

| Explore FactIn...lesReason Table | Sales Reason [Online] | Adventure Works |

| Table | Pivot Table | Chart | Pivot Chart | |

	SalesOrderNumber	SalesOrderLineNumb	SalesReasonKey
▶	SO43697	1	5
	SO43697	1	9
	SO43702	1	5
	SO43702	1	9
	SO43703	1	5
	SO43703	1	9
	SO43706	1	5
	SO43706	1	9
	SO43707	1	5
	SO43707	1	9
	SO43709	1	5

Figure 6-12. *Many-to-many dimensions require at least three source tables. One of the tables establishes the relationship between the dimension table attributes and the rows in the destination fact table. In the AdventureWorks example, this is the* FactInternetSalesReason *table.*

You can also see whether you've modeled the relationship correctly by reviewing the participating tables in the DSV as shown in Figure 6-13.

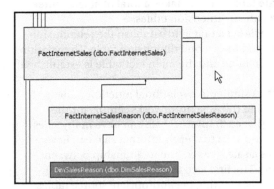

Figure 6-13. *You can verify that you've modeled the many-to-many relationship in the DSV for your cube. The intermediate table will appear as an additional fact table in this view. A portion of the AdventureWorks sample is shown here.*

After you've correctly modeled the many-to-many dimension, you establish the relationship using the Dimension Usage tab of the cube designer. While working in the Define Relationship dialog box, you select the Many-to-Many dimension type as shown in Figure 6-14.

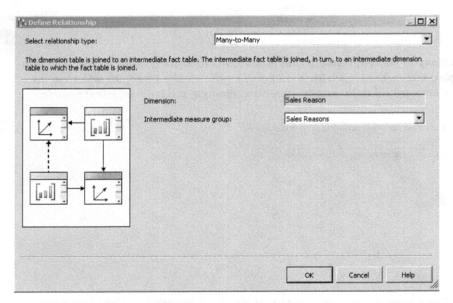

Figure 6-14. *After selecting the Many-to-Many relationship type in the Define Relationship dialog box, you must select a table in the Intermediate measure group list box.*

Role-Playing Dimensions

Role-playing dimensions are set up via modeling as well. A typical example from the AdventureWorks sample (from the time dimension) is shown in Figure 6-15—the three instances of the Date dimension in the Dimension Usage tab.

Role playing means joining rows from a dimension to a fact table more than once. The example for this case is Date, Ship Date, and Delivery Date. To do this, you join more than one dimension based on the same source table by simply adding (or referencing) the same source table multiple times as the basis for cube dimensions and giving each dimension a different dimension name. In other words, you add new dimensions based on the same table multiple times. The example from AdventureWorks is the most typical implementation of a role-playing dimension, that is, adding a time dimension multiple times to create different time-based dimensions.

Figure 6-15 shows the modeling of this type of dimension in the Dimension Usage tab of the cube designer in BIDS.

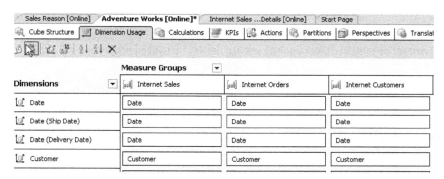

Figure 6-15. *Role-playing dimensions are modeled as regular dimensions in the Dimension Usage window. You model this type of dimension by creating multiple dimensions based on the same source table. A typical use of this is with a time dimension.*

Writeback Dimensions

Writeback dimensions require the Enterprise Edition of SSAS. You enable writeback for a dimension by setting the WriteEnabled property value of a dimension to True. You can also use the Business Intelligence Wizard to enable writeback for a dimension. Figure 6-16 shows the property value interface for a dimension to enable writeback for an entire dimension (which means all attributes at all levels). You cannot enable writeback for any subset from a dimension, which means that you cannot enable writeback for a particular attribute of a dimension. Writeback is an "all or nothing" option for a particular dimension.

With writeback dimensions, you need to verify that your selected client applications support writeback. Also, you must confirm that allowing writeback is consistent with your project's business requirements. Another consideration is that you must specifically grant read/write permissions to write-enabled dimensions for those end users who will need to write to a dimension. In my experience, writeback is not commonly enabled for BI projects. One case where it may be enabled is when a cube is used for financial forecasting, particularly "what if" scenarios.

Figure 6-16. *You can write-enable dimensions by setting the* WriteEnabled *property of an entire dimension to* True.

Note Writeback is *not* supported for certain dimensions types, including referenced dimensions, fact dimensions, many-to-many dimensions, and linked dimensions. As previously mentioned, you can only enable writeback for entire dimensions, not specific attributes of a dimension.

Modeling Changing Dimensions and More

After you've selected the type of dimension to be used for your particular business scenario, another important concept is whether and how your model will support update behavior for the dimensional attribute values.

To understand how to model for updates, consider that updates in SSAS need to be divided into two types: new values (or inserts) and changes (or updates or deletes of existing attribute values). Allowing inserts of new values for the dimension or fact tables does *not* require you to use any special modeling techniques. However, the business rules required for *changes* to dimensional attributes *will* affect the way you model those attributes.

In Chapter 2, I introduced the topic of modeling slowly (or rapidly) changing dimensions. At this point in your BI solution, you now have six considerations. These considerations include modeling for the rate of change (that is, slow or rapid), and configuring error definitions (that is, "Are changes allowed at all?" "Are nulls allowed?"). The options and support for updating the various types of dimensions via the SSIS transformation "update slowly changing dimension" are listed next. The reason for this last point is that you will probably want to automate the process of dimensional attribute updates via SSIS packages.

The considerations are as follows:

- *Slowly Changing Type 1*: Any submitted changes overwrite previous values. The SSIS "update slowly changing dimension transformation" calls this type Changing. If you choose this method, you may want to add a column to your dimension table called dateLoaded, if your business requirements call for this.

- *Slowly Changing Type 2*: Any submitted changes will result in a new record (or row) being added. The SSIS "update slowly changing dimension transformation" calls this type Historical. The structure of your dimension tables must accommodate this in one of two ways: either by having columns for start and end dates or by having a column that allows you to record historical attributes.

- *Slowly Changing Type 3*: Adding more attributes (or column values) when the dimension member value changes. The SSIS "update slowly changing dimension transformation" does not support this type. The structure of your dimension tables must accommodate this. This type requires a source table structure, which includes as many columns (and corresponding date effective columns) for the number of changes you want to capture.

- *Rapidly Changing*: The dimensional attributes change constantly, for example, fast-food restaurant location employee names. In this case, you would usually process your dimension differently altogether. If your business requirements include a rapidly changing dimension, then you can use ROLAP (or relational OLAP storage).

  This means that the dimension metadata is not copied to SSAS; rather, it is read "live" from the star schema. This option is discussed in more detail in Chapter 7. This type of dimension does not require any special modeling. You simply set the storageMode property of the dimension to ROLAP. Be aware that this can result in significantly slower query processing. Also, this option requires the Enterprise Edition of SSAS.

- *No changes allowed*: Requests for changes are treated as errors (and are usually logged as errors). The SSIS "update slowly changing dimension transformation" calls this type Fixed. You configure a custom error configuration to support this business requirement. This is discussed in more detail in the next paragraph.

- *Nulls allowed*: If you choose to allow null values on load, then you should establish a standard method of "handling" or renaming those null values. This is configured via the UnknownMember dimension property. The SSIS "update slowly changing dimension transformation" calls this type an inferred member. This property is discussed further in subsequent paragraphs of the next section.

Error Handling for Dimension Attribute Loads

If your business needs require more granular control over error handling, you can set several properties in the SSAS dimension editor, at the dimension level.

First, let's consider what types of errors could occur. These could include loading nulls, loading mismatched (to the rows in the fact table) key values, and loading duplicate key values. You should capture desired error-handling behavior for each dimension during the requirements gathering phase of your BI project.

The first consideration when implementing those requirements is whether you'll need to include a custom error configuration. If you set the ErrorConfiguration property to (custom), then several properties become available for you to configure in BIDS via the dimension property sheet. These properties are shown in Figure 6-17; all the values are the defaults, with the exception of the KeyErrorAction property value, which I have changed from the default value of ConvertToUnknown to the optional value of DiscardRecord for this example.

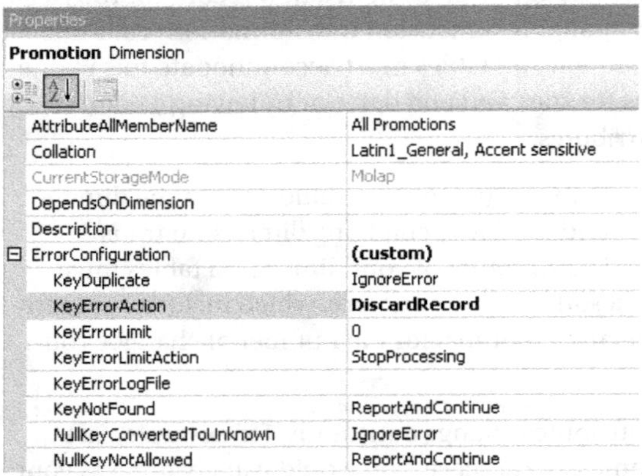

Promotion Dimension	
AttributeAllMemberName	All Promotions
Collation	Latin1_General, Accent sensitive
CurrentStorageMode	Molap
DependsOnDimension	
Description	
⊟ ErrorConfiguration	**(custom)**
KeyDuplicate	IgnoreError
KeyErrorAction	**DiscardRecord**
KeyErrorLimit	0
KeyErrorLimitAction	StopProcessing
KeyErrorLogFile	
KeyNotFound	ReportAndContinue
NullKeyConvertedToUnknown	IgnoreError
NullKeyNotAllowed	ReportAndContinue

Figure 6-17. *You set the behavior of key errors at the level of the entire dimension in SSAS.*

Along with custom error handling, you may want to control the value of nulls loaded into a dimension by changing the UnknownMember property of the dimension to a nondefault value for a dimension as shown in Figure 6-18.

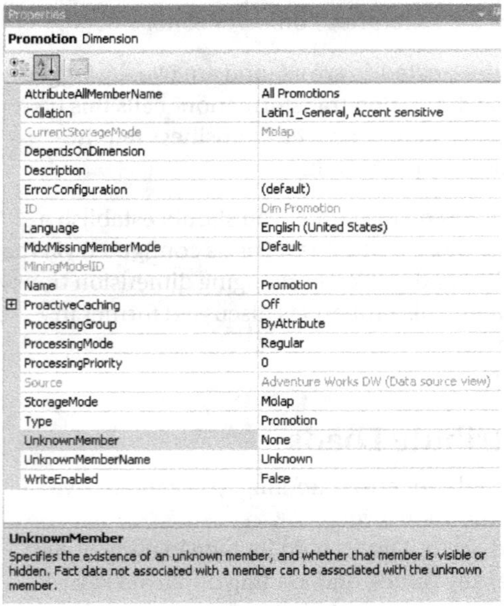

Promotion Dimension	
AttributeAllMemberName	All Promotions
Collation	Latin1_General, Accent sensitive
CurrentStorageMode	Molap
DependsOnDimension	
Description	
ErrorConfiguration	(default)
ID	Dim Promotion
Language	English (United States)
MdxMissingMemberMode	Default
MiningModelID	
Name	Promotion
⊞ ProactiveCaching	Off
ProcessingGroup	ByAttribute
ProcessingMode	Regular
ProcessingPriority	0
Source	Adventure Works DW (Data source view)
StorageMode	Molap
Type	Promotion
UnknownMember	None
UnknownMemberName	Unknown
WriteEnabled	False

UnknownMember
Specifies the existence of an unknown member, and whether that member is visible or hidden. Fact data not associated with a member can be associated with the unknown member.

Figure 6-18. *The* UnknownMember *property of a dimension allows you to control the behavior of nulls (if you choose to load null values into a dimension).*

It is still best practice to cleanse all data prior to loading into your cube via the ETL processes (using SSIS). Most of my clients prefer to refrain from loading nulls into both the dimension and fact tables. However, should your business requirements be such that you load nulls, BIDS gives you many options for working with them.

Using the Business Intelligence Wizard

After you've added the fact tables and dimensions to your cube and configured the properties for both, the next option for you to consider is whether to use the Business Intelligence Wizard to add still more sophisticated options to your BI solution. This wizard presents you with a different list of options depending on whether you've opened it from the cube or from the dimension designer. The complete list of options (for both types) is as follows:

- *Add Writeback*: (For dimensions only) Requires the Enterprise Edition of SSAS. Using this wizard simply sets the WriteEnabled property of a dimension to True.

- *Add Semiadditive Measures*: (For cubes only) Allows you to set the aggregationFunction property for a cube measure to something other than the default (sum). The choices are Average of Children, By Account, Count, Distinct Count, FirstChild, FirstNonEmpty, LastChild, LastNonEmpty, Max, Min, None, Sum. These options are discussed in more depth in Chapter 12.

- *Add Account Intelligence*: Allows you to assign accounting types, that is, income, expenses, and so on, to dimension attributes. Specifically, you associate one dimension attribute with one of the following: Chart of Accounts, Account Name, Account Number, or Account Type. The default is to set measures to be semiadditive based on account type. The wizard will set the aggregationFunction property to the value byAccount. The Configure Dimension Attributes page of the wizard is shown in Figure 6-19.

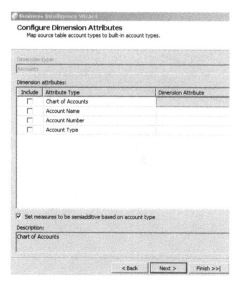

Figure 6-19. *In the Business Intelligence Wizard's Add Account Intelligence Configure Dimension Attributes page, you can associate attribute types with specific attributes.*

- *Add Time Intelligence*: (For cubes only) Generates a MDX script that creates calculated members (which appear in the cube as regular measures) based on common time-based comparisons that you've selected in the wizard page that lists a selection of common comparison values.

Some examples are Quarter to Date, Three Month Moving Average, and Year Over Year Growth. Figure 6-20 shows the list of options. Figure 6-21 shows a sample generated MDX script.

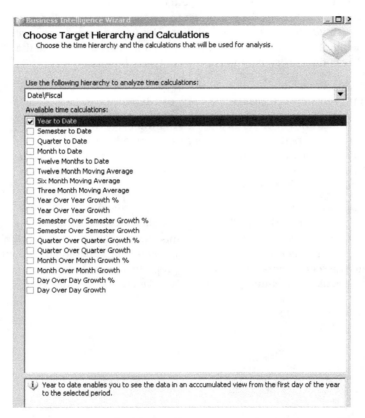

Figure 6-20. *In the Business Intelligence Wizard's Add Time Intelligence selection, you select common time-based scenarios, and SSAS generates a MDX script for you. This script will add calculated members to your OLAP cube.*

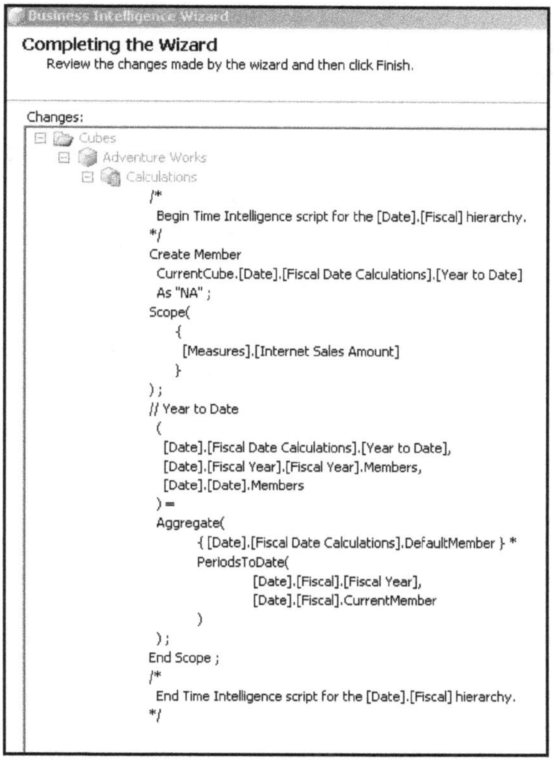

```
Business Intelligence Wizard

Completing the Wizard
    Review the changes made by the wizard and then click Finish.


Changes:
□ 📂 Cubes
    □ 🗐 Adventure Works
        □ 📇 Calculations
                /*
                Begin Time Intelligence script for the [Date].[Fiscal] hierarchy.
                */
                Create Member
                CurrentCube.[Date].[Fiscal Date Calculations].[Year to Date]
                As "NA" ;
                Scope(
                    {
                      [Measures].[Internet Sales Amount]
                    }
                ) ;
                // Year to Date
                (
                    [Date].[Fiscal Date Calculations].[Year to Date],
                    [Date].[Fiscal Year].[Fiscal Year].Members,
                    [Date].[Date].Members
                ) =
                Aggregate(
                        { [Date].[Fiscal Date Calculations].DefaultMember } *
                        PeriodsToDate(
                                [Date].[Fiscal].[Fiscal Year],
                                [Date].[Fiscal].CurrentMember
                        )
                ) ;
                End Scope ;
                /*
                End Time Intelligence script for the [Date].[Fiscal] hierarchy.
                */
```

Figure 6-21. *In the Business Intelligence Wizard's Add Time Intelligence selection, SSAS generates a MDX script that creates a calculated member in the cube.*

- *Add Dimension Intelligence*: Allows you to associate metadata with dimension attributes by setting the type property. For example, for the customer dimension, you can associate a particular dimension attribute with the address type, the city type, or the company type. Some client applications use this type information to present information to end users in a more friendly fashion and to assist end users in adding calculated members by using GUI tools included in their particular client application, rather than by having to manually author MDX scripts.

- *Add Unary Operator*: (For cubes only) Allows you to specify a unary operator to replace the default aggregation (which is to sum all measures) for noncalculated hierarchy members in parent-child hierarchies. You can specify either regular or weighted aggregations. Like the Add Account Intelligence option, this option is often used when your business requirements include modeling to support an organization's balance sheets.

- *Add Custom Member Formulas*: Allows you to specify a column with a custom MDX formula that will override the default rollup. The default rollup is to Sum all measures. This sets the CustomRollupColumn property of the selected dimensional attribute to the selected column.

- *Add Attribute Ordering*: (For dimensions only) Allows you to override the default setting, Order by member name, to replace with Order by key or Order by name of a
  different attribute in the same dimension.

- *Add Currency Conversion*: (For cubes only) Allows you to add a dimension that is used
  to translate one or more currencies in the fact table to one or more new currencies.
  I covered the implementation of this option by reviewing the steps in the wizard in
  detail in Chapter 5.

What's Next?

Now that we've reviewed most aspects of logical cube design, in Chapter 7, we'll discuss
physical cube design. That chapter will include cube and dimension processing, partitions,
and much more.

Summary

This chapter covered many advanced OLAP modeling techniques. These methods included
using multiple fact tables and various types of dimensions. SSAS 2005 has added quite a bit of
flexibility in its capacity to allow for modeling scenarios that more closely match that of your
actual business data. Remember that several of these features require the Enterprise Edition of
Analysis Services.

The other important consideration with these techniques is to always use business
requirements as a justification for adding the complexity that any of these new capabilities
bring to your BI solution. I've seen many BI solutions in both SSAS 2005 and 2000 that were
overcomplicated, which made them difficult to maintain, to administer, and most important,
to use. Favor simplicity in cube design.

In the next chapter, you'll learn about physical storage mechanisms for cube and dimension data and metadata. This is the world of MOLAP, HOLAP, or ROLAP—multidimensional,
hybrid, or relational OLAP. You'll also learn about what exactly is happening when you
"process" a cube or dimension. Finally, we'll explore a feature new to SSAS 2005: Proactive
Caching.

CHAPTER 7

■ ■ ■

Cube Storage and Aggregation

Now that you've completed your cube's logical design, it's time to design the physical storage mechanisms, including file placement and aggregations.

This chapter covers the details of physical cube processing and storage, including an explanation of the what, when, and why to use any of the three cube storage methods: MOLAP, HOLAP, or ROLAP. These storage-type acronyms stand for multidimensional, hybrid, or relational OLAP. The chapter also explains cube aggregations—what they are and when and when not to use the default cube-processing settings (which uses 0% aggregations). Following is a complete list of topics for this chapter:

- Using default storage: MOLAP, no aggregations

- Designing custom aggregations

- Understanding advanced storage: MOLAP, ROLAP, or HOLAP

- Working with Proactive Caching—welcome to the (near) real-time

- Designing relational partitions and SSAS partitions

- Planning for rapidly changing (ROLAP) dimensions

- Selecting appropriate cube-processing options

Using the Default Storage: MOLAP

From earlier chapters, you may remember that to view structural changes to your cube, you must process the cube in BIDS and then deploy the changes to Analysis Services. To understand what is happening during this process, you must first be aware of what you are creating when you design and build BI objects (such as DSVs, cubes, dimensions, and so on) using BIDS. Although you are working in a GUI environment, commands in the XMLA SSAS metadata language are being generated.

XMLA (XML for Analysis)

XMLA (XML for Analysis) is an open standard XML dialect that is used for client-server communications between OLAP servers. XMLA describes its messages in a SOAP-style format designed to access multidimensional databases that contain OLAP cubes. (SOAP, Simple Object Access Protocol, is a type of XML dialect.) XMLA will sometimes also contain

Multidimensional Expressions (MDX) queries. XMLA is the language of cube metadata. This language includes many methods that allow you to view or modify cube information; two examples are the `Discover` and `Execute` methods. For an example of XMLA that uses the `Create` method, see Figure 7-1. For a complete list of XMLA methods, see the BOL topic "Using XML for Analysis in Analysis Services (XMLA)."

```
WEBFLUENT\mo...LAQuery1.xmla | Summary
<Create xmlns="http://schemas.microsoft.com/analysisservices/2003/engine">
    <ParentObject>
        <DatabaseID>Adventure Works DW Standard Edition</DatabaseID>
    </ParentObject>
    <ObjectDefinition>
        <Dimension xmlns:xsd="http://www.w3.org/2001/XMLSchema" xmlns:xsi="http://www.w3.org/2001/XMLSchema-instance">
            <ID>Dim Customer</ID>
            <Name>Customer</Name>
            <Annotations>...</Annotations>
            <Source xsi:type="DataSourceViewBinding">
                <DataSourceViewID>Adventure Works DW</DataSourceViewID>
            </Source>
            <Type>Customers</Type>
            <UnknownMember>Visible</UnknownMember>
            <Language>1033</Language>
            <Collation>Latin1_General_CI_AS</Collation>
            <UnknownMemberName>Unknown</UnknownMemberName>
            <Attributes>
                <Attribute>
                    <ID>Full Name</ID>
                    <Name>Customer</Name>
                    <Type>Customers</Type>
                    <Usage>Key</Usage>
                    <EstimatedCount>18484</EstimatedCount>
                    <KeyColumns>
                        <KeyColumn>
                            <DataType>Integer</DataType>
                            <DataSize>-1</DataSize>
                            <Source xsi:type="ColumnBinding">
                                <TableID>dbo_DimCustomer</TableID>
                                <ColumnID>CustomerKey</ColumnID>
                            </Source>
                        </KeyColumn>
                    </KeyColumns>
                    <NameColumn>
                        <DataType>WChar</DataType>
                        <DataSize>152</DataSize>
                        <Source xsi:type="ColumnBinding">
                            <TableID>dbo_DimCustomer</TableID>
                            <ColumnID>FullName</ColumnID>
                        </Source>
                    </NameColumn>
                    <AttributeRelationships>
                        <AttributeRelationship>
                            <AttributeID>Date First Purchase</AttributeID>
                            <Name>Date of First Purchase</Name>
                        </AttributeRelationship>
                        <AttributeRelationship>
                            <AttributeID>Phone</AttributeID>
```

Figure 7-1. *The metadata language of SSAS is an XML dialect called XMLA.*

■**Note** To generate the XMLA for an SSAS object, you must use SSMS, not BIDS! In SSMS, you connect to SSAS, right-click the object you want to script, click Script to, New Query Window, and so on.

I'm opening this discussion of cube data storage with the XMLA because you must understand what Analysis Services considers to be data and what it considers to be metadata as you begin to plan your cube storage options.

The simplest way to think of this is as follows: Data is the content (rows) in the fact table. Metadata is everything else. By "everything else," I mean cube definitions, dimension names, attribute names, hierarchy names, and, most important, dimension attribute values. This list provides some examples from the samples available with SSAS to help explain this concept more fully:

- *Data*: All fact table rows from Fact Internet Sales, Fact Internet Sales Reason, and so on. Data does *not* include rows from the dimension tables; those rows are metadata and treated differently from data during dimension and cube processing.

- *Metadata*: Names and all attributes for the `Customer` dimension called "Customer," Customer dimensional hierarchy called "Customer Geography," Customer Attribute called "Marital Status," Customer attribute values called "Married, Single or Unknown."

When you design storage for your cube, your primary concern is how to store the *data* (or the fact table rows, *not* the dimension table rows). This is because the largest amount of data in any cube is generally contained in the facts (or fact table rows.). There can be exceptions to this in the case of huge dimensions. We will discuss this case in more detail later in this chapter.

We'll start our discussion of storage with storage of data only. We'll cover storage of metadata later in this chapter. For data storage, you have three choices at the topmost level:

- *MOLAP*: Multidimensional OLAP stores a copy of the fact table rows (or facts) on SSAS. This is not a one-for-one storage option. Due to efficient storage mechanisms used for cubes, the resultant storage is approximately 10–20% the size of the original data; that is, if you have 1GB in your fact table, plan for around 200MB storage on SSAS. However efficient, when you chose MOLAP, be aware that you are choosing to make a copy of all source data.

- *HOLAP*: Hybrid OLAP does *not* make a copy of the facts in SSAS. It reads this information from the star schema source. This is covered in greater detail later in this chapter.

- *ROLAP*: Relational OLAP does *not* make a copy of the facts on SSAS. It reads this information from the star schema source. This is covered in greater detail later in the chapter.

Aggregations

The other major consideration is the quantity of and the storage of aggregations. An *aggregation* is a calculated, stored intersection of fact values that is calculated at a level higher than that of the load of the fact table. In other words, if your fact table holds a fact (say sales amount) for each product sold on each day by each employee, a possible aggregation would be to sum (and store) that information at the week level or for each week for all rows in the fact table.

An important difference between OLAP aggregations and materialized (or stored) indexes on calculated columns in a relational database such as SQL Server is that the SSAS can use aggregations from *any* level in response to a query. The result is that full cube aggregation is *never* needed to optimize queries. In fact, overaggregation of OLAP cubes is a common design mistake. Baseline values for aggregation are defined a bit later in this section.

For example, SSAS uses aggregations to efficiently and quickly return query results by writing a query that looks for the sales amount for each product, for each employee by year (from the scenario described in a previous paragraph). If there were aggregations at the week level, then SSAS would use them to calculate the results of the query for the yearly results and would not have to read each cell of the cube, which is based on each row of the fact table (assuming the cube was loaded at the day level).

The storage type you select impacts where any aggregations are stored. MOLAP, by default, creates no aggregations. Should you choose to add any aggregations, those will be stored in the native SSAS format on SSAS as well as the fact data. For HOLAP, only aggregations—not data (or fact table rows)—will be stored on SSAS. For ROLAP, aggregations will be "written back" to the relational database. Figure 7-2 shows a conceptual rendering of a ROLAP aggregation table as part of a star schema. Note that the column names reflect the positions in the hierarchy that are being aggregated and the type of aggregation performed.

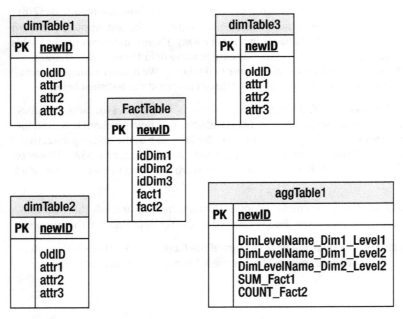

Figure 7-2. *ROLAP storage creates and stores aggregations in the star schema source relational database. A side benefit of this storage is that these aggregations can be queried using T-SQL.*

Note MOLAP is your only storage option if you are working with the Standard Edition of SSAS. If you are working with the Enterprise Edition of SSAS, you may choose MOLAP, HOLAP, or ROLAP storage.

MOLAP as Default in SSAS

So, which type of storage is best? Why is MOLAP with 0% aggregations the default mechanism? In my experience, most of you will use only or primarily MOLAP because it provides efficient storage and the fastest query results. Although the default level of aggregations is 0%, most of my customers choose to add at least some aggregations to their production cubes. The reason for doing this is that SSAS is optimized to quickly and easily add aggregations during cube- and dimension processing, and the improvement in query results usually offsets the overhead in processing time and cube storage file sizes. We will drill into this topic a bit more deeply in the next section as well.

MOLAP is the storage default because the SSAS query engine is highly optimized for calculating aggregates on large quantities of data; the SSAS engine is really more like Excel's calculation engine than that of SQL Server (or any other relational database). Relational database engines, such as SQL Server 2005, are designed to fetch subsets of data efficiently, not necessarily to sort, filter, or aggregate that data. For many customers, MOLAP with 0% aggregations (or some small amount such as 20%) will produce queries that run quickly enough for all of their end users.

Adding Aggregations

Why is it so important to add the correct amount of aggregations to your cube(s)? As stated previously, it may not be. It's important to remember that some SSAS cubes do not require aggregations to function acceptably. Similar to the the idea that tiny OLTP databases need no relational indexes, if your cube is quite small (under 1GB), and if you have a small number of end users (100 or fewer), then you probably won't have to add any aggregations at all.

Unlike adding indexes to a relational database, (which can be time-consuming if manually done), adding aggregations to an SSAS cube can be done pretty quickly via a couple of wizards (or tools) in BIDS. There are a couple of considerations when adding aggregations to a cube: aggregations increase cube processing times, and aggregations increase the storage space required for the cube on disk.

There are two tools to help you design appropriate aggregations. The first tool, the Aggregation Design Wizard, is available in BIDS (and SSMS). You access the wizard by clicking the `Design Aggregations` link on the partitions tab in BIDS as shown in Figure 7-3.

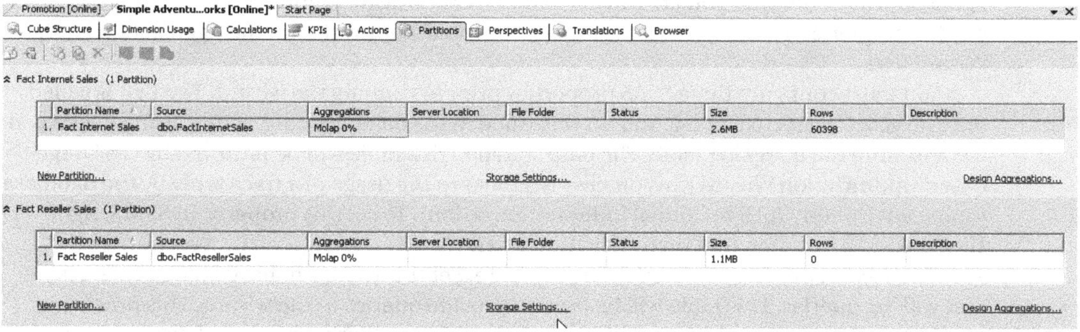

Figure 7-3. *BIDS provides you with an Aggregation Design Wizard to assist you with intelligent aggregation design for your cube.*

In the first dialog box of the wizard, you are asked to provide a count of the rows in the fact table, or you can ask SSAS to "count" the rows for you. In the next step, you'll be presented with a couple of options for aggregation design:

- *Estimated storage reaches*: SSAS designs aggregations up to the size limit you input here (in megabytes or gigabytes) for storage of the resulting aggregations on disk.

- *Performance gain reaches*: SSAS designs aggregations up to this threshold that you input as a percentage increase in query performance speed.

- *I click stop*: The wizard stops adding aggregations when you click stop.

- *Do not design*: The wizard does not design any aggregations.

If you select the Performance gain reaches option in the wizard, then a good starting value for you to choose is 20%. As discussed earlier, there is no need to aggregate an SSAS cube 100% because SSAS's can use intermediate aggregations to answer queries. In fact, aggregating more than 50% is usually detrimental, as this increases cube-processing times and storage space without positively impacting query response times. Another consideration is that when the wizard completes its recommendations, you can chose whether to process the cube using those recommendations immediately, or to save the results for later processing.

Note A new capability in SSAS 2005 is generating aggregations via XMLA batch processing. For more information see the BOL topic "Designing Aggregations (XMLA)."

The second tool you can use to more granularly define aggregations—the Usage-Based Optimization Wizard—is available in SSMS and in BIDS (using the Partitions tab). This wizard works by saving actual queries sent to the SSAS database. The saved queries are based on parameter values that you specify, such as start and end time, user name, and so on. The wizard then figures out which aggregations will best improve the performance of the queries that are run and which fall within the configured parameters. Because query performance is determined as much by the selected (and filtered) queries coming from your client applications as it is by the data. This makes effective use of the Usage-Based Optimization Wizard a very intelligent approach because you are causing SSAS to create aggregations specifically for the particular queries, rather than just using the "blanket" approach that the Aggregation Design Wizard uses.

You must configure three SSAS properties prior to running the wizard. The first is called the QueryLogConnectionString. You set this value to the database connection string where you want to store the query log table. The data stored in this table will be retrieved by the Usage-Based Optimization Wizard (this process is similar to the usage of a trace table by the database tuning advisor for OLTP relational index optimization). To set this property, in SSMS, right-click the SSAS instance, and then click Properties.

The second property is CreateQueryLogTable. Set this to True to have SSAS create a table that will log queries. This table will be used to provide queries to the wizard. This process is similar to using a trace table to provide queries to SQL Profiler for relational database query tuning. You can optionally change the default name of the query log table for the database you previously defined. This value is set to OlapQueryLog by default.

The third property to set is `QueryLogSampling`. The default is to only capture one out of ten queries. You will probably want to set this to 1 for your sampling purposes, so that every query within the defined parameter set is captured. Figure 7-4 shows the properties window for SSAS inside of SSMS where you can set all of these properties.

Name	Value	Current Value	Default Value
BackupDir	C:\Program Files...	C:\Program Files...	
CommitTimeout	0	0	0
CoordinatorExecutionMode	-4	-4	-4
DataDir	C:\Program Files...	C:\Program Files...	\data
DataMining \ AllowAdHocOpenRowsetQueries	false	false	false
DataMining \ AllowSessionMiningModels	false	false	false
DataMining \ MaxConcurrentPredictionQueries	0	0	0
Feature \ ComUdfEnabled	false	false	false
Feature \ LinkFromOtherInstanceEnabled	false	false	false
Feature \ LinkInsideInstanceEnabled	true	true	true
Feature \ LinkToOtherInstanceEnabled	false	false	false
Feature \ ManagedCodeEnabled	true	true	true
Feature \ UseCachedPageAllocators	false	false	false
ForceCommitTimeout	30000	30000	30000
Log \ ErrorLog \ ErrorLogFileName			
Log \ ErrorLog \ ErrorLogFileSize	4	4	4
Log \ ErrorLog \ KeyErrorAction	0	0	0
Log \ ErrorLog \ KeyErrorLimit	0	0	0
Log \ ErrorLog \ KeyErrorLimitAction	0	0	0
Log \ ErrorLog \ KeyErrorLogFile			
Log \ ErrorLog \ LogErrorTypes \ KeyDuplicate	0	0	0
Log \ ErrorLog \ LogErrorTypes \ KeyNotFound	1	1	1
Log \ ErrorLog \ LogErrorTypes \ NullKeyConver...	0	0	0
Log \ ErrorLog \ LogErrorTypes \ NullKeyNotAllo...	1	1	1
Log \ Exception \ CrashReportsFolder			
Log \ Exception \ CreateAndSendCrashReports	1	1	1
Log \ Exception \ CriticalErrorHandling	1	1	1
Log \ Exception \ ExceptionHandlingMode	0	0	0
Log \ FlightRecorder \ Enabled	true	true	true
Log \ QueryLog \ CreateQueryLogTable	false	false	false
Log \ QueryLog \ QueryLogConnectionString	Provider=SQLN...	Provider=SQLN...	
Log \ QueryLog \ QueryLogFileName			
Log \ QueryLog \ QueryLogFileSize	4	4	4
Log \ QueryLog \ QueryLogSampling	10	10	10
Log \ QueryLog \ QueryLogTableName	OlapQueryLog	OlapQueryLog	OlapQueryLog
Network \ ListenOnlyOnLocalConnections	false	false	false

Figure 7-4. *You must capture queries by setting the database connection string property for the* `QueryLogConnectionString` *value and setting the* `CreateQueryLogTable` *switch to* `True` *before you can use the Usage-Based Optimization Wizard in SSMS.*

To run the wizard, connect to SSAS in SSMS, right-click a cube partition in Object Explorer, and then click Usage-Based Optimization. Every cube will have at least one partition. We'll talk more about partitions later in this chapter. After you start the wizard, you ask SSAS to design aggregations based on any combination of the following parameter values: beginning date, ending date, specific user, and quantity of queries by percentage to total. Figure 7-5 shows a sample list of queries. In the wizard, you select which queries you want SSAS to design aggregations for.

Figure 7-5. *The Usage-Based Optimization Wizard in SSMS allows you to select which queries you want SSAS to design aggregations for.*

Another interesting tool that you can use to design aggregations more intelligently is SQL Server Profiler. You may be familiar with Profiler's capability to capture whatever traffic and information that you set in the trace definition for OTLP databases. What is new in 2005 is that you can use Profiler to capture activity on Analysis Services.

This will allow you to easily see which MDX queries are taking up the most resources on the server. As is with any type of query tuning, adding aggregations is only half of the solution. The other method of improving query performance is to rewrite the query in a more optimal way. Although this is possible, it is done much less often in the world of SSAS (than, for instance, rewriting T-SQL queries for SQL Server) because of the inherent complexity of MDX. Using SQL Server Profiler to identify those queries placing the heaviest load on the server will help you effectively target your tuning efforts (which more often involve adding aggregations than rewriting the MDX queries) for those queries that need it the most.

Later in this book, Chapter 10 is devoted to introducing MDX syntax. Figure 7-6 shows output from Profiler while tracing SSAS activity.

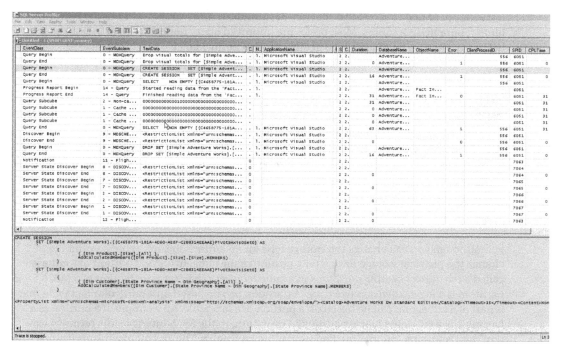

Figure 7-6. *Profiler allows you to trace any activities that you include in the trace filter for Analysis Services 2005. This can assist you with identifying long-running queries as candidates for aggregations.*

Advanced Storage: MOLAP, HOLAP, or ROLAP

Most production BI cubes will work just fine with the default storage type of MOLAP, with one caveat: they should not be huge. (I'll define "huge" in the next section.) The one default that I most often change is *not* the storage mechanism; rather it's the amount of aggregations. Remember that the default is 0%. It is most typical to use the Storage and Design Aggregation Wizard to add between 20% and 30% increase in query performance in aggregation values.

Considering Other Types of Storage

Storing cube data and metadata in MOLAP results in the best query performance, so why use any other type of storage? Most typically, you will only be interested in these options if your cube is relatively large, 250GB or greater, for example, or if storage space is problematic. Another reason to consider ROLAP or HOLAP storage is if cube-processing times are excessive for your particular business needs. Also huge dimensions sometimes warrant the use of ROLAP storage—huge being defined as those dimensions containing millions of members. A final consideration for nondefault storage is the business case, which requires real-time information. Be diligent in understanding requirements for this last situation. Using the new Proactive Caching feature (described more fully in the upcoming section of the same title) allows for near real-time results—latency of seconds in some cases—without the performance hit that pure ROLAP causes. Most prefer the improved query performance of MOLAP and are willing to "trade" a bit of latency to get that level of performance.

■**Tip** Before changing storage settings for a cube, you may want to review aggregation design. Remember that the default aggregation is 0%. If you are considering changing the storage method primarily to improve query performance, then you'll first want to look at adding aggregations using one or more of the techniques already discussed in this chapter. However, if you choose to add aggregations, you'll need to be sure not to overaggregate your cube (as discussed in the "Adding Aggregations Section"). Overaggregation will result in excessive disk storage space and slow cube-processing times. As a rule of thumb, aggregating more than 50% is considered overaggregating.

Although you can change the storage type for an entire cube, it is more common to change the physical storage design for a portion of the cube. In SSAS, a portion of a cube is called a *partition*. Creating partitions in a cube requires the Enterprise Edition of SSAS. A SSAS partition is a logical division of a cube. A partition can be based on a particular fact table that is part of a cube, or it can be based on a portion of a fact table. An example of a portion of a fact table is a fact table that is partitioned by month. In the SSAS interface, the terms "partition" and "measure group" are often used interchangeably. This is a bit of a misnomer because even cubes with a single (default) partition can have more than one measure group associated with that partition. In other words, there is not necessarily a one-to-one ratio between a measure group and a partition.

To create a partition in BIDS, you click the partition tab on the cube design surface, and then click the New Partition link on the design surface as shown in Figure 7-7. You are asked to select which Measure Group and Partition (Fact Table) Source you want to partition in the wizard. The Partition Source is a DSV in the SSAS database. Alternatively, you can enter a table name in the Filter tables text box and then click the Find Tables button to restrict the source to a particular source table. This dialog box is shown in Figure 7-8.

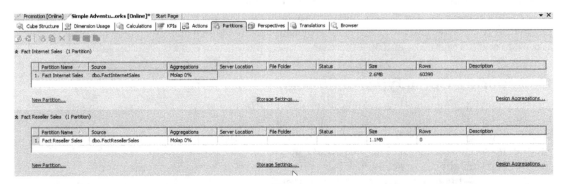

Figure 7-7. *If you want to vary the cube storage by a subset of the cube, then you must first create partitions in BIDS.*

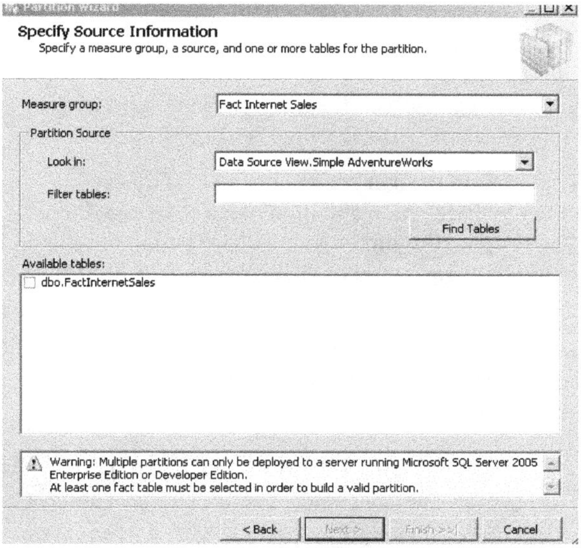

Figure 7-8. *The Partition Wizard asks for information about which measure group you want to partition.*

Whether you want to implement some type of nondefault storage for the entire cube or for one of the partitions in a cube, the procedure is identical. In the BIDS cube designer, you click the Storage Settings link on the Partitions tab. This displays a wizard that you can adjust either by sliding the slider bar or by setting custom storage options. Figure 7-9 shows the default setting, MOLAP.

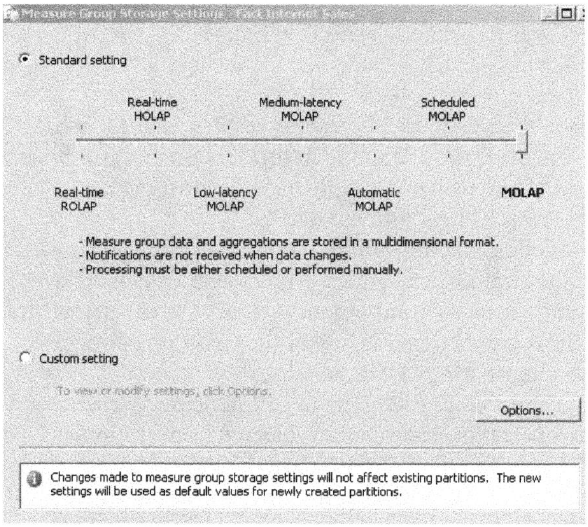

Figure 7-9. *To adjust the default storage setting of MOLAP for a cube or for a partition (which is associated with a particular measure group in SSAS), you access the Measure Group Storage Settings dialog box using the Partitions tab of the cube browser in BIDS.*

Although the slider provides a brief explanation of the other settings, you probably need a fuller explanation to effectively select something other than the default. Note that a new feature called Proactive Caching is enabled for all storage modes other than the default (simple MOLAP). Proactive Caching is covered in the next section of this chapter. Here's a list of the impact of changing the default setting in the Measure Group Storage Settings dialog box.

- *(default) MOLAP*: Source *data* is copied from the star schema fact tables to SSAS as MOLAP data; source *metadata* (which includes cube and dimension structure and dimension data) and *aggregations* are copied (for dimension data) or generated (for all other metadata and aggregations) and then are stored in MOLAP format on SSAS; and Proactive Caching is not used.

- *(nondefault) MOLAP*: Source *data* is copied, *metadata* and *aggregations* are stored in MOLAP format on SSAS, and Proactive Caching is enabled. This includes scheduled-, automatic-, medium-, and low-latency MOLAP.

- *HOLAP*: Source *data* is *not* copied, *metadata* and *aggregations* are stored in MOLAP format on SSAS, and Proactive Caching is enabled.

- *ROLAP*: For a cube, source *data* is *not* copied, *metadata* is stored in MOLAP format on SSAS, and *aggregations* are stored in the star schema database. For a dimension, *metadata* is *not* copied but is simply read from the star schema database table(s), and Proactive Caching is enabled.

Note ROLAP storage can also be used for a dimension as discussed in Chapter 8.

ROLAP Dimensions

ROLAP dimensions have been available since SSAS 2000. In the 2005 release, Microsoft has worked to improve their performance, which was unacceptable in production environment in the SSAS 2000 release. ROLAP dimensions are used in a couple of situations: rapidly (nearly constantly) changing dimensions and/or huge dimensions.

For example, let's say that you are modeling a dimension that contains employee information for a fast-food restaurant chain. The chain has very high employee turnover, as is typical in the fast-food industry. However, a business requirement is to be able to retrieve the most current employee name from the employee dimension at all times with no latency. This type of requirement may lead you to choose a ROLAP dimension.

Another example is if you have a huge number of members in a dimension. A business example is that you are modeling the customer dimension for an international shipping company. It is a business requirement to have the name of every customer for all time included in your cube. This may mean that you must include millions, or eventually even billions of customer names in the dimension. The storage limits for SQL Server tables (that is, maximum number of rows) are still larger than those in SSAS dimensions.

Despite the fact that you may have business situations that warrant the consideration of ROLAP dimensions, you should test to make sure that your infrastructure (that is, hardware and software) will provide adequate performance given the anticipated load. Although the performance has been improved, some of my customers have still found that the performance in SSAS 2005 is too slow to use ROLAP dimensions for production cubes. If you are considering this option, be sure to test with production level of data before you deploy this configuration into a production environment.

Huge Dimensions

Like so many of the advanced storage features, ROLAP dimensions require the Enterprise Edition of Analysis Services. You would use this typically only for dimensions with millions of members; an example might be the customer dimension. What this means is that the dimensional attribute values will not be copied to and stored on SSAS, rather they will be retrieved directly from the relational source table or tables. To set a dimension as a ROLAP dimension in the Properties window for that dimension, change the StorageMode property from the default MOLAP to ROLAP as shown in Figure 7-10.

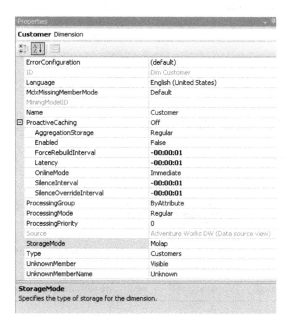

Figure 7-10. *You can change the default dimension storage mode from MOLAP to ROLAP if your business scenario warrants it. This is usually done for very large dimensions, that is, millions of members.*

As mentioned in the introduction to this section, although ROLAP dimensions increase the flexibility of your cube, I've not seen them used frequently in production BI solutions. The reason is that any queries to the relational source will always be significantly slower than queries to MOLAP data or metadata.

Summarizing OLAP Storage Options

If you are working with the Standard Edition of SSAS, the only consideration for you is whether or not to add aggregations to your cube because non-MOLAP storage and cube partitions are enterprise-only features. In my experience, for cubes of 100GB or less, it is often prudent to add aggregations to the 20% to 30% query-improvement level. If particular queries are problematic, you can use the Usage-Based Optimization Wizard to capture them and have SSAS add aggregations specifically for those queries. The procedure for this was described in the "Adding Aggregations" section earlier in this chapter.

If you are working with the Enterprise Edition of SSAS, you have several choices in terms of cube storage and aggregation. These include the following:

- *Should I use partitions?* If your cubes are 250GB or larger, you'll probably want to partition them by either months, quarters, or years (assuming your time granularity is "day" and not "hour" or "minute").

- *Should I add aggregations?* If you are considering partitioning your cubes due to size, then you should also consider customizing the amount of aggregations based on the size of partition and frequency of query. In addition to the tools reviewed previously (Usage-Based Optimization Wizard and so on), you may also choose to use SQL Profiler to more granularly track activity on your cubes so that you can aggregate appropriately.

- *Should I use MOLAP, ROLAP, or HOLAP?* Generally, you'll use something other than MOLAP only if you choose to use partitions. Typically, current data (partitioned on some time value, for example, months) is stored as MOLAP with a relatively high level of aggregation (25%–30%) with "older" data partitions stored as HOLAP or ROLAP with a lower level of aggregation.

Table 7-1 summarizes storage information.

Table 7-1. *Storage Options for SSAS Cubes*

Type	Data (Facts)	Metadata	Aggregations	Reason
MOLAP cube*	SSAS (copied)	SSAS	SSAS	Default/fastest query**
HOLAP*** cube	Not copied	SSAS	SSAS	Good for archive partitions
ROLAP*** cube	Not copied	SSAS	Written to SQL	Good for storage issues
ROLAP*** dimension	Not copied	Not copied	Written to SQL	Real-time dimensions

*Cube or cube partition

**SSAS Standard Edition supports only MOLAP storage with the default (1) partition per cube.

***Requires the Enterprise Edition of SSAS

If you are using the Enterprise Edition of SSAS, you have one additional storage configuration to consider: Proactive Caching.

Using Proactive Caching

Proactive Caching enables your BI solution to allow end users to access the data with all of the speed and power of SSAS and also allow them to use a solution that doesn't require the typical latency (often one business day) between the OLTP source and OLAP data. Configuring Proactive Caching is the method by which you manage the MOLAP cache.

The *MOLAP cache* is an in-memory storage location created automatically by SSAS. The cache includes actual data and sometimes aggregations. This information is placed in the cache area after MDX queries are executed against the SSAS cubes. Figure 7-11 shows a conceptual rendering of the MOLAP cache.

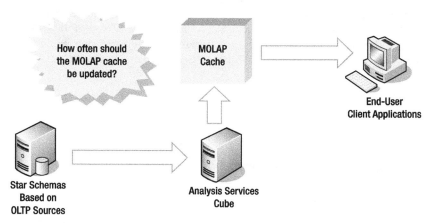

Figure 7-11. *Proactive Caching settings allow you to manage the update/rebuild frequency of the MOLAP cache for your cube or partition(s).*

Note One of the reasons queries in SSAS are so much faster than queries to a relational data store is the use of the MOLAP cache. When you are considering configuring manual settings to manage cache refreshes, you can use the Analysis Server: Query object in System Monitor to measure which queries are being answered by cache hits versus disk calls.

Now the catch is that Proactive Caching is near real time but not exactly real time. Also, the nearer to real time, the more overhead is added to the system. That's why SSAS has six different options for you to choose from when configuring Proactive Caching using the measure group processing tool. Also, there is the possibility of still more finely grained control using the Custom Options dialog box in this section, and even more control by configuring the property section for any particular measure group. Also, remember that you can only configure storage and caching settings at the level of the partition (or subset of the measure group or fact table) if you have already set up partitions in your solution.

■**Note** Proactive Caching is *not* for every BI solution. Using it effectively necessitates that you either read your OLTP data directly as the source for your cube, or you read a replicated copy of your data. Another option is to read your OLTP data using the new snapshot isolation level available in SQL Server 2005 (assuming, of course, that your source data is stored only in SQL Server 2005). To use any other of these options, your source data must be very clean. If you need to do cleansing, validation, and/or consolidation during ETL processing, then Proactive Caching is not the best choice for your solution.

Let's start with a more complete explanation of the choices available in the Measure Group Storage Settings dialog box (shown earlier in Figure 7-9) as they relate to Proactive Caching settings. The first choice you'll make is whether to use MOLAP, HOLAP, or ROLAP data storage for your cube. In most cases, due to the superior query performance, you'll select some version of MOLAP. The Proactive Caching configuration choices for MOLAP are as follows:

- *Scheduled MOLAP*: In this setting, the MOLAP cache is updated per a schedule (whether the source data changes or not); the default is once daily. This sets the rebuild interval to one day.

- *Automatic MOLAP*: In this setting, the cache is updated whenever the source data changes. It configures the silence interval to 0 seconds and sets no silence override interval.

- *Medium-latency MOLAP*: In this setting, the outdated caches are dropped periodically (the default is a latency period of 4 hours). The cache is updated when data changes (defaults are a 10-second silence interval and a 10-minute silence override interval).

- *Low-latency MOLAP*: In this setting, outdated caches are dropped periodically (the default is a latency period of 30 minutes). The cache is updated when data changes (defaults are a 10-second silence interval and a 10-minute silence override interval).

■**Tip** To understand the "silence interval" property, think of this question: "how long should the cache wait to refresh itself if there are no changes to the source data?" To understand the "silence override interval" property think of this question: "what is the maximum amount of time after a notification (of source data being updated) is received that the cache should wait to start rebuilding itself?"

If you select HOLAP or ROLAP, then Proactive Caching settings are as follows:

- *HOLAP*: In this setting, outdated caches are dropped immediately (configures the latency period to 0 seconds). The cache is updated when data changes (defaults are a silence interval of 0 seconds and no silence override interval).

- *ROLAP*: In this setting, the cube is always in ROLAP mode, and all updates to the source data are immediately reflected in the query results; the latency period is set to 0 seconds.

Selecting the Options button on this same property sheet allows you to manually adjust the cache settings, options, and notification values as shown in Figure 7-12.

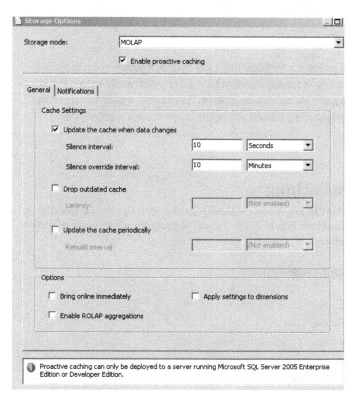

Figure 7-12. *The custom settings for Proactive Caching include the General and Notifications tabs of the Storage Settings dialog box in the Partitions tab of BIDS. Here you can more granularly adjust the cache and notification settings.*

Notification Settings for Proactive Caching

You can adjust the notification settings (regarding data changes in the base OLTP store) by using the Notifications tab of the Storage Options dialog box. Notification Services is a new feature set in SQL Server 2005 that allows clients to subscribe to "interesting" events and receive notification of changes. There are three types of notifications possible using this dialog box:

- *SQL Server*: For this option, you'll need to specify tracking tables in the relational source database. This option uses trace events and requires that the service account for SSAS has dbo permissions on the SQL database that contains the tracking table.

- *Client Initiated*: As for SQL Server, you'll need to specify tracking tables in the relational source database. This is used when notification of changes will be sent from a client application to SSAS.

- *Scheduled Polling*: For this option, you'll need to specify the polling interval time value and whether you want to enable incremental updates and add at least one polling query. Each polling query or queries is also associated with a particular tracking table.

Tip Notification Services includes an adaptor for SSAS. Using this adapter, a custom client application could subscribe to an interesting event by specifying a custom MDX query (which would include the data to be inspected, the frequency of polling, and the notification scheme). For example, a plant manager could request notification if the defects per hour of a particular product had risen above a specified level.

Fine-Tuning Proactive Caching

Finally, here's the most specific way to set Proactive Caching settings is the Properties dialog box for a particular measure group (see Figure 7-13). Table 7-2 provides a summary of the settings available for Proactive Caching.

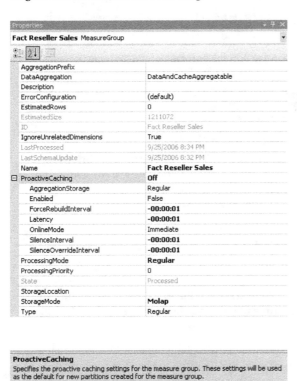

Figure 7-13. *You can control the Proactive Caching settings to a fine degree of granularity using the properties section for a particular measure group.*

Table 7-2. *Proactive Caching Settings*

Setting	Choices	Description
Aggregation Storage	Regular; MOLAP only	Applies to partitions only
Enabled	True; False	Turns Proactive Caching on or off
ForceRebuildInterval	Time value	Max time increment to rebuild the cache whether the source data has changed or not; default is -1 = infinity
Latency	Time value	Max time to wait to rebuild cube; default is -1 = infinity
OnlineMode	Immediate; OnCacheComplete	Tells whether new cache will be available immediately, or only after it's been completely rebuilt
SilenceInterval	Time value	Max time the source data has no transactions before the cache is rebuilt; default is -1 = infinity
SilenceOverrideInterval	Time value	Max to wait after a data change notification in the source data to rebuild the cache; override SilenceInterval value; default is -1 = infinity

Proactive Caching is a powerful new capability that some of you will find invaluable in enhancing the usability of your BI solution. As mentioned earlier, the key consideration when deciding whether to use Proactive Caching is the quality of your source data. It must be very pristine for this feature to be practical.

Deciding Among OLTP Partitioning, OLAP Partitioning, or Both

If you are working with the Enterprise Edition of SQL Server 2005, you now have the ability to do relational table partitioning in your star schema source tables. This strategy can complement any partitioning you choose to do using SSAS (that is, cube partitions), or you can choose to partition only on the relational side. The consideration then becomes which type of partitioning is appropriate for your BI solution?

Relational Table Partitioning in SQL Server 2005

Table partitioning is the ability to position data from the same table on different physical locations (disks), while that data appears to continue to originate from the same logical table from the end-user's perspective. This simplifies management of VLDBs (very large databases), in particular, management of very large tables. The large tables that we are concerned about here are, of course, fact tables.

Fact tables commonly contain millions or tens of millions of rows. In fact, support for these huge (over four billion rows) fact tables is one of the reasons that the BIGINT datatype was introduced in SQL Server 2005. Relational table partitioning can simplify administrative tasks and general management of these, often large or even huge, data sources. An example of this is that backups can be performed much more efficiently on table partitions, rather than on entire (huge) fact tables.

Implementing Relational Table Partitioning

Although relational table partitioning is relatively simple, several steps are involved in implementing it.

Tip For an excellent, detailed description of how to implement relational partitioning in SQL Server 2005, see Kimberly Tripp's whitepaper at `http://msdn.microsoft.com/library/default.asp?url=/library/en-us/dnsql90/html/sql2k5partition.asp`.

Here's a conceptual overview of the technique:

1. Identify the tables that are the best candidates for partitioning. For OLAP projects, as mentioned, these will generally be the fact tables.

2. Identify the value (or column) to be used for partitioning, usually a date field; a unique constraint must be implemented on this column of the tables that will participate in partitioning.

3. Implement the physical architecture needed to support partitioning, that is, install the physical disks.

4. Create filegroups in the database for each of the new physical disks or arrays.

5. Create .ndf files (or secondary database files) for the SQL Server 2005 database where the tables to be partitioned are contained, and associate these .ndf files with the filegroups you created in Step 4.

6. Create a partition function. This creates the "buckets" to distribute the sections of the table into. This is most often done by date range, that is from *xxx* to *yyy* date (most often monthly or annually).

7. Create a partition scheme. This associates the buckets you created previously to a list of filegroups, in which there is one filegroup for each time period (that is, month or year).

8. Create the table (this is usually the fact table) on the partition scheme that you created earlier. This "splits" the table into the buckets you've created.

Other OLAP Partition Configurations

One other consideration in the world of partitions returns us to SSAS cube partitions. With the Enterprise Edition of SSAS, it is possible to define cube partitions as local (the default) or remote.

The primary reason to consider using remote partitions is to do a kind of "load balancing" in the SSAS environment. You would use remote partitions to implement load-balancing situations where your primary SSAS server was stressed due to (usually) a large number of users executing complex queries. By using remote partitions, you can split the processing work across multiple physical servers. Additional considerations with remote partitions include the following:

- *Remote partitions*: These partitions can use MOLAP, HOLAP, or ROLAP storage. They can also use Proactive Caching. Remote partitions store information on the remote server.

- *Remote MOLAP*: Data and aggregations for the remote partition are stored on the remote server.

- *Remote HOLAP*: Aggregations for the remote partition are stored on the remote server; data is read from the OLTP source.

- *Remote ROLAP*: Nothing is stored on the remote server; both data and aggregations are read from the OLAP source.

Cube and Dimension Processing Options

Now that we've covered storage, aggregations, partitions, and caching, we are (finally!) ready to review cube and dimensions processing option types. Dimensions must be completely and correctly processed either prior to or at the beginning of a cube process. The best way to understand this is to remember that dimensional data is the metadata or the structure of the cube itself. So the metadata must be available before the data can be loaded into the cube.

During development, you will most often do a *Full process* on your cube whenever you need to view the results of a change that you've made. This option completely erases and rebuilds all data and metadata. For some customers, this simple method of updating the cube can be used in production as well. A Full process is, of course, a complete overwrite on rebuild. This is only practical for the very smallest cubes—a couple of gigabytes in size maximum.

The majority of you will choose to use the more granular processing options after you move your cube to a production environment. The first consideration is the ability to separate processing of dimensions from the cube. In this chapter, we'll review the process for processing using BIDS. In Chapter 8, I'll discuss automating these cube and dimension refreshes using SSIS tasks and workflows.

To process a cube, you right-click the cube name in the Solution Explorer in BIDS, and then select Process. You'll see the dialog box shown in Figure 7-14.

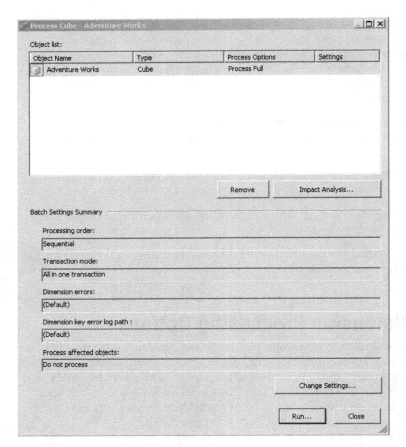

Figure 7-14. *To process a cube, right-click the cube name in BIDS, click Process, and then select the process type and options in the dialog box.*

The following is a more complete explanation of the available selections for process options for both cubes and dimensions. Some options are only available for cubes or for dimensions as noted in the list:

- *Default*: SSAS detects the current state of the cube or dimension, and then does whatever type of processing (full or incremental) that is needed to return the cube or dimension to a completely processed state.

- *Full*: SSAS completely reprocesses the cube or dimension. For a cube, this will include all the objects contained within it, for example, dimensions. Full process is required when a structural change has been made to a cube or dimension. For a dimension, one example would be when an attribute hierarchy is added, deleted, or renamed.

- *Data*: SSAS processes data only and does not build any aggregations or indexes. SSAS indexes are not the same as relational indexes; SSAS indexes are generated and used by SSAS internally during the aggregation process.

- *Unprocess*: SSAS drops the data in the cube or dimension. If there are any lower-level dependent objects, for example, dimensions in a cube, those objects are dropped as well. This option is often used during the development phase of a BI project to quickly "clear out" erroneous results.

- *Index*: SSAS creates or rebuilds indexes for all processed partitions. This option results in no operation on unprocessed objects.

- *Structure (cubes only)*: SSAS processes the cubes and any contained dimensions, but does not process any mining models.

- *Incremental (cubes only)*: SSAS adds newly available fact data and processes only the affected partitions. This is the most common option used in day-to-day production.

- *Script Cache (cubes only)*: Per BOL, "This feature will be removed in the next version of Microsoft SQL Server. Do not use this feature in new development work, and modify applications that currently use this feature as soon as possible."

- *Update (dimensions only)*: SSAS forces an update of dimension attribute values. This value is to dimension processing as the incremental value is to cube processing; that is, update adds new members for dimensions just as incremental adds new facts for cubes.

Note Aggregation processing behavior in dimensions depends on the `AttributeRelationship` `RelationshipType` property. If this property is set to the default value (`Rigid`), then aggregations are incrementally updated on incremental process of the cube or update of the dimension. If it is set to the optional (or nondefault) value (`Flexible`), then aggregations are fully reprocessed for cube/dimension incremental updates. Also, if you set the dimension processing mode for a dimension to `lazyAggregations`, then flexible aggregations are reprocessed as a background task, and end users can browse the cube while this processing is occurring.

An optimization step you can take to reduce processing times for your dimensions is to turn off the `AttributeHierarchyOptimized` property for dimensional attributes that are only viewed infrequently by end users.

Tip To identify infrequently queried attributes, you could either use a capture of queries from SQL Server Profiler, or you could read the content of the `LogTable` after running the Query Optimization Wizard.

To adjust the `AttributeHierarchyOptimizedState` property, you'll open the Properties dialog box for the particular `DimensionalAttribute` and then set the property value to `NotOptimized`. Figure 7-15 shows the property sheet for the `Education` attribute in the `Customer` dimension. Setting the value to `NotOptimized` causes SSAS to not create supplementary indexes (usually created by default) for this particular attribute on dimension or cube process. This can result in slower query times, so change this setting only for rarely browsed attributes.

Figure 7-15. *You can improve dimension processing times by adjusting the*
AttributeHierarchyOptimizedState *property of rarely browsed* DimensionalAttributes.

The final consideration when processing cubes and dimensions is whether you'll need to
adjust any of the processing options. You access these options using the Change Settings button on the Process Cube dialog box as shown in Figure 7-14. Here you have two tabs to work
with. In the first tab, Processing Options, you can set the following values:

- *Parallel or Sequential processing*: If parallel, maximum number of parallel tasks

- *Single or multiple transactions*: For sequential processing

- *Writeback table*: Use existing or create new

- *Process dependent objects*: Off or on

The second tab, Dimension Key Errors, allows you to configure the behavior of errors during processing (see Figure 7-16). You can either use the default error configuration, or you can
set a custom error configuration. When using a custom error configuration, you can specify
the Key Error Action (shown in the figure as Convert to Unknown), the Processing Error Limit
(shown as Stop Processing on first error), the behavior to result for reaching Specific Error
Conditions (Key Not Found, Duplicate Key, Null Key Converted to Unknown, Null Key Not
Allowed), and the Error Log Path location.

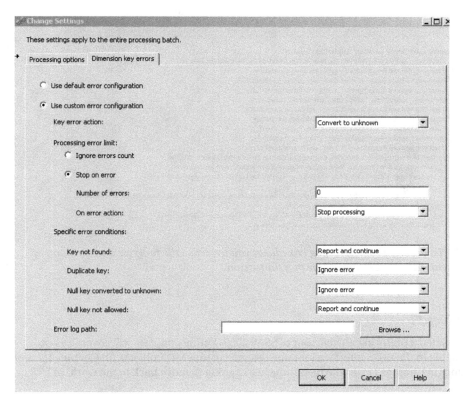

Figure 7-16. *The Dimension Key Errors tab in the Change Settings dialog box of the Process Cube dialog box allows you to specify custom error behavior responses when processing a cube.*

Although you had probably been processing test cubes for awhile prior to reading this chapter, you've probably gained a bit more insight into what actually happens when you run the process action. Figure 7-17 shows the output from the Process Cube dialog box. You can also direct this process information to a log file. In production, you would normally automate the cube/dimension processing via SSIS packages, using the cube- or dimension-processing tasks.

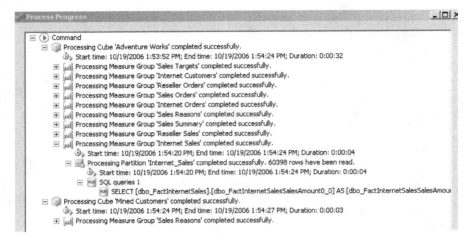

Figure 7-17. *The Process Progress dialog box allows you to review the progress and duration of each step involved in processing a cube or a dimension.*

What's Next?

We've completed a pretty exhaustive tour of SSAS 2005. Future chapters will cover the last items available in the BIDS interface for cube design: custom MDX objects (in Chapter 10) and data mining (in Chapter 11). In the meantime, we're going to move back to the world of ETL using SSIS.

Summary

This chapter covered the processes for designing physical storage for your cube. You learned about the capabilities of the three core storage modes: MOLAP, HOLAP, and ROLAP and about aggregation design and partitioning. Remember that several of these features require the Enterprise Edition of SSAS, as noted for each feature in the text of this chapter.

The most important consideration for physical cube storage design is to get the correct balance between performance and manageability. Many customers are satisfied with MOLAP for their entire cube, with just a bit of added custom-designed aggregations.

In the next chapter, we'll return to the world of SSIS. You'll learn how to design basic SSIS packages, and in the process, you'll learn to use the BIDS interface for SSIS 2005. The discussion will include the use of control flow tasks and data transformations.

CHAPTER 8

■ ■ ■

Intermediate SSIS

By now, you've translated your business requirements into an SSAS cube. The next task in implementing your BI project is to execute an ETL solution from your detailed data map.

As discussed in Chapter 3, data maps are used as a basis for beginning ETL design. In my experience, up to 75% of the initial work on a BI project consists of ETL process design, development, and debugging. I assume that you've completed your data map and created a simple package or two using the Import/Export Wizard or by using the SSIS package template in BIDS. In this chapter, we'll cover the following topics:

- Considering general ETL package-design best practices

- Understanding control flow tasks

- Understanding data flow transformations

- Using the Dynamic Configuration Wizard and property expressions

General ETL Package-Design Best Practices

Whether you start with the blank SSIS package project-type template in BIDS, or by using the Import/Export Wizard in BIDS (or in SSMS) to create simple starter packages, your ETL solution will ultimately consist of many SSIS packages.

Before you begin implementing any packages, you should take a bit of time to plan your ETL approach and high-level package design principles. The most common practices are listed here:

- Create one set of packages for inserts and a different set for updates. Name the packages according to function.

- Create a minimum of one package for each dimension and fact table per action type (insert or update), for example, `insertCustomerDim`, `updateCustomerDim`.

- If you have a large number of data sources, then consider creating one package per data source per dimension per action type. For example, one BI project I recently worked on had 16 data sources. Our naming convention was something like this: `insertCustomerDimFromCust1_xls`, `insertCustomerDimFromClient2_xls`.

- Use self-documenting naming conventions throughout each package. That is, apply common-sense names not only to package names but also to all items contained in packages (tasks, steps, and so on). Also, you can put notes on the design surfaces using the annotation capability in BIDS. This is a step that will pay for itself many times over; each time new ETL developers need to work on a package, they can read your notes, instead of emailing you or coming to your office to ask you questions. This is sounding better and better already, isn't it?

- Avoid hard-coded connection strings, user names/passwords, file paths, computer names, and so on in all packages using dynamic configuration (which will be explained in detail later in this chapter). This is critical to creating packages that can easily run in development, test, and production environments.

- If source data needs significant cleansing, validation, and/or consolidation, use an interim staging database in your ETL process. Disk space is cheaper than additional RAM or CPUs, which would be needed to execute complex packages. Also simpler packages are easier to work with, as mentioned next.

- Break complex processing down into discrete steps for finer-grained control over performance and debugging. For very complex scenarios, use multiple packages.

- Consider that some capabilities of SSIS are available in the Enterprise Edition of SQL Server only. I will note these features in this chapter's text, as they are discussed.

Tip Because the initial project work using SSIS is often extensive in BI projects and for speed and convenience, I've often contracted out this part of my production projects to absolute experts in SSIS for BI. Although the many enhancements in this version of SSIS 2005 (vs. DTS 2000) have improved usability tremendously, my experience is that mastering this rich toolset takes a significant amount of time. Whether you do it yourself or hire it out, my final piece of advice for SSIS is to be diligent about using accurate estimations. Again, experience is the most valuable skill to bring to the table. If you do not have the time or inclination to immerse yourself in SSIS, then you would be wise to engage someone else with extensive experience. Many a BI project has been derailed by a lack of appropriate resources being assigned to the ETL processes.

Creating the SSIS Package from Scratch

In this chapter, we'll work either from scratch or from the samples available with SQL Server 2005. If you chose to install the samples, you will find the SSIS samples at this location: C:\Program Files\Microsoft SQL Server\90\Samples\Integration Services. If you did not choose to install the samples, you can install them from the source media.

Tip If you do not have access to your source media and wish to install the samples, you can download them from http://www.microsoft.com/downloads/
details.aspx?FamilyID=E719ECF7-9F46-4312-AF89-6AD8702E4E6E&displaylang=en.

As with designing your first cube, developing SSIS packages requires that you use BIDS to create a new project. You no longer use the SQL Server administrative interface (SSMS) to design packages as you did using Enterprise Manager in SQL Server 2000. To get started, in BIDS, you'll select a project template of type Business Intelligence, then a subtype of Integration Services Project. Give your project a name, pick a directory location, and then click OK to create the project. After you do that, you'll see the development environment shown in Figure 8-1.

Figure 8-1. *You author SSIS packages using BIDS with a project template type of Integration Services Project.*

We'll review each section of the designer now. First, to the left is the Toolbox. The items displayed depend on which section you are working on in the (center) SSIS package designer area. If you are working with the Control Flow, Event Handlers, or Package Explorer tabs, then the Toolbox will display the Control Flow Items; if you are working with the Data Flow tab, then the Toolbox will display the Data Flow transformations; and if you don't have any package design surface selected, your Toolbox will be empty.

We'll be discussing both the control flow task and the data flow transformation types in greater detail later in this chapter.

Tip If you're feeling overwhelmed by all the different windows in BIDS and wondering how you're going to keep track of them all, relax! If you press Ctrl+Tab within BIDS, you'll get a list of all the open documents and a list of all the BIDS windows, and you can select the desired window by using the arrow keys. This technique should be a huge time-saver for you.

You may also choose to display variables associated with a package by clicking the SSIS item on the top menu bar, and then clicking Variables. The Variables window will display in the same location as the Toolbox by default (see Figure 8-2). In this section, you can view package variables and add variables to the package as well. It is also important to remember that variable names are case-sensitive in SSIS. In Figure 8-2, the icon next to the last variable (TestVar) is blue to indicate that the variable is user-defined. The other variables that are listed in Figure 8-2 are created automatically when you create a new SSIS package using that template in BIDS, and they are colored gray.

Name	Scope	Data Type	Value
CancelEvent	Package	Int32	0
ContainerSta...	Package	DateTime	10/24/2006 10:53 AM
CreationDate	Package	DateTime	10/24/2006 10:53 AM
CreatorComp...	Package	String	WEBFLUENT
CreatorName	Package	String	WEBFLUENT\llangit1
ExecutionInst...	Package	String	{C21C69E0-5B23-42E1...
InteractiveM...	Package	Boolean	False
LocaleID	Package	Int32	English (United States)
MachineName	Package	String	WEBFLUENT
OfflineMode	Package	Boolean	False
PackageID	Package	String	{A8DFEFE4-8EB6-4C1F...
PackageName	Package	String	Package
StartTime	Package	DateTime	10/24/2006 10:53 AM
UserName	Package	String	WEBFLUENT\llangit1
VersionBuild	Package	Int32	0
VersionComm...	Package	String	
VersionGUID	Package	String	{A611635-596C-4A8...
VersionMajor	Package	Int32	1
VersionMinor	Package	Int32	0
TestVar	Package	Int32	1000

Figure 8-2. *You can view variables associated with SSIS packages in BIDS by clicking the SSIS menu, and then on Variables. You can also add variables via this interface.*

Also, when you're working with the Control Flow, Data Flow, or Event Handlers tabs, the BIDS designer will display the Connection Managers work area at the bottom of the screen. The Connection Managers area displays an icon for each connection used in the package. You can add new connections by right-clicking in this area, selecting the connection type from the menu, and then configuring the connection.

On the right side of the BIDS SSIS package designer interface is Solution Explorer. When you open the SSIS template, you are actually working with a Visual Studio 2005 project template. SSIS projects in Visual Studio are containers for multiple files, in this case, multiple

.dtsx files or packages and related files, like data sources (or connections) and DSVs. Projects allow the information in them to be shared between files in the same project. In the case of SSIS, the most common items to be shared (data sources and DSVs) are represented as folders in the Solution Explorer tree.

On the bottom right (by default) of the BIDS interface is the properties area. As we saw with SSAS projects, you can select a particular item from the drop-down list in the property area, or you can simply click the item you want to set the properties for on the (center) design surface. After you've selected the appropriate item, the properties for that item will appear. Read-only properties are "greyed-out." Most properties are configurable.

The last part of the SSIS interface is the SSIS menu, which contains the following items:

- *Logging*: Allows you to create package logs in up to five different destination types (such as file, SQL Server, and so on). These logs capture runtime events that are enabled for logging. This option is covered in more detail in Chapter 9.

- *Package Configurations*: Starts the Package Configuration Wizard. This wizard allows you to dynamically configure various package properties. The implementation of this wizard is covered in more detail later in this chapter.

- *Digital Signing*: Allows you to associate a certificate with your SSIS package. Signing a package will allow you to prevent it from running if its contents have been altered.

- *Variables*: Displays the package variables window on top of the Toolbox by default. It allows you to view package variables and add variables as needed.

- *Work Offline*: Allows you to work in a disconnected fashion. The default is to work in connected mode so that connections to data sources and DSVs can be used to retrieve metadata (for example, source table column names and data types) that is used to populate SSIS tasks.

- *Log Events*: Displays the Log Events window over the top of the Toolbox by default as shown in Figure 8-3.

Figure 8-3. *The Log Events window is displayed in BIDS after you open it from the SSIS menu. It shows information about events you've chosen to capture for a particular SSIS package.*

- *New Connection*: Allows you to create a new connection for use in the package. These connections can be based on data sources (global to the project) or can be local to the specific package that you are working on. All connections will appear in the Connection Mangers window at the bottom center of the design area after you add and configure them.

- *View*: Allows you to switch between tabs in the SSIS designer, that is, Control Flow, Data Flow, and so on.

Note When you execute a package in BIDS, for example, by clicking the green triangle on the toolbar, an additional tab becomes available in the BIDS designer. There are other ways to execute packages, such as right-clicking the .dtsx file in Solution Explorer and then clicking Execute Package. The new tab is called Progress, and its windows will show you step-by-step execution results. A sample is shown in Figure 8-4.

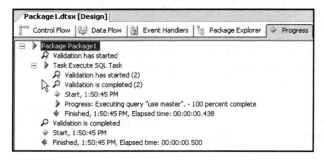

Figure 8-4. *The Progress tab is displayed in BIDS after you execute an SSIS package. It shows detailed execution information for the package down to the step level.*

Now that we've thoroughly reviewed the BIDS design environment, you're ready to create your first SSIS package by designing it from scratch (rather than by running the Import/Export Wizard from SSMS as we did in Chapter 3). You still may choose to use the Import/Export Wizard as a starting point in your production BI solutions. The wizard works great to quickly create simple template package prototypes. You can save those packages and then edit them in BIDS. Most of the time, however, you'll probably start your package implementation from within a blank BIDS design surface.

Note You can also import a DTS package created in SQL Server 2000. For more detail about the import processes, see the BOL topic "How to: Ensure Support for Data Transformation Services Packages." Be aware that attempting to migrate all but the simplest DTS packages to SSIS will probably be more trouble than it's worth. Remember that Microsoft completely redesigned the SSIS object model in SQL Server 2005 SSIS, so many DTS tasks (and even sometimes entire packages) will fail to migrate properly.

To best understand what is now possible with SSIS, you should consider an SSIS package to be an executable file that will perform a data workflow. You can combine the traditional ETL data for BI projects with many other types of tasks to create whatever type of customized data workflow that best suits your particular business needs.

Another important point to consider is that neither the data sources nor the data destinations need to be any version of SQL Server. SSIS can connect to anything for which there is a supplied provider. There are 17 provider types supplied with SSIS. SQL Server 2005 SP2 adds provider types to SSIS as well.

CHAPTER 8 ▓ INTERMEDIATE SSIS   **165**

With all this power, you may be wondering where to start. All data workflows need to connect to something, so the logical starting point is configuring connections.

Configuring Connections

Although it is possible to define connections only within each package, as a matter of convenience, you will most often find yourself reusing connections across multiple packages. To create a new connection in this way, right-click the Data Sources folder in the Solution Explorer window for your project. After you do this, you'll see a Data Source Wizard dialog box in which you can either reuse a previously defined connection (for any other SSIS package designed on your computer), or you can create a new connection. The Create a data source based on an existing connection option in the Data Source Wizard dialog box is shown in Figure 8-5.

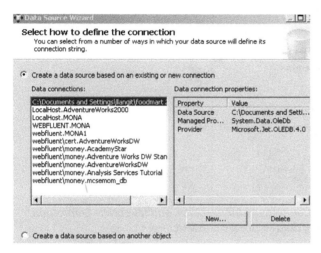

Figure 8-5. *In the Data Source Wizard dialog box in BIDS, you configure reusable connection based on existing connections, other objects, or new information.*

The next step is to associate this global connection with the specific package that you are working on. To do this, right-click the bottom center Connection Managers area, click New Connection from Data Source, and select the connection name that you previously created.

It's useful to review the broad variety of data source types that can be used in SSIS packages. Figure 8-6 shows this list of Connection Manager types that are available to you (choosing SSIS ➤ New Connection, and then right-clicking the Connection Managers work area presents you with a subset of these options only). New in SSIS 2005 are these types: MSMQ, MultiFile, MultiFlatFile, SMOServer, SQLMobile, and WMI.

Tip An interesting type of connection is to use an OLE DB connection to connect to and retrieve data from the Active Directory (AD). To do this, you need to create a linked server to AD, and then you can use a T-SQL statement with OPENROWSET, which includes a LDAP string inside of the T-SQL query. The BOL topic "OLE DB Provider for Microsoft Directory Services" provides an example.

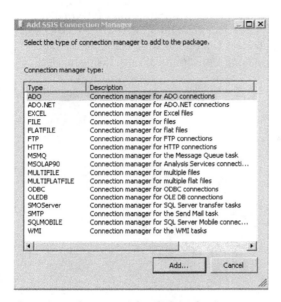

Figure 8-6. *When you right-click in the Connection Manager area, and select New Connection, you are presented with a wide variety of data source types to select from.*

Interestingly, different types of connections are available when you right-click the Connection Managers area of the SSIS design surface versus those that are available if you right-click the Data Sources folder in the Solution Explorer list. Figure 8-6 shows the connection types available for you from the former area. Generally these include more file-based types, such as FLATFILE, EXCEL, MULTIFLATFILE, and so on.

The top-level types of connections available for you from the latter area are .NET Providers, .NET Providers for OLE DB, and Native OLE DB providers. These types are more relational in nature, that is, SQL, Oracle, and so on. You can see the list of specific providers when you expand each of these three folder types; for example, the .NET Providers include SqlClient Data Provider, OracleClient Data Provider, and Odbc Data Provider.

Using Data Source Views (DSVs)

Another type of component shared across packages is a Data Source View (DSV). DSVs function identically to the way they work in the SSAS designer in this designer. As with SSAS, you use (and customize) DSVs when you do not have permissions to create views or other types of abstractions, such as calculated columns, in the underlying data source.

An interesting option available to you when creating DSVs is the ability to restrict the view to a particular schema in the source database. This option supports the new capability in SQL Server 2005 to group objects in a relational database together by schema. If you are not familiar with the concept, you can think of schemas like folders on the file system. In SQL Server 2000, formal relational object names included the object owner's name, in the format of `server.database.owner.object`. This has been modified in SQL Server 2005 to this structure: `server.database.schema.object`. The Advanced Data Source View Options dialog box is shown in Figure 8-7.

Figure 8-7. *When you create a DSV, you can restrict the view to a particular schema in the source database via this dialog box.*

Another useful aspect of using DSVs while working in BIDS is the ability to explore the data contained in the view. To do this, you just right-click any table in the DSV work area. As was mentioned in Chapter 4, you can then view a subset of the data as a table, chart, pivot table, or pivot chart. This can help you better understand the type and quality of the source data before you start creating your SSIS package. Again, you'll find this capability most helpful when you are not permitted to directly query the source data.

Although using shared objects can be useful for your ETL solution development, you do not have to use shared data sources or DSVs to create an SSIS package. This differs from the process of creating a SSAS cube, where using both a shared data source and a shared DSV are required.

Reviewing the Included Samples Packages

Now that we've completed our tour of the BIDS environment and the common areas, we'll start working through the sample packages. These packages are located by default at C:\Program Files\Microsoft SQL Server\90\Samples\Integration Services. We'll use these packages as a platform to build our understanding of two of the core parts of the SSIS design interface: using the control flow tasks and data flow transformation.

The first package we'll start with is the Execute SQL Statements in Loop sample. To open this package in BIDS, locate the samples folder (C:\Program Files\Microsoft SQL Server\90\Samples\Integration Services), then double-click the ExecuteSqlStatements InLoop.sln file. This opens the SSIS solution (and project) file in BIDS. Next, double-click the same file name under the packages node in Solution Explorer (or ExecuteSQLState- mentsInLoop.dtsx). This opens the package to the Control Flow design surface and is shown in Figure 8-8.

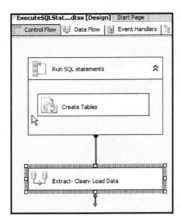

Figure 8-8. *The first sample package we are going to work with is called Execute SQL Statements in Loop. This package is a good example of using the new Control Flow* Foreach *loop container.*

Adding Control Flow Tasks

Your next step in package design will be to select one or more control flow items from the Toolbox and drag them to the Control Flow design surface section. As mentioned in Chapter 3, SSIS now separates control flow tasks from data flow transformations. You have 28 different task types to select from, 11 of which were not available in SQL 2000 DTS. Figure 8-9 shows the Toolbox for the control flow items.

Figure 8-9. *The Control Flow Items Toolbox in BIDS allows you to add 28 different types of control flow tasks to your SSIS package. Of these, 11 were not available in SQL 2000 DTS.*

To best understand all of these tasks, we'll group them into types. We'll also refer to our sample package for this discussion. The task type groups for the control flow tasks are as follows:

- *Containers*: Allows you to group one or more tasks inside of it. These include the For loop, the Foreach loop, and the Sequence containers. There is also a container object called the TaskHost that is designed to encapsulate a single task. The TaskHost object is not visible in the Control Flow Toolbox. For more information, see the BOL topics "TaskHost Container" and "TaskHost Class." You also have the ability to group tasks together. This grouping of tasks places grouped tasks inside of a container-like Group object.

- *SQL*: Allows you to perform some T-SQL action. These include the Bulk Insert, Data Flow, Execute DTS 2000 package, Execute package, Execute SQL, Transfer Database, Transfer Error Message, Transfer Jobs, Transfer Logins, Transfer Master Stored Procedures, and Transfer SQL Server objects tasks. You'll probably find yourself using tasks from this category frequently.

- *File System*: Allows you to work with the local file system. These include the Bulk Insert, Execute Process, File System, and XML tasks.

- *Operating System*: Allows you to work with the local operating system. These include the Message Queue, WMI Data Reader, and WMI Event Watcher tasks.

- *Script*: Allows you to execute some type of script. These include the ActiveX Script and Script tasks. ActiveX Script tasks are deprecated and are included in SSIS 2005 for backward compatibility with DTS 2000 only.

- *Remote*: Allows you to work with remote systems. These include the FTP, Send Mail, and Web Service tasks.

- *SSAS*: This type allows you to perform some sort of processing on SSAS objects. These include the SSAS Execute DDL, SSAS Processing, and Data Mining query tasks.

You can also extend the set of control flow tasks or data flow transformations available in BIDS by downloading, purchasing, or developing your own SSIS tasks and then installing them into the BIDS environment. You install new components by right-clicking the Toolbox, and then clicking Choose Items. This brings up a dialog box that allows you to add the appropriate .dll as shown in Figure 8-10.

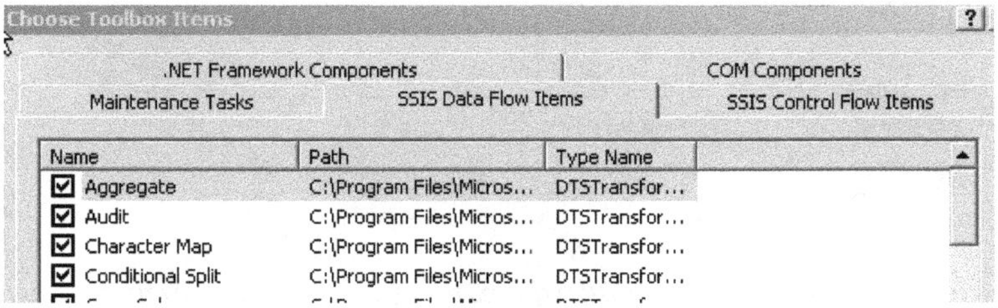

Figure 8-10. *You can install new components that you download, purchase, or create into the BIDS SSIS control flow or data flow transformations by right-clicking the Toolbox and then clicking Choose Items. You then navigate to the .dll you want to add and then add it to the appropriate dialog box tab (data flow or control flow) as shown here.*

Tip A great source of additional downloadable SSIS tasks is Darren Green's SSIS Web site: http://www.sqlis.com/.

Now that we've grouped the control flow tasks by type, let's dig in a bit deeper to the capabilities of the tasks most frequently used in BI ETL solutions.

Container Tasks

Container tasks, new in SSIS 2005, allow you to group and iterate over contained tasks. They include the For loop, Foreach loop, and Sequence tasks in the Control Flow Toolbox.

You also have the option to simply group multiple child tasks together by selecting the tasks on the design surface, right-clicking, and then choosing Group. This type of an object looks like an SSIS container (that is, shows up on the SSIS design surface as a collapsible rectangle with other tasks inside of it), however, it is really more like a code region in VS 2005 in that it allows you to collapse complex sections of packages, thereby making them more human-readable. Refer to Figure 8-8 to see a use of the Foreach container task.

To use this task, you must configure the properties of the enumerator by right-clicking the task on the design surface. You select from these choices: Foreach file, Item, ADO, ADO.NET, From Variable, NodeList, and SMO. When you do so, you'll see the Foreach Loop Editor dialog box shown in Figure 8-11.

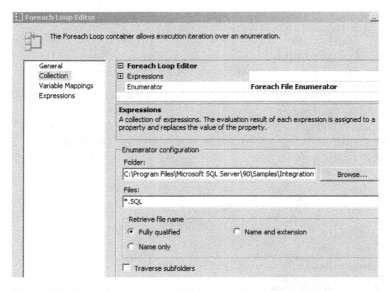

Figure 8-11. *Using the new* Foreach *loop container task requires that you configure the enumerator.*

Note SMO (SQL Management Objects) is the management object model used in SQL Server 2005.

SQL Tasks

The next group of tasks allows your SSIS package to execute some kind of SQL statement. The most commonly used task is the Execute SQL task. In our sample package, shown earlier in Figure 8-10, the execute SQL task will create tables based on information contained in a SQL script file.

The script file is configured in the property sheet for this task as shown in Figure 8-12. Note also that this task will iterate because in the example package, it's nested in a Foreach loop container.

Another consideration with Execute SQL tasks is the ability to associate parameters with a query. This is configured in the same dialog box.

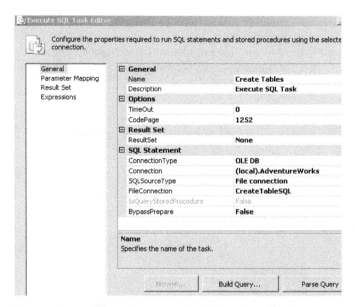

Figure 8-12. *In the configuration dialog box for the Execute SQL task, you can associate the SQL query with a connection to a file (which tells the task to get the SQL to execute from the file contents) by configuring the* SQLSourceType *property to the file connection. Also note that you can map parameters via this dialog box.*

The next most common type of SQL control flow task used in ETL solutions is the data flow task. The data flow task is shown as a task rectangle on the Control Flow area in Figure 8-8 (shown previously); for our example, this has been named Extract – Clean – Load Data.

Note If you've used DTS 2000, you've got some "unlearning" to do! This task is the equivalent of the "black arrow" between data source and destination in that version.

In SSIS 2005, the data flow task detail is exposed via an entirely new work window: the Data Flow window. To get there, double-click the data flow task on the Control Flow design surface. You'll then be taken to the Data Flow work area for that particular data flow task as shown in Figure 8-13.

Figure 8-13. *The Data Flow work area in BIDS allows you to visually configure a data flow for a particular data flow task from the control flow area of your SSIS package.*

Once in the Data Flow area, you can configure the data flow by using data flow source and destination components and data flow tranformation components available in the Data Flow Toolbox. You'll learn more about the procedure for doing this later in this chapter. For now, however, you may be interested in what the Data Flow area looks like for our particular sample package. Figure 8-14 shows the Data Flow area.

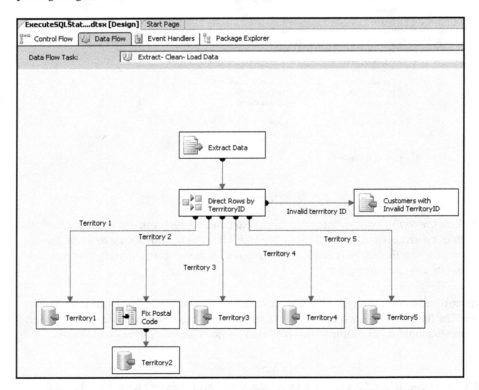

Figure 8-14. *The Data Flow work area for the sample package shown in Figure 8-8.*

Another commonly used SQL/file system control flow task is Bulk Insert. The functionality is similar to that of DTS 2000. I've listed this task in both categories because it executes a SQL BULK INSERT to move text data from the file system into a SQL Server table.

File System Tasks

As mentioned in the previous paragraph, Bulk Insert is one of the most commonly used ETL file system tasks. There is, however, a new kid on the block—the XML task—that supports the industry direction to move away from .txt or .csv files toward "more intelligent" .xml files.

The samples include a ProcessXMLData.dtsx package that shows the use of this task. To open this package, navigate to the sample files, and open the .sln file with the same name. Open the package in BIDS by double-clicking it, and you'll see two XML tasks on the control flow design surface.

To configure the XML task, right-click it, choose Edit, and select first the type of operation you want to perform. The selection you make here changes the dialog box to add/remove additional configurable supporting properties. Here are your choices:

- *Validate*: Allows you to specify that the package should validate an XML document against some type of XML schema, DTD, XSD, and so on.

- *XSLT*: Allows you to specify that the package should perform an XSLT transformation against the configured XML document.

- *XPath*: Allows you to specify that the package should run an XPath query and then do some sort of evaluation against the named section of the configured XML document.

- *Merge*: Allows you to specify that the package should merge two XML documents.

- *Diff*: Allows you to specify that the package should compare two XML documents and return some result based on the comparison, that is, fail on difference, return a DiffGram, and so on.

- *Patch*: Allows you to specify that the package should apply a DiffGram to a configured XML document, with the result being a combined, new XML document. A DiffGram is an XML format that identifies current and original versions of data elements.

Figure 8-15 shows the configuration dialog box for the XML task with the XPath operation type selected.

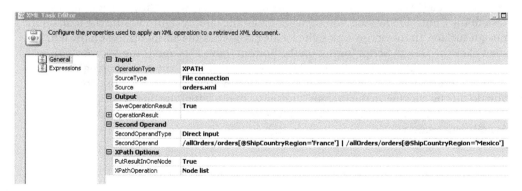

Figure 8-15. *The XML task has six different types of XML operations for you to select from when configuring this task. This example shows the configuration values for the XPath option.*

Operating System Tasks

New for SSIS 2005, in this type of task are the two WMI (Windows Management Instrumentation) tasks: the WMI Data Reader and the WMI Event Watcher. Both of these tasks allow you to add the ability for your SSIS package to "listen" to values associated with the operating system—for example, hot fixes installed or events that have fired—and then continue on with the control flow of the SSIS package based on the results of this listening. WMI uses a query language that is similar to T-SQL, which is called WQL (WMI Query Language).

To use either of these tasks, you must add a connection of type WMI to your package. Then you associate that connection with whichever type of WMI task you are working with. To configure the properties of that task, you right-click it. The most important property is the WMI Query. BOL has several examples.

■**Tip** If you do use the WMI tasks, there are some tools that can help you to quickly author WQL queries. A freely downloadable WMI query builder is available at http://www.microsoft.com/downloads/details.aspx?FamilyID=2cc30a64-ea15-4661-8da4-55bbc145c30e&DisplayLang=en.

The MSMQ (or Message Queue) task is also available in this category. It allows you to configure your SSIS package to send or receive particular messages in a Microsoft Message Queue.

Script Tasks

If you choose to add any script to the control flow area of your package, you now have two choices regarding the language. The ActiveX Script task (which uses VBScript) is still available. As mentioned previously, be aware that the ActiveX Script task is included for backward compatibility. Microsoft states in BOL: "This feature will be removed in the next version of Microsoft SQL Server. Do not use this feature in new development work, and modify applications that currently use this feature as soon as possible."

New in 2005 is the ability to add scripts using VB.NET. To do this, you add the script task to the Control Flow area. You then configure the task by right-clicking the icon on the design surface. In the Script Task Editor dialog box, click the Script option on the left, and then click the Design Script button on the bottom right. This opens the Microsoft Visual Studio for Applications scripting window. Here you can write your script using VB.NET with full IntelliSense. You also can set breakpoints to assist you with script debugging. You do this by clicking in the margin (grey area) to the left of the line of script you want to "break" at. A sample script is shown in Figure 8-16, using the sample package SyncPartitions.dtsx.

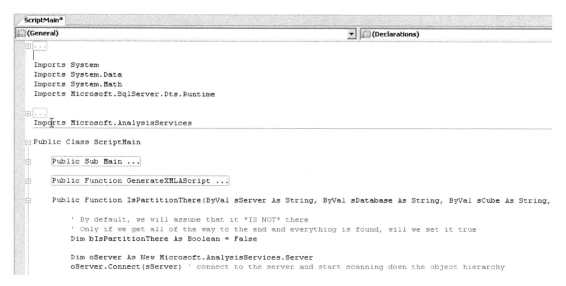

```
ScriptMain*

(General)                                                        ▼   (Declarations)

    ...

    Imports System
    Imports System.Data
    Imports System.Math
    Imports Microsoft.SqlServer.Dts.Runtime

    ...
    Imports Microsoft.AnalysisServices

  Public Class ScriptMain

      Public Sub Main ...

      Public Function GenerateXMLAScript ...

      Public Function IsPartitionThere(ByVal sServer As String, ByVal sDatabase As String, ByVal sCube As String,

          ' By default, we will assume that it "IS NOT" there
          ' Only if we get all of the way to the end and everything is found, will we set it true
          Dim bIsPartitionThere As Boolean = False

          Dim oServer As New Microsoft.AnalysisServices.Server
          oServer.Connect(sServer) ' connect to the server and start scanning down the object hierarchy
```

Figure 8-16. *The new script task allows you to write scripts using VB.NET. The text editor gives you full IntelliSense.*

Remote Tasks

The new task available with SSIS 2005 in this category is the Web Service task. This task is not only new, but also it is enhanced after you install SP1 for SQL Server 2005. This task requires that you set up a connection manager of type HTTP. It also requires a local copy of a WSDL file to define the programmatic interface of the Web Service to be called. After you've met these two prerequisites, then you can execute any permitted Web Service method as part of the control flow for your SSIS package. SP1 added the ability to configure parameters for the Web Service task.

Another task available in this category is the FTP task. This task allows you to configure your package to send or receive files via FTP. It also allows you to copy or move files on the remote server or local file system, or to create or delete files and folders.

SSAS Tasks

One of the most important sets of control flow tasks in the toolset for your BI project is, of course, the set of tasks that affect SSAS objects. We'll review the newly added Execute SSAS DDL (Data Definition Language) task and the SSAS processing tasks here. (The Data Mining Query task will be covered in Chapter 13 with all of the rest of the information about data mining.)

The Execute DDL task allows you to add the ability for the control flow in your package to create, alter, or drop cubes and dimensions. There are a couple of interesting considerations when configuring this new task type. The first is that two new languages are used:

- *ASSL (Analysis Services Scripting Language)*: This language is used to define the particular instance of the object type that your want to affect, that is, the dimension named `CustomerDim` in the cube named AdventureWorks, and so on.

- *XMLA (XML for Analysis)*: This language sends the action commands, that is, create, alter, or drop, to SSAS. It does this via its `execute` method. There are 24 supported commands as of this writing. They are listed in BOL under the topic "Command Element (XMLA)." Some example commands are alter, create, drop, insert, and process.

An example of using this new task type for a BI project is included with SSIS samples. Open the SyncPartitions.sln file from the samples, and then open the SSIS package of the same name in BIDS as shown in Figure 8-17.

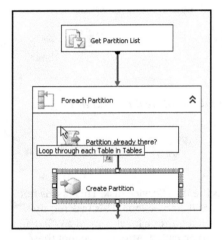

Figure 8-17. *The sample package SyncPartitions shows an example of using the new Analysis Services Execute DDL task to loop through the partitions and take actions appropriately.*

The Analysis Services Processing task is virtually unchanged from the version shipped with DTS 2000. The task, however, has been updated to support all of the various processing types for cubes and dimensions that we reviewed in Chapter 7. This task will be one of your workhorses, especially after you move the solution into production, because you will normally want to automate the processing of cubes, dimensions, and mining models. In my experience, it is most typical to run an update-type of process on a nightly basis. This package would include success logging and failure notification. Figure 8-18 shows the configuration options for the Analysis Services Processing task.

After you've selected your particular control flow tasks, then you'll want to configure the particular workflow for these tasks. You do this by configuring the precedence constraints. These are shown on the design surface as colored lines (by default green) between control flow tasks or components.

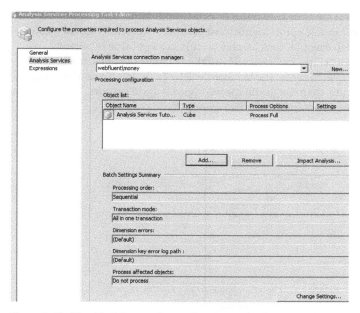

Figure 8-18. *The SSAS Processing task mirrors the functionality of cube and dimension processing you have access to via the SSAS template in BIDS. In SSIS, of course, you can incorporate this task into any sort of workflow that suits your business needs.*

Precedence Constraints

Precedence constraints link executables, containers, and tasks in packages into a control flow and specify conditions that determine whether control flow tasks or event handlers run. There are three types of constraints: Success (shown with a green line), Failure (shown with a red line), or Completion (shown with a blue line). To add a Success constraint between components, click the green arrow on the design surface from the source component and drag it to the destination component. Figure 8-19 shows an example of two Control Flow components that must run successfully for the subsequent destination Control Flow component to run.

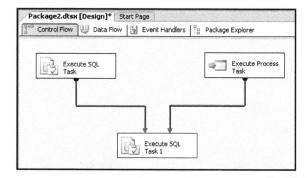

Figure 8-19. *Success constraints, indicated by green lines with arrows, allow you to establish workflow paths in your SSIS packages.*

The default condition when multiple constraint lines go to the same destination task is a logical AND. That means that *all* source components must execute successfully for the destination component to be allowed to execute. You can change this to a logical OR by selecting all constraint lines and then right-clicking Properties. If you then change the default setting of the LogicalAnd property from True to False, the behavior will be such that if *any* of the source components successfully execute, then the destination component will execute. This is shown on the design surface with dotted constraint lines in Figure 8-20.

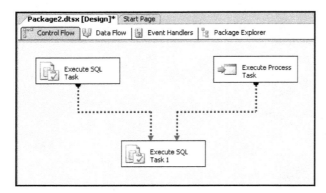

Figure 8-20. *Dotted success constraint lines indicate a logical* OR *condition.*

Using Expressions with Precedence Constraints

Another capability in SSIS is to associate expressions with constraints. One way to do this is to right-click the particular constraint line of interest, and then click Edit. This will open the Precedence Constraint Editor dialog box, which is shown (with its default values) in Figure 8-21.

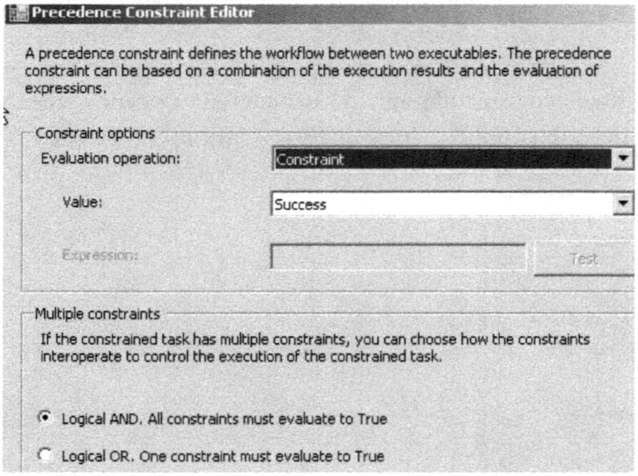

Figure 8-21. *One way to alter the behavior of a precedence constraint is to right-click it and add or change the appropriate information. Note that you can add expressions to the evaluation path. You can also use the Properties window to change these values.*

When combining expressions with constraints, you have these options in the Evaluation operation drop-down list:

- *Constraint*: This default option adds only a constraint, no expression.

- *Expression*: This adds only an expression, no constraint.

- *Expression and Constraint*: This adds both an expression and a constraint, both of which must evaluate to True to allow the destination component to execute.

- *Expression or Constraint*: This adds both an expression and a constraint, either of which must evaluate to True to allow the destination component to execute.

If you choose any of the previous three options from the Evaluation operation drop-down list, then the Expression text box and Test button will become available as shown in Figure 8-22.

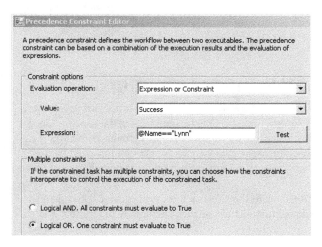

Figure 8-22. *You can associate expressions with precedence constraints by configuring the Precedence Constraint Editor dialog box.*

Tip If you include an expression in a precedence constraint, then BIDS will place an icon on the design surface of the control flow (next to the affected precedence constraint), and the tooltip on the icon will display the configured expression (see Figure 8-23).

Now that we've reviewed control flows tasks and precedence constraints in detail, the next step is to dive in to the details of the data flow sources, destinations, and, most importantly, transformations.

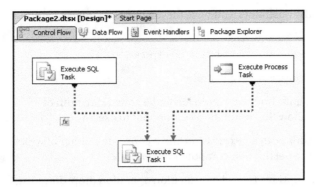

Figure 8-23. *Expressions that are associated with constraints will be indicated by a small button labeled "fx" next to the affected constraint line. This figure shows another example of dotted success constraint lines that indicate a logical* OR *condition.*

Understanding Data Flow Transformations

As mentioned previously, in DTS 2000, the data flow was shown on the same surface as the control flow items. A black arrow represented the data flow by connecting data sources and destinations. Configuration of data flow was done by right-clicking the black arrow and navigating a through a series of dialog boxes. The DTS-style interface has been replaced by a separate work area in BIDS: the Data Flow tab. Microsoft introduced this new design to make SSIS packages easier to design, debug, and use.

When you double-click the data flow task in the Control Flow area, you will be taken to the Data Flow window for that particular data flow task (shown previously in Figure 8-14).

Understanding Data Sources and Destinations

To begin work in the Data Flow area, you will select at least one data flow source component. Usually, you will select at least one data flow transformation and at least one data flow destination. Figure 8-24 shows all data sources and all data destinations from the BIDS Toolbox.

Note When should you use a DataReader source (or destination) and when should you use an OLE DB source (or destination)? Use a DataReader when consuming or providing data to any .NET data provider. Use a OLE DB task when consuming or providing data to any OLE DB provider.

New source types are DataReader, Raw File, and XML. New destination types are DataReader, Dimension Processing, RawFile, Recordset, and SQL Mobile. The *Raw File Source* type is used to retrieve raw data that was previously written by the SSIS Raw File destination. It works more quickly on this type of file than using the Flat File or OLE DB Source. You could use this source as the intermediate step in processing to more quickly move data that would be undergoing subsequent additional transformations within a package.

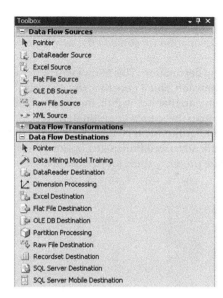

Figure 8-24. *Data Flow Sources and Data Flow Destinations from the Toolbox in BIDS reflect a wide variety of interoperability in SSIS packages.*

The XML Source allows you to use an XML file with or without an associated XSD schema as a source. The schema can be inline, a separate file, or generated by the task itself. XSD schemas are used to validate the format of the contents of XML files. All of these options are configured by right-clicking the task and working with the XML source editor property page as shown in Figure 8-25.

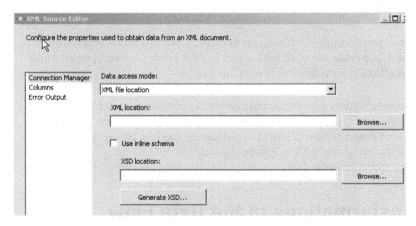

Figure 8-25. *You can associate an XSD schema with an XML file as a source for your data flow by using the XML Source Editor property page.*

Data Flow Destinations

As with Data Flow Sources, this section provides more explanation for some of the new Data Flow Destination types that are used in BI scenarios.

The first one to consider is the Dimension Processing destination. This allows you to map and insert the results of a data flow into a SSAS cube dimension. You'll note that you can select the Processing method that meets your business requirement, that is, the Full, Incremental, or Update Processing method. On the Mappings page, you map the source to destination columns, and on the Advanced page, you set the error configuration behavior (that is, key error behavior, and so on). This last page is identical to the Advanced Processing options page available for cube and dimension processing in BIDS. The property sheet for this destination is shown in Figure 8-26.

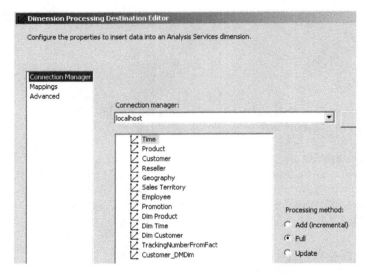

Figure 8-26. *BIDS allows you to configure dimension processing (using a subset of available processing types) as a data flow destination. To have access to all possible processing types, you'd have to use the control flow Analysis Services Processing task.*

The Partition Processing data flow destination presents you with a similar subset of partition processing options: Add (incremental), Full, or Data Update Again, if your business scenario calls for a more granular type of partition processing (such as Process Index), then you'd use the control flow Analysis Services Processing task.

The Data Mining Model Training destination will be discussed in Chapter 13.

Adding Transformations to the Data Flow

After you've added and configured your data sources and data destinations, you'll usually then add one or more data transformations to your SSIS package. Figure 8-27 shows the transformations available in BIDS.

Figure 8-27. *SQL Server 2005 SSIS has 28 data flow transformation types to select from.*

An SSIS data flow transformation is a type of component that takes some source data, applies a type of change to any defined subset of the source data, and then makes the changed data available for output to whatever configured data flow destinations your business requirements necessitate. A great way to begin to understand the types of data flow transformations available for use in SSIS packages is to simply open the BIDS Toolbox while working in the Data Flow tab for any SSIS package and then pass your mouse over each transformation. When you do this, a tooltip with a brief explanation will pop up over each transformation.

In this version of SSIS (if using the Enterprise Edition of SQL Server), you now have a mind-boggling array of 28 types of data transformations to use in your SSIS packages. As with control flow tasks, you can best understand what these transformations do by grouping them into categories. The following lists the transformation groups by priority order; the first group transformation types are the most commonly used in ETL projects.

- *Add*: This type allows you to add or combine data. These include Aggregate, Copy Column, Import column, Merge, Merge Join, and Union All transformations.

- *Split*: This type allows you to split data. These include the Conditional Split, Derived Column, and Export Column transformations.

- *Translate*: This type allows you to change or to sort the data. These include Character Map, Data Conversion, Lookup, Pivot, Sort, and Unpivot transformations.

- *SSAS*: This type is specific to SSAS object processing. These include the Audit, Data Mining Query, and the Slowly Changing Dimension transformations. The Audit transformation isn't specific only to SSAS, but we'll discuss its use in this context.

- *Sample*: This type allows you to count or sample the data. These include Percentage Sampling, Row Count, and Row Sampling transformations.

- *Run command*: This type allows running a command against the data. These include Multicast, OLE DB command, and Script component transformations.

- *Enterprise Edition*: This type is available only in the Enterprise Edition of SQL Server. These include the Fuzzy Grouping, Fuzzy Lookup, Term Extraction, and Term Lookup transformations.

Note Some transformation types are only available in the Enterprise Edition of SQL Server 2005, for example, the fuzzy lookup transform. For a complete list, see `http://www.microsoft.com/sql/prodinfo/features/compare-features.mspx`.

As with the control flow transformations, you can extend the transformations available in the data transform transformations by downloading, purchasing, or creating your own transformations and then installing them in the BIDS interface.

We'll continue our tour of the data transformation types by group, as we did with control flow tasks.

Adding Data Transformations

The sample package calculatecolumns.dtsx shows examples of the Aggregate (also Derived Column and Sort) data flow transformations. The Aggregate transform allows you to easily perform aggregations of types GroupBy, Count, Count Distinct, Sum, Average, Minimum, or Maximum against your data flow by simply configuring the aggregate dialog box. The Data Flow work area for the Calculated Columns SSIS sample package is shown in Figure 8-28.

The Add transformation group contains some of the data flow transformation types that are most often used in BI projects: Copy Column, Import Column, and Union All. All of these transformations are self-explanatory.

The transformation group also contains the new Merge and Merge Join transformations. The Merge Join transformation allows you to configure your SSIS package to perform a left, right, or full join on two sorted inputs with matching metadata. While configuring this transform, you must also specify null handling behavior.

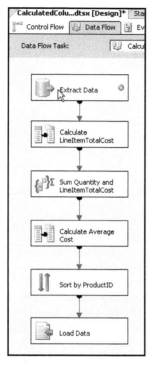

Figure 8-28. *The Data Flow work area in BIDS allows you to visually configure a data flow for a particular data flow transformation from the Control Flow area of your SSIS package. This example shows the use of the Aggregate, Derived Column, and Sort data flow transformations.*

Tip You can use the Sort transformation to properly sort inputs prior to performing a merge join on them. If you choose not to do this, then you must configure the inputs as sorted by using the isSorted property on them. This process is described in more detail in the BOL topic "How to: Set Sort Attributes."

Split Data Transformations

Another handy new transform type is the Derived Column transformation. This is also shown in the calculatecolumns.dtsx data flow sample. Figure 8-29 shows the dialog box where you configure the new column. In this work area, you can use the SSIS expression language, which is like T-SQL, but is *not* T-SQL itself.

Note For more information about SSIS expression syntax, see the BOL topic "Syntax (SSIS)."

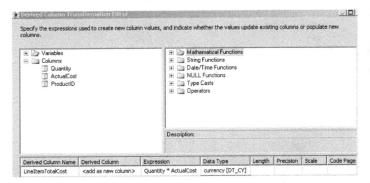

Figure 8-29. *The Derived Column Transformation Editor in BIDS allows you to write expressions to create derived columns in your SSIS package.*

You use the SSIS expression in your statement to derive the new column or columns. The dialog box includes a function reference for your convenience. It also includes the list of all available columns in the data flow as well a list of all of the package variables.

The new Conditional Split transformation shown in "execute SQL statements in loop.dtsx" is yet another helpful tool for you. The Conditional Split transformation routes rows to different destinations depending on the content of the data using a CASE-like decision structure. The transformation evaluates expressions, and based on the results, directs particular data rows to the specified outputs. The data flow for this package is shown in Figure 8-30, and the Conditional Split dialog box is shown in Figure 8-31.

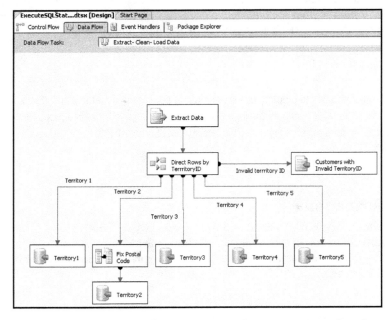

Figure 8-30. *The sample package ExecuteSQLStatementInLoop.dtsx shows off the new Conditional Split data flow transformation type.*

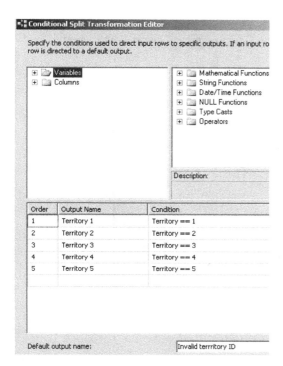

Figure 8-31. *The Conditional Split Transformation Editor dialog box allows you to specify the split conditions via expressions.*

Translate Data Transformations

The Lookup and Union transformations are showcased in the complex sample datacleaning.dtsx. The Lookup transformation performs lookups by joining data in source columns with columns in a reference table.

The Fuzzy Lookup transformation is contrasted to the regular Lookup transformation because it uses fuzzy matching. The Lookup transformation returns either an exact match or nothing from the reference table. The Fuzzy Lookup transformation uses fuzzy matching to return one or more close matches from the reference table.

Tip A Fuzzy Lookup transformation frequently follows a Lookup transformation in a package data flow (as is shown in the sample package). First, the Lookup transformation tries to find an exact match. If it fails, the Fuzzy Lookup transformation provides close matches from the reference table.

The Data Cleansing sample is, by far, the most complex of all the samples. It includes not only the two transformations mentioned previously but also uses many others, including the very powerful Fuzzy Lookup and Fuzzy Grouping. The Fuzzy transformation types require the

Enterprise Edition of SQL Server. This sample is also a very good example of using annotations on the design surface to make SSIS packages "self-documenting." Figure 8-32 shows the data flow for this package.

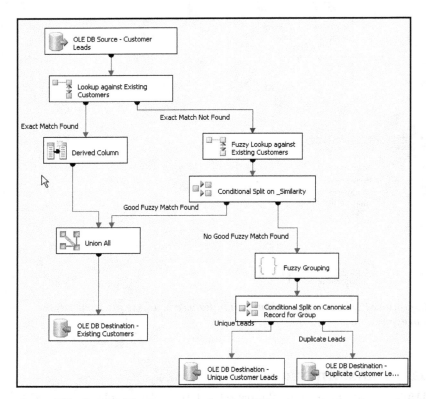

Figure 8-32. *The DataCleansing sample SSIS package uses the most complex data flow sequence of the samples included with SQL Server 2005. It includes the following data transformation types: Lookup, Derived Column, Union, Conditional Split, Fuzzy Lookup, and Fuzzy Grouping. It is also a good example of documenting functionality on the design surface via annotations.*

The Lookup transformation has some new configurable capabilities via the Advanced property sheet. The new functionality allows you to more granularly control the overhead associated with the performance of the lookup activity. You configure this on the Advanced tab of the Lookup Transformation Editor dialog box. This enhancement was made in response to customer feedback about the slow performance of the Lookup capabilities in DTS. The Advanced tab is shown in Figure 8-33.

Tip Lookup transformations are case-sensitive. You can use UPPER or LOWER T-SQL functions to convert lookup source data to the correct case prior to using them in a Lookup transformation.

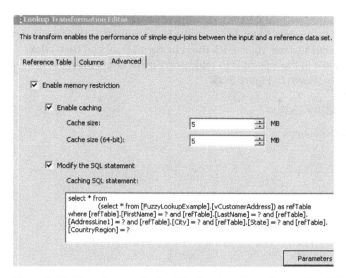

Figure 8-33. *The advanced tab of the Lookup Transformation Editor allows you to configure additional settings on it. This allows you greater control over the performance overhead generated by this transformation.*

SSAS Data Transformations

An interesting SSIS sample package showcases the new Audit transformation from the SSAS transformation category. This package also demonstrates a common BI scenario: tracking data lineage. Lineage is a formal way for saying that your business requirements include the need to track package execution history. The CaptureDataLineage.dtsx package includes an Audit transformation. Part of the Audit Transformation Editor dialog box is shown in Figure 8-34.

Audit Transformation Editor

Configure the properties used to insert audit information into the data flow.

Output Column Name	Audit Type
Username	User name
Execution Start Time	Execution start time

Figure 8-34. *The Audit data flow transformation allows you to capture lineage or package execution information easily for logging.*

Slowly Changing Dimension Transformation

The Slowly Changing Dimension transformation is probably the most important data transformation in the Toolbox for BI solutions. Using it properly requires that you understand the concepts behind changing dimensions (type 1, 2, or 3) and what structures are required to support them. (This was discussed in Chapters 2 and 6.)

When using this transformation type, you'll have to configure several options via the Setup Wizard. To open the wizard, you select a Slowly Changing Dimension transformation, drag it onto the data flow SSIS design surface, right-click the transformation, and then click Edit. The first choice for you to make in the wizard is to select the Business key from the Key Type column of the source table as shown in Figure 8-35.

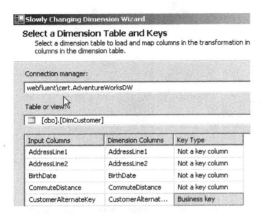

Figure 8-35. *When using the Slowly Changing Dimension data flow transformations, the first step is to select the source table and its Business key.*

The next step is to configure the change type for each attribute in the table. The choices are Fixed attribute (no overwrite), Changing attribute (overwrite), or Historical attribute (write new record and mark previous values as outdated).

This corresponds to SCD (or slowly changing dimension) type 1 for changing or overwriting and type 2 for historical records. Type 3 (adding an additional dimension attribute) for each change is *not* supported by this transformation type. These options are shown in Figure 8-36.

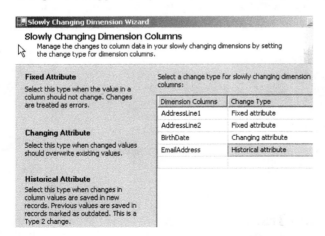

Figure 8-36. *When using the SCD data flow transformation, the second step is to configure the change type for each attribute of the dimension table.*

The next step is to configure the optional behavior for fixed attributes and changing attributes. These options, which include failing the transformation if changes are detected in a fixed attribute and/or cascading changes to all affected records for attributes marked as changing type, are shown in Figure 8-37.

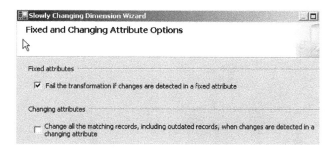

Figure 8-37. *When using the SCD data flow transformation, the third step is to configure the optional behavior for fixed and changing attributes.*

The next step is to configure the storage location for historical attribute values. These options are shown in Figure 8-38.

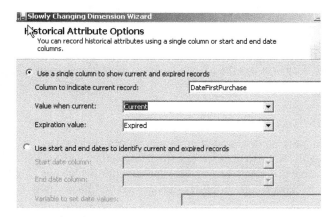

Figure 8-38. *When using the SCD data flow transformation, the fourth step is to configure the storage location and values for historical attributes.*

The next step is to configure the behavior for inferred dimension members. These options are shown in Figure 8-39.

Although the wizard has a large number of steps and options, it's actually an incredibly powerful and useful tool. It has been designed to help you quickly implement the most common SCD scenarios from your particular BI solution's requirements.

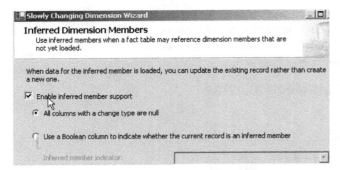

Figure 8-39. *When using the SCD data flow transformation, the fifth step is to configure the behavior for inferred members via the options in the wizard.*

Sample Data Transformations

The Percentage Sampling, Row Count, and Row Sampling transformations included in this group are pretty straightforward to use. They all allow you to sample or to count and to send output, if sampling, to a configured destination. You configure the number (or percentage) of rows to be sampled, and you can also configure a random seed value via the property sheet.

These transformations can be particularly useful in BI projects because you may be working with huge volumes of data. Using transformations from the Sample data group can help you to quickly (that is, with very little overhead) get a view of what you are working with.

Run Command Data Transformations

The new script component transformation requires a bit of explanation. As mentioned in the "Adding Control Flow Tasks" section, you have two choices for associating scripts with your SSIS package in the control flow workspace: the ActiveX task used for VBScript (which has been depreciated and is included for backward compatibility only) and the Script task used for VB.NET script.

So, why the need for an additional script component transformation in the data flow transformations area? You'll see that the key to understanding the difference between the Script task and the script component is to be found by looking at the first dialog box that you must configure when using the script component. In this dialog box shown in Figure 8-40, you must select whether the component will be used to associate a script with a data flow source, destination, or transformation.

Because the Script Component task output becomes part of the data flow, rather than the more general output of the more general control flow Script task, there are several syntax differences when writing your scripts between these two transformations. For a more detailed discussion see the BOL topic "Comparing the Script Task and the Script Component."

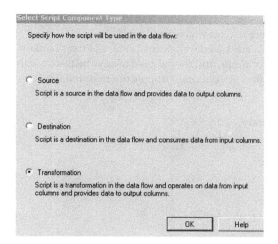

Figure 8-40. *The Script Component data flow transformation requires that you associate the VB.NET script with a data flow source, destination, or transformation.*

Enterprise Edition Only Data Transformations

The Fuzzy Logic, Fuzzy Grouping, Term Extraction, and Term Lookup transformations are only available in the Enterprise Edition of SQL Server 2005. Both types of fuzzy transformations are shown in the sample package named datacleaning.dtsx. The data flow for this package was shown earlier in Figure 8-32.

■**Note** What does "fuzzy" mean? In a word, inexact; the difference between a typical database lookup and a fuzzy lookup is that the database lookup is Boolean. That is, either there is a match to a string, to a portion of a string, or no match at all. Fuzzy lookups and groupings use a much more sophisticated algorithm that finds the "nearest neighbor." The result is that lookups and groupings will be more flexible, inclusive, and ultimately useful.

Term Extraction tasks and Lookup tasks use the same powerful fuzzy type of logic in your package's data flow. The Advanced property sheet for the Term Extract transform type allows you to even more finely configure the type of term you are looking for, that is, whether it's a noun or not. Your input will impact the algorithm because different linguistic pattern matching is used for different parts of speech. For example, nouns are searched for both in singular and plural format; verbs are searched for using all possible declensions, and so on.

Figure 8-41 shows the Advanced property sheet for the Term Extraction transformation.

A primary consideration when using the wide variety of transformations now available in BIDS is the execution overhead and complexity that you are adding to your package. Execution overhead includes stressing processors, memory, and IO. The components most affected depend on the type of transformations, quantity of data, and other factors. You can use the

Windows System Monitor Counter Object SQLServer:SSIS Pipeline and its associated 12 counters to help to determine whether and where you may have bottlenecks.

As with SSAS advanced cube design options, advanced transforms, such as Fuzzy Lookup, should only be used when business needs call for them, and they should always be tested with production levels of data to ensure that production systems can process the required loads given the resources that they have available.

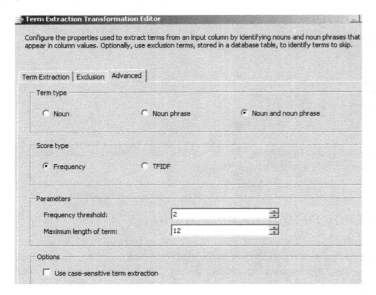

Figure 8-41. *The Term Extraction Transformation Editor allows you to more granularly configure this transformation. In the Score type section, TFIDF refers to Term Frequency and Inverse Document Frequency.*

Using the Dynamic Package Configuration Wizard

An important, and practical, consideration when implementing SSIS packages is creating packages that can easily be moved from a development environment to a production environment. As stated in the "General ETL Package-Design Best Practices" section of this chapter, this means that many package values, such as connection string, should never be hard-coded into a package.

The revamped Dynamic Package Configuration Wizard (the previous version with a somewhat similar subset of this functionality is called the Dynamic Properties Task in DTS 2000) will help you accomplish this goal. To access this wizard, you choose SSIS ➤ Package Configurations. Once in the wizard, you can set most properties of an SSIS package via a number of dynamic methods. Figure 8-42 shows the wizard's interface for selecting the property you want to configure dynamically.

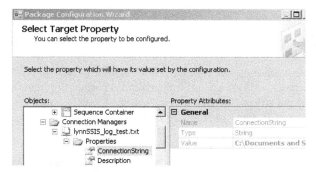

Figure 8-42. *The Package Configuration Wizard allows you to set SSIS package properties dynamically by showing you a hierarchical view of all objects (such as Connection Managers, Properties, Variables, and Executables) contained in the package.*

The wizard provides you with a number of options to set whatever properties you are working with dynamically. An example of a property that you may choose to use this functionality to configure could be the connection strings values for data sources or destinations. The sources for property values can originate from any of these options: XML configuration file, Environmental Variable, Registry Entry, Parent Package Variable, or SQL Server.

SSIS Expressions

In some ways, I've saved the best for last. A new jewel in SSIS is the ability to configure expressions for nearly every control flow task type property value. You learned earlier in this chapter that SSIS expressions could be used in conjunction with control flow precedence constraints; they can also be used with particular control flow tasks. So, why are expressions associated with tasks or components so wonderful? These expressions can be assigned to most any read/write property in the entire SSIS package, which, in effect, enables dynamic update of the associated property at runtime. Figure 8-43 shows the interface for expression definition using the Execute SQL control flow task.

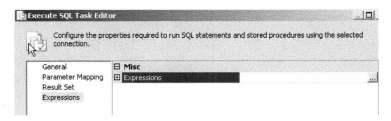

Figure 8-43. *The Expressions section of control flow tasks allows you to dynamically set read/write property values.*

One common use of property expressions is to allow for dynamic update of a connection string using a value that is stored in a variable. Expressions can be added to a package, task, event handler, connection manager, log provider, or (as discussed earlier in this chapter) precedence constraint. (Event handlers and log providers are covered in Chapter 9.)

Summary

SSIS provides you with an incredible degree of flexibility and power when implementing your ETL solution. This chapter covered the foundations of using the tools available in BIDS to create the SSIS packages that will be the workhorses of your ETL processes for BI. You learned more about common objects—data sources and DSVs—and then explored connection managers. The heart of this chapter covered the core of the ETL toolset—control flow task and data flow transformations. You also learned about using the Dynamic Package Configuration Wizard.

Believe it or not, there is still much more to learn about creating data workflows using SSIS. In Chapter 9, we'll explore debugging, error handling, event handling, logging, and using transactions in SSIS packages in BI projects.

CHAPTER 9

■ ■ ■

Advanced SSIS

We just completed an extensive tour of SSIS, including most all of the design surfaces in BIDS (the notable exception is the Error Flow design surface). What else could we possibly have to cover in the SSIS area?

Actually there is still a great deal more to learn. The focus of this chapter is on using BIDS to make your packages even more useful by adding or using features that will improve your ability to reuse, deploy, and debug them. Also, we'll look at error handling in depth. In this chapter, we'll cover the following topics:

- Understanding package execution—viewers and BIDS

- Debugging—breakpoints, watch windows, and more

- Logging—new log providers and error handling

- Deploying packages

- Setting runtime properties

- Defining security

- Placing checkpoints

- Using transactions

Understanding Package Execution

The BIDS environment is not only conducive to implementing elegant data workflow packages but it also has a large number of features that allow you to understand the implications of package execution.

The most basic of these tools are the Package Explorer view, the package Progress window view, and the design surface itself. When you execute packages in BIDS, all of these areas dynamically reflect a large amount of important information about each step in the package as it executes. The Package Explorer view is a quick list of all objects associated with a package as shown in Figure 9-1.

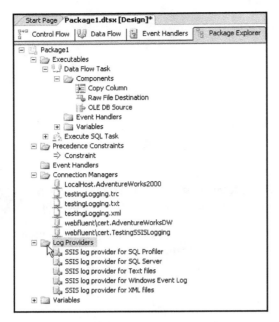

Figure 9-1. *The Package Explorer view shows a complete list of all objects in a particular package. Objects are categorized and grouped into folders by type of object. This hierarchical display of objects is identical to the one used in the Package Configuration Wizard (Select Target Property dialog box) discussed in Chapter 8.*

The next areas for you to work with to get more insight into the execution overhead associated with your package are the Control Flow work area and Data Flow work area. As you execute your package by clicking the green triangle on the toolbar (or by right-clicking the package file in Solution Explorer and then clicking Execute Package), each task item on the Control Flow and transformation on the Data Flow work areas changes color to indicate status: yellow for executing, red for failure, and green for success. Also the Data Flow area shows the number of rows output by each transformation (see Figure 9-2).

■ **Note** You cannot make any changes to the package while it is executing. To alter the package, you must stop the execution by clicking the Stop Debugging button (small, square, blue button on the top toolbar).

Yet another informational indicator available to you in BIDS is the Progress window. When you start a package executing, the Progress tab will become available at the top of the SSIS design area. This window shows you detailed information about the runtime details associated with executing each step of your package. Warnings or errors may be included in this information. In Figure 9-3, for example, the last item shows a warning message indicating that unused columns are included in the data flow. It advises removing them to improve package performance.

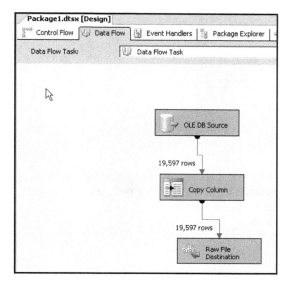

Figure 9-2. *As you execute SSIS packages in BIDS, you can view the progress of each task on the Control Flow design surface and each transformation on the Data Flow design surface: yellow for executing, green for success, and red for failure. BIDS will also report the number of rows output for each transformation on the design surface.*

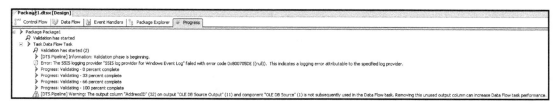

Figure 9-3. *The Progress window reports detailed information about the execution of each task. It can also report warnings and errors.*

Data Viewers

Another useful new capability in SSIS is the feature that allows you to add data viewers to one or more paths in your package's data flow. A *data viewer* is a visual tool or debugger that will help you understand the data flow. To add a data viewer, you right-click a data flow path arrow (which is represented as a green line) that connects any data flow transformations. You then click Data Viewers. You can insert multiple data viewers into any one section of your data flow. Each data viewer can have its own configuration settings.

In the configuration settings, you select one or more columns from the data flow to include based on the type of viewer you've selected. Figure 9-4 shows a configuration that uses two of the possible four data viewer types: Grid, Histogram, Scatter Plot, and Column Chart.

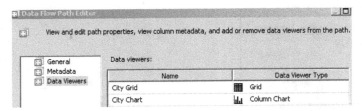

Figure 9-4. *The Data Flow Path Editor allows you to add multiple data viewers to a data flow. You can add Grid, Histogram, Scatter Plot, or Column Chart data viewers.*

After you've added a data viewer to a particular data flow, BIDS indicates this on the Data Flow design surface by placing a small table-shaped icon (with glasses) next to the data flow path arrow where the data flow has been configured (see Figure 9-5).

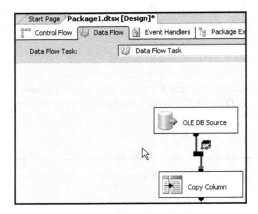

Figure 9-5. *After you've added a data viewer to a data flow of an SSIS package, the package will show the small table-shaped icon (with glasses) next to the data flow path arrow where the data flow has been configured.*

After you've added a data viewer, when you execute the package in BIDS, package execution will halt or break to display the data viewer. The associated data will be shown in a pop-up window. You can then manually continue package execution by clicking the small green triangle on the data viewer window. This process is a type of visual debugging. You can also detach and/or copy the data in the window to the clipboard. The transformation status execution will be paused (the components will be colored yellow) until you manually allow the package to continue by clicking the green triangle on the data viewer window. The data grid type data viewer for an executing package is shown in Figure 9-6.

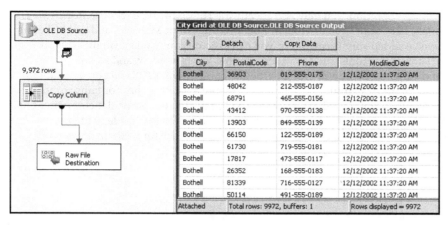

Figure 9-6. *Executing a package with an associated data grid data viewer allows you to review the data as it flows through the pipeline.*

Debugging SSIS Packages

We've already seen the first type of debugging now available in SSIS—using data viewers to debug data flows. New to SSIS 2005 is the ability to add breakpoints to a package or a control flow task. An SSIS package breakpoint adds the ability for a package or an individual component to be paused when a certain condition (or event) fires. Additionally, you can configure breakpoints to fire when a certain condition fires at a precise number of times.

To add a breakpoint to a package, right-click the control flow design window and then click Edit Breakpoints. To add a breakpoint to a particular task, right-click the task and then click Edit Breakpoints. Breakpoints are set on one or more of ten included break conditions. A *break condition* is the name for an SSIS event. Figure 9-7 shows the list of available SSIS events.

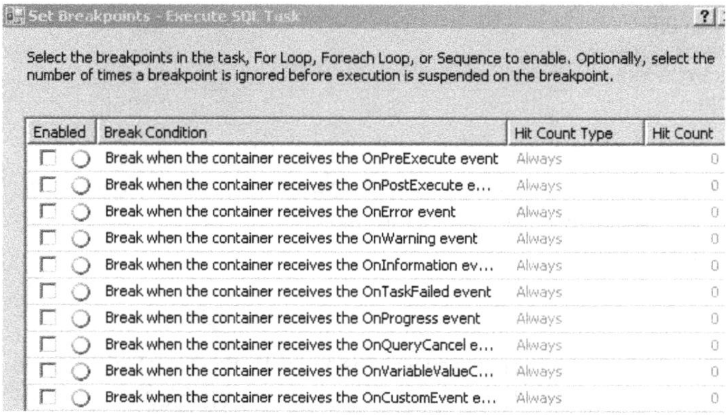

Figure 9-7. *New to SSIS 2005 is the ability to set breakpoints on a package or task for one or more break conditions.*

For each break condition, you may also specify the Hit Count Type (choose from Always, Hit Count Equals, Hit Count Greater Than or Equal To, Hit Count Multiple) and/or Hit Count Value. After you've added your breakpoints, you can execute your package in BIDS and use all of the "classic" debugging tools, such as watch window, locals window, and so on.

After you configure a breakpoint for a particular component, BIDS will add a red dot to that component on the design surface. When you execute a package that contains components with breakpoints configured, your package will show that the particular component has stopped at the configured breakpoint by adding a yellow arrow to the inside of the red dot that is placed on that component. Figure 9-8 shows the design surface for a task in break mode.

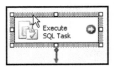

Figure 9-8. *When you configure a breakpoint for a task, BIDS adds a small red dot to that task on the design surface. When an executing package halts at a breakpoint, the red dot shows a yellow arrow inside it to indicate that the package is in break mode and has halted at this task.*

While in break mode, you can use the Debug menu (choose Debug ➤ Windows ➤ Breakpoints) to open debug windows to see even more information about your executing package. Figure 9-9 shows an example of the output available in the Locals window (which shows the current values of local variables) for a particular task of a running package.

Name	Value	Type
⊟ Variables		
System::ContainerStartTime	{10/27/2006 8:48:15 AM}	DateTime
System::CreationName	{Microsoft.SqlServer.Dts.Tasks.ExecuteSQLTask.ExecuteSQLTask, Microsoft.SqlSe	String
System::LocaleID	{1033}	Int32
System::TaskID	{{4D6FD634-2D29-4DA9-8038-D577FB3CDC6E}}	String
System::TaskName	{Execute SQL Task}	String
System::TaskTransactionOptio	{1}	Int32
System::CancelEvent	{2832}	Int32
System::ContainerStartTime	{10/27/2006 8:48:15 AM}	DateTime
System::CreationDate	{10/24/2006 1:49:58 PM}	DateTime
System::CreatorComputerNam	{WEBFLUENT}	String
System::CreatorName	{WEBFLUENT\\llangit1}	String
System::ExecutionInstanceGU	{{203BE993-9F53-4BBA-B4F2-2E210FE4C3E1}}	String
System::InteractiveMode	{True}	Boolean

Figure 9-9. *When you run a package with an associated breakpoint in BIDS, you can open various debug windows to see even more detailed information about package or task information. This example shows part of the Locals window for a particular task.*

■**Tip** You can also add breakpoints to to the VB.NET scripts you write using the Control Flow Script task as well as by using the Data Flow Script component. You do this by right-clicking in the left (grey) margin next to the line of code where you want the application to break in the Script Design window.

The vastly expanded debugging capabilities included with SSIS 2005 greatly improve your productivity when implementing an ETL solution for your BI project, particularly as your SSIS packages increase in complexity. Also, if you use any scripts inside of your packages, you'll particularly appreciate the ability to work with breakpoints.

Most BI projects also require extensive attention to logging and error handling; both of these subjects are covered in the next section in detail.

Logging Execution Results

Execution and error logging in SSIS 2005 have been completely revamped as compared to what was available in DTS 2000. To access the new logging capabilities, you choose SSIS ➤ Logging, or you right-click the package design surface work area and then click Logging. You'll then be working with the Configure SSIS Logs dialog box. Your execution logging options include selecting which control flow task execution outputs you want to log and to which destinations you want to send these logs. You have a choice of five different types of destinations for logs. Also, you can send more than one log to the same destination type. Figure 9-10 shows the Configure SSIS Logs dialog box and the five destination options: a SQL Server table, a SQL Profiler trace file, a text file, a Windows event log, or an XML file.

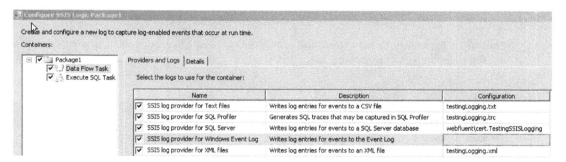

Figure 9-10. *You can add five types of destination locations for your package execution logs in the Configure SSIS Logs dialog box. You also select which control tasks and which event outputs you want to capture.*

After you've selected the control flow tasks and log locations, you then use the Details tab of the dialog box, as shown in Figure 9-11, to select the particular events that you are interested in logging. Figure 9-11 shows the selection of events you have to pick from. Note that Figure 9-11 shows one of the most commonly selected events, OnTaskFailed, for logging.

After logging is enabled, executing the package in BIDS generates all of the configured logs for you and allows you to view the logged information in the Log Events window. To view this window, choose SSIS ➤ Log Events. The Log Events window will open over the Toolbox window by default. Figure 9-12 shows an example of this window for an executing package.

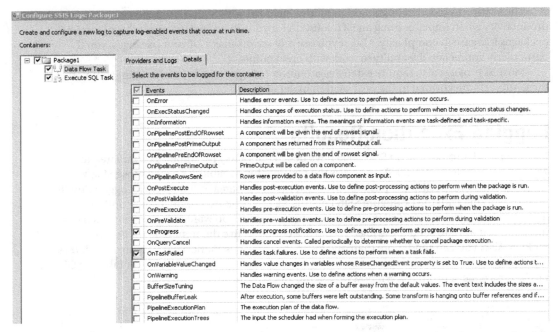

Figure 9-11. *In the Details tab of the Configure SSIS Logs dialog box, you select the events that you are interested in capturing in your logs.*

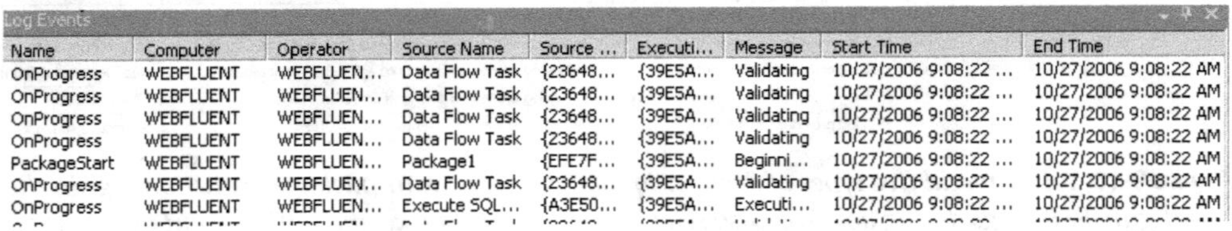

Figure 9-12. *You can view the logged events in an executing package in BIDS by choosing SSIS ➤ Log Events.*

Tip To see more detail about any listed event in the Log Events window, just double-click the event to open a details window in BIDS.

My favorite new log type is to log events to a SQL Server Profiler trace file. To open the resulting log file (the file type is .trc) in Profiler, just double-click the file. Once inside Profiler, you can view the file and, importantly, further analyze the file using the associated tools (Database Engine Tuning Advisor, and so on).

For example, you could create a log file destination in SQL Server Profiler for an SSIS package and then save that file as a trace or .trc file. You could subsequently use that trace file as input to the Database Engine Tuning Advisor (DETA). You could expect to see results from the DETA, including optimizing SSIS data flows by adding, removing, or changing indexes on SQL Server source or destination data, for example. Figure 9-13 shows a log trace file opened in Profiler. Of course, tools like DETA are designed to work only with SQL Server source and destination data.

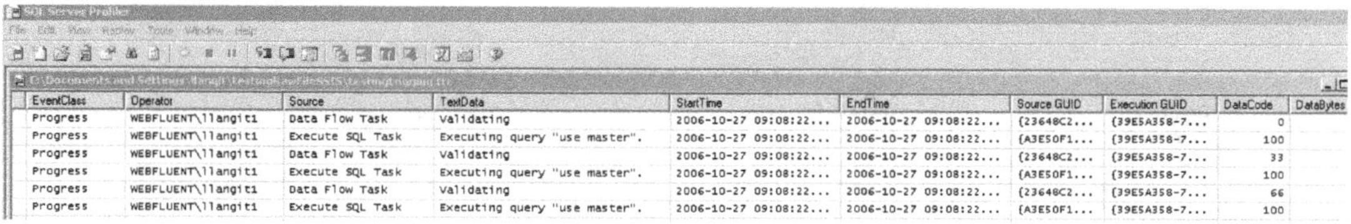

EventClass	Operator	Source	TextData	StartTime	EndTime	Source GUID	Execution GUID	DataCode	DataBytes
Progress	WEBFLUENT\llangit1	Data Flow Task	Validating	2006-10-27 09:08:22...	2006-10-27 09:08:22...	{23648C2...	{39E5A358-7...	0	
Progress	WEBFLUENT\llangit1	Execute SQL Task	Executing query "use master".	2006-10-27 09:08:22...	2006-10-27 09:08:22...	{A3E50F1...	{39E5A358-7...	100	
Progress	WEBFLUENT\llangit1	Data Flow Task	Validating	2006-10-27 09:08:22...	2006-10-27 09:08:22...	{23648C2...	{39E5A358-7...	33	
Progress	WEBFLUENT\llangit1	Execute SQL Task	Executing query "use master".	2006-10-27 09:08:22...	2006-10-27 09:08:22...	{A3E50F1...	{39E5A358-7...	100	
Progress	WEBFLUENT\llangit1	Data Flow Task	Validating	2006-10-27 09:08:22...	2006-10-27 09:08:22...	{23648C2...	{39E5A358-7...	66	
Progress	WEBFLUENT\llangit1	Execute SQL Task	Executing query "use master".	2006-10-27 09:08:22...	2006-10-27 09:08:22...	{A3E50F1...	{39E5A358-7...	100	

Figure 9-13. *A new destination for SSIS package logs is a SQL Server Profiler trace (or .trc) file.*

Whatever your business requirements for logging execution results in your SSIS packages, SSIS 2005 has the flexibility to meet your needs. At this point, I need to remind you about the data flow Audit task. It is quite common in BI solutions for SSIS logging to include requirements regarding logging data lineage. The Audit transformation discussed in Chapter 8 allows you to capture selected types of information during the execution of your SSIS package.

Another consideration when implementing logging is the configuration of error handling. We'll cover this in the next section.

Error Handling

By default, one error is permitted in an SSIS package or control flow task. If this default is exceeded, then either the control flow task or the entire package will halt execution and return failure. You can change the number of allowed errors at either the control flow task or the entire package level by configuring the `MaximumErrorCount` property at the appropriate level.

You also can configure several additional properties that control the error behavior. Following is a list and brief explanation (all are shown in Figure 9-14 in the task Properties dialog box as well) of each of these six properties:

- `FailPackageOnFailure`: This means to fail the entire package on the first task or transformation failure.
- `FailParentOnFailure`: This means to fail the parent package or task if this, the child package or task, fails.
- `ForcedExecutionValue`: This means return the actual result of the `ForceExecutionValue` for the package (if that value has been set to `true`).
- `ForcedExecutionValueType`: This is the data type of the `ForcedExecutionValue` property.
- `ForceExecutionResult`: This is the result from a `TaskHost` container.
- `ForceExecutionValue`: This means force or always try to execute the package; the default is `false`.

Tip For a more detailed explanation of all six properties, see the BOL topic "Setting Package Properties."

Properties	
Execute SQL Task Task	
BypassPrepare	False
CodePage	1252
Connection	webfluent\cert.TestingSSIS|
DelayValidation	**False**
Description	**Execute SQL Task**
Disable	**False**
DisableEventHandlers	**False**
ExecValueVariable	<none>
Expressions	
FailPackageOnFailure	**False**
FailParentOnFailure	**False**
ForcedExecutionValue	**0**
ForcedExecutionValueType	**Int32**
ForceExecutionResult	**None**
ForceExecutionValue	False
ID	{A3E50F14-2C90-4C5F-B83
IsolationLevel	**Serializable**
IsStoredProcedure	False
LocaleID	**English (United States)**
LoggingMode	**UseParentSetting**
MaximumErrorCount	**1**

Figure 9-14. *By configuring the* `MaximumErrorCount` *and the other properties that affect error handling (*`Fail – Forced`*), you have complete control over error-handling results in your SSIS packages.*

In additon to specifying how you want a package's or a particular control flow task's errors handled, you also can configure error handling for most data flows. This is done by right-clicking the data source or destination icon on the Data Flow design surface, clicking Edit on the shortcut menu, and then clicking Error Output in the dialog box. This custom configuration is available only for the OLE DB, Excel, Flat File, and XML data flow sources.

This selection brings up a dialog box (see Figure 9-15) that allows you to configure error output for each column in the data flow source or destination item. For each column, you have three choices for errors or truncations (truncations mean conversions that could result in data loss due to narrowing of the destination data type, for example, using a ten-character string source and a two-character string destination): Ignore Failure, Redirect Row, and Fail Component. Following are more complete descriptions of each option:

- *Ignore Failure*: The error (or truncation) is ignored, and the row is sent to the output of the transformation or source.

- *Redirect Row*: The error (or truncation) row is sent to the error output of the source, transformation, or destination.

- *Fail Component*: The data flow task will fail whenever an error or a truncation occurs. Fail Component is the default value.

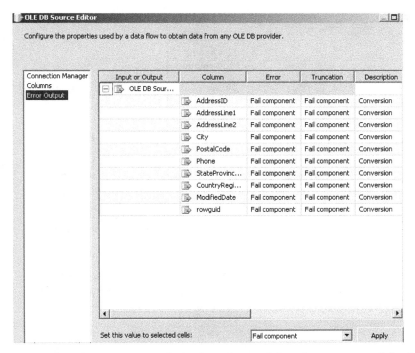

Figure 9-15. *The error output dialog box of several data flow source and destination types allows you to specify the error behavior of your package at the level of individual column errors. You have three options to chose from: Fail Component (default), Redirect Row, or Ignore Failure.*

In addition to configuring logging and error handling, you can add control flows in response to various event handlers firing in your packges via the BIDS interface. We'll cover the details of doing this in the next section.

Event Handlers

SSIS 2005 includes an easy method for you to use from inside BIDS that allows you to add custom control flows to your SSIS packages as a result of package or control flow task events firing. To do this, click the Event Handlers tab of the SSIS BIDS designer. You'll see the Executable drop-down list and the Event handler drop-down list. In the Executable list, select either the entire package or a specific control flow task. In the Event handler list, select the particular event for which you want to design a control flow. An example of creating a simple control flow for a data flow task using the OnProgress event is shown in Figure 9-16.

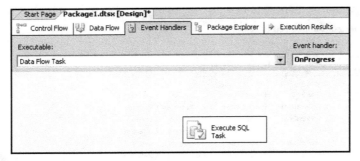

Figure 9-16. *The Event Handlers tab of the SSIS designer allows you to easily create control flows that are associated with a particular event handler for the entire package or for a particular event handler for a control flow task.*

Tip The most commonly used event handler is OnError. Your BI scenario may have requirements that call for the use of one of the other event handlers. BOL has a detailed description of each type of event handler under the topic "Integration Services Event Handlers." All the events are also listed in this section.

After you've created a control flow for a particular event handler that event name text is shown in bold on the drop-down list called Event handler on the right side of the BIDS design surface (as shown previously in Figure 9-16). The list of events available in the SSIS event handler interface is as follows:

- OnError is raised by an executable when an error occurs.

- OnExecStatusChanged is raised by an executable when its execution status changes.

- OnInfomation is raised during validation or execution of an executable and displays only information, not errors or warnings.

- OnPostExecute is raised by an executable after it has completed running.

- OnPostValidate is raised by an executable after it has completed validation.

- OnPreExecute is raised by an executable before it runs.

- OnPreValidate is raised by an executable when its validation starts.

- OnProgress is raised by an executable when it makes measurable progress.

- OnQueryCancel is raised by an executable to decide whether it should stop.

- OnTaskFailed is raised by a task when it fails.

- OnVariableValueChanged is raised by an executable when the value of an associated variable changes.

- OnWarning is raised by an executable when a warning runs.

As with many other aspects of SSIS, you can, of course, create event handlers programatically. BOL has complete descriptions and sample code if you want to do this.

Deploying the Package and Configuring Runtime Settings

When you've completed implementing your SSIS package (or packages) in BIDS, you'll next want to deploy the package to a testing and, eventually, into a production environment. To start this process, you must first validate the SSIS packages you've created in BIDS by working with the SSIS project menu. When you right-click the SSIS project name in the Solution Explorer, three options are available: Build, Rebuild, and Clean. What exactly do these options do?

To understand this you need to understand what exactly you are creating in the SSIS designer. Although you are working visually, you are creating an executable file. As with SSAS and SSIS 2005, the underlying object model has been completely rearchitected as compared to DTS 2000. The code that you are writing when you create an SSIS package is a dialect of XML.

If you want to view this XML, right-click any .dtsx package in the Solution Explorer and then click View Code. You'll see something similar to Figure 9-17.

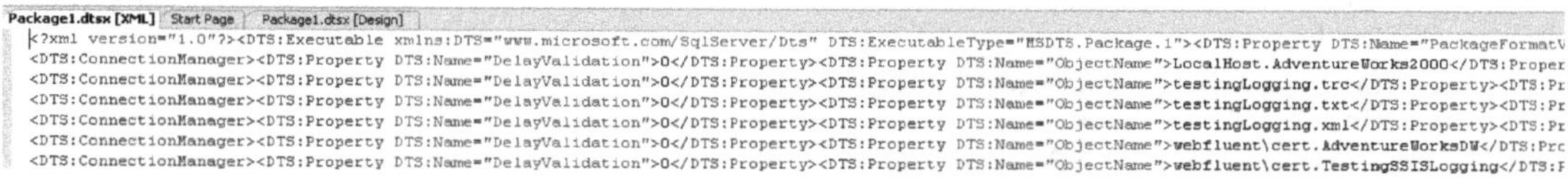

Figure 9-17. *You are actually creating XML metadata when you visually design .dtsx packages using the SSIS template in BIDS.*

Note that you're validating either the entire output or the changed output of each XML file for each .dtsx package against the associated specialized XSD schema when you select the Build or Rebuild options in Solution Explorer. Rebuild includes the Clean functionality in SSIS. If there are validation errors, BIDS will show them to you in the Error List window so that you can resolve those errors prior to package deployment.

After your package or packages have been built successfully, your next step is to deploy them to a testing or production server. You have a couple of different options for deploying your packages.

SSIS Package Deployment Options

Although you could deploy and run your SSIS packages manually, you'll rarely manage and execute your SSIS packages this way unless you are in a development and testing environment. Rather, you'll prefer to automate and run your packages in most production BI environments.

BIDS includes a Package Installation Wizard (tool) that can simplify deployment of your SSIS packages. To deploy your package using the SSIS Package Installation Wizard, you first set the package properties by right-clicking the SSIS project name in the Solution Explorer and selecting Properties. Set the CreateDeploymentUtility property to true, and then build your project. This will create an SSIS manifest file at the location configured in the DeploymentOutputPath property as shown in Figure 9-18.

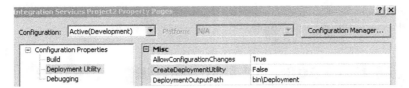

Figure 9-18. *Configure the* `CreateDeploymentUtiltiy` *property to generate an SSIS manifest file.*

Next, you locate the manifest file (which has the name format of `<ProjectName>.SSISDeploymentManifest` and contains package metadata in an XML format), and double-click it. This launches the SSIS Deployment Utility Wizard. Using the wizard, you can select whether to have your packages deployed to the file system or SQL Server. You can also optionally validate packages after installation. The Deploy SSIS Packages section of the Package Installation Wizard is shown in Figure 9-19. If you choose to validate your package, then a Package Validation section in the wizard will list invalid or inefficient task configurations in your package.

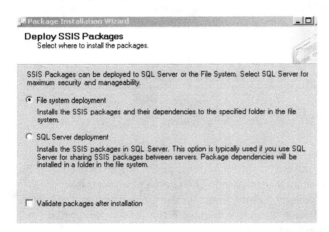

Figure 9-19. *You can select the destination for installation for your SSIS packages using the Package Installation Wizard.*

Another option for package deployment is to use the command-line tool dtutil.exe to copy, move, delete, or take other actions on your SSIS package. You will often choose this option in production because you can script SSIS package deployment with this tool. The syntax for this command is shown in Figure 9-20.

Still another option for deployment is to simply import the packages into the desired location. You do this using SSMS by right-clicking the node in the SSIS tree (file, MSDB, and so on) and then clicking Import Package. Figure 9-21 in the next section shows the SSMS SSIS interface.

After you've deployed your packages to one of the three possible locations—SQL Server MSDB (Multisource Database), default file system, or specified location on the file system—then you have a couple of choices about how you'll run them.

```
C:\WINDOWS\system32\cmd.exe
C:\Documents and Settings\llangit>dtutil /?
Microsoft (R) SQL Server SSIS Package Utilities
Version 9.00.1399.06 for 32-bit
Copyright (C) Microsoft Corp 1984-2004. All rights reserved.


Usage: DTUtil /option [value] [/option [value]] ...
Options are case-insensitive.
A hyphen (-) may be used in place of a forward slash (/).
The vertical bar (|) is the OR operator and is used to list possible values.
For extended help use /help with an option.  For example: DTUtil /help Copy

/C[opy]              {SQL | FILE | DTS};Path
/Dec[rypt]           Password
/Del[ete]
/DestP[assword]      Password
/DestS[erver]        Server
/DestU[ser]          User name
/DT[S]               PackagePath
/En[crypt]           {SQL | FILE | DTS};Path;ProtectionLevel[;Password]
/Ex[ists]
/FC[reate]           {SQL | DTS};ParentFolderPath;NewFolderName
/FDe[lete]           {SQL | DTS};ParentFolderPath;FolderName
/FDi[rectory]        {SQL | DTS}[;FolderPath[;S]]
/FE[xists]           {SQL | DTS};FolderPath
/FR[ename]           {SQL | DTS};ParentFolderPath;OldFolderName;NewFolderName
/Fi[le]              Filespec
/H[elp]              [Option]
/I[DRegenerate]
/M[ove]              {SQL | FILE | DTS};Path
/Q[uiet]
/R[emark]            [Text]
/Si[gn]              {SQL | FILE | DTS};Path;Hash
/SourceP[assword]    Password
/SourceS[erver]      Server
/SourceU[ser]        User name
/SQ[L]               PackagePath
```

Figure 9-20. *The command-line tool dtutil.exe allows you to script actions on your SSIS packages.*

SSIS Package Execution Options

A first option for package execution is to use SSMS. This method of SSIS package execution is usually primarily used for development and testing. The second and third options are to use either a GUI package execution tool (dtexecui.exe), which runs outside of SSMS, or to use a command-line tool, which also runs outside of SSMS (dtexec.exe). The latter two are the preferred methods in production environments.

To run SSIS packages from within SSMS, you'll first connect to SSIS from SSMS. Once connected, you can view a list of packages grouped by storage location and then configure execution properties for any package you want to execute. You then right-click any package to execute it. Figure 9-21 shows a connection to SSIS in SSMS. Note that you can view packages in two locations: file system or MSDB nodes in Object Explorer.

A large number of configurable runtime properties are available for packages in SSMS. For example, Figure 9-22 shows the reporting options for packages. The Reporting options include selecting the level of verbosity for logging console events and the type of information to capture in console logs.

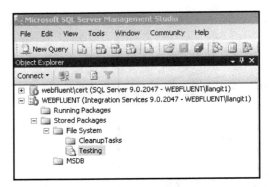

Figure 9-21. *You can view SSIS packages grouped by storage location, configure execution properties, and execute packages after connecting to SSIS in SSMS.*

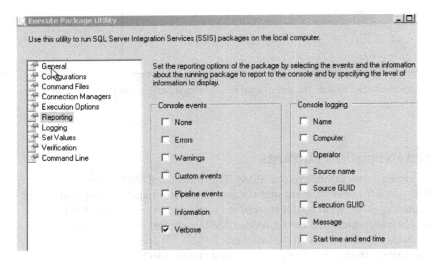

Figure 9-22. *The Execute Package Utility dialog box in SSMS allows you to configure many types of reporting events and logs for each executing package.*

Continuing with another example, Figure 9-23 shows the Log providers configuration area. In production, business requirements often drive logging requirements for your production SSIS packages. Sometimes this will be more formal than others; that is, you may be subject to regulatory requirements such as SOX, HIPPA, and so on.

After you've executed the associated package as least once, one way to view the logs that you have configured in the procedure described previously is to right-click the top node (SSIS) in SSMS and then click View Logs. You'll see the output similar to what is shown in Figure 9-24.

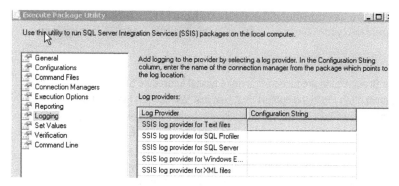

Figure 9-23. *By using the logging section of the Execute Package Utility dialog box, you can associate one or more logs with the package.*

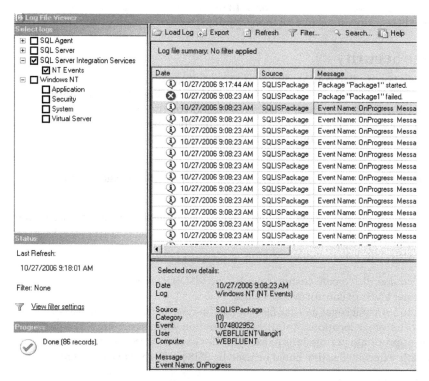

Figure 9-24. *You can view any logs that you've configured via the Execute Package Utility in SSMS by right-clicking the top node (SSIS) in SSMS and then clicking View Logs.*

As you may have noticed, you can configure many additional runtime package properties by using the Execute Package Utility dialog box. In production systems, the most commonly configured properties belong to the Connection Managers, Reporting, and Logging categories of the Execute Package Utility properties. Microsoft has created five SSRS reports to help you understand SSIS log data. You can download these reports from http://www.microsoft.com/ downloads/details.aspx?familyid=526e1fce-7ad5-4a54-b62c-13ffcd114a73&displaylang=en.

Tip After you move your BI solution to production, it is more typical to execute SSIS packages by using scripts. These scripts are most often run in the context of dtexec.exe. You can run these scripts from the command line, you can use Windows Task Scheduler to regularly schedule these executables, or you can use SQL Server Agent jobs to schedule these executables. Also, you can start the Execute Package Utility outside of SSMS by running dtexecui.exe for the GUI version or dtexec.exe for the command-line verison. As with other command-line tools, in production, you'll often use dtexec.exe (rather than the SSMS GUI) because you can more easily automate package execution via scripts using the command-line tool.

Of course, another important consideration with deployment of packages is security. We'll look at the SSIS security model in a bit more depth in the next section of this chapter.

SSIS Package Security

The security options you have to consider for your SSIS packages depend on where you choose to store them. You have three options: within a SQL Server instance in the MSDB, in the default location on the file system, or in a named location on the file system.

If you choose to store your packages in MSDB (which is the most typical case for production solutions), then you can use the built-in SQL Server security roles to limit access to your packages:

- db_dtsadmin: This role has full administrative rights on all SSIS packages stored in MSDB.

- db_dtsltduser: This role can view, execute, change, or export only its own packages and can import any packages.

- db_dtsoperator: This role can view, execute, and export packages.

You could, of course, also create custom roles for the MSDB if your business requirements call for more granular levels of control over packages.

If you choose to store packages as .dtsx files on the file system, then you will assign NTFS permissions to those storage locations. Another consideration when assigning NTFS permissions is assigning appropriate permissions to external files used by SSIS packages. Some examples of possible external files that could be used by SSIS packages are listed here:

- *Data source files*: Excel, Text, XML

- *Configuration files*: XML, Text, SQL scripts

- *Package execution log files*: Text, XML, trace files

Another aspect of securing your SSIS packages involves configuring the ProtectionLevel property of the package. Here you'll specify whether sensitive data should be protected by encryption, or whether the sensitive data should be removed before saving the package by choosing one of the following options:

- `DontSaveSensitive`: Removes any data that is tagged as "sensitive" from the package when it is saved. When the package is opened, after having been saved with this protection level, the end user must provide the values for the properties that were marked sensitive.

- `EncryptSensitiveWithUserKey`: Encrypts sensitive package data with a key from the user profile. Only the same user with the same profile can run the package. This is the default option for SSIS packages.

- `EncryptSensitiveWithPassword`: Encrypts sensitive package data with a user-supplied password. To run the package, the end user must supply the password.

- `EncryptAllWithPassword`: Encrypts all package data with a user-supplied password. To run the package, the end user must supply the password.

- `EncryptAllWithKey`: Encrypts all package data with a key from the user profile. Only the same user with the same profile can run the package.

- `ServerStorage`: Protects the package based on SQL server database roles. This option is only available for packages stored in MSDB.

Note You cannot control which property values are considered sensitive. SSIS sensitive information includes the password portion of connection strings, some XML node information, and certain other properties, according to BOL "The marking of variables (as sensitive) is controlled by Integration Services."

Although you set the initial package protection level when designing the package in BIDS, you can update this setting after the package has been deployed. Some of the `ProtectionLevel` options require that you associate a password with your package. You do this by configuring the `PackagePassword` property.

The final security option you can consider is whether you need to guarantee the integrity of packages, or to more formally prevent tampering with the contents of packages. If this is a requirement for your project, you'll sign your packages with certificates. This option requires associating a certificate that has been created for code-signing purposes with your package. To do this in BIDS, you choose SSIS ➤ Digital Signing, and then click the Sign... button. A Select Certificate dialog box appears. You select the appropriate certificate and then click OK twice.

Placing Checkpoints

A new capability in SSIS 2005 is checkpointing within packages. *Checkpointing* refers to placing a checkpoint, or a marker, in the control flow so that if that package fails, you can restart the package from the point of failure. Execution information is saved into a checkpoint file. Figure 9-25 shows this property option. If you choose to use checkpointing in SSIS packages, then you'll want to include this capability in the initial package design of all affected packages.

Figure 9-25. *To enable checkpointing in a package, you must set the* CheckpointUsage *property to either* IfExists *or* Always *and then set three other properties.*

To implement checkpointing in your SSIS package, you must configure four properties:

- CheckpointUsage: This must be set to IfExists or Always.

- CheckpointFileName: This is the path to the checkpoint file.

- SaveCheckpoints: This must be set to True to enable package checkpoints.

- FailPackageOnFailure: This must set to True to enable package checkpoints.

■**Caution** Checkpointing only allows package restart for failures that occur during the execution of control flow tasks. You must implement other error-handling and recovery methods to recover from data flow transformation failures. Also, if the checkpoint file is deleted or altered, it cannot be used for recovery.

One method of recovering from data flow task failures is to use transactions. We'll get a brief introduction to this very advanced technique in the next section.

Using Transactions in SSIS Packages

SSIS packages support the grouping of tasks into transactions by using one of two methods. You can either use the Distributed Transaction Coordinator (DTC), or you can use the transactions that are built in to SQL Server 2005 or any other Relational Database Management System (RDMS), such as Oracle. The primary factor to consider is the span of the tasks. If your business needs call for transactions that must go across multiple data sources or connections, then you must use DTC transactions. If your transactions will take place within the same RDMS, such as SQL Server, then you can use RDMS-native transactions. For our example, we'll discuss SQL Server transactions.

To use DTC transactions, you must ensure that the DTC service is installed and running (use Services in Control Panel). You then configure the transaction option at a package or task level by setting the TransactionOption property to either Required or Supported. You'll also use sequence containers within SSIS as transactional boundaries.

■**Note** You can also configure the TransactionOption property to the value NotSupported to specifically exclude a component from participating in a package transaction.

The TransactionOption property for an SSIS package is shown in Figure 9-26. You also may configure the IsolationLevel property for the transaction. The IsolationLevel property setting affects the locking behavior of the involved data sources during the execution of the transaction.

Figure 9-26. *If your SSIS package needs to support transactions at the task or package level, you configure the* TransactionOption *property value to either* Required *or* Supported *for the task or the package.*

If you want to use native SQL transactions in your SSIS packge, all tasks participating in the transaction must be configured to use the same Connection Manager. Then you must first configure the RetainSameConnection property of that Connection Manager to the value true, and then you simply use the T-SQL Begin Transaction syntax within your package. The T-SQL transaction syntax should include a Begin Transaction and a Commit Transaction statement at minimum. It will typically also include at least one Rollback Transaction statement as well; this code would, of course, be most often encapsulated in a T-SQL stored procedure called from an SSIS Execute SQL Task control flow task inside of the particular SSIS package of interest.

Summary

We've now completed our tour of SSIS. From the simple, for example, using the Import/Export Wizard to quickly move data between a source and a destination, to the complex, for example, transactional data workflows, SSIS really does it all. SSIS is an invaluable tool for implementing BI solutions.

Now we move on to an equally complex and important topic for BI solutions—Multidimensional Expressions (MDX). In the next chapter, we'll begin to explore the intricacies of MDX, the native query language for SSAS.

CHAPTER 10

■ ■ ■

Introduction to MDX

In this chapter, we'll work with Multidimensional Expressions (MDX), which is the native query language for SSAS. MDX is a SQL-like language used to query SSAS cubes.

Although there will be situations that cause you to write MDX expressions or queries "from scratch," the design of the BIDS interface really minimizes your need to author much of the MDX that you'll need for your BI project in this way. A large number of MDX templates, samples, and wizards are available in BIDS and SSMS for you to use and customize.

Unlike working with relational databases where you are probably accustomed to authoring many T-SQL scripts, when working with SSAS cubes, you need more of a reading than a writing knowledge of MDX for typical BI projects. Given that framework, in this chapter, we'll cover:

- Understanding basic MDX query syntax

- Adding calculated members, script commands, and named sets to your cubes

- Understanding the most commonly used MDX functions

- Understanding MDX functions that are new to SSAS 2005

- Adding .NET assemblies to your SSAS project

Understanding Basic MDX Query Syntax

To understand basic MDX syntax, we'll discuss some core OLAP terms used in SSAS:

- *Cube*: Also called an implementation of the UDM (Unified Dimensional Model), this is the core structure in SSAS. Unlike in previous versions, in SSAS 2005, it will be most typical for all of your enterprise data to be placed in a single cube. MDX also contains the concept of subcubes, which, as the name suggests, are subsets of your enterprise cube.

- *Dimension*: In this version of SSAS, a dimension is a collection of attributes. You can think of it as being based on a group of columns from one or more source tables. The default member of a dimensional attribute is the first member loaded into the dimension. For example, for a customer's dimension, last name attribute, the first value would be alphabetized, so customer "Aand" would appear first by default. You can adjust the default member for a dimensional attribute for all users of the dimension, or you can adjust this value for members of particular SSAS security groups.

- *Hierarchy*: This is an optional grouping of dimensional attributes into a rollup grouping. Hierarchies can either be "regular" (or "pyramid-like"), which means that as you travel downward, each lower level has progressively more members, or "irregular" (or "ragged"), which means that as you travel downward, lower levels don't always have more members.

  An example of an irregular hierarchy can be found in some Geography dimensions. You may have a hierarchy that consists of the following levels: All, Country, State, and City. You may have data in your dimension source table for particular countries that do not have any states.

  You can create as many hierarchies of dimensional attributes as are needed to satisfy the business requirements of your project. It is quite common to have several hierarchies in certain dimensions, such as time, where you might have a Calendar Time, Fiscal Time, 4-5-4 (retail) Time, and so on.

Note In SSAS 2005, hierarchies are optional and flexible (as compared to SSAS 2000 where they were both rigid and required). Hierarchies are either created automatically by the Cube Wizard (based on inferences made against the source data), or manually when you build your cube.

- *Level*: This is a position in the hierarchy. For example, in a time dimension, it is typical to have a year, quarter, month, and day level. You could, of course, also have a half-year level or a week level in your particular time dimension. You can think of levels as being based on column names from the source table or tables for the dimension. The default level for every dimension is the top or "All" level. You can adjust which level appears by default—either for everyone or for members of particular security groups.

- *Data member*: This is the actual dimensional data value for an attribute or the member of a level. Another way to think of this is as a particular cell value in your cube. For example, "July 25, 1975" is a member of the time dimension at the day level. As mentioned earlier, by default, the first member loaded into an attribute value is the one that all end users will see in their dimension and cube browser.

- *Measure*: In the world of MDX, a measure is just another dimension. It does, however, have three particular characteristics:

  - The first is that the measures dimension has containers called measure groups to associate measures of a similar type or from a particular source fact table together. These measure groups are *not* levels; they are simply display containers.

  - The second characteristic is that the measures dimension is always flat; that is, it never has any hierarchies. A couple of examples of measures would be "Internet Gross Sales" and "Internet Freight Costs." There is, of course, an "All" level, but this has little meaning in the measures dimension and is hidden by default.

- The third characteristic is that nearly all cube browser clients display measures by default in an area called "data," rather than on the rows, columns or filter areas, as other dimension data are displayed. So, measures have a particular default display location in most pivot-table style OLAP client applications. Also, as with other types of dimensional attributes, the first measure created is the one that is displayed in client applications by default. As with other attributes, this can easily be adjusted either globally or for particular groups of end users. You should also remember that measures originate from facts (or rows) in one or more source fact tables. Very frequently in the OLAP literature, the terms *measures* and *facts* are used interchangeably.

Figure 10-1 shows a sample dimension to help illustrate some of the terms in the preceding list. The dimension name is Time, the hierarchy name is Calendar Time, the selected level name is the Calendar Quarter level, and the selected level member is Q1 CY 2003. You can also see the Month and Day levels, with the Data Member value "February 1, 2003" being the lowest level value viewable in the figure.

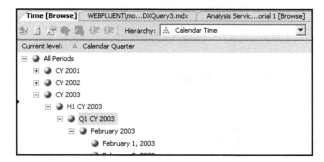

Figure 10-1. *It's important to understand the terms—dimension, hierarchy, level, and member— when beginning to write MDX queries.*

Your next consideration when working with MDX is to understand its basic syntax. Like T-SQL, MDX is *not* case sensitive or space sensitive. Also, similar to T-SQL, you can add comments to MDX script commands by using the -- (double dash – to comment out single lines) or the /* (to comment out multiple lines, used at the beginning *and* end of the commented section) syntax.

New to SSMS 2005 is an integrated MDX query tool. (In SSAS 2000, the MDX query tool was accessed as a separate item, like the Query Analyzer for T-SQL queries.) To access this tool, you connect to SSAS using SSMS, and then click the Analysis Services MDX query button on the toolbar. You also have access to a set of MDX query templates in SSMS. The MDX Template Explorer in SSMS is shown in Figure 10-2.

Tip The Template Explorer is not displayed by default in SSMS. To open this window, you can either click the MDX button (second-to-last) on the toolbar, or from the choose View ➤ Template Explorer. To display MDX templates in the Template Explorer, click the Cube button on the toolbar inside the Template Explorer.

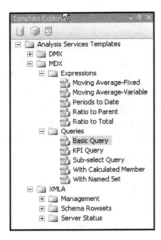

Figure 10-2. *SSMS includes an MDX query execution environment and an MDX template tool with commonly used MDX sample queries and expressions.*

Note What is the difference between an *MDX query* and an *MDX expression*? A query returns a result set, which is called a *cellset* in MDX. Cellsets are displayed in a tabular format in SSMS. An expression evauates to one or more values. Expression templates in SSMS create objects such as *calculated members*, and those calculated members are included in an MDX query as part of the template—so that you can view the result of the expression. Calculated members will be explained in the "Defining Calculated Members" section of this chapter.

Another useful enhancement to the SSMS environment is the inclusion of an SSAS meta-data browser. This allows you to drag and drop cubes, dimensions, hierarchies, levels, or members into MDX queries or query templates. It is nearly always quicker to drag and drop dimension, hierarchy, level, and member names to the query surface than to type them because of the object-naming syntax requirements for MDX objects. It is quite tedious to type object names.

Manually typed object names can also be a source of code errors. One example of this is the use of square brackets to qualify portions of object names. Strictly speaking, qualifiers, or square brackets, are only required if object names contain embedded spaces or are keywords; however, every GUI tool throughout the BI suite puts square brackets around every object name, which is, in fact, a best coding practice. So, if you drag and drop a measure, dimensional attribute, and so on from any of the metadata browser areas to the MDX query design area, then square brackets will always be added automatically for you.

Another example is the peculiarity of MDX that results in object attributes sometimes being listed by name (or string value) and, at other times, being listed by number (or ordinal position). This is determined based on whether or not member values have been designated as unique at a particular level in a dimensional hierarchy. Because of vagaries like this,

dragging and dropping objects from MDX metadata browsers to query windows is a best practice when you are creating MDX queries or MDX expressions. Figure 10-3 shows the SSAS
metadata browser included in SSMS.

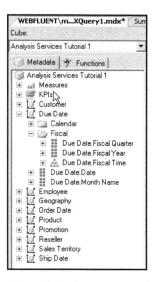

Figure 10-3. *The SSAS metadata browser included in the SSMS MDX query window allows you to
drag and drop cube objects such as measures, KPIs, or dimensions into the MDX query window.*

Now that you've learned a bit about the MDX query environment, you're probably
anxious to write your first query. Before you do that, however, take a minute to explore the
automatic query-writing capabilities of the built-in cube browser (either in BIDS or SSMS).
Many common queries are available from the shortcut menu on the cube browser surface.
To access the cube browser from within SSMS, you right-click any cube in the Cubes folder in
Object Explorer and then click Browse.

As mentioned in the introduction to this chapter, SSAS requires mostly reading (rather
than writing) knowledge of MDX, so before you "jump in" to the world of MDX queries, make
sure you've exhausted the built-in capabilites of the cube browser in SSMS, which is identical
to the cube browser built in to the BIDS interface. In the cube browser, you can sort, filter, and
drill-through cube data, and more. The most useful shortcut menu option is Show As. It allows
you to see the selected measure in five alternate configurations (Percent of Row Total, Percent
of Parent Item, and so on).

Tip New to SSAS 2005 is the ability to use SQL Server Profiler to capture activity on SSAS. If you want
to create template queries using the built-in Show As menu options in the SSAS cube browser, then just
turn on Profiler before you run those queries, and you'll be able to capture the generated MDX statements
in your trace.

Writing Your First MDX Query

The best place to start when you are ready to write your first MDX query is with the MDX templates. You'll work in SSMS with the MDX interface to do this. Figure 10-4 shows a simple query. As mentioned, MDX uses a syntax that is similar to T-SQL. We'll start with the FROM portion of the example—FROM most generally takes a cube name as a source. New in 2005, the FROM clause can also reference a subcube (that is written in the form of a nested SELECT statement).

Next is the SELECT clause. You'll note the on Columns and on Rows clauses—these clauses take axis values and are used to "flatten" the results (or cellset) into a table structure. You can include up to 128 axes in the SELECT clause. If you include multiple hierarchies on the same axis, then the result set will display those results combined on whichever axis (that is, columns or rows) you've chosen to combine them on.

You will sometimes see queries that use the shortcut syntax on 0 (for columns) and on 1 (for rows). You must, however, reference axis values in order; that is, if you want to use an on Rows clause, then you must include an on Columns clause in your query.

The WHERE clause functions similarly (but not identically) to a T-SQL WHERE, in that it "slices" the cube along an axis. You can visualize this slice as literally a slice (or portion) of a cube. In the query shown in Figure 10-4, we are restricting the returned measure value to a count of only those Products that exist in the Product Line name that start with the letter "R". You can have more than one member in a slice, but each member must come from a different dimension. The WHERE clause member illustrates the member-naming concept discussed in the previous section; that is, the member is listed by ordinal or position in the list of attribute members that starts (at the default ordering) or the letter "R" (&[R]) rather than by actual full name.

You may have expected the rows and columns in this query to show a list of all members in the Customer and Time dimensions; however, MDX is NOT identical to T-SQL. What's being shown is the default member of those dimensions (which is, in this case, the "All" member).

Note Also the default member of the measures dimension is being shown. The default member of the measures dimension is the first measure added to the cube. You can adjust the defaultMember property of the measures dimension to something other than the first member added to the cube, or you could include a specific member name is your query, if that is what you want to see returned in your query. Also you can assign particular default members to particular end users by creating SSAS security roles. SSAS security roles are covered in Chapter 13.

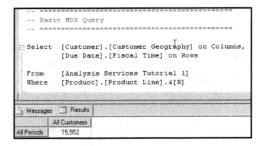

Figure 10-4. *A simple MDX query using SSMS. Note that the default members of the* Customers, Time, *and* Measures *dimensions are returned by this simple query.*

So, to return a list of members, rather the (single) default member, from a dimension as a result of your query, you need to understand two additional concepts: tuples and sets.

Members, Tuples, and Sets

As described in the "Understanding Basic MDX Query Syntax" section of this chapter, a data *member* is an item in a dimension of a cube. In MDX, a member is designated by listing the position of the item in the dimension members between square brackets with periods separating the levels in the dimensional hierarchy. Here's an example: `[Time].[Years].[2004]`.

■ **Tip** Square brackets surrounding object names are required only for certain conditions, for example, object names that have spaces in them and object names that use reserved keywords. However, it's common in MDX queries to put square brackets around *all* object names. I would suggest that you follow this guideline as a best coding practice.

A *tuple* is a location or a cell in a cube made up of one or more members from each involved hierarchy. In MDX, a tuple is designated by listing the position of all involved dimension members between parentheses, with each member separated by a comma. Here's an example: `( [Time].[Years].[2004], [Measures].[Periods To Date])`.

If you do not specify a complete tuple in an MDX query, then the default member of the dimension will be returned, which is why the default member of all three dimensions is returned in Figure 10-4.

A *set* is a defined portion or subset of a cube that consists of one or more ordered tuples from different dimensions, surrounded by curly braces and separated by commas. Here is an example: `{([Time].[Years].[2004]), ([Product].[Product Line].&[R])}`. Sets can be created by listing tuples, by using MDX set-generating functions, or by some combination of both techniques. If you create a set by using an MDX function rather than by explicitly listing the members, then you do not need to surround your set with curly braces.

In Figure 10-5, you can see a modified version of the original query using the MDX `CHILDREN` function. Note that the result set now displays the data members directly below the top level of the hierarchy for both the `Customer.Customer Geography` and `Due Date.Fiscal Time` dimensions.

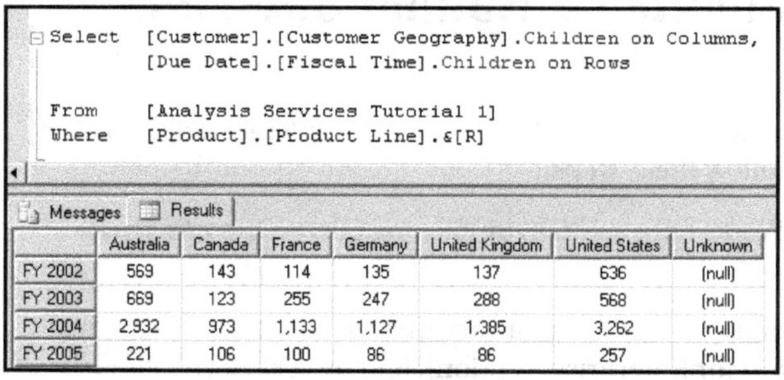

```
Select  [Customer].[Customer Geography].Children on Columns,
        [Due Date].[Fiscal Time].Children on Rows

From    [Analysis Services Tutorial 1]
Where   [Product].[Product Line].&[R]
```


	Australia	Canada	France	Germany	United Kingdom	United States	Unknown
FY 2002	569	143	114	135	137	636	(null)
FY 2003	669	123	255	247	288	568	(null)
FY 2004	2,932	973	1,133	1,127	1,385	3,262	(null)
FY 2005	221	106	100	86	86	257	(null)

Figure 10-5. *You can display the members of a set by using an MDX function in your query. This query uses the* `CHILDREN` *function to do just that.*

SSMS includes an MDX function browser in the MDX query tool interface. This helps you to work with the most commonly used MDX functions. Note that the function browser does *not* contain all MDX functions. If you click and drag any MDX function to the MDX query surface, you'll see the function and any arguments that it takes. Arguments are shown between chevrons (<<and >>). Optional arguments are enclosed in square brackets, such as [<<optional argument>>]. MDX functions are color-coded in brown text on the MDX query surface; MDX keywords are colored blue. The SSMS function browser is shown in Figure 10-6.

░**Tip** You may use IntelliSense in the design surface by clicking Edit ➤ IntelliSense ➤ List Members. After you select a function, a tooltip will pop up on the design surface with a brief description of what the function does.

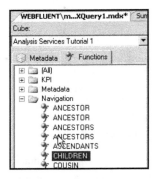

Figure 10-6. *The SSMS MDX query area includes an MDX function browser. When you drag the function to the query surface, an argument list will be generated as well.*

Although authoring and executing MDX queries in SSMS is helpful to learning MDX syntax, this is not the most common production task you'll use in your BI solutions. In the next section, we'll discuss the Calculations tab in BIDS, which is where you'll do most of your MDX work. Here you'll add MDX calculated members, named sets, or script commands.

Adding Calculated Members, Named Sets, and Script Commands

The interface for adding MDX objects to your SSAS cube has been completely redesigned in SSAS 2005. To access this interface, follow these steps:

1. Open the sample AdventureWorks cube in BIDS by clicking File ➤ Open Analysis Services Database.

2. In the Connect to Database dialog box, click your servername and database names (AdventureWorks DW Standard [or Enterprise] Edition), and then click OK.

3. Double-click the AdventureWorks cube in Solution Explorer.

4. Click the Calculations tab in the cube designer.

You will work with three windows in this tab: the Script Organizer, the Calculation Tools, and the (MDX) Script Designer. The Script Organizer contains a list of script objects, listed in the order they will run in your cube. The Calculation Tools window contains the useful metadata browser, function references, and templates (similar to what you already worked with in SSMS). The MDX Script Designer window has two views: a guided GUI interface for calculated members (called Form View) and named sets, and a native script window (called Script View) for any of the three types of MDX objects: calculated members, named sets, and MDX script commands. Figure 10-7 shows the Script Organizer section.

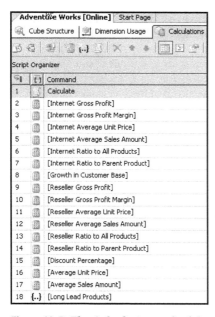

Figure 10-7. *The Calculations tab of the cube designer allows you to add three types of MDX objects to your cube: calculated members, named sets, and MDX script commands.*

Calculated members are very similar to calculated cells in Excel workbooks, in that an expression (in our case, an MDX expression) returns a value that can be displayed for the end user. The key difference is that the MDX expression returns a set of members rather than a single value.

Similiar to cell expressions in Excel, MDX expressions can be created by simply adding, subtracting, and so on existing member values (or tuples). MDX functions also can be used. An example of a calculated member expression (to determine Net Profit) that contains only existing members is [Measures].[Gross Sales] –[Measures].[Expenses].

An example of a calculated member expression (to determine an aggregated or combined value for a certain amount of time periods to date) that contains two MDX functions (Aggregate and PeriodToDate) is a bit more complex:

```
Aggregate (PeriodsToDate([<<Target Dimension>>].[<<Target ➥
Hierarchy>>].[<<Target Level>>],[<<Target Dimension>>].
[<<Target Hierarchy>>].CurrentMember),[Measures].[<<Target Measure>>])
```

Here's how it works. The Aggregate function combines all results. The PeriodsToDate function takes two dimensions and hierarchies as arguments. For the first argument, you must also supply the level from the dimension that you are interested in, that is, [Time].[CalendarTime].[Quarters]. For the second argument, you must also specify a member. Usually, you are interested in the currently viewed member, so you just use the current member function. For the last argument, you specify which measure you want to aggregate.

Despite the power of MDX (and a certain subset of unique MDX functions), you'll find that some MDX functions are actually similar to those found in Excel, for example, Sum, Mix, Max, Avg.

The Calculation Tools work area in the Calculations tab in BIDS includes an MDX Function reference area and Metadata areas (identical to the ones found in SSMS when executing an MDX query). It also includes a Template area. The MDX templates in BIDS are different from the ones available in SSMS. In BIDS, the MDX templates are examples of calculated measures or named sets (rather than MDX queries as are available in SSMS), and the BIDS templates are organized by business scenario. The Templates tab of the Financial section of the Calculation Tools area in BIDS is shown in Figure 10-8. All of these templates are examples of calculated measures, as indicated by the small calculator-shaped icon next to each one.

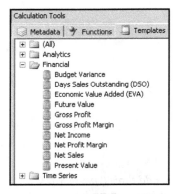

Figure 10-8. *The Calculation Tools section on the Calculate tab in BIDS includes many templates for calculated measures. These are grouped by business scenario, that is, Financial, Time Series, and so on.*

To take a closer look at the MDX syntax associated with a calculated member, you can double-click the first example in the Script Organizer section of the Calculate tab in BIDS. This will load the MDX associated with the sample calculated measure called Internet Gross Profit into the Form View window. You'll see that calculated measures consist of a couple of items:

- *Parent properties*: This indicates which dimension the member is to be calculated in. Most often, this will be the measures dimension. Because the measures dimension is flat, that is, never has any hierarchies associated with it, you'll leave the parent member property blank in this case.

- *Expression*: This is the MDX expression that will be evaluated to produce the result set. In this case, Internet Gross Profit, we are using a simple subtract between two other members of the measures dimension.

- *Additional properties*: These include formatting, empty display behavior, and visibility. Also, you can further format by adding information to the color or font expressions areas.

Using Calculated Measures

The most interesting question when working with calculated measures is when you should use them. To answer that you should consider the following questions:

- *How frequently will this measure be accessed?* If only a small subset of end users needs access to a measure, consider using a calcuated measure. Performance for calculated measures is very good, much faster than SQL Server retrieving calculated column information out of an OLTP store; however, be aware that calculated measures will not be as fast as retrieving information from a stored measure. If the majority of the end users will access a measure that is not present in the source data, it is preferred to calculate the new measure value during the ETL process, store it in the star schema (fact table), and load it into the cube during cube processing.

- *Am I concerned about increasing cube size?* Storing additional information will add to cube storage space time; using calculated members will not add to it.

- *Am I concerned about increasing cube processing times?* Storing additional information will add to cube processing time; using calculated members will not add to it.

- *Do I need measures that do not aggregate (like averages)?* Calculated measures (unlike stored measures) do not aggregate. A common use of calculated measures is to produce average values for a source set.

- *Do I wish to add the complexity of calculating and storing measures to my ETL processes?* An alternative to creating calculated members by writing MDX expressions is to generate the calculated values during the ETL process, store them in the star schema, and load them into the cube.

- *What is my level of proficiency with MDX?* Although Microsoft does provide some calculated member templates, the reality is that if you intend to add a large number of calculated members, you'll probably have to become pretty familiar with the vagaries of MDX. It is important for you to accurately assess the time you'll spend authoring the MDX expressions if you choose to use this approach.

I've found calculated members to be quick and easy to add cubes and pretty solid in the performance department. In the BI projects I've been involved with, all have used at least a couple of calculated measures, and some of the projects have used tens or even hundreds of them. Figure 10-9 shows an example of a calculated member from the sample Adventure-Works cube in the BIDS Calculations tab, showing just the calculated member designer.

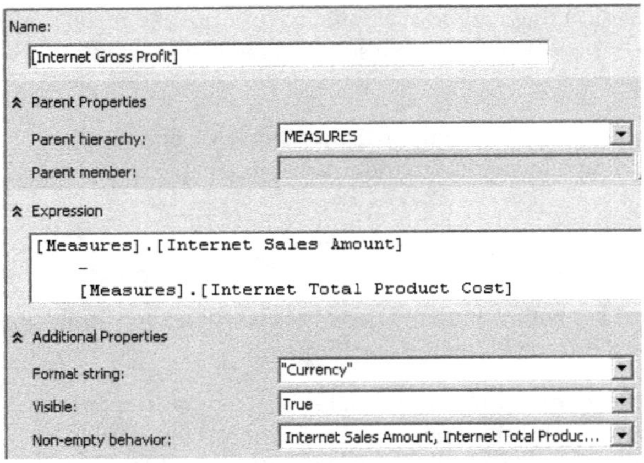

Figure 10-9. *The Calculations tab in BIDS presents you with a graphical interface to help you add calculated members to your cube quickly and easily. This figure shows the Form View section of the Calculations tab.*

If you want to view or edit the complete MDX statement that the calculated member UI builds for you, then you click the small Script View button on the toolbar just below the Calculations tab. You will then be presented with the MDX script for not only the calculated measure that you have been working with but also for all items listed in the Script Organizer window. Figure 10-10 shows the script for the calculated measure shown in the GUI view in Figure 10-9.

```
Create Member CurrentCube.[Measures].[Internet Gross Profit]

  As [Measures].[Internet Sales Amount]
      -
      [Measures].[Internet Total Product Cost],

Format_String = "Currency",
Non_Empty_Behavior = { [Internet Sales Amount],
                       [Internet Total Product Cost] } ;
```

Figure 10-10. *If you click the Script View button in BIDS, you can see the complete MDX script for a calculated measure.*

Tip You can use either `With Member` or `Create Member` when you are creating calculated members. The difference is that `With` creates a temporary member, which only lasts for the duration of that particular MDX query, and `Create` creates a durable member, that is, one that can be viewed by any client application that supports calculated members (most do).

Named Sets

Named sets are simply aliases for sets. Sets consist of one or more tuples that are grouped together to define some portion of the cube. Named sets usually contain tuples from within the same dimension. Named sets are most often used to create filters or slices for your queries. In the cube browser, you place them on the (top) filter portion of the interface to use them as filters. Using the named set called Long Lead Products is shown in Figure 10-11. We'll look at the MDX syntax used to create this named set in the next paragraph of this section.

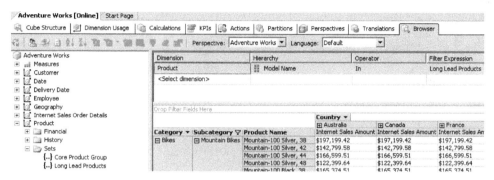

Figure 10-11. *Named sets appear in a Sets folder under the dimension where they are created. To use them in the cube browser in BIDS, drag the named set to the (top) filter portion of the UI.*

If you want to use your named set as a slicer (`WHERE` clause), then you'll have to write an MDX query. Slicers restrict results to the set values included. I've included a query in SSMS using one of the named sets defined for the AdventureWorks sample cube. You'll note that the named set appears in the `WHERE` clause of the MDX query statement as shown in Figure 10-12.

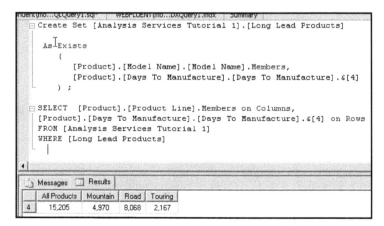

Figure 10-12. *To better understand named sets, you should consider that they are created to be used in the* `WHERE` *(slicer) or* `FILTER` *(which returns the set that results from filtering a set) portion of an MDX query statement.*

> **Note** The MDX Members function returns a list of members at the level immediately below the level specified in the query object; that is, for Product Lines, the members mountain, road, and touring are returned on the columns axis in the sample.

Named sets are really just a convenience (like relational T-SQL views). They allow you to read a specific subset of a cube. Using them can speed up development because they can be used multiple times to refer to complex definitions. They are unlike relational views in that they are *not* security mechanisms. To set security for specific portions of a dimension, you can use SSAS security roles. The procedure for implementing these roles is covered in Chapter 13.

Script Commands

The third type of object that you can add to your SSAS cube via the Calculations tab in BIDS is the MDX script command. This name isn't really accurate, as this feature hasn't been enabled to allow you to add all types of MDX script commands to your cube, rather (usually) one particular type: a script using the MDX Scope keyword.

Similar conceptually to a named set, a script with a Scope keyword allows you to define a subset of your cube (sometimes called a subcube). Unlike a named set, this subcube is usually created so that you can read it and also make changes, or *write*, to it. To enable writing by end users to any portion of the cube, you must enable both the Writeback property and Writeback permissions for the particular portion of the cube of interest.

> **Note** You can also use the MDX keywords Calculate (which creates a subset of a cube, or a subcube) or Freeze (which locks cell values in a subcube) in an MDX script. For more information, see the BOL topics "The Basic MDX Script" and "MDX Scripting Statements."

There are two parts to a script command. The Scope statement creates the subcube. The This function applies whatever change you want to make to the subcube. The sample script called Sales Quota Allocation is a good example of using script commands. Switch to the Script View on the Calculations tab in BIDS, and you'll see two complete script commands (using both the SCOPE and the THIS keywords) as shown in Figure 10-13.

The most common scenario for subcubes is the one shown in this example, that is budget allocations based on past history and other factors. In this script, the Scope statement defines subsets of the cube (called subcubes), and the This keyword applies new values to the named members of the subcube. This example is typical of the reason you would use MDX script commands, that is, to faciliate budgeting "what if" scenarios.

Subcubes are convenient for these kinds of scenarios because business budgeting is typically based on a number of factors, some past known values combined with some future predicted (or unknown) values. These factors often need to be applied to some named subset (or subcube) of your enterprise data.

```
/*-----------------------------------------
| Sales Quota Allocation |
-------------------------------------------

I

/*-- Allocate equally to quarters in H2 FY 2005

 Scope
 (
    [Date].[Fiscal Year].&[2005],
    [Date].[Fiscal].[Fiscal Quarter].Members,
    [Measures].[Sales Amount Quota]
 ) ;

   This = ParallelPeriod
         (
            [Date].[Fiscal].[Fiscal Year], 1,
            [Date].[Fiscal].CurrentMember
         ) * 1.35 ;
```

Figure 10-13. *The new* SCOPE *and* THIS *MDX keywords allow you to create subcubes and write changes to the MOLAP data.*

Note The ParallelPeriod function will be explained in the next section.

Another consideration when using the Calculations tab in BIDS to design MDX script objects is the order you add the script objects. Script commands are evaluated and then executed in the order (top-to-bottom) listed in the Script Organizer window. You can change the order of execution by right-clicking any one script and then clicking Move Up or Move Down. You can also change the order of execution for calculated members (or cells) by using the MDX keyword SOLVE_ORDER inside of the affected script commands.

The final consideration when using the Calculations tab in BIDS to design any of the supported MDX objects—calculated members, named sets, or MDX script commands—is that you now can debug any portion of the resultant script. All MDX objects that you add to your OLAP cube are added by the execution of one, ordered MDX script.

To enable debugging in this script, you must be working with the objects in the Calculations tab in Script View. Once there, you simply click once in the gray margin next to the line of the MDX object for which you want to set a breakpoint. An example is shown in Figure 10-14. While you are in break mode, you can examine the value of variables, as you do in traditional debugging. Also, BIDS presents you with a series of SSAS-specific "watch" windows, where you can execute MDX queries by dragging and dropping items from the metadata browsers to those debugging windows.

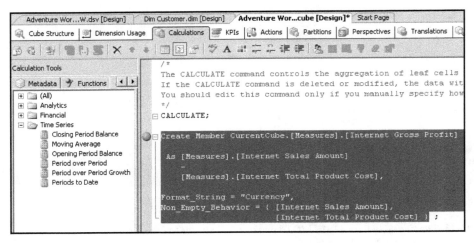

Figure 10-14. *Using the Script View in the BIDS Calculations tab, you can set breakpoints in the MDX script associated with your cube.*

Understanding Common MDX Functions

To give you a "flavor" for working with MDX, here's a brief list of commonly used MDX functions types. Figure 10-15 shows the list of functions and the arguments for each function that we will discuss in this section.

```
--common MDX functions,showing argument lists
--<<arg>> is mandatory, [<<arg>>] is optional

«Set».CURRENT

DISTINCTCOUNT( «Set» )

FILTER( «Set», «Search Condition» )

GENERATE( «Set1», «Set2»[, ALL] )

GENERATE( «Set», «String Expression»[, «Delimiter»] )

IIF( «Logical Expression», «object»,  «object» )

PARALLELPERIOD( [«Level»[, «Numeric Expression»[, «Member»] ] ] )

SETTOARRAY( «Set»[, «Set»...][, «Numeric Expression»] )
```

Figure 10-15. *When you add MDX functions to the MDX query area in SSMS using the function browser, the argument list is provided for your reference.*

Now on to discussing how each function works:

Current: This function returns the current tuple from a set. You should note that this function only works with named sets. You can think of this function as a kind of a CurrentMember function, but one that is specific to named sets.

DistinctCount: This function returns a count of unique, nonempty tuples in a set. BOL erroneously says that DistinctCount "can be applied only on calculated measures," however, the AdventureWorks sample cube stored OrderCount measure (in the Sales Orders measure group) uses a DistinctCount aggregation.

IIF: This function works similarly to IIFs (Immediate If) in other applications (Excel, for example). It takes three arguments, an expression, a value to be returned if the expression evaluates to true, and an alternate value to be returned if the expression evaluates to false. The IIF function is commonly used in the Status expression for many KPIs, such as the Customer Profitability template (along with many others). You'll note that KPIs return either 1 (for a positive result) or -1 (for a negative result). The Status expression section of the template, illustrating the IIF function, is shown in Figure 10-16.

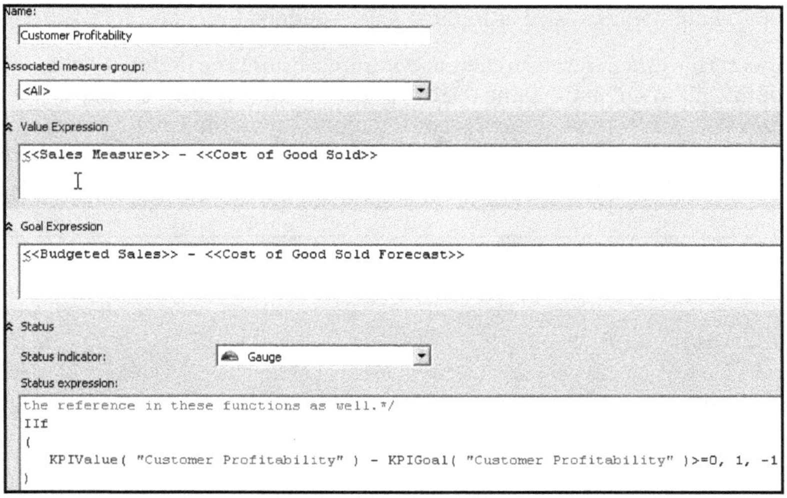

Figure 10-16. *The MDX function* IIF *is commonly used when creating KPIs.*

Filter: This function returns a subset of the listed set based on the action of a filter (which contains a condition). Using this function makes your queries more efficient, as it reduces the amount of data being returned. The Filter function is used in MDX queries to restrict data on one of the axes. Figure 10-17 shows an example query.

```
With
        Set [Big Sales] AS
        ([Measures].[Internet Sales-Sales Amount],
        [Measures].[Reseller Sales-Sales Amount])

Select  [Big Sales] on Columns,
        FILTER(([Due Date].[Fiscal Time].Members),[Geography].[Geographies]<>'Australia') on Rows

From    [Analysis Services Tutorial 1]
Where   [Product].[Product Line].&[R]
```

Figure 10-17. *The* FILTER *function allows you to reduce the set you are working with by using a condition.*

Generate: This function has two types of functionality, which are shown in the argument lists in Figure 10-15. The first functionality applies the second set to each member of the first set in the argument list and then joins the resulting sets by union. The Generate function eliminates duplicates by default but does provide you with the option of including them (by specifying the optional "all" third argument).

The second functionality returns a concatenated string created by evaluating a string expression over a set. You have the option, using the third argument, to specify a particular delimeter in the results.

The Generate function is often used when creating calculated members to write MDX queries that perfom operations on multiple sets in a more concise way.

SetToArray: This function converts a set (or sets) to an array. The optional arguments are the second set and the numeric expression. The return value, which is the datatype variant (VT_ARRAY), should only be used as input to a user-defined function.

ParallelPeriod: This function returns a member from a prior time period (that is, year, quarter, month, and so on) in the same relative position as a member listed. It is often used with the MDX CurrentMember and Parent functions. An example of this function is shown in one of the scope script commands provided with the AdventureWorks sample. This is shown in Figure 10-18.

```
// Scope on month level in FY 2003 and onwards
Scope
(
    [Date].[Fiscal Year].&[2003] : Null,
    [Date].[Fiscal].[Month].Members
) ;

// Compute weights based on reseller sales ratio in previous year
This =
(
    ParallelPeriod          // Fetch reseller sales amount in previous year
    (
        [Date].[Fiscal].[Fiscal Year], 1,
        [Date].[Fiscal].CurrentMember
    ),
    [Measures].[Reseller Sales Amount]
)
/
(
    ParallelPeriod          // Divide monthly value by quarterly value to obtain ratio
    (
        [Date].[Fiscal].[Fiscal Year], 1,
        [Date].[Fiscal].CurrentMember.Parent
    ),
    [Measures].[Reseller Sales Amount]
) ;

// Allocate quarterly values to months according to weight
This = [Measures].CurrentMember * [Date].[Fiscal].Parent ;

End Scope ;
```

Figure 10-18. *The scope script sample from AdventureWorks illustrates the use of the* ParallelPeriod *MDX function.*

New or Updated MDX Functions

This section covers some of the more interesting new or updated MDX functions since SSAS 2000. Curiously, even though most of these functions are commonly used, some of them are not listed in the function browser in BIDS. Figure 10-19 shows the function arguments.

```
AGGREGATE( «Set»[, «Numeric Expression»] )

EXISTS( «Set1», «Set2» )

--this is not a function
EXISTING

--all of the KPI functions take the same arg list
KPIVALUE( «String Expression» )

«Member».MEMBERVALUE

UNKNOWNMEMBER

UNORDER( «Set» )
```

Figure 10-19. *This figure shows the argument lists for the functions we will discuss in this section.*

Aggregate: This function has been enhanced in SSAS 2005 to now allow it to work with `DistinctCount` measures, as well as with the various semiadditive measures. Note that numeric expression is an optional argument.

Freeze: This statement (not function) locks the specified value of the current subcube to the specified values. It is used in MDX script commands to "pin" a subcube (or exempt it from updated) during the execution of a script using the `Scope` statement and `This` function. In the example shown in Figure 10-20, the `Freeze` statement is used to "lock" the current quarterly values of the Sales Amount Quotas in a cube that uses a `Scope/This` statement to assign new values (weights) to the Sales Amount Quotas at the month level. Without the `Freeze` statement, these updates would aggregate up to the Quarter level. In this particular business scenario, that behavior is undesirable.

```
/*-- Weighted allocation to remaining months ---------------------------*/

    // Pin quarterly values prior to assigning weights for months
    // This is done in order to avoid overwriting the quarterly values
    // once weights are entered for monthly values.
    Freeze
    (
        [Date].[Fiscal].[Fiscal Quarter].Members,
        [Measures].[Sales Amount Quota]
    ) ;
```

Figure 10-20. *A* Freeze *statement pins a subcube during the execution of a* Scope/This *script so that the range that it defines will not be updated.*

Exists: This function takes one or more sets that can be filtered and returns the set of membes that exist with the other sets. The [Filtered Set of Attribute Members] named set template illustrates the use of the Exists function. Note the comment in Figure 10-21.

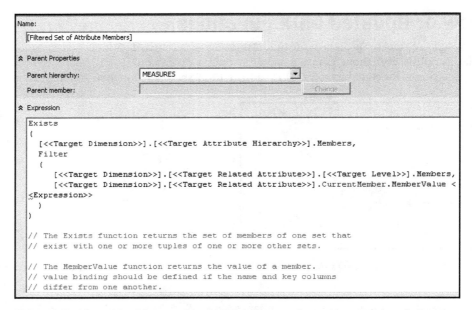

Figure 10-21. *The Named Set template* [Filtered Set of Attribute Members] *demonstrates the new* EXISTS *function.*

KPICurrentTimeMember, KPIGoal, KPIStatus, KPITrend, KPIValue, KPIWeight: These functions are used in the KPI tab in BIDS when adding KPIs to your cube (as discussed in Chapter 5). They all basically function as aliases for MDX (usually CASE) expressions that are defined in the KPI builder area of BIDS. The KPIValue function is shown in Figure 10-16 as well.

MemberValue: This function allows you to directly retrieve (or use for comparison) a value associated with a dimension attribute (configured via the ValueColumn property). In SSAS 2000, you had to use the conversion function (Val) to peform this type of operation, which was not only more cumbersome to write but also did not perform very efficiently. The ValueColumn property page for a dimensional attribute is shown in Figure 10-22.

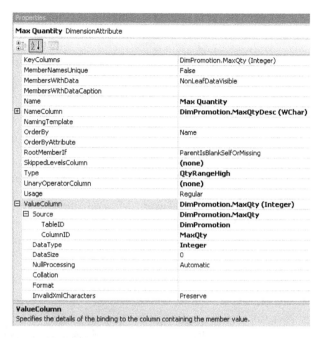

Figure 10-22. *The* .MemberValue *function allows you retrieve or make comparisons with the value associated with a dimensional attribute (stored in* ValueColumn *properties) with a more concise and efficient syntax than was used in SSAS 2000.*

This: This function allows you to apply an update to the MOLAP data as defined in a subcube (usually by using the MDX keyword Scope to define the subcube). This is illustrated in a script in Figure 10-13 earlier in this chapter.

UnknownMember: This returns the unknown member value for a level or member. Remember that you have the ability to configure an unknown member value for an entire dimension by setting the property values for both the UnknownMember and the UnknownMemberName.

Unorder: This function allows you to improve the efficiency of MDX queries by specifying that you have no need for specifically ordered results. Some MDX functions use Unorder automatically (Sum, for example). If you would like to verify whether a function you are using does this, you can open a trace in Profiler to see the internally generated MDX query.

Note If your BI solution requires extensive custom MDX queries or scripting, you will probably want to pick up a reference to MDX. *MDX Solutions*, 2nd Edition by George Spofford (Wiley, 2006) is the best available book devoted entirely to MDX.

Several Web sites are devoted to reviewing MDX functions. A very concise page listing nearly all MDX functions, arguments, and functionality can be found at http://mondrian. pentaho.org/documentation/mdx.php. Also, a series by William Peason for the site Database Journal provides a thorough reference to many MDX functions: http://www.databasejournal. com/features/mssql/article.php/1495511.

Adding .NET Assemblies to Your SSAS Project

A new capability in SSAS 2005 is the ability to add COM DLLs or .NET assemblies to your installed instance of SSAS or to a particular SSAS database. The primary question for you to consider is why would you want to take the trouble to write .NET assemblies that will be called via MDX queries or script commands as functions? To best understand the answer to that, you really have to understand the capabilities of the .NET Framework. Conceptually, what you are able to now do is harness the power of the framework inside of SSAS.

Our discussion will include only .NET assemblies. We'll reference some examples that have been written specifically for SSAS to help you understand "why" you may choose to use .NET assemblies.

■**Tip** The open source community has a sample project showcasing several examples of using .NET assemblies with SSAS. This is available on Microsoft's CodePlex site (http://www.codeplex.com/Wiki/ View.aspx?ProjectName=ASStoredProcedures). The project includes downloadable source code using C# functions and sample MDX queries that call those functions. The entire project is very well commented and documented.

One example showcased in the CodePlex samples (mentioned in the preceding tip) is using the .NET RegEx (or Regular Expressions) class to efficiently search for a string pattern in SSAS cube data. In this case, using .NET to perform this functionality is not only quicker and easier to write in C# than in MDX (assuming you know both languages, which is, of course, a big assumption!), but also the .NET assembly will perform more efficiently than the same functionality written only in MDX.

There are eight different examples in the CodePlex sample. If you are inclined to include .NET assemblies in your BI project, investigate these samples thoroughly.

■**Tip** If you do choose to write your own .NET assembly for use in SSAS, you'll get better performance if you mark all functions that you intend to call in MDX expressions or queries as static (if using C#) or shared (if using VB.NET). This is the equivalent of marking the functions as global. It results in better per-formance because there is no need to instantiate the class each time the function is called. Rather, the function is directly invoked by SSAS as soon as the assembly is loaded. Assembly load usually happens only once, whereas class instantiation could occur on each function call.

Configuring Assemblies

After you (or a .NET developer) has written an assembly, then you must make it available to SSAS. You can do this in SSMS by right-clicking either the main Assemblies folder in Object Explorer (to associate an assembly with SSAS itself), or by right-clicking the Assemblies folder inside of a particular database in Object Explorer (to associate an assembly with a particular database). In both cases, you'll then click New Assembly and then configure the Register Server Assembly dialog box shown in Figure 10-23. In this dialog box, you'll add the File name, Assembly name, Permissions, and Impersonation information for the assembly.

Note You can also reference a .NET assembly (or COM DLL) in BIDS. The process is slightly different from doing so in SSMS. In BIDS Solution Explorer, you right-click the Assemblies folder, and then on New Assembly Reference. Then, you select the particular assembly from the Add Reference dialog box. After you add a .NET assembly, you'll right-click the assembly in Solution Explorer and then click Properties. In the Properties dialog box, you'll configure the Permissions and Impersonation information.

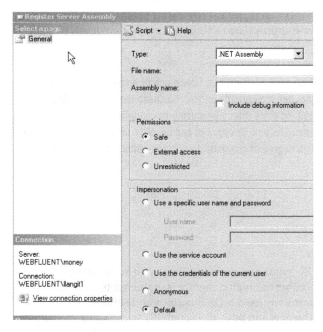

Figure 10-23. *To add a COM DLL or a .NET assembly to your SSAS project in SSMS, you right-click the assembly node after connecting to SSAS in SSMS and then configure the Register Server Assembly dialog box.*

You may be wondering about the Permssions section of the Register Server Assembly dialog box. In this area, you set the .NET CAS (Code Access Security) permissions for the assembly. This setting is a group of code-level permissions (for example, permission to read from or to write to the Registry) that will apply to your DLL. You will usually select either Safe for assemblies that do not access any resources outside of SSAS, or External access for assemblies that do access resources outside of SSAS. Unrestricted is the equivalent of "full trust," so you should use it only when absolutely necessary. Some of the samples that are in the Code-Plex project do require you to configure them to use the Unrestricted CAS assembly permission.

Note Although a complete discussion of CAS is beyond the scope of this book, it is vital that you fully understand the implications of using External Access or Unrestricted assemblies before using these settings, as they can potentially pose a security risk or reduce the stability of your server if the assembly is not written correctly.

The Impersonation section of this same dialog box allows you to set the access credentials for the assembly. If you select the Use the service account option, then you are requesting to use the service account set that SSAS is using.

Using .NET assemblies is a very specialized technique. Like many of the subjects discussed in this chapter, you should use this functionality only if your business requirements mandate it and only after you have done appropriate testing with production levels of load.

Tip MDX is a deep topic. Entire books have been written on it. How much of an expert you need to become to implement a successful BI project depends greatly on your business requirements. Some projects require very minimal MDX, which is nothing more than customizing the supplied templates. Other projects require quite a bit more customization. As with any type of coding, MDX adds time and complexity to your project. For BI projects with a high degree of customization, it sometimes makes sense to hire a specialist in MDX.

Summary

In this chapter, we reviewed basic MDX syntax and querying. We then discussed the core objects that you might add to an SSAS cube: calculated members, named sets, and script commands. We next reviewed the most commonly used MDX functions and some of the new ones as well. The last area we covered was the new and powerful capability to associate assemblies with SSAS.

In the next chapter, we'll explore the greatly enhanced toolset available in SSAS for data mining.

CHAPTER 11

■ ■ ■

Introduction to Data Mining

In this chapter, we'll explore the incredibly powerful tools included with SSAS for use in data mining solutions. You can begin by thinking of data mining as a terrific "value add" to your BI solution. Although SSAS 2000 included two data mining algorithms, very few of my clients actually implemented them because deep knowledge about data mining algorithms had not been a typical attribute of SQL Server professionals, and that level of knowledge was necessary to implement data mining using SSAS 2000. As with SSAS OLAP cubes in this 2005 release, Microsoft has made a concerted effort to improve the usability of data mining in SSAS 2005, in part by including a large number of easy-to-use wizards. These wizards contain consistently and remarkably well-documented dialog boxes. However, data mining *is* a complex topic, and it's important to understand that this chapter is an introduction to this topic.

Tip Microsoft's data mining team has a terrific Web site with tips, notes, samples, and much more: http://www.sqlserverdatamining.com/DMCommunity/default.aspx.

The SSAS 2005 data mining facilities are among the brightest of the gems in the entire BI feature set because of the included power and the improved ease of implementation. We've got a great deal of ground to cover here, and this is what we'll discuss in the chapter:

- Defining SSAS data mining

- Reviewing data mining structures

- Explaining the nine SSAS data mining algorithms

- Processing mining models

- Using the data mining language: Data Mining Extensions (DMX)

Defining SSAS Data Mining

Data mining is a set of sophisticated tools and algorithms that allow analysts and end users to solve problems that would otherwise take huge amounts of manual effort or else would simply remain unsolved. We will discuss examples of business problems that data mining can impact later in this chapter.

You can also think of data mining as a set of tools to help you enable your end users to discover patterns and trends based on defined subsets of enterprise data. Such analysis is useful in many types of business situations, such as predicting future values and better understanding why your business got the past results that it did. Using SSAS, you can create data mining structures, which contain mining models. *Mining models* represent implementations of specific data mining algorithms. Algorithms are mathematical functions that perform specific types of analysis on the associated data set. One example is the Microsoft Time Series algorithm. This algorithm will predict a specific value, for example, rate of sale (or quantity) of a particular item, over time.

These mining models can be built using OLAP cubes or on relational tables as source data. Data mining is usually (but not always) meant to be complementary to an SSAS cube. A cube is often used to verify results, that is, "We think this happened, does the data support our belief?" You can use mining structures (and their contained models) to discover correlations, patterns, and other "surprises" in the data, that is, "what will happen?" Another common use of mining is when businesses buy data from data-collection companies that represents competitive information (this type of data is often called "competitive data"). Data mining can be used to help businesses consider what would happen if they got into a certain type of new business, what would happen if they started doing business in certain locations, and so on.

Some of the focus areas for this release of SSAS data mining are as follows:

- Make data mining easier to implement. Data mining has traditionally been one of the most challenging types of data analysis solutions to put into operation, due to the need to deeply understand the various algorithms involved. The tools provided in BIDS make the creation of mining structures much easier by including intelligently designed wizards with (mostly) self-documenting dialog boxes. Also, importantly, there are now tools to help you verify the accuracy of your mining model. This can help you select the most useful algorithms.

- Make it easy for end users to work with the results of mining structures in ways that are meaningful to them. To this end, SSAS includes a broad variety of data mining model viewers in BIDS, many new types of client integration (discussed in detail later in the chapter), and an API for custom viewer development.

Note The model viewers in BIDS are not intended to be used by end users; rather, they are provided for you so that you can better understand the results of the various mining models included in your mining structure. Interestingly, Microsoft has included these same viewers in Excel 2007, so if you implement Office 2007, you'll be able to allow end users to have the same rich views as you do during mining model development.

This version of SSAS has tremendously enhanced the available data mining methods. These methods are expressed as algorithms; there are nine algorithms included in SSAS 2005 (as compared to only two in SSAS 2000). In addition, the UI and object model for data mining has been completely revamped and is both powerful and easy to use.

One the most challenging parts of data mining in SSAS is understanding what the various models (algorithms) actually do and then creating a mining structure that includes the appropriate algorithm or algorithms to best support your specific business requirements. Also, some algorithms function more effectively after you configure some of their available properties. Understanding how to best configure the algorithm properties can also be challenging. We will review some of the more important algorithm properties in this chapter. Another important consideration is how you will present the completed data mining model results to your end users.

To help you select the most appropriate data mining algorithm or algorithms, we'll start by thinking about some of the business problems that SSAS data mining can impact. Later, we'll tie these types of problems to particular algorithms. Here's just a partial list:

- What characteristics do our customers share? How could we group them or put the types of customers into "buckets"? This type of information could be used, for example, to improve effectiveness of marketing campaigns by targeting different campaign types more appropriately, that is, use magazine ads for customers who read magazines, TV ads for customers who watch TV, and so on.

- What situations are abnormal for various groups? This type of analysis is sometimes used for fraud detection. For example, purchasing behavior outside of normal locations, stores, or total amounts might be indicative of fraud for particular customer groups.

- What product or services should be marketed or displayed next to what other products or services? This is sometimes called *market-basket* analysis and can be used in scenarios such as "brick-and-mortar" store shelf product placement when considering which products should be next to each other, or for Web marketing when considering which ads should be placed on which product pages.

- What will a certain value be (for example, rate of sales per week) for an item or set of items at some point in the future, based on some values (for example, the price of the item) that the item had in the past? An example of this would be a retailer that adjusts the price of a key item upward or downward based on the sell-through rate for that price point for that type of item for particular groups of stores in an effort to control the amount of inventory of that particular item over time in each store.

The best way to start working with SSAS data mining is by exploring the models that ship with the sample AdventureWorks cube. To do this, you'll open the AdventureWorks sample in BIDS. You'll note that the sample includes five data mining models. We'll use these for the basis of the data mining discussion in this chapter.

Figure 11-1 shows the sample data mining containers, which are called mining structures, in the Solution Explorer in BIDS. Each mining structure showcases using one or more mining models (with each mining model containing a particular set of algorithms applied to source data) to impact a different type of business problem.

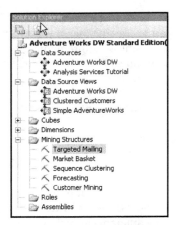

Figure 11-1. *The sample AdventureWorks cube contains five different mining structures. Each mining structure contains one or more data mining models. Each data mining model is built using a particular set of data mining algorithms.*

More Data Mining Concepts

The Data Mining Wizard simplifies creating a mining structure in SSAS. To start the wizard, you right-click the Mining Structures folder in Solution Explorer in BIDS, and then click New Mining Structure. Your first choice when using the wizard is the location of the source data for the mining structure. Here you'll select either a subset of a defined DSV (which is, most often, based on relational data) or a dimension from one of the cubes in the same SSAS project. Your next choice is to select one of the nine available data mining algorithms.

Before we start exploring the individual algorithms, we'll first discuss general categories of data mining algorithms, the types of business problems those categories are designed to impact, and which SSAS data mining algorithms are available in which category or categories. A nice feature included in SSAS is the ability to easily add additional mining models (using different algorithms and/or different input columns) to the same mining structure. Often using more than one mining model is the most effective strategy when implementing data mining as part of your BI solution.

Here's a list of categories or types of data mining tasks:

- *Classification*: This involves predicting the value of one or more fixed variables, based on multiple input variables (or attributes). These types of algorithms are often used when a business has a large volume of high-quality historical data. The included algorithm most often used to implement this technique is Microsoft Decision Trees. The Microsoft Naïve Bayes and the Microsoft Neural Network algorithms can also be used. The Naïve Bayes algorithm is so named because it assumes all input columns are completely independent. The Microsoft Neural Network algorithm is often used with very large volumes of data that have very complex relationships. With this type of source data, Microsoft Neural Network can sometimes produce the most meaningful results of all supplied algorithms.

- *Clustering*: This involves grouping source data into categories (sometimes also called segments or buckets) based on a set of supplied values (or attributes). All attributes are given equal weight when determining the buckets. These types of algorithms are often used as a starting point to help end users better understand the relationships between attributes in a large volume of data. Businesses also use them to make more intelligent "like-for-like" predictions, such as this store is like that store in these categories, and so it should perform similarly in this category. The included algorithm most often used to implement this technique is the Microsoft Clustering algorithm.

- *Association*: This involves finding correlations between variables in a set of data. This is often called *market basket* analysis. The goal of the algorithm is to find "sets of items" that show correlations (usually based on rates of sale). It is used to help businesses improve results related to cross-selling. In "brick-and-mortar" locations, the results can be used to determine shelf placement of products. For virtual businesses, the results can be used to improve click-through rates for advertising. The included algorithm most often used to implement this technique is the Microsoft Association algorithm.

- *Forecasting or Regression*: This involves a process that is similar to classification, that is, predicting a value based on multiple input variables. The difference is that the predictable value is a continuous number. In the case of a forecasting, the input usually contains a time series. Businesses use regression algorithms to rate a sale of an item based on retail price, position in store, and so on or to predict the amount of rainfall based on humidity, air pressure, and temperature. The included algorithm most often used to implement this technique is the Microsoft Time Series. The Microsoft Linear and Microsoft Logistical Regression algorithms can also be used.

- *Sequence Analysis and Prediction*: This involves finding patterns in a particular subset of data. Businesses could use this type of algorithm to analyze the click-path of end users through a commercial Web site. These paths or sequences are often analyzed over time, that is, what items did the customer buy on the first visit? What did the customer buy on the second visit? Sequence and Association algorithms both work with instances (called "cases" in the language of data mining) that contain a set of items or states. The difference is that only sequence algorithms analyze the state transitions (that is, the order or time series that cases occurred); association algorithms consider all cases to be equal. The included algorithm most often used to implement this technique is Microsoft Sequence Clustering.

- *Deviation Analysis*: This involves finding exceptional cases in the data. In the language of data mining, this is often called *outlier cases*. Businesses use this type of algorithm to detect potential fraud; one example is credit card companies who use this technique to initiate alerts (which usually result in a phone call to the end user, asking for verification of a particularly unusual purchase due to location, amount, and so on). The most commonly used algorithms for this type of analysis are Microsoft Decision Trees used in combination with one or more other algorithms (often Microsoft Clustering).

Architectural Considerations

To implement data mining in a BI solution, you will need to consider your requirements in light of the following architectural concerns:

- Determine what type of business problems you want to impact.

- Review the quality of the source data. Is additional ETL warranted to clean or validate that data? These processes may include aggregating source data, removing nulls, and removing abnormal data points (or outliers).

- What data should be included in your model? Here you'll select tables and columns from relational data or dimensions, attributes, and measures from your cube. Will any source data be from related (or nested) tables? What columns will be marked as keys, as inputs, as predictable (more on what these terms mean later in this chapter)?

- Which algorithms will you begin with in your data mining structure? Remember, it's relatively easy to add additional algorithms as you continue to work with your project.

- How will you validate the results of your models? Which algorithms prove to be most useful for presenting you with useful information regarding your particular business scenario? Also, which algorithms prove to be most accurate? We'll discuss more about the tools included in BIDS to do this later in this chapter.

- Who will view the results of your mining structure? What client tools will end users use? Will custom application development be required?

- How will your mining model be maintained? How often will new data be added?

- At what intervals will the model be reverified? What metrics or baselines will be used to "prove" the validity and usefulness of your models?

Tip If you are looking for more information about lifecycle processes for data mining, you can review the standard model for the data mining lifecycle. It's called the Crisp-DM method and is described at http://www.crisp-dm.org/Process/index.htm.

The next step in our journey is to dig a bit deeper into the sample mining structures supplied with the AdventureWorks cube.

Reviewing Data Mining Structures

As discussed in the previous section, to begin to create your first mining structure, you open the AdventureWorks sample in BIDS, and then right-click the Mining Structures folder in the Solution Explorer. After you click Mining Explorer, you are asked to select either a DSV or an existing cube as a source for your model. The next step is to select the mining algorithm. After you've done that, you are asked to select the specific source columns or dimensional attributes and then select what is called a *nested table*.

Note A case table contains the entities that you want to analyze, and a nested table contains additional information (often transactions) about each item listed in the case table. For example, if you wanted to analyze sales for customer types, then the Customer table would be the case table, and the CustomerOrders table would be the nested table.

Figure 11-2 shows the interface for defining a nested table (if you have selected an existing cube) as a source for your mining model.

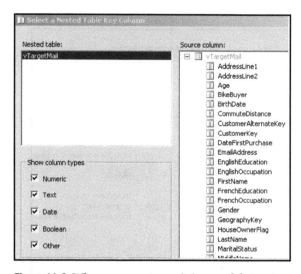

Figure 11-2. *When you create a mining model structure, you will sometimes elect to add a nested table.*

After you select your source data, then you must complete one or more additional configuration steps in the wizard, depending on which algorithm you've selected. When you complete the wizard, the BIDS interface allows you to make further refinements to any mining model within your mining structure.

We'll explore the BIDS mining structure in more detail now. The first tab in the work area is the Mining Structure tab. Here you can see the source data included in your mining model (in a DSV-like format). An important difference between this view and the DSV container in a BI project is that you can only view the source data in the Mining Structure view. You cannot add calculated columns, and so on, and you have to use the *original* DSV defined at the level on the SSAS database (as you do when creating a cube) to make any structural changes to the DSV used as a source for your mining structure. If you need to add or remove columns (or nested tables), you'll use the original level view.

There are several properties that you can configure for both the entire source or for individual columns in this view. An example is the CacheMode property. Your choices are KeepTrainingCases or ClearAfterProcessing.

Note What is "training data?" During this chapter, we'll often use this term. It means to provide the data mining models with sample data so that the model can "learn" from the sample cases. In SSAS, "process" is equivalent to "train."

The latter option is often used during the early development phase of your mining project. You may process the model, only to find that the data used needs further cleaning. In this case, you would perform the subsequent clean, and then reprocess the model. Figure 11-3 shows the properties for the targeted mailing sample.

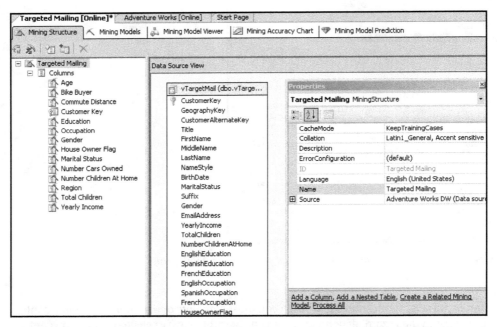

Figure 11-3. *In the Mining Structure tab of BIDS, you can view the source data and add or remove columns and nested tables.*

The next tab in the mining structure designer in BIDS is the Mining Models tab. Here you view the one or more mining models that are included in the particular mining structure that you are editing. You can easily add new models to your structure by right-clicking the surface and then clicking New Mining Model. Also, you can change the source data associated with a type of mining model by creating more than one instance of that model and "ignoring" one or more columns from the the mining structure DSV. You may choose to do this to test the level of impact that a particular attribute has to a mining model. This is shown for the Yearly Income column using the Microsoft Naïve Bayes algorithm in Figure 11-4.

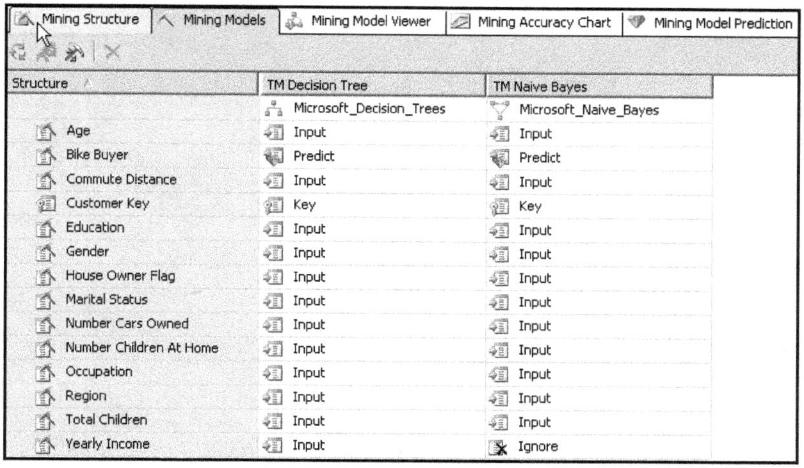

Figure 11-4. *Two mining models, one based on Microsoft Decision Trees and one based on Microsoft Naïve Bayes, are included in the mining structure shown.*

You can change the use of the associated (nonkey) source columns in the following ways:

- *Ignore*: This setting causes the model to remove the column from the model.

- *Input*: This setting causes the model to use that column as source data for the model.

- *Predict*: This setting causes the model to use that column as both input and output.

- *PredictOnly*: This setting causes the model to use that column as output only.

Note There are specific requirements about Input and Predictable columns for each type of algorithm. These are discussed later in this chapter.

You can configure the algorithm parameters for each mining model in the mining structure by right-clicking the mining model on the design surface and then clicking Set Algorithm Parameters. These parameters vary depending on which mining algorothm you are working with. Figure 11-5 shows the configurable parameters for the Microsoft Decision Trees model. Note that when you select one of the properties, the configuration dialog box shows you a brief definition of the configurable property value. Figure 11-5 shows the definition for the COMPLEXITY_PENALTY property.

You may be surprised to see the configuration of parameters being included at this point in this chapter, assuming that such configuration is for advanced users of data mining only. Actually, you will find yourself exploring (and changing) many of the parameters as you begin to tinker with data mining. The UI does a pretty good job explaining each of them; also there is additional documentation in BOL.

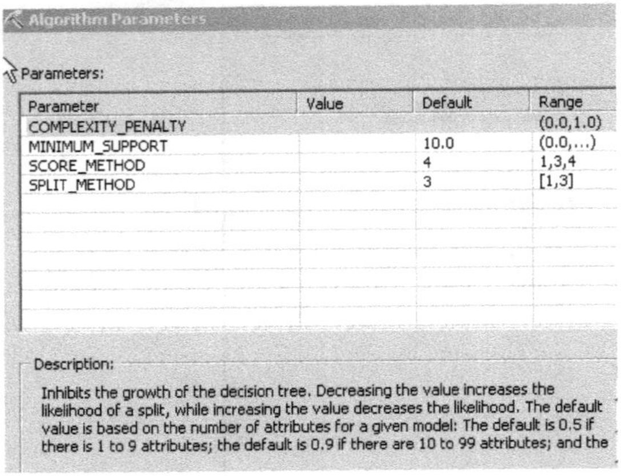

Figure 11-5. *Right-clicking any mining model in BIDS allows you to do an additional property-level configuration that is specific to the particular algorithm type that you are working with.*

Also, as you become a more advanced user of data mining, for certain algorithms, you may choose to add your own custom parameters (and configure their values) via this dialog box.

Mining Structure Viewers

The next tab in the BIDS mining structure designer is the Mining Model Viewer. An interesting aspect of this tab is that each mining model algorithm includes one or more types of mining model viewers. These viewers are for you, as the mining model designer, and not for end users. The purpose of the broad variety of viewers is to help you to determine which mining model algorithms are most useful for your particular business scenario.

In our case, we'll look at the included TM Decision Trees sample in AdventureWorks. This model shows information correlated to bicycle purchasing, that is, "number of cars owned," "number of children at home," and so on.

The viewers include both graphical and text (rows and columns of data) representations of data. Some of the viewers include multiple types of graphical views of the output of the mining model data. Additionally, some of the viewers include a mining legend in the properties area of the design surface.

Tip The Mining Structure Viewers are available in SSMS. To access them, connect to SSAS in SSMS, right-click the particular mining structure in the Object Explorer, and then click Browse. Also Microsoft has included a set of Data Mining Web Controls (and Plug-In Algorithms) as part of SSAS. You can use these to create custom applications for end users. If you choose to install the samples, you will find them at `C:\Program Files\Microsoft SQL Server\90\Samples\Analysis Services\DataMining`.

For example, the Microsoft Decision Trees algorithm includes two types of viewers. These are the Microsoft Tree Viewer and the Microsoft Content Viewer. The tree viewer itself has two different views of the mining model output: the decision tree view and the dependency network view.

Figure 11-6 shows a portion of the Decision Tree Viewer for the targeted mailing sample mining structure and the associated mining legend. It shows the most closely correlated information at the first level, in this case, "Number Cars Owned." The depth of color of each node is a visual cue to the amount of association; darker colors indicate more association. Note that the mining legend reflects the exact number of cases (or rows) for the particular node of the model that is selected. It also shows the information via a probablity column (percentage) and a histogram (graphical representation). In the diagram, the selected node is "Number Cars Owned = 2" so the detailed (Case) data in the mining legend reflects the selection.

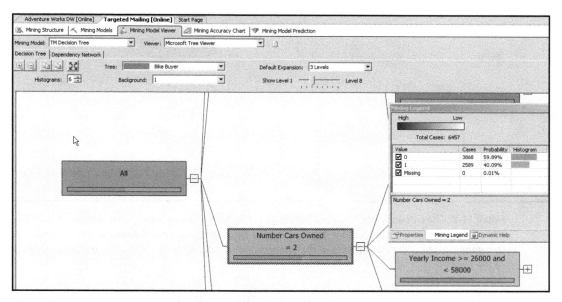

Figure 11-6. *The Microsoft Decision Tree Viewer allows you to understand dependency relationships in your mining model.*

The other type of viewer for the Microsoft Decision Trees algorithm is the Dependency Network Viewer. This allows you to quickly visualize which data has the strongest correlation to a particular node. You can adjust the strength of association being shown by dragging the slider on the left of the diagram up or down.

Figure 11-7 shows the Dependency Network for the same mining structure that we've been working with. You'll note that the three most correlated factors for bike purchasing are yearly income, number of cars owned, and age.

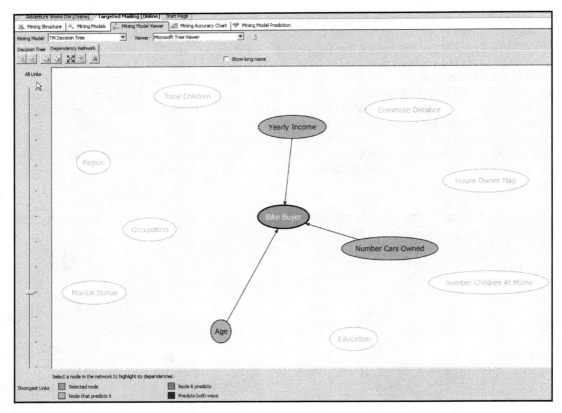

Figure 11-7. *The Dependency Network Viewer provides you with a quick visual representation of the most closely correlated factors. You can adjust the strength of correlation by clicking and dragging the slider on the left side of the viewer up or down. Note the legend on the bottom left of the figure.*

The Mining Model Content Viewer allows you to review the greatest level of detail in your mining model. It shows the processed results in rows and columns of data. For certain mining models, this viewer will include nested tables in the results as well.

As mentioned earlier, different algorithms have different types of associated viewers. For example, the Microsoft Naïve Bayes algorithm includes the following additional viewers: Attribute Profiles, Attribute Characteristics, and Attribute Discrimination. Figure 11-8 shows the Attribute Profiles view and includes the mining legend (which shows the color-coded "buckets" of data). This is showing the distribution of various attributes, that is, "age," "commute distance," and so on for the entire population (or complete data set), then for the the bike buyers—indicated by a 1 value—and the nonbike buyers—indicated by a "0" value.

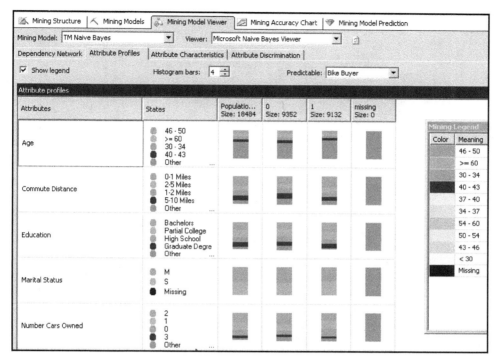

Figure 11-8. *The Attribute Profiles Viewer for a mining model built using the Microsoft Naïve Bayes algorithm allows you to review the populations of created clusters. These are called Attribute Profiles.*

Tip If you are new to data mining concepts, a great way to better understand what the different included algorithms do is to look at the output from the included sample mining structures using each of the included viewers.

Mining Accuracy Charts

The next tab in the BIDS designer is the Mining Accuracy Chart tab. Here you can validate (or compare) your model against some actual data to understand how accurate your model is. You'll do this by using a specific type of chart called a Lift Chart. This chart will show a "perfect" result and then compare the results of your particular mining model to that result.

You will commonly validate the various mining models inside of a mining structure, so that you can understand which mining models will be most accurate (and, therefore, most useful) to understanding and impacting the particular business problems you want to forecast, predict, cluster, classify, and so on. Figure 11-9 shows the configuration of the Mining Accuracy Chart tab in BIDS.

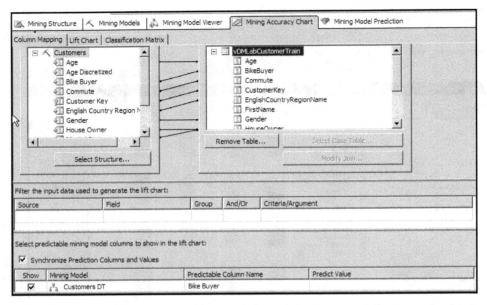

Figure 11-9. *You associate a subset of data with the training (or source) data to work with the accuracy of your mining models. The output type varies depending on the algorithm used. For this example, the output is a Lift Chart.*

To further explain the outputs of the Mining Accuracy Chart tab, you need to understand a bit more about Lift Charts and Profit Charts. A Lift Chart compares the accuracy of the predictions of each model included in your structure to an average guess and a perfect prediction. This guess is shown in the middle of the chart, and the perfect value is shown as a line at the top of the chart. "Lift" is measured by how much your model results improve (or lift) the predictive values above that average guess. A Profit Chart displays the theoretical increase in profit that is associated with using each model.

Mining Prediction Viewers

The next tab in the BIDS designer is the Mining Model Prediction tab. Here you can create predictions based on the mining models that a mining structure contains. What you are actually doing is writing a query using the native mining model language—Data Mining Extensions (DMX)—by using a GUI interface. You can use DMX to create the structure of new data mining models, to train (or populate) your models, and to browse, manage, and predict against them. DMX contains Data Definition Language (DDL) statements, for example, `CREATE MINING STRUCTURE`; Data Manipulation Language (DML) statements, for example, `SELECT FROM <model>`; and functions and operators, for example, `Predict` or `PredictAssociation`. We will look in more detail at DMX sample statements later in this chapter.

Figure 11-10 shows the interface in BIDS for creating a data mining prediction query. In this example, we are working with the DMX `PredictProbability` function to determine the probability of an individual (or case) becoming a bike buyer.

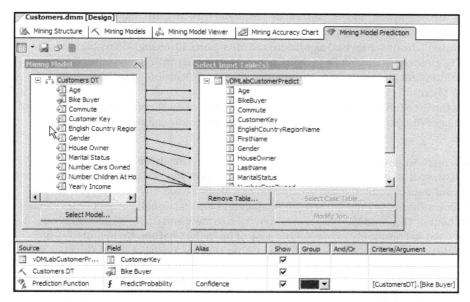

Figure 11-10. *The BIDS interface for generating a mining model prediction query allows you to easily create predictive queries.*

Understanding the Nine Included Data Mining Algorithms

Before we start reviewing the individual algorithms, there's a concept that will help you understand how to select the mining algorithm that best matches your business needs: *supervision*. The options are to use a supervised or an unsupervised algorithm.

Supervised mining models require you to select both input and predictable columns. This type is used when you not only know the values (or columns) that should serve as inputs but also when you have determined which value you want to predict.

Unsupervised mining models require you only to select input columns. This type is used earlier in your project when you are just trying to understand the data you are working with, rather than to predict a specific outcome.

Note An *input column* is any column from source data that should be considered when executing the mining algorithm. A predictable column is any column that you want the algorithm to predict values for. Not all algorithms support prediction (some support only clustering or grouping data together).

When you build your models, you will be presented with an error dialog box if you don't configure your model per the supervision requirements for the particular algorithm that you've selected. The unsupervised algorithms are Microsoft Clustering, Microsoft Linear or Logistical Regression, Microsoft Sequence Clustering, and Microsoft Time Series. The supervised algorithms are Microsoft Association Rules, Microsoft Decision Trees, Microsoft Naïve Bayes, and Microsoft Neural Networks.

Here's the list of all the algorithms in descending order of most common use. The list also includes a brief discussion of some of the more important configurable attributes for each algorithm.

- *Microsoft Naïve Bayes*: One of the simplest algorithms available to you in the SSAS toolkit, so it is often used as a "starting point" to help you understand basic groupings in your data. It's called *naïve* because no one attribute has any higher significance than another. Also only discrete (or distinct and not fractional) content types can be evaluated. This model type is most often used to view and understand data better; it's not used as commonly to predict because of its "naïve" nature. No included configurable properties are used with this algorithm that are available when you click the algorithm parameters property Build button in the Solution Explorer in BIDS. The most commonly used viewer in BIDS for this type of model is the dependency network. This was shown earlier in Figure 11-7.

■**Tip** The Algorithm Parameters dialog box in Solution Explorer in BIDS only shows a partial list of the configurable properties for each algorithm. For several algorithms, it shows none at all. If you want to add a configurable property and a value, click the Add button at the bottom of the dialog box. If you search on the name of the particular algorithm in BOL, you can review the complete list of configurable properties for each algorithm.

- *Microsoft Decision Trees*: Probably the most commonly used algorithm, due to its flexibility. It works with discrete and continuous (numbers that represent some unit of measure, which can include fractions) attributes, and the richness of its included viewers. It's quite easy to understand the output via these viewers. This algorithm is used to both view and to predict. There are four configurable properties with this algorithm. The most import property is the COMPLEXITY_PENALTY. By adjusting this number (usually downward), you can decrease the complexity of your model by reducing the number of inputs to be considered and literally reducing the size of your decision tree, that is, the number of nodes in the result set. Figure 11-11 shows the dialog box for adjusting this setting.

The most commonly used viewer for this algorithm is the Decision Tree Viewer. It allows you to view the nodes representing the most closely aligned factors predicting the value you select, and includes supporting information that shows detail about the values and the number of cases for each node. This was shown previously in Figure 11-6.

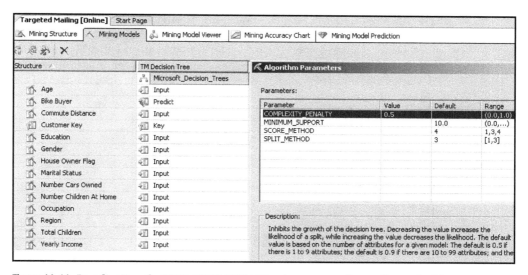

Figure 11-11. *By adjusting the* COMPLEXITY_PENALTY *value, you can "prune" your decision tree. This can make the tree easier to work with.*

- *Microsoft Time Series*: Used to impact a common business problem: accurate forecasting. This algorithm is often used to predict future values, for example, rates of sale of a particualar product. The configurable properties include the interesting PERIODICITY_HINT property. Supplying a value for this setting allows you to "nudge" the algorithm into better understand the way the data is distributed across time. For example, if sales vary by year, and the unit of measurement in the series is quarters, then the periodicity would be 4. This property is shown in Figure 11-12.

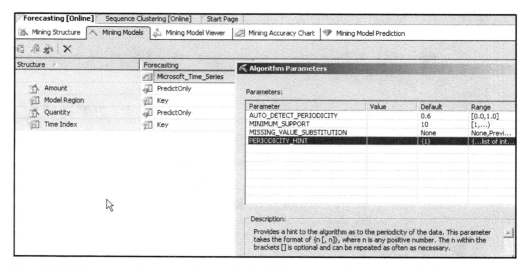

Figure 11-12. *You can configure a value for the* PERIODICITY_HINT *if you want to "help" the Microsoft Time Series algorithm better understand the temporal breakout of your data.*

The Time Series Chart view helps you to understand the output of your model by showing the predicted values over the configured time series in an easy-to-understand graphical format. You can also configure the number of prediction steps (the number of data points along the time axis) and whether or not you want to show deviations (or outliers) by using the controls on the viewer design surface. This is shown in Figure 11-13.

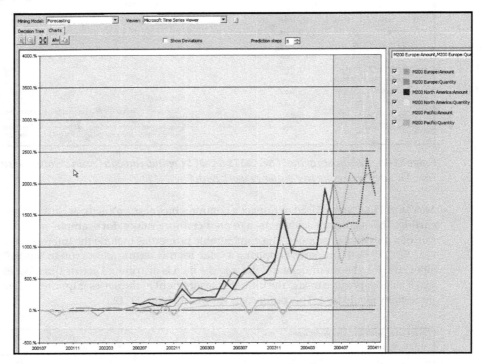

Figure 11-13. *The Time Series chart allows you to see the selected, predicted values over the time series.*

- *Microsoft Clustering*: Separates your data into "intelligent" groupings by using iterations to group cases into clusters that contain similar characteristics. This algorithm will help you to "bucketize" types of customers, for example.

You can configure CLUSTERING_METHOD using the properties available for this algorithm as shown in Figure 11-14. The choices are Scalable EM (Expectation Maximization), Nonscalable (vanilla) EM, Scalable K-means, or Nonscalable K-means. The default is scalable EM. K-type clustering is considered "hard" clustering in that it creates buckets or grouping and then assigns your data into only one bucket—there is no overlap. EM clustering takes the opposite approach and allows overlaps. This type is sometimes called "soft clustering."

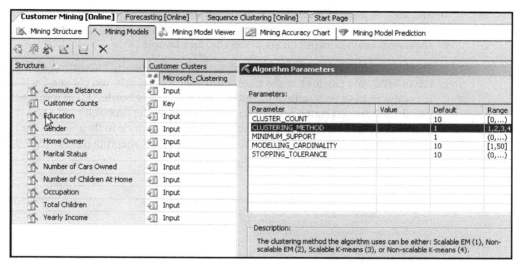

Figure 11-14. *You have a choice of four different methods of implementing the clustering algorithm. You configure your choice by using the* CLUSTERING_METHOD *property.*

After you've created your model, it's important to use the associated viewers to better understand the clusters that have been created. You can also rename the clusters shown on the Cluster Diagram Viewer as you work with the other tabs to better understand the traits associated with a particular cluster. Figure 11-15 shows the Cluster Diagram Viewer with a node renamed to Education Important based on a review of the information contained in that particular cluster's data.

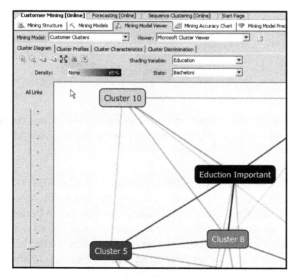

Figure 11-15. *The Cluster Diagram Viewer allows you to rename clusters as you begin to understand the traits associated with particular clusters better. The other types of viewers— Cluster Profiles, Cluster Characteristics, and so on—are designed to help you with this task.*

- *Microsoft Sequence Clustering*: Does the same thing as clustering with one important addition—it monitors the states between values. You can use this to get a sense of page sequences customers use on your Web site, for example.

The State Transitions Viewer for this algorithm is particularly interesting. Using that tab in BIDS, you can look at the state transitions for any selected cluster. Each square (or node) represents a state of the model, such as "water bottle." Lines represent the transition between states, and each node is based on the probability of a transition. The background color represents the frequency of the node in the cluster. The number displayed next to the node represents the probablity of affecting the associated node. This viewer is shown in Figure 11-16.

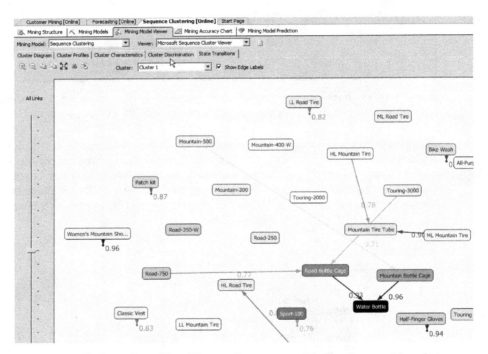

Figure 11-16. *The State Transitions Viewer allows you to visualize the transitions between states for each cluster in your model. Note that in this view, cluster one has been selected as a filter.*

The most interesting configurable property for this algorithm is the CLUSTER_COUNT. This allows you to set the number of clusters that the algorithm will build. As with Microsoft Clustering, by adjusting the number of clusters, you can gain a better perspective on the data. Most often, you will reduce the number of clusters, so that you can focus on the most important results-generating clusters for your particular business scenario. The default number of clusters generated is ten. Figure 11-17 shows this property.

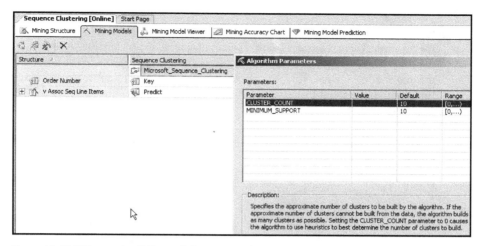

Figure 11-17. *When using Microsoft Sequence Clustering, you may want to change the number of clusters that will be built. You do this by setting a value for the* CLUSTER_COUNT *property. The default value is ten clusters.*

- *Microsoft Association Rules*: Produces itemsets or groups of related items from the source attribute columns, which are called itemsets. The results of this algorithm is often called "market-basket" analysis.

There are four configurable properties for Microsoft Association Rules. Included in the configurable properties is the ability for you to adjust the maximum size of the discovered itemsets (MAXIMUM_ITEMSET_SIZE). This property is set to a value of 3 by default, which means that the three items that are sold most often together will be shown as itemsets in the results viewers. The algorithm's configurable properties are shown in Figure 11-18.

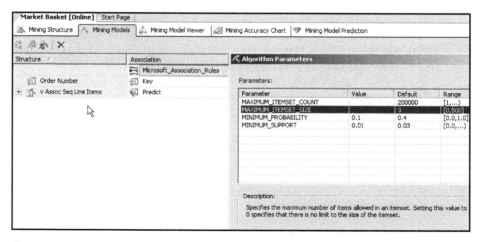

Figure 11-18. *You can adjust the size of the itemsets via the* MAXIMUM_ITEMSET_SIZE *property when using the Association Rules algorithm.*

The most interesting viewer for the Association Rules algorithm is the Rules Viewer. It shows whatever subset groupings of itemsets per your configuration parameters; for example, if you've stayed with the default value of 3 for the MAXIMUM_ITEMSET_SIZE property, then you'll see groupings of up to three related items in the associated mining model viewers.Note that you can adjust the view by setting or adjusting filters, min/max probability settings, and other properties. This viewer is shown in Figure 11-19.

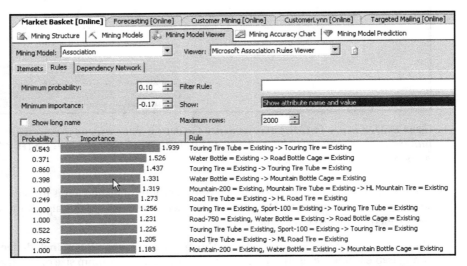

Figure 11-19. *The Rules Viewer for the Microsoft Association Rules algorithm allows you to review itemsets from the results of your mining model.*

- *Microsoft Neural Network*: By far, the most powerful and complex algorithm, which is often used when other algorithms fail to produce meaningful results. Using the Microsoft Neural Network algorithm against large data sources should always be well-tested using near production-level loads. This is because of the amount of overhead needed to process these types of models. The algorithm itself uses a very complex network called the Multilayer Perceptron network. This network uses three types of objects, called neurons. They are intput, hidden, and output neurons.

It has no configurable parameters in the associated dialog box in the BIDS GUI. However, there are parameters that you can add and configure, such as MAXIMUM_INPUT_ATTRIBUTES and MAXIMUM_OUTPUT_ATTRIBUTES, both of which have a default value of 255. You may choose to adjust either of these to improve both the performance and the usability of the results of this algorithm.

For more information about the details of how this algorithm processes data and the possible configurable parameter names and values that you may add to it, see the BOL topic, "Microsoft Neural Network Algorithm (SSAS)." Figure 11-20 shows output from one of the built-in viewers for this algorithm.

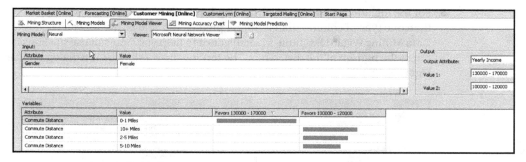

Figure 11-20. *The built-in Mining Model Viewer for the Microsoft Neural Network allows you to visualize the output of this algorithm. In this model, the configured output shows there is a strong correlation to high income for women who work at home—maybe they are writers!*

- *Microsoft Linear Regression*: A variation of the Microsoft Decision Trees algorithm that works like "classic" linear regression; that is, it fits the best possible "straight line" through a series of points. It has no included configurable parameters.

- *Microsoft Logistic Regression*: A variant of the Microsoft Neural Network algorithm (with a HIDDEN_NODE_RATIO parameter set to 0), which makes its output more like a variant of linear regression. One example is when the dependent variable is a dichotomy, such as success/failure. It has no included configurable parameters.

Now that we've reviewed the nine mining algorithms, your next step is to consider the complete set of information that you'll need to use to create your mining model and how exactly to implement data mining structures and models in BIDS.

Using the Mining Structure Wizard

To start the wizard, right-click the Mining Structures folder in Solution Explorer in BIDS. As you work with the wizard's dialog boxes to create a structure, you'll need to consider these questions:

1. What type of data can you include? Relational (from a DSV) or multidimensional (from a cube in your project). For the purpose of creating a mining structure, you can use either type of data. The wizard supports both types equally well. Your selection of data source should be based on where the data that you need is stored.

2. For relational sources, which table is the case table (that is, describes the main entity, for example, customers)? Which is the nested table (that is, has information related to each case or entity; in a "many" relationship, for example, sales transactions for each customer)? Do the case and any nested tables have columns that form a relationship between rows in the case (one: primary key) table and rows in the nested (many: foreign key) table(s)? What other columns will you include from both tables?

3. For OLAP sources, what dimensions, attributes, and facts will you include?

4. Which algorithm will you start with? Remember you can easily add additional algorithms to your mining structure after you've completed the wizard.

5. For the included columns, which are key, input, or predictable? You can select more than one type of column (that is, input, predictable, and so on) for each column. The Data Mining Wizard has built-in intelligence to help you. You can use the Suggest button at the bottom of the dialog box. The result will be a shown via a dialog box (see Figure 11-21).

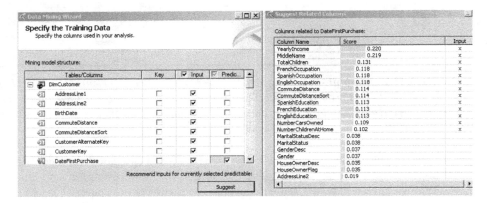

Figure 11-21. *The Data Mining Wizard can help you select input columns for your mining structure by showing you which columns are most related to your predicted attribute after you click the Suggest button on the wizard's dialog box.*

Tip If you make a selection in the wizard that will result in an error during mining structure processing, the wizard will prompt you with an informational dialog box. The error messages are specific and thoughtfully written. This is yet another way that Microsoft has made it easier for you to successfully build mining structures, even if you are a novice. An example is shown in Figure 11-22.

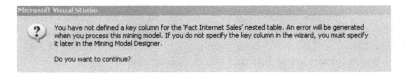

Figure 11-22. *Intelligent error messages are returned to you during the creation of a mining model.*

6. What are the content and data types of the columns?

In the next step of the wizard, you are presented with a dialog box that shows you the content type and data type of the involved columns. You can make adjustments as needed in this dialog box. There is also a handy Detect button at the bottom right that can be used to help you configure the appropriate content type (that is, continuous or discrete) for a numeric column (see Figure 11-23). These two concepts are discussed in greater detail in the next section of this chapter.

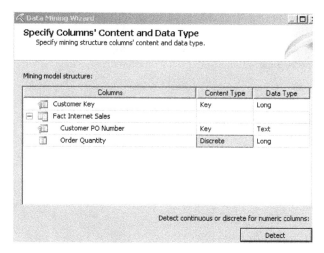

Figure 11-23. *The Detect button can help you determine the appropriate content type setting for numeric columns: continuous or discrete.*

Content and Data Types

SSAS data mining structures use data and content types that are specific to the Microsoft implementation of data mining. It's important that you understand these types when you build your mining structures. Also, certain algorithms only support certain content types. A *content type* is an additional attribute that the mining model uses to understand the behavior of the data; an example is *cyclical*. Marking a source column as a cyclical content type tells the mining algorithm that the order of the data is particular, important, and repetitive, or has a cycle to it, for example, the month numbers of more than one year in a time table.

A *data type* is the same as what you already understand data type to mean from relational database modeling, that is, integer, string, and so on. The difference here is that the data types are based on C++, rather than the typical relational database data types that you are probably more familiar with. The rule of thumb is for you to determine the data type first and then verify (and sometimes adjust) the appropriate content type in your model. Remember that certain algorithms only support certain content types; for example, Naïve Bayes does *not* support continuous content types.

Here's a list of the content type attributes:

- *Discrete*: This column (or attribute type) contains values which are distinct, for example, number of children. Another way to think about this is that there are no fractional values. It is worth noting that marking a column as discrete does *not* indicate that the order (or sequence) of the information is important. You can use any data type with this content type.

- *Continuous*: This column has values that are a set of numbers which represent some unit of measurement, for example, outstanding loan amount. These values can be fractional. You can use the date, double, or long data types with this content type.

- *Discretized*: This column has continuous values that are grouped into buckets. Each bucket is considered to have a specific order and to contain discrete values. An example of this is shown in Figure 11-24 using the Age column in the Targeted Maining sample. You can can use dates, doubles, longs, or text data types with the discretized content type.

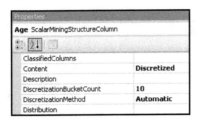

Figure 11-24. *If you choose to mark a mining model column as Discretized, you can also configure the method and bucket count properties for the discretization.*

Note You can adjust the DiscretizationMethod (which determines how the data will be grouped—AUTOMATIC | CLUSTERS [for numerics only; works well for any type of distrubution curve], EQUAL_AREAS [for strings; works best for standard distribution curves]) and the DiscretizationBucketCount (which specifies the number of discrete buckets that the data in this column should be divided into) if you mark your column as Discretized.

- *Key*: This column is used as a unique identifier for a row. You can use date, doubles, longs, or text for this.

- *Key Sequence*: This column is a type of a key; the sequence of key values is important to your model. You can use doubles, longs, text, or dates with this content type. By using this content type, you are identifying the importance of the sequence (or order) or the key values, in addition to noting that the values are identifiers or keys.

- *Key Time*: This column, similar to a key sequence, is a type of key where the sequence of values is important. Additionally, by marking your column with this content type, you are indicating to your mining model that the key values run on a time scale.

- *Ordered*: This column contains data in a specific order that is important for you mining model. Also, when you mark a column with the Ordered content type, SSAS considers that all data contained is discrete. You can use any data type with this content type.

- *Cyclical*: This column has data that is ordered and represents a set that cycles (or repeats). This is often used with time values (months of year, for example). Data marked as Cyclical is considered both ordered and discrete. You can use any data type with this content type.

For your reference, I've "pivoted" the information presented in the preceding list in Table 11-1 so that you can see which data types are supported by which content types. Understanding this concept is very important to successful model building.

Table 11-1. *List of Data Types and Supported Content Types for Each One*

Data Type	Content Types Supported
Text	Supports discrete, discretized, or sequence
Long	Supports continuous, cyclical, discrete, discretized, key sequence, key time, ordered, sequence, or time
Boolean	Supports discrete
Double	Supports cyclical, discrete, discretized, key sequence, key time, ordered, sequence, or time
Date	Supports continuous, discrete, discretized, or key time

As you complete the wizard, you'll be asked to name your mining structure. You have the option to allow drillthrough for your mining structure here as well. Drillthrough in this context functions similiarly to drillthrough in a SSAS cube; that is, it gives the end users with appropriate permissions the ability to right-click a data mining model to see a list of the source data columns that "lead" to the result that they are viewing. Remember that in SSAS 2005 (unlike SSAS 2000), any columns that are included in drillthrough must be included in the particular model; that is, end users can no longer drill through to data that is part of the source start schema but has not been included in the SSAS database.

If you select From Existing Cube as your data source for your mining model, you'll be presented with one additional dialog box before you complete the wizard. This dialog box allows you to define a particular slice of the cube for your mining structure. Figure 11-25 shows an example of this, using the slice "show only customers who are home owners."

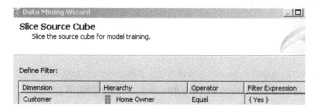

Figure 11-25. *The Data Mining Wizard allows you to define slices of the source cube when you select From Existing Cube as the data source for your mining structure.*

Tip If you are creating a model based on an existing cube that contains a time series, then you'll need to slice the time dimension to remove all future members, assuming those members have been loaded into your cube already.

Another difference in the wizard, if you base your mining model on an existing cube (and you use any of these three algorithms: Microsoft Clustering, Microsoft Decision Trees, or Microsoft Association Rules), is that in the final dialog box, you are also asked whether you want to create a new dimension in your existing cube or create a new cube with a data mining dimension in it. This is shown in Figure 11-26.

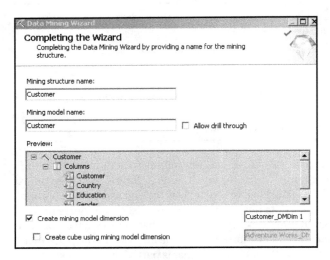

Figure 11-26. *The Data Mining Wizard allows you to create a new dimension in your existing cube using the information in your mining model, or you can create an entirely new cube containing the new dimension.*

One interesting aspect of creating a new dimension, whether in the existing cube or in a new cube, is that a new DSV will be created representing the information in the model. Unlike most typical DSVs, this one cannot be edited, nor can the source data (the model output) be viewed via the DSV interface.

Caution Not all features of data mining are included in all editions of SSAS. If you are working with the Standard Edition of SSAS, you should review the list of features that are included in this edition. A good reference can be found at `http://msdn2.microsoft.com/en-us/library/ms143761.aspx`. If you try to use a feature that is not included in the Standard Edition, SSAS will present you with a warning dialog box as shown in Figure 11-27.

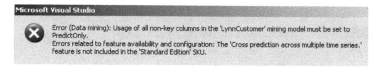

Figure 11-27. *If you are working with the Standard Edition of SSAS, you should be aware that you are only able to use a subset of the data mining features available in SSAS Enterprise Edition.*

Processing Mining Models

After you complete the design of your mining structure, you must process it. You can process some types of included mining models individually, or you can process all models included in the particular mining structure that you are working with. Processing methods for mining structures are as follows:

- *Process Full*: Drops all data and metadata and completely reprocesses the selected object.

- *Default*: Detects the selected object's current state and then determines the appropriate processing method, that is, Full, and so on.

- *Process Structure*: Populates only the mining structure but not the mining models with source data.

- *Process Clear Structure*: Removes all training data from the selected object.

- *Unprocess*: Deletes the data in the object selected and any lower-level associated objects.

Process methods for mining models are as follows:

- *Process Full*: Drops all data and metadata and completely reprocesses the selected object.

- *Default*: Detects the selected object's current state and then determines the appropriate processing method, that is, Full, and so on.

- *Process Unprocess*: Deletes the data in the object selected and any lower-level associated objects. After the data is deleted, it is not reloaded.

As with cube processing, you can configure error handling during processing by clicking the Change Settings button on the Process Model (or Structure) tab dialog box.

Figure 11-28 shows you the detailed output window that is generated in BIDS when you choose to process your mining model.

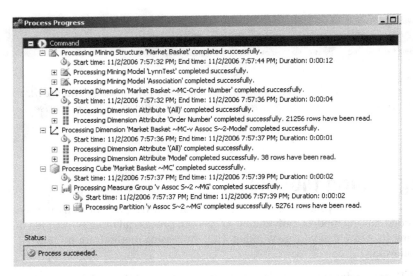

Figure 11-28. *The Process Progress dialog box for data mining structures shows a detailed record of all activities performed during mining structure processing.*

After you move to production, you will want to "automate" the processing of your mining structures. You can easily do this by creating a SSIS package and including the Analysis Services Processing Task. You'll configure the task to perform the type of processing that your business requirements necessitate for the particular mining structure. Figure 11-29 shows this dialog box. This task is encapsulating the XMLA `Process` command, so if you wanted to script this process using only XMLA, and not SSIS, you could do that as well.

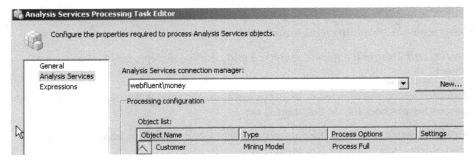

Figure 11-29. *The Analysis Services Processing Task Editor in SSIS allows you to automate the processing of your mining structures by including them in an SSIS control flow.*

In addition to automating model structure processing, there are a couple of other areas of integration between data mining and SSIS. We'll review those in the next section.

SSIS and Data Mining

Data mining by DMX query is supported in SSIS. You have one control flow SSIS task and one data flow transformation to select from. The Data Mining Query Task is available on the Control Flow Toolbox. The editor for this task is shown in Figure 11-30.

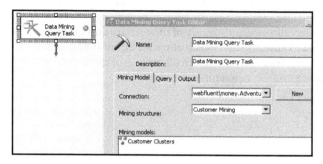

Figure 11-30. *The new Data Mining Query Task allows you to associate a data mining query with the control flow of an SSIS package.*

The Data Mining Query Transformation is available in the Data Flow Transformation Toolbox. As with the control flow task, the data flow transformation allows you to associate a data mining query with an SSIS package. One difference between the two objects is, of course, where they are used in your package. One is for control flow (which is connecting various activities together, such as T-SQL queries, FTP, WMI, and so on), and the other is for data flow (which is impacting a specific set of data flowing through the package by extracting, transforming, and then loading the transformed data to one or more destinations).

An example of where the Data Mining Query Transformation can be used is in a situation where you have a large amount of "unclean" data. This transformation can be used to help determine possible values for "partially dirty" data by splitting this data into clusters. The dialog box for this Transformation is shown in Figure 11-31. Note that both of these objects are only available with the Enterprise Edition of SQL Server.

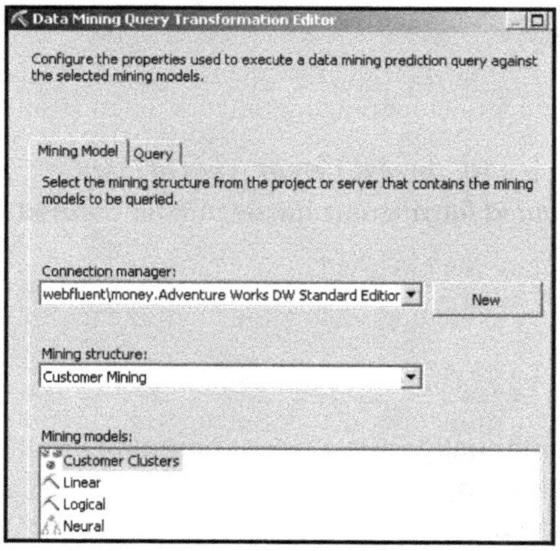

Figure 11-31. *The new Data Mining Query Transformation allows you to associate a data mining query with the data flow of an SSIS package.*

Working with the DMX Language

If your business requirements call for custom client development using the data mining API, you can begin to familiarize yourself with the DMX language by reviewing the supplied templates in SSMS. As with creating an SSAS query, you first connect to SSAS in SSMS, display the Template Explorer, and then click the DMX node to view and work with the included templates. Figure 11-32 shows the included DMX templates.

They include Model Content (which allows simple query of model data and metadata, such as return model attributes), Model Management (which allow for administration, such as create, rename, export model), and Prediction Queries (which allows use of model content in conjunction with other data using the OPENQUERY operator).

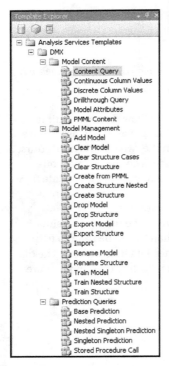

Figure 11-32. *The Template Explorer in SSMS provides you with three different types of DMX queries. There are three different types of templates provided for you as a starter: Model Content, Model Management, and Prediction Queries.*

A Simple DMX Query

As with MDX, in my experience, you'll seldom have to manually write a large amount of DMX queries in production BI solutions. One obvious exception to this general guideline is, of course, if your BI project work was primarily focused on implementing data mining. Microsoft has provided you with a large number of tools, templates, and wizards so that you can implement DMX queries without having to take the time to master the language from scratch. Because of this, we'll simply review the basic DMX syntax at this time.

SSMS included a DMX query tool. You access this tool in a similar fashion to the way you worked with the MDX query tool; that is, you open SSMS, and click the Analysis Services DMX Query button on the toolbar in SSMS to open a DMX query window. Figure 11-33 shows the results of a simple DMX query in SSMS.

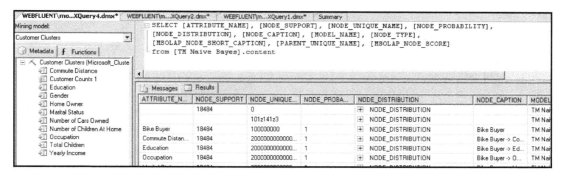

Figure 11-33. *You can write and execute custom DMX queries in SSMS.*

The query shown allows you to view metadata about a particular mining model. I built this query by customizing one of the included DMX templates. These templates are a very good starting location for learning DMX. Like any query language, if you are going to be doing extensive DMX work, you should probably pick up a reference book on it. You will also want to refer to the BOL topic, "Data Mining Extensions (DMX) Reference."

Tip To better understand what type of DMX query you might choose to implement using either of the SSIS objects, you may want to explore the DMX language in a bit more detail. A great way to learn any new language is by reading queries generated by client tools before you begin to attempt to write queries. For data mining, you can do this by capturing queries that data mining client tools (including the BIDS viewers) generate using the SQL Server capture tool—SQL Server Profiler. SSAS 2005 DMX queries can be captured using tracing with Profiler. DMX queries are noted in the Event Subclass column (type = 1) of Profiler traces.

Data Mining Clients

One of the most important considerations when determining whether (and how) to implement SSAS data mining in your BI solution is the selection of end user or client tools. The lack of available client tools has definitely hurt the adoption of data mining in SSAS 2000 and SSAS 2005. However, that void has been filled as of late. As of this writing, you have a couple of choices: you can write your own client tools, you can purchase third-party vendor client tools, or you can use Excel 2007 with the newly available data mining addins (covered in Chapter 14).

Note If you want to write your own client, there is a tutorial for constructing a viewer at `http://msdn2.microsoft.com/en-us/library/ms345129.aspx`. Also, you can read about using the data mining Web control at `http://msdn2.microsoft.com/en-us/library/ms160727.aspx`, and download these controls as part of the Feature Pack at `http://www.microsoft.com/downloads/details.aspx?familyid=d09c1d60-a13c-4479-9b91-9e8b9d835cdc&displaylang=en`.

Summary

Are you now intrigued about the possibilities of adding data mining to your BI solution? I hope so! We covered data mining concepts, conducted a brief tour of the BIDS data mining UI using one of the AdventureWorks samples, and then went on to cover building data mining structures in more detail We discussed each of the supplied algorithms and looked at their content, data types, and other key properties.

We then discussed the practical matters of processing your mining structures. We then took a quick look at SSIS integration. We ended our tour of SSAS data mining by looking at the basic syntax of DMX.

In the next chapter, we'll explore the world of end-user client applications or reporting clients. We have a lot to cover there: Microsoft client tools for BI, third-party tools, and custom development.

CHAPTER 12

■ ■ ■

Reporting Tools

This chapter will cover the ins and outs of selecting, designing, and implementing one or more reporting clients for your BI solution. The focus of the chapter will be on using Microsoft clients. Many third-party options are available as well but discussing them is beyond the scope of this book.

The selection of an appropriate set of client tools can make or break your BI solution. Ideally, you will select your client strategy near the beginning of your project, as support (or lack of) for various SSAS features in the selected client tools is an important design consideration. Given that backdrop, this is what we'll discuss in the chapter:

- Using Excel 2003 pivot tables and more

- Using SQL Server Reporting Services (SSRS)

- Producing reports with Report Builder

- Working with .NET 2.0 report viewer controls

- Understanding SharePoint 2003 Web parts

- Examining Business Scorecards Server 2005 and ProClarity

- Considering ProClarity and data mining clients

By the time this book is published, you'll have the option to work with Office 2007. Because of the large amount of new functionality included in that release, Chapter 14 is devoted to BI integration in Office 2007 applications.

Using Excel 2003: Pivot Charts and More

The simplest choice for reporting is to use an Excel 2003 pivot table or pivot chart. As discussed in Chapter 1, it is quick and easy to establish a connection from Excel to SSAS. Because we covered the process for creating a pivot table in Chapter 1, this section covers the procedure for creating a pivot chart from your SSAS database.

Note Remember, you must install the (nondefault) Office component called Microsoft Query so that you can connect from Excel 2003 to SSAS.

As with creating a pivot table, to create a pivot chart, you start by choosing Data ➤ Pivot Table and Pivot Chart Report to open the PivotTable and PivotChart Wizard. The first step asks you to select the location of the source data and the type of pivot structure you want to create. As shown in Figure 12-1, you'll select External data source and PivotChart report (with PivotTable report) in this step of the wizard.

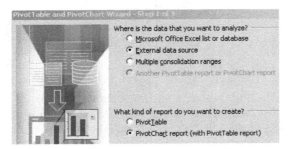

Figure 12-1. *To create a pivot chart using your SSAS database as a source, select the displayed values on the first step of the PivotTable and PivotChart Wizard.*

In the next step of the wizard, you'll click the Get Data button (as you did to create the connection for the pivot table in Chapter 1), and then configure the connection to the SSAS database the same way you did in Chapter 1 as well. Be sure to use the OLAP provider called Microsoft OLE DB for Analysis Services 9.0, which is required to connect to SSAS 2005. The connection dialog box is shown in Figure 12-2.

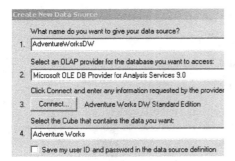

Figure 12-2. *To connect to the sample SSAS database in Excel, you must configure the Create New Data Source dialog box.*

You can then complete the wizard and begin to format your pivot chart. The wizard will create both a pivot table and a pivot chart—both of these items are linked to each other. The pivot chart design area contains "hint" text (for example, "Drop Page Fields Here") in all of the design areas of the pivot chart. These hints are designed to help you to understand which type of items (that is, dimensional attributes, measures [or data items], and so on) you may drag from the PivotTable Field List to the design surface. The pivot chart design surface is shown in Figure 12-3.

Figure 12-3. *The pivot chart design surface contains hints that help you understand what types of data items you can drag and drop to which parts of the pivot chart design surface.*

The PivotTable Field List displays all of the selected cube's dimensions, dimension attributes, and measures. You can drag items from this list to the various design surface areas. After you have dragged an item to the design surface, the item name text becomes bold in the PivotTable Field List to indicate that it has been selected. You can then continue to design and format your pivot chart, until it has the appearance that you need. Figure 12-4 shows a pivot chart created using the sample AdventureWorksDW cube.

You also have the option to save your pivot table or chart as a Web page. This page can be saved with or without (pivot) interactivity, which allows your end users to manipulate the resulting pivot chart by using the pivot functionality (that is, add or remove fields, rotate fields from one position to another, and so on). To save your pivot chart and allow interactivity, you choose File ➤ Save as Web Page. In the Save As dialog box, click the Selection: Chart radio button. If you want to add interactivity, then click the check box next to that value. You may also add additional functionality by clicking the Publish button on the lower-right side of the dialog box. The options that you can configure via the Publish as Web Page dialog box are shown in Figure 12-5. These options include the ability to add interactivity through the use of an ActiveX control, to auto-republish the pivot chart on open, and to preview the results in a browser.

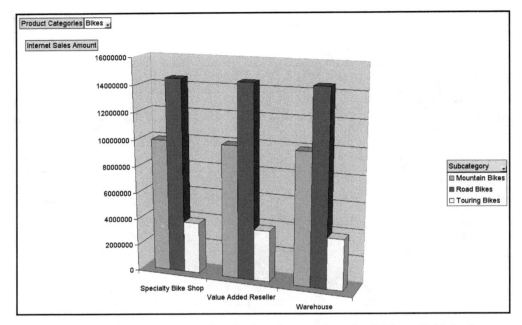

Figure 12-4. *You configure your pivot chart by dragging and dropping fields available in the fields list to the pivot chart design surface areas.*

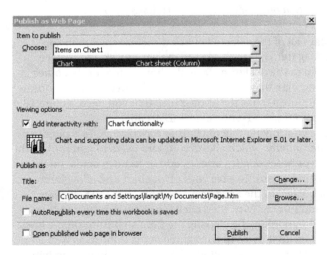

Figure 12-5. *You can add pivot interactivity to your pivot chart when you save it as a Web page in this dialog box.*

The pivot (or interactivity) functionality requires the execution of a specific ActiveX control in Internet Explorer. For this to run correctly, the end user must have permission to run this control.

Caution ActiveX controls, such as those that are required to enable pivot chart interactivity, are typically only permitted in intranet (not Internet) usage scenarios to prevent potential security risks.

Figure 12-6 shows the result of saving this pivot chart as an interactive HTML page. Note that a linked pivot table is also saved as part of this Web page.

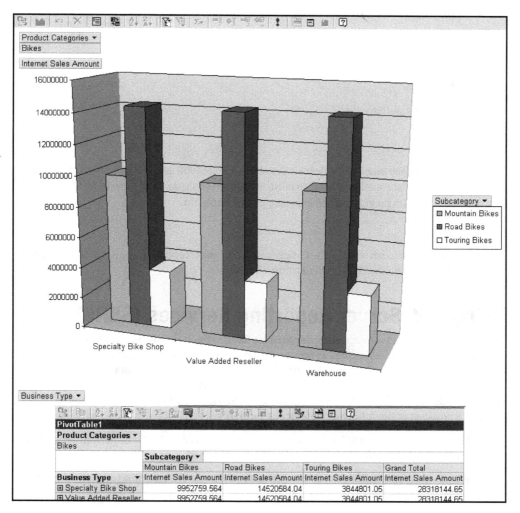

Figure 12-6. *Saving a pivot chart as an interactive HTML page allows end users to manipulate both the pivot table and chart built against the sample SSAS cube in a browser. This functionality requires the execution of an ActiveX control in the browser.*

Limitations of Excel 2003 as an SSAS Client

Although pivot tables and pivot charts are easy to implement and are somewhat adequate as clients for some BI solutions, it is important to understand and consider some of the limitations of using Excel 2003 as a client for SSAS cubes. Quite a few features that are available in SSAS are not supported by Excel 2003. Here's a list of the most commonly requested features that are *not* supported in Excel 2003.

- Actions

- Drillthrough

- KPIs

- Perspectives

- Translations

- Data mining: all aspects

Note Microsoft is well aware of the deficiencies of using Excel 2003 as a client for SSAS 2005. In Excel 2007, Microsoft has made a major effort to improve the support and usability of Excel as an SSAS client. This expanded feature support is covered in more detail in Chapter 14.

The next step is to review another Microsoft Web-based reporting solution: SQL Server Reporting Services (SSRS) 2005 as a client for SSAS cubes.

Using SQL Server Reporting Services (SSRS)

This version of SQL Server Reporting Services (SSRS) has been significantly enhanced to make creating reports using SSAS cubes as source data much easier and more flexible. SSRS is designed to be an enterprise-capable reporting solution for all types of data sources (relational, multidimensional, text, and so on). This section mostly focuses on using SSRS as a reporting client for only SSAS cube data. However, before we do that, let's discuss SSRS in general.

SSRS consists of the following default components:

- *Web Service hosted in IIS 6.0, called ReportServer*: This required component is one of the areas where the core report processing is done in SSRS.

- *Windows Service called SQL Server Reporting Services*: This required component is the other area where the core report processing is done in SSRS.

- *Web Site (or application) hosted in IIS 6.0, called Reports*: This is the default user interface for the results of the Web Service. End users access this ASP.NET 2.0 Web application, which is also called Report Manager, by navigating to the (default) URL: `http://localhost/reports`. Figure 12-7 shows a named instance (`Reports$Enterprise`) of SSRS in IIS.

Figure 12-7. *SSRS uses both a Web service and a Web application in IIS.*

Note You can develop alternate user interfaces (Web forms, Windows forms, or other types) by connecting to published reports hosted on the ReportServer or by writing your own .NET applications, which call the ReportServer Web Service APIs.

- *Report development environment:* This is a template that is added in to Visual Studio 2005 (or available in BIDS, if you do not have VS 2005 installed on your development machine). BIDS, which is built on VS 2005, is the default development environment for report queries, layout, and structure. You can use other report development tools to author reports, including Report Builder, discussed later in this section.

Tip If you are hosting other Web sites on the same IIS 6.0 server as SSRS, you will probably want to isolate SSRS to its own application pool in IIS as shown in Figure 12-7. This improves the manageability and security of your SSRS installation by allowing you to isolate resources (such as CPU utilization) for your particular SSRS instance.

Although sample SSRS reports are included with the SQL Server samples (located by default at `C:\Program Files\Microsoft SQL Server\90\Samples\Reporting Services\ Report Samples\AdventureWorks Sample Reports`), it will be valuable for you to build a report from scratch, so we'll now review the steps involved to build a report using the sample AdventureWorks cube as a data source.

> ■**Note** The included samples contain not only sample reports but also a number of different interesting samples of other types of functionality, such as SSRS management samples, custom delivery and authentication samples, and more. The default location for all SSRS samples is `C:\Program Files\`
> `Microsoft SQL Server\90\Samples\Reporting Services`.

To build a report against an SSAS cube for SSRS, you open BIDS, and then choose File ➤ New ➤ Project. In the New Project dialog box, you'll select the BI template type. You have three template types to choose from when building reports: Report Server Project Wizard, Report Server Project, or Report Model Project. For this discussion, we'll use the Report Server Project Wizard template as shown in Figure 12-8.

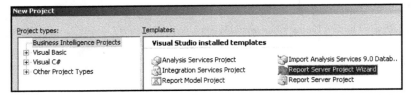

Figure 12-8. *To create a report, you open BIDS and select one of the three types of report templates.*

After you select this template type, the wizard presents you with a series of dialog boxes. In the Select the Data Source dialog box (see Figure 12-9), you are asked to configure a data source. Although this process is similar to configuring a data source in SSAS, there are some important differences. One of these differences is the option to create the data sources as "shared" or global to the entire report solution. It is a best practice to create shared data sources because you'll spend less time creating connections (that is, you can just reuse the global one you've created for multiple reports), and you can easily update any of the values (that is, the connection string information) in the data source, which will affect every report in the project.

You can either type the desired connection string directly into the Connection String list box, or you can use the Edit or Credentials buttons to quickly generate a connection string based on your input values.

> ■**Note** If you click the Credentials button, the only available connection type is Use Windows Authentication (Integrated Security). The other choices, Use a specific username, Prompt for credentials, and so on, are greyed out and not available for connections to SSAS using SSRS.

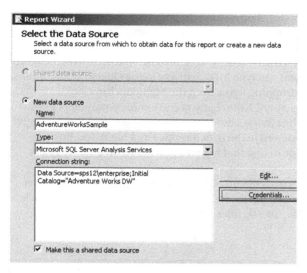

Figure 12-9. *In the Select the Data Source dialog box, you configure the connection to SSAS.*

The next step is to write the MDX query to retrieve the values from your cube. The Report Wizard has a built-in visual query designer, which you access by clicking the Query Builder button. The Query Builder interface is much like the cube browser in BIDS as shown in Figure 12-10. To generate a MDX query, you simply drag and drop items from the Metadata section onto the design areas. This built-in visual MDX query designer greatly reduces the amount of manual query writing you'll need to do to build a reporting solution for SSAS and results in the ability to generate reports much more quickly.

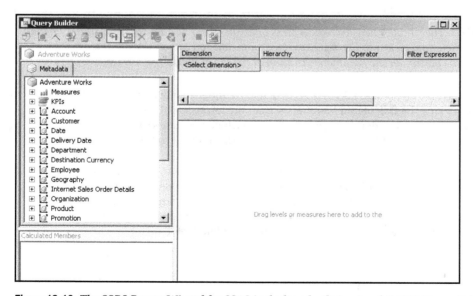

Figure 12-10. *The SSRS Report Wizard for SSAS includes a built-in visual (MDX) Query Builder. This greatly reduces the need for you to manually write MDX queries.*

The visual Query Builder has two modes of operation: design mode and native query mode. It opens in design mode. This means that you drag and drop items from the Metadata viewer to the blank windows on the right to generate a MDX query.

If you want to manually write (or use) a MDX query, click the last button on the toolbar to switch to native query mode, and then you can type MDX natively in the Query Builder interface in combination with dragging and dropping items from the Metadata browser.

Figure 12-11 shows a drag-and-drop query. Note that you can enable parameters in your report interface by simply checking the box in the filter section at the top of the query design work area. These parameters can be presented in the user interface as a blank text box or a drop-down list (showing a list you provide or one that is generated based on another query) that shows a default value.

Another enhancement to this version of SSRS for SSAS is that multiple query parameter values can be selected as default (and can be passed by the end user by making multiple selections in the drop-down list). In SSRS 2000, only a single query parameter value could be passed to a MDX query.

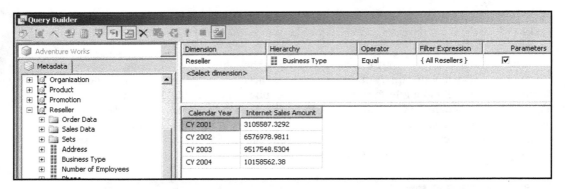

Figure 12-11. *The simplest way to create a MDX query in Query Builder is to drag and drop items from the Metadata viewer to the design surface. Note that you can enable parameters by simply checking the box under the Parameters column at the top of the design surface.*

You can also create and add MDX-calculated members while in visual design mode by right-clicking the Calculated Members area at the lower-left of the design surface. The Calculated Member Builder dialog box appears in which you can write the MDX for the calculated member (see Figure 12-12). Normally you will generate, rather than manually author, the MDX.

Remember that the calculated members you are creating here are specific to the particular report that you are creating. In other words, they are visible only to this report. You can think of this type of calculated member as "local." This differs from creating calculated members as objects for a particular cube using the cube designer (Calculations tab) in BIDS. Calculated members created for the cube can be considered "global."

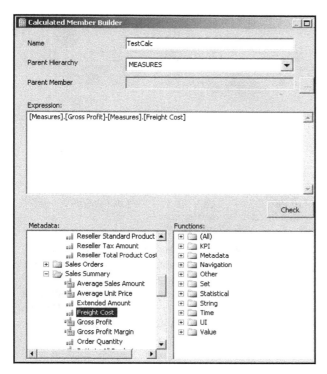

Figure 12-12. *You can add calculated members to your report by adding them to the query while using the Query Builder. To do this, right-click the Calculated Members surface, and then enter your MDX query into the the Calculated Member Builder dialog box.*

Tip To generate, rather than manually write the MDX calculated member expression, you can drag and drop measures, dimensions, and so on from the Metadata area of the Calculated Member Builder dialog box to the Expression area. You can also drag or double-click Functions to add them to the expression that you are building.

Figure 12-13 shows the same query as was generated in Figure 12-11, now rendered in the Query Builder so that the MDX statement is visible. You can edit this query by simply typing directly into the interface. Note also that the Metadata viewer includes the MDX Functions and Templates libraries. As in BIDS and SSMS, you can also generate the MDX query by selecting and then dragging and dropping Metadata items, Functions, or Templates into the MDX work area.

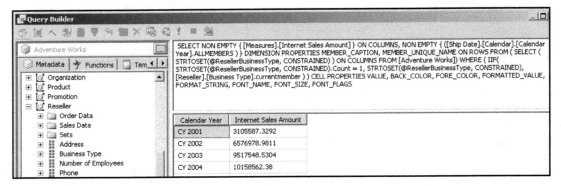

Figure 12-13. *You can switch from visual design to native MDX query mode in the Query Builder by clicking the Design Mode button (the last button) on the toolbar.*

Another change to the interface when you are working in native query mode is the availabilty of two additional buttons on the toolbar: the Query Parameters (fifth button from the right) and Prepare Query buttons (fourth button from the right).

When you click the Query Parameters button, the Query Parameters dialog box allowing you to visually configure the query parameters becomes available (see Figure 12-14). Here you can specify parameter names; associate those names to dimensions, attributes, or hierarchies (using the Hierarchy section); allow multiple values; and set a default value.

Query Parameters

Specify details of the parameters defined in the query:

Parameter	Dimension	Hierarchy	Multiple values	Default
ProductProductLine	Product	Product Line	☑	Mountain

Figure 12-14. *When working in native MDX query mode in the Query Builder, you can use the Query Parameters dialog box to view and adjust the query parameters as needed.*

The Prepare Query button acts much like the "blue check" button in SSMS T-SQL query mode; that is, when you click it, the query syntax is checked and any errors are returned to you via a pop-up window. The one item that is lacking in this view is also similar to a missing feature in the T-SQL query interface: IntelliSense. If you had a need to author most of your MDX queries manually, you could use one of the query interfaces, like the SSMS Analysis Services MDX Query tool, which does support IntelliSense to write your query, and then copy and paste it into the SSRS Query Builder dialog box.

■**Caution** If you make changes to the MDX query in native query mode in SSRS and then switch back to visual design mode, all of the changes that you made will be lost.

The next few dialog boxes of the wizard ask you a series of questions about the visual design of the report (that is, layout, styles, colors, and so on). This process is very similar to other visual report design wizards, particulary Access. After you've run through the wizard, you will have three work areas to continue to work with your report: the Data tab, Layout tab, and Preview tab. The Preview tab is shown in Figure 12-15.

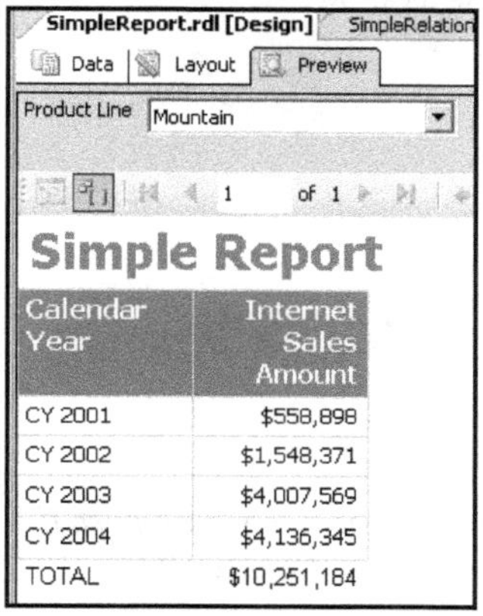

Figure 12-15. *The Report Design interface includes a Preview tab so that you can review the report you've created as you continue to enhance the design.*

If you want to alter your query, then you click the Data tab and make changes to the MDX query either by dragging and dropping items from the Metadata view (using visual design mode) or by a combination of typing MDX and dragging items from the Metadata, Functions, or Templates tabs (using native MDX query mode). Of course if the changes you make to the MDX query invalidate the report layout, for example, if you remove an item from the On Columns clause of the MDX query, then you would also have to update your report by using the Layout tab to remove that information from the report layout.

You can associate more than one query with a report. To do so, click the drop-down list next to Dataset and then click New Dataset. Associating more than one query with a report is commonly done to populate parameter lists with dynamic values. In fact, when you add a parameter to your report using the visual query designer, a separate data set is automatically created for you. The MDX syntax used to create the data set for the parameter ProductLine is shown in Figure 12-16.

```
WITH MEMBER [Measures].[ParameterCaption] AS '[Product].[Product Line].CURRENTMEMBER.
MEMBER_CAPTION' MEMBER [Measures].[ParameterValue] AS '[Product].[Product Line].CURRENTMEMBER.
UNIQUENAME' MEMBER [Measures].[ParameterLevel] AS '[Product].[Product Line].CURRENTMEMBER.LEVEL.
ORDINAL' SELECT {[Measures].[ParameterCaption], [Measures].[ParameterValue], [Measures].
[ParameterLevel]} ON COLUMNS , [Product].[Product Line].ALLMEMBERS ON ROWS FROM [Adventure Works]
```

Figure 12-16. *Parameters that are added to your MDX queries generate calculated member MDX statements.*

After you're satisfied with the values retrieved by your MDX query (or queries), then you may want to modify the layout of your report. To do so, click the Layout tab in the report designer. While there, you may place the available data fields onto the available design surfaces. The example uses a simple table. Your choices are Table, Matrix, Chart, List, or Subreport. I added a total amount by right-clicking the table and then clicking Table Footer. Then, I dragged the Internet_Sales_Amount from the Datasets viewer to the Footer cell. Note that the SUM function was automatically applied to the field value as shown in Figure 12-17.

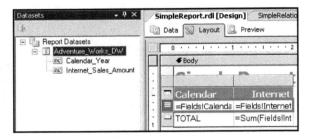

Figure 12-17. *Drag fields from the Datasets view to the Layout tab to add them to your report. If you drag a field to the Table Footer area, the SUM function will be added automatically.*

Another area you may want to work in while in Layout view is the Report Parameters area. To access this, choose Report ➤ Report Parameters. You can then further configure the parameters per the values available in the dialog box; for example, you can allow null values, blank values, multiselects; populate a drop-down list with values from the cube; and so on (see Figure 12-18).

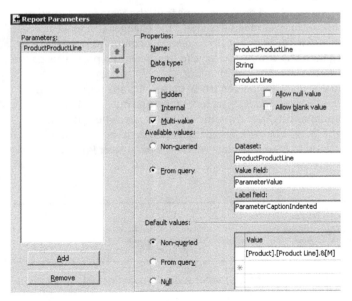

Figure 12-18. *The Report Parameters dialog box allows you to configure the parameters for your report. Note that for our sample the parameter values are populated from the second MDX data set.*

If you're satisfied with your report, you can now deploy it to the ReportServer Web Service. To do this, first right-click the name of your solution in the Solution Explorer window, and then verify that the TargetServerURL address is correct for your particular installation of SSRS. The example shown in Figure 12-19 is installed as a named instance to a nondefault port.

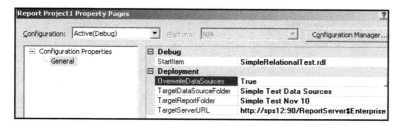

Figure 12-19. *Be sure to verify the* TargetServerURL *location on the Report Project Property Pages prior to attempting to deploy your reporting project.*

The StartItem property lists the first report that you created in the project. Note that the file name ends in .rdl. This is the XML dialect (Report Definition Language) that the Report Designer generates in Visual Studio. When you build or deploy a report or report project, the .rdl syntax is validated against a specialized type of XSD schema. Be aware that .rdl and .rds files are not compiled during this process.

Note You can actually see (and manually edit) the RDL being generated in Visual Studio 2005 by right-clicking any report in Solution Explorer and then clicking View Code. You will want to avoid editing the .rdl files manually whenever possible because it is easy to make a mistake that will invalidate the entire file. Be sure to back up an .rdl file *before* editing it manually. Remember that RDL (being an XML dialect) is both case sensitive and space sensitive.

A portion of the RDL for a report is shown in Figure 12-20.

If you have made errors in configuring your report, those errors may appear when you attempt to deploy the project. Any designtime errors will be shown in BIDS at the bottom on your work area in the Error List window. These errors result when you create a configuration that is invalid for the schema, for example, binding a field in a table (or any other type of data bindable container) using the Layout tab with an Expression that contained invalid syntax.

You can also create report configurations that result in runtime errors (these are most often due to incorrect data source connection string information). You will discover these types of errors when you attempt to view the report you've created in BIDS by using the Preview tab. BIDS displays a description of the runtime error on the Preview design surface.

After you've successfully deployed your report, you can then view it using the Report Manager Web interface installed with SSRS, or you can use the Web Service APIs to create your own customized user interface if the included Report Manager Web site doesn't meet your business requirements. Your end users can also use the available drop-down list on that Web site to render the report in formats other than the default HTML. These formats include .xls,

.pdf., .csv, and .xml. Also you can configure security and other runtime settings (for example, execution and caching behavior) via Report Manager. Figure 12-21 shows a sample report rendered in Report Manager.

```
SimpleReport.rdl [XML]   SimpleReport.rdl [Design]   SimpleRelation...st.rdl [Design]   Start Page
    <?xml version="1.0" encoding="utf-8"?>
    <Report xmlns="http://schemas.microsoft.com/sqlserver/reporting/2005/01/reportdefinition
      <DataSources>
        <DataSource Name="Adventure Works DW">
          <ConnectionProperties>
            <IntegratedSecurity>true</IntegratedSecurity>
            <ConnectString>Data Source=sps12\enterprise;Initial Catalog="Adventure Works DW"
            <DataProvider>OLEDB-MD</DataProvider>
          </ConnectionProperties>
          <rd:DataSourceID>04eeed2b-0fe5-4575-80d8-819dde55d36c</rd:DataSourceID>
        </DataSource>
      </DataSources>
      <BottomMargin>1in</BottomMargin>
      <RightMargin>1in</RightMargin>
      <ReportParameters>
        <ReportParameter Name="ProductProductLine">
          <DataType>String</DataType>
          <DefaultValue>
            <Values>
              <Value>[Product].[Product Line].&amp;[M]</Value>
            </Values>
          </DefaultValue>
          <Prompt>Product Line</Prompt>
```

Figure 12-20. *To view or edit the RDL associated with a report, you right-click the report in Solution Explorer and then click View Code.*

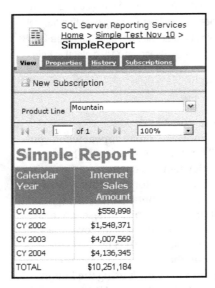

Figure 12-21. *You can use Report Manager to present your SSAS reports to end users. Note that the interface supports the use of parameters.*

Another method of producing reports from SSAS cube data sources using SSRS is to use the new Report Builder interface. More about that in the next section.

Producing Reports with Report Builder

The new Report Builder tool included with SSRS 2005 is a Windows application that you, or authorized users, can launch directly from Report Manager. Report Builder provides you (or authorized end users) with a simplified interface for report development. Using Report Builder is an alternative to creating report definitions using BIDS or Visual Studio 2005.

Before you launch Report Builder, you must first create a report model. A *report model* is a specific type of an XSD schema called Semantic Model Definition Language (SMDL), which is generated for SSAS cubes by clicking a button in Report Manager. An SMDL model is a way to describe the underlying database in business terms, so that the end user does not need to know about tables, relationships, measures, dimensions, and the like.

There is only one way to create a report model for SSAS (unlike for models run against SQL Server data, where you have multiple methods of creating a report model) using the GUI interfaces and tools. You do this by generating the schema from inside Report Manager. First, you must navigate to the data source properties for the SSAS connection in Report Manager. Once there, you click the Generate Model button at the bottom of the page to create a model that can be used by the Report Builder. This interface is shown in Figure 12-22.

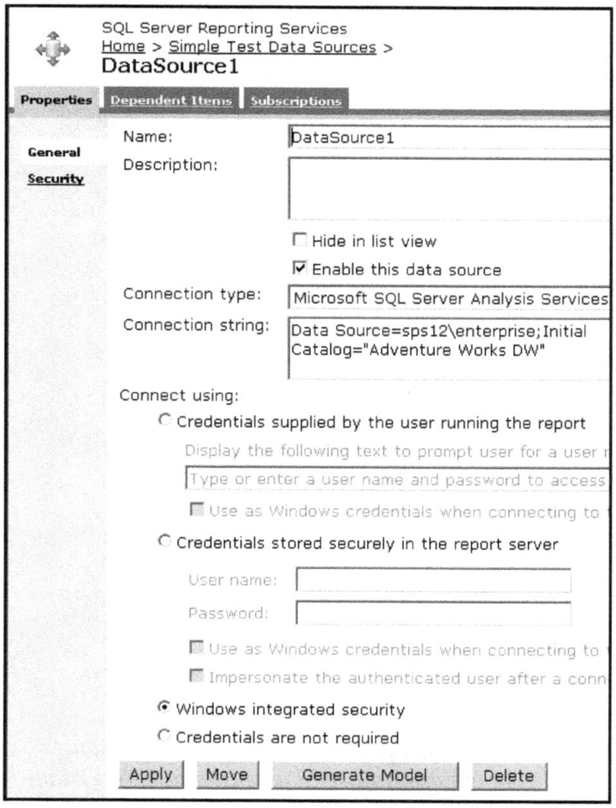

Figure 12-22. *To create a Report Model from an SSAS data source, you navigate to the properties of the data source, and then click Generate Model.*

Interestingly, you *cannot* create (or edit) a report model of an SSAS database using the BIDS Create a Report Model template. The BIDS template only allows relational data sources using that template because you have created an appropriate level of abstraction when you created your cube, and you don't need to repeat that process. Instead, you just need to create a copy of that abstraction in the language required by Report Builder or SMDL.

After you've created a model, you can then launch the Report Builder application by clicking the Report Builder button on the Report Manager toolbar. This launches the Report Builder application by using ClickOnce technologies. The button is associated with this URL by default: `http://<yourserver>/reportserver/reportbuilder/reportbuilder.application`. You could, of course, access this URL by embedding the link in your own custom client application as well. After you click the link and agree to Run the application, the application downloads from SSRS and launches. You must have permissions to run this application as well. For more information about the required permissions, see the BOL topic "Securing Report Builder."

The first step in using the Report Builder is to select the report model source and report type that you want to use as a basis for your report. You'll note that the top-level SampleModel is greyed out, indicating that you must select one of the items listed below it as a source for your report model. These items are the cubes and cube perspectives that are contained in your SSAS database. Generating a report model from the sample AdventureWorks SSAS presents you with the choices shown in Figure 12-23.

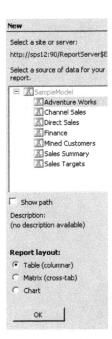

Figure 12-23. *The first choice you'll make in Report Builder is to select the source of the data for your report. Then you'll select the report type. For our example, we'll use AdventureWorks data source and a matrix-type report layout.*

The next choice is which entity you want to use as the basis for the report. Report Builder reports are built around the concept of displaying a single entity and some or all of its related attributes (or fields). So, what's an *entity*? Per BOL, an entity is "a logical collection of model items, including source fields, roles, folders and expressions, presented in familiar business terms." For SSAS Report Builder models, entities are created for each dimension and for most fact tables. Another way to think of an entity is as a particular business object, such as customer, product, marketing campaign, and so on.

To continue working toward building a report using Report Builder, you select an entity, and then select the desired field from the available (associated) fields (or attributes) list, which is shown in the Fields box. To use a particular entity, you need to drag it to the design surface. After you drag an entity to the design surface, then the available entities displayed are restricted to the particular selected entity and all child entities associated with it. If you want to reset the Entities list back to the original (master) set, then you simply drag all items off of the report design surface. Figure 12-24 shows the Entities and Fields selection list boxes in the Report Builder.

Figure 12-24. *To configure your report, you drag an entity to the report design surface. You then drag associated fields (or attributes) to the design surface.*

You may also add Filters to your report by clicking the Filter button and then configuring the filter conditions that are appropriate for your business scenario. Figure 12-25 shows the dialog box you use to add filters to your report. It's interesting to see that the filters are generated from your "natural language" inputs. This is yet another time-saving feature built into this product. The idea is that nonprogrammers can quickly and easily generate, in this case, filters using natural langauge rather than having T-SQL or MDX programmers writing code.

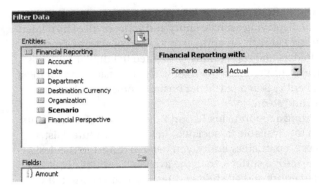

Figure 12-25. *The Filter Data dialog box allows you to add filters to your report. These filters are generated based on your natural language inputs (shown as Financial Reporting on the right side of this dialog box).*

The Sort and Group button on the toolbar allows you to perform those actions using the simple GUI interface, rather than by writing code, on your report as well. The Sort dialog box is shown in Figure 12-26.

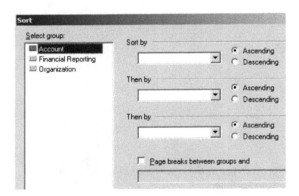

Figure 12-26. *The Sort dialog box allows you to sort the data displayed in your report.*

You may also add a calculated field to your report by choosing Report ➤ New Field. The Define Formula dialog box appears that lists the currently available entities and fields and a subset of functions that are appropriate to the particular selection. If you add a function to the formula area, the formula definition and arguments are displayed as shown in Figure 12-27.

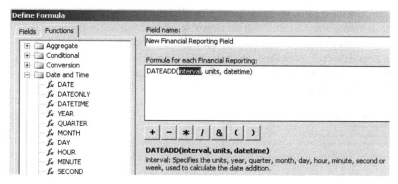

Figure 12-27. *The Define Formula dialog box allows you to add a calculated field to your report.*

Tip You can also edit the formula for any calculated field in your report (represented by values on the design surface or by a numeric value) by right-clicking the cell and then clicking Edit Formula.

The last area for you to configure prior to running your report is accessed by choosing Report ➤ Report Properties. In the Report Properties dialog box, you can configure advanced properties, including User Sorting, Drillthrough, Fixed Headers, Drilldown, and Server Totals. Figure 12-28 shows the default settings for this dialog box.

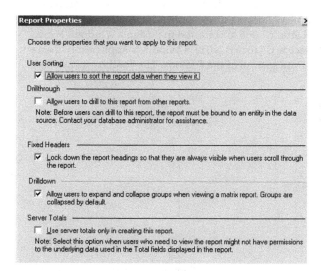

Figure 12-28. *The Report Properties dialog box allows you to set a number of options for your report.*

After you've configured your report, you may view it by clicking the Run Report button on the toolbar. If you want to create a report that will be viewable after this session (by you and anyone else to whom you grant permission) using Report Builder, then you may save the report definition to the ReportServer (provided you have the appropriate permissions). When you choose File ➤ Save, you are prompted to name your report and are then directed to the ReportServer location by default. Figure 12-29 shows a portion of this dialog box.

Figure 12-29. *You have the option to save your report definition to the ReportServer. If you choose to do this, you can then access the report that you built in Report Builder using Report Manager.*

Report Builder is a great addition to the tools available for you to build .rdl reports against your SSAS cubes. Third-party vendor RDL generators are also available. An important consideration for your BI project is the determination of which tools will be used to create reports and which end users will be involved in report writing.

Working with .NET 2.0 Report Viewer Controls

Two report controls ship with .NET 2.0. One can be used with Windows Forms, and one can be used with Web Forms. Both appear in the toolbox inside of Visual Studio 2005 after you've started developing an application using either the Windows or Web development templates.

For this example, we'll create a simple Windows Forms application to display our SSAS cube report. After you've opened Visual Studio 2005 and started to design a Windows Forms application by clicking File ➤ New Project ➤ C# (or VB.NET) ➤ Windows Application, then you will find the Report Viewer icon on the Data section of the Toolbox. The Toolbox section is shown in Figure 12-30.

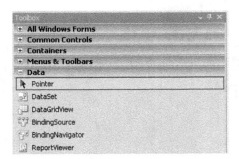

Figure 12-30. *The Report Viewer control allows you to add SSRS reports (which use your SSAS cube as a data source) to your Windows Forms application. There is also a Report Viewer control included in Visual Studio 2005 for use with ASP.NET 2.0 Web applications.*

Drag the Report Viewer onto the Windows Forms design surface and you'll see that a smart tag pops up at the upper-right side of the control. This smart tag allows you to enter the URL to an existing report (called remote processing mode), or to design a new one (called local processing mode) by clicking the `design a new report` link on the smart tag. If you use local processing mode, no license for SSRS is needed, and all processing is done locally. Also, the type of RDL produced is slightly different; it's called .rdlc. Unfortunately, this mode does *not* support SSAS cubes as a data source. It does, of course, support using SQL Server (and other types of relational data) as data sources.

If you use local processing mode with some relational data as your data source, a new report design area opens up. This file is called Report1.rdlc by default and is shown in Figure 12-31.

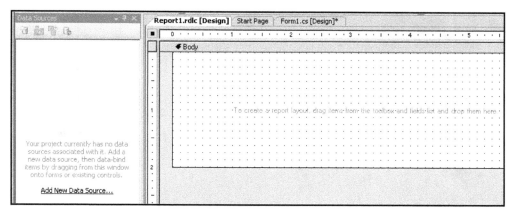

Figure 12-31. *If you choose to design a new report using the Report Viewer control, you'll be presented with a work area to create that report. Unfortunately, development of locally processed reports using an SSAS database as a data source is not supported.*

Because you will use only remote processing mode to display reports built on your SSAS cubes, your considerations when using the Windows Forms ReportViewer control will be the following:

- `URL to reportServer`: This string is configured in the smart tag on the ReportViewer control in the form of `http://<yourserver>/reportserver`.

- `URL to report`: This string is configured in the smart tag on the ReportViewer control in the form of `/report folder/report name`, for example, `/AdventureWorks Sample Reports/Company Sales`.

- `Security Credentials`: The credentials being passed will vary depending on how the application developer has configured the application. Be sure to verify that the credentials being used in the Windows Forms application have access to the desired report on the SSRS. If you are working with WebForms, you'll need to consider authentication and authorization strategies related to that type of UI.

- `Parameter values`: If the report to which the control is connecting expects parameter values, then the ReportViewer control header area will automatically provide a UI for entering or selecting the particular parameter value.

Figure 12-32 shows the ReportViewer control used in a Windows Forms application, displaying the simple sample report that we've been working with in this chapter. When you work with the ReportViewer control you can optionally set the Dock in Parent Container option to true, and then the report surface fills the entire Window Forms display area (as is shown in Figure 12-32).

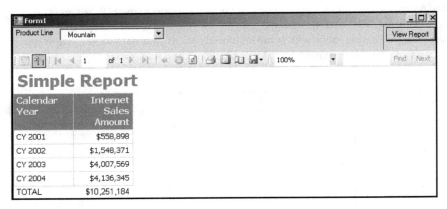

Figure 12-32. *The ReportViewer control allows you to quickly add server-based SSAS reports to Windows Forms or WebForm applications.*

■ **Note** VS 2005 SP1 includes some enhancements to the ReportViewer controls. Read more details at http://prologika.com/CS/blogs/blog/archive/2006/12/20/Report-Viewer-Enhancements-in-VS.NET-2005-SP1.aspx.

Understanding SharePoint 2003 Web Parts

The SharePoint 2003 reporting Web parts are specialized report viewer controls. The two types of Web parts available for this release of SharePoint are the Report Explorer and the Report Viewer Web parts. As with the remote processing mode for the .NET 2.0 ReportViewer control, the SharePoint ReportViewer Web part allows you to display an SSRS based on an SSAS database on a SharePoint Portal site (which is a specialized type of an .aspx page). Also similar to the .NET ReportViewer control, the logged-on user to SharePoint must have appropriate permissions to view the report on SSAS via the SharePoint Web part. Figure 12-33 shows the Report Explorer and the Report Viewer controls.

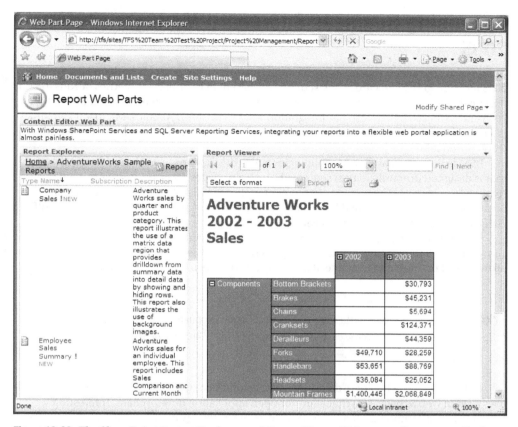

Figure 12-33. *The SharePoint Report Explorer and Report Viewer Web parts allow you to display reports in your portal.*

You can use the controls independently; that is, the Report Explorer can list all the reports available in a particular folder on your ReportServer, and the Report Viewer can display a particular report. You can also connect the two Web parts by configuring the Report Explorer to pass the selected value (report name) to the Report Viewer.

It is also possible to develop custom Web parts for SharePoint to display reports in other types of configurations by creating Web parts that display data returned from SSRS in whatever method that you needed to satisfy your business requirements. A key component in this type of development is the creation of custom XSLT stylesheets to transform the XML results from SSRS into the appropriate output format.

Tip Development of Web parts for future versions of SharePoint has been made much simpler with the introduction of several new base classes in the .NET 2.0 framework (included with VS 2005). Note, however, that SharePoint 2003 is based on .NET 1.1, which means that custom Web part development for this version of SharePoint would entail writing a large amount of code manually.

Examining Business Scorecard Manager (BSM) 2005

This product is a server that hosts scorecards. This Web-based server is built on SharePoint 2003 technologies. Scorecards consist of reports based on key business metrics or KPIs. BSM is designed to work with Office 2003 applications such as Excel and SharePoint, as well as SSAS 2005 and SSRS 2005. BSM also has integration with Microsoft Dynamics. Microsoft Dynamics is a customer-relationship management (CRM) product and Enterprise Resource Planning (ERP) product line.

BSM is built on SharePoint technologies and is the first product released from Microsoft that is designed primarily to host scorecards. It also provides other functionality, such as "what if" forecasting. The previous implementation was called Microsoft Office Business Scorecards Accelerator and had been made available to selected partners only. It wasn't officially a product, rather a solution accelerator or group of files and templates.

BSM consists of a client component, a server component, and a builder (or developer) component. All three components can be placed on separate physical machines, or they can all be placed on the same machine, depending on your business requirements.

Note BSM has very specific installation requirements. More information can be found at http://office.microsoft.com/en-us/performancepoint/HA101956241033.aspx.

BSM uses a set of business definitions that are defined by XSD (XML) schemas. It also uses a set of Web Service APIs that allow for open application development. Interestingly, there is a also a component that allows you to create a *strategy map* in Visio and then use that map to associate business data results with the goals listed in the map. This is called a *data-driven strategy map*.

Note Microsoft has renamed BSM for its next release as PerformancePoint Server (PPS). PPS is in CTP release at the time of this writing (January 2007), and is expected to be in final release in late 2007. We'll discuss that new product in more detail in Chapter 14.

Considering ProClarity and Data Mining Clients

I have two final thoughts on current client tools before this chapter ends. The first regards a very popular product that, until recently, was a third-party tool for SSAS called ProClarity. The second thought is consideration for the lack of support for data mining clients in the 2003 client products.

ProClarity

ProClarity is a power tool for sophisticated end users of SSAS, with the typical audience usually being financial analysts. It allows direct MDX query authoring and provides many other high-end features. ProClarity is also known for a powerful type of visualization, called the decomposition tree. As of this writing, Microsoft has recently acquired ProClarity and has announced plans to integrate its functionality into the Performance Point Server. We'll discuss ProClarity's integration to PPS in more detail in Chapter 14.

Data Mining Clients

The last item worth mentioning in this chapter is the lack of support for SSAS data mining in the 2003 client products. Microsoft has announced deep support for data mining in Excel 2007 and has made a CTP release of the Data Mining Add-Ins for Office 2007 available. We will review that release in Chapter 14.

Several other third-party vendors will likely develop client tools in the near term as well. Also, the data mining API is publicly available, so if you have .NET developers on staff or want to contract developers, you could design and implement your own custom client tools for data mining. Microsoft has also released some very useful documentation, samples, and tools to help you to develop your own data mining clients:

- *Data Mining Web Controls information on MSDN*: `http://msdn2.microsoft.com/en-us/library/ms160727.aspx`.

- *Data Mining Web Controls download on MSDN*: `http://www.microsoft.com/downloads/details.aspx?familyid=50b97994-8453-4998-8226-fa42ec403d17&displaylang=en`.

- *Feature Pack for SQL Server 2005 download (which includes the data mining controls and more)*: `http://www.microsoft.com/downloads/details.aspx?familyid=d09c1d60-a13c-4479-9b91-9e8b9d835cdc&displaylang=en`.

Tip The choice of a reporting tool will greatly influence the acceptance of a BI solution in your enterprise. There are many factors to consider, including license cost, usability, and SSAS feature support.

Plan to spend time at the beginning of your BI project evaluating and selecting possible reporting tools. The other consideration is that while there are several Microsoft SSAS reporting tools to select from, depending on your particular business needs, you may want to consider third-party client tools as well. It is, of course, also possible to build your own custom client tools.

Summary

In this chapter, we reviewed capabilities of currently available client tools for SSAS. These included Excel 2003 pivot charts, SSRS, the .NET 2.0 ReportViewer controls, and SharePoint Portal Server Web parts. We also took a look at the Report Builder.

In the next chapter of the book, we'll discuss deploying and managing your BI solution in a production environment. We'll discuss disaster recovery strategies and techniques for health monitoring and then review information about improving scalability and availability of your BI solutions.

CHAPTER 13

■ ■ ■

SSAS Administration

This chapter covers the processes and methodologies used to administer your SSAS cubes, including some discussion on methods of moving or copying the SSAS cubes from development or test environments to production. We'll focus here only on SSAS cube deployment, not SSAS data mining structures, SSIS packages, or SSRS reports, as these topics are beyond the scope of this chapter. We'll also discuss monitoring, scalability, and availability techniques—so that your SSAS cubes will perform consistently well, no matter how large or distributed your environment is. In this chapter, we'll cover the following:

- Understanding offline vs. online mode in BIDS

- Reviewing SSMS/SSAS administration

- Using XMLA scripting in SSMS

- Thinking about Disaster Recovery: backup/restore

- Considering security: roles and permissions

- Understanding health monitoring and performance tuning

- Applying scalability: load balancing

- Using high availability SSAS clustering

Understanding Offline vs. Online Mode in BIDS

To understand the processes included in deployment of SSAS cubes and data mining structures, you must understand two concepts. The first is working with your SSAS solution in either offline mode or online mode in BIDS, and the second is understanding the differences among the terms Build, Rebuild, Clean, Deploy, and Process.

When you begin to work with SSAS in BIDS, you'll first create your SSAS project in offline (or disconnected) mode. To do this, you open BIDS, click File ➤ New (or Open) ➤ Project ➤ BI Project ➤ SSAS project, and then give a name to your project.

Note It is important to understand the concept of projects and solutions when you are working in BIDS. A project is designated by a .proj file extention (sometimes a prefix is added to designate the type of project, such as .csproj for C# projects, and so on). A project is a container for folders and files. The meta-container for (multiple) projects is called a solution file. Solution files end in the .sln file name extension.

You'll now be working in disconnected mode. You are creating metadata (for example, the definition of a dimension, including its name, attribute names, hierarchy and level names, and so on) in this mode, but you cannot browse the cubes or mining structures you are creating because the metadata has not yet been made available to the SSAS server. This mode is also called project mode. When you've completed your design, your processing options are Build, Rebuild, Deploy, Process, and Show Deployment Process. Deploy makes your metadata available to the SSAS server instance that you've configured in the <Projectname> Property Pages, Deployment dialog box, and Target Server and Database values. The default Server location is localhost. After you've successfully deployed your initial model, then you can choose to work subsequently in either connected (online) or disconnected (offline) mode.

To work in disconnected mode, follow the same process as described previously, open the <Projectname> .sln file associated with your BI project to launch it. Although disconnected mode reduces the load on the server, you must be careful to manually synchronize your work with any other SSAS developers because SSAS does not perform this task for you. If there are conflicts during deployment, you will simply see a dialog box warning you that conflicts exist but not telling you what those conflicts are or allowing you to control the overwrite behavior. Instead, you are asked whether you want to globally overwrite the existing SSAS database.

Note There is a large body of knowledge on how to manage this aspect of software development projects; many books and many tools focus exclusively on this topic. Although it's beyond the scope of this book to dig into these details, be aware that the same best practices apply to BI projects and tools as well.

Because of this, if you work with a development team and you all work in disconnected mode, your team will need to use another tool to maintain source control, such as Visual Source Safe, Team Foundation Server, or Visual Studio Team System.

Your other option (after you've completed an initial deployment) is to work in connected or online mode. To do this, open BIDS, click File ➤ Open ➤ SSAS database, and then select the SSAS server and database you want to connect to in the dialog box. When working in online mode, the only processing option available to you is to Process some or all of your solution. There is no need to Build (validate schema) or Deploy (send files) because you are working with the live server. If you are working with a team in your project, then online mode is probably not feasible, unless team members work in nonoverlapping areas of development.

■**Caution** There is a risk, of course, if you choose to work in online mode in a cube that has been deployed into production. An erroneous configuration made while you are working in online mode could cause the cube to become unavailable for anyone attempting to browse the data.

Reviewing SSMS/SSAS Administration

If you want to use a GUI environment, then general administration for SSAS is done in the SSMS interface. You can also use scripts (which are discussed in detail later in this chapter). A simple but usable capability built into SSMS is the ability to generate reports that display metadata in SSMS. You can view the built-in reports or open reports written in RDLC. To view the default reports, you right-click the item you are interested in from the Object Explorer window, and then click Reports ➤ Standard Reports ➤ General. Figure 13-1 shows the output for a general report generated off of the Adventure Works sample cube.

Cube: Adventure Works

sps12\enterprise.Adventure Works DW - 11/15/2006 11:54:42 AM

Description:	
Estimated rows:	0
Date created:	11/8/2006 7:02:00 PM
Date last updated:	11/14/2006 6:57:20 PM
Date last processed:	11/8/2006 7:15:18 PM
Visible:	True
Language:	English (United States)
Collation:	Latin1_General_CI_AS
Storage mode:	Molap
Processing mode:	Regular

Figure 13-1. *You can view SSAS object metadata in SSMS by right-clicking any object in the Object Explorer tree and then clicking Reports ➤ Standard Reports ➤ General. This report is for the Adventure Works cube sample.*

Other tasks that you can perform in an SSAS database in SSMS are as follows:

- *Browse objects*: The cube and dimension browsers that are available in BIDS can also be used in SSMS; for data mining structures, you can browse using the various types of browsers associated with the different mining algorithms. You can also view lift charts and build prediction queries.

- *Manage the SSAS service*: You can start, pause, and stop the SSAS service. You can also configure properties by right-clicking the SSAS instance name in Object Explorer and then clicking Properties.

- *Process objects*: You can implement all the various process types (full, incremental, and so on) for all of the objects in your SSAS database. Processing methods for cubes, dimensions, and data mining structures were discussed in Chapters 7 and 11.

- *Set properties on most objects*: In SSMS, you set runtime properties, which are a subset of all properties for each object. For example, for a cube, you can set Processing Mode, Proactive Caching, and Error Configuration settings. All other properties are read-only in this view.

- *Script objects*: You can generate an XMLA script (more about XMLA in the next paragraph) to create, alter, and drop each object.

- *RUN queries*: You can run MDX, DMX, or XMLA queries in SSMS. The Template Explorer provides sample queries in each of the three SSAS languages.

XML for Analysis (XMLA)

XMLA (XML for Analysis) is a new XML scripting language introduced in this version of SSAS that you'll use to administer your SSAS solution. Like any other scripting language, XMLA is a great efficiency tool for routine administrative tasks, such as performing backups, monitoring loads, and so on. XMLA is open standard supported by other OLAP vendors. In this release, Microsoft has also extended the 1.1 specification to include features specific to SSAS databases.

You can use XMLA scripts in SSAS to perform Data Definition Language (DDL), Data Manipulation Language (DML), and Data Control Language (DCL) tasks. You can also use XMLA to work with data mining using schema rowsets to query mining models using the XMLA Discover method.

To run an XMLA query, you connect to SSAS in SSMS and then click the XMLA query button on the toolbar to launch the query window. Alternatively, you can use any of the built-in templates in the Template Explorer. Microsoft has provided XMLA templates for the most routine tasks (for example, backup, restore, and so on) in this template (see Figure 13-2).

When you run an XMLA query in SSMS, the results will be returned in XML format.

Figure 13-3 shows the results of running the templated XMLA query (called Connections, which returns information about current connections to SSAS) in SSMS. You'll note in the figure that the `<Restrictions>` and `<Properties>` elements are collapsed (or closed), so that the code is simpler to read. To see the contents of the collapsed sections, you click the plus sign to the left of either of those two elements.

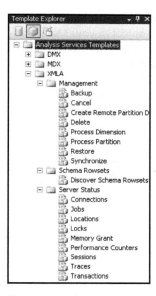

Figure 13-2. *The SSMS Template Explorer includes XMLA templates for the most common administrative SSAS tasks.*

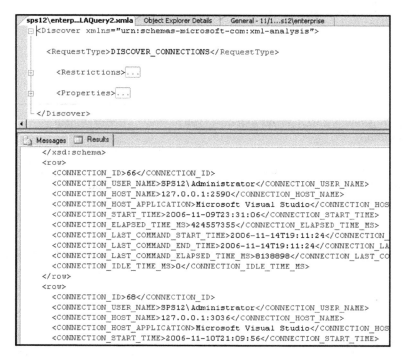

Figure 13-3. *XMLA query results are returned in XML. Here you see information about the current connections to SSAS.*

In addition to running a template query or simply typing XMLA into the query window, you can also generate an XMLA script to create, alter, or drop any object in your SSAS database by right-clicking the object in the SSMS Object Explorer; clicking Script Database (or whatever object name you want to script); clicking Create To, Alter To, or Drop To; and then clicking the location (New Query Window, Clipboard, and so on). Also, most dialog boxes in SSMS (Backup Database and others) have a Script button that allows you to generate XMLA script. Figure 13-4 shows the results of generating an `Alter` XMLA script for a particular data source.

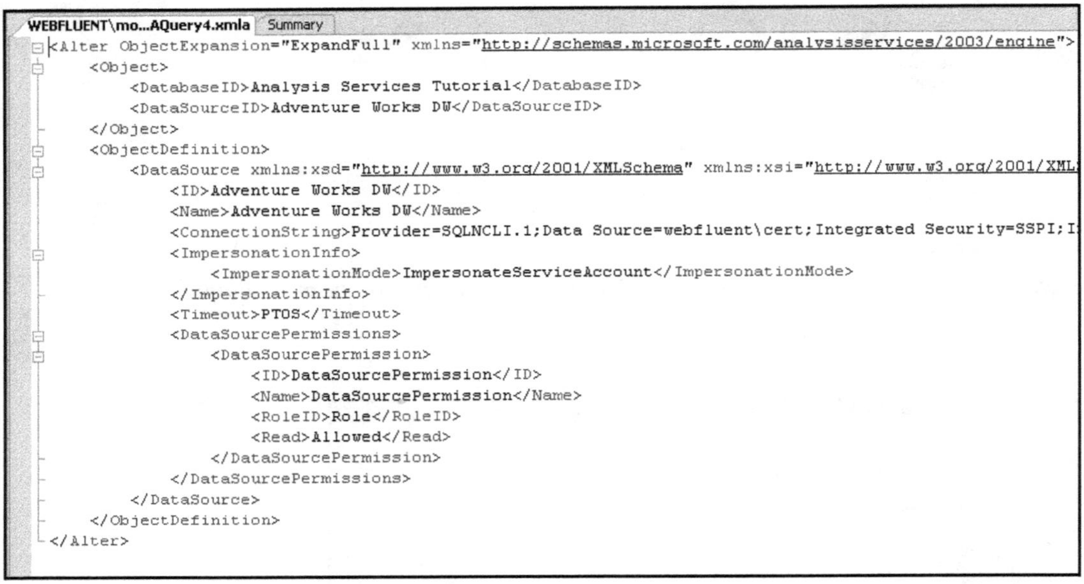

Figure 13-4. *You can easily generate XMLA scripts that allow you to create, alter, or drop any objects in your SSAS solution.*

XMLA scripts are a great new tool for you to use to automate management and maintenance of your BI solution because they allow you to easily generate reusable and schedulable tasks, such as backup.

Tip For a complete reference to the XMLA scripting language, see the BOL topic "Using XML for Analysis in Analysis Server (XMLA)."

SSAS Deployment Wizard

The SSAS Deployment Wizard allows you to copy an SSAS database (and to select which data and metadata you want to include) by using a series of dialog boxes that allow you to configure various options for generating an XMLA script and/or implementing the copy immediately. To launch this tool, you click Start ➤ Programs ➤ Microsoft SQL Server 2005 ➤ Analysis Services ➤ Deployment Wizard.

To use the tool, you navigate to the <projectname>.asdatabase file, which for the AdventureWorks sample database is located in this default location: C:\Program Files\ Microsoft SQL Sever\90\Tools\Samples\Adventure Works Analysis Services\Standard\Bin. You then name the server and the SSAS target database locations. In the next dialog box of the wizard, Specify Options for Partitions and Roles, you select the behavior for Partitions (Deploy partitions or Retain partitions [which means do not change *existing* partitions] only) and security Roles and Members (Deploy roles and members, Deploy roles and retain members, or Retain roles and members) as shown in Figure 13-5.

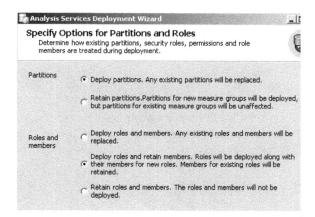

Figure 13-5. *You can specify the XMLA script options for Partitions/Roles and Members.*

In the next Specify Configuration Properties dialog box (see Figure 13-6), you can select whether you want the new XMLA script to Retain configuration settings for existing objects and Retain optimization settings for existing objects. If you select either of these options, your XMLA script will include associated, advanced attribute properties, which you may have configured. Some examples of this are the values for the properties AttributeHierarchyOptimized and MemberNamesUnique. In this same dialog box, you can also adjust the Connection String, Default Data Source Impersonation Information, and Key error log file names and locations for individual cube objects (that is, measure groups, dimensions, and so on).

In the next dialog box, you can specify a Processing method (Default, Full, or None) and can choose to include all processing in a single transaction. In the next dialog box, you can choose to implement the deployment immediately, or you can create deployment script and specify the location where the script will be saved. You can manually edit the generated script in an SSMS XMLA query window and then execute it at your convenience (on that same server with a different database name as the destination) or on any other server. You can use this wizard to quickly create a script for the purposes of deployment from one environment (such as development or test) to another one (such as production). Because the wizard is quick and easy to use, it's a great tool for simple movement from development to production. However, if your migration is complex, repetitive, and/or incremental in nature, you will probably prefer to use XMLA that you've generated, rather than relying on the wizard.

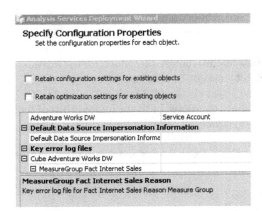

Figure 13-6. *You can specify the XMLA script options for connection, impersonation, and error log locations in this dialog box.*

Note SSAS also includes a command-line verison of the SSAS deployment wizard called the Microsoft.AnalysisServices.Deployment Utility. This tool is located by default at C:\Program Files\Microsoft SQL Server\MSSQL.2\OLAP\bin. For more information, see the BOL topic "Microsoft.AnalysisServices.Deployment Utility."

Server Synchronization

The Synchronize command synchronizes one SSAS database with the data and metadata of another database on a different server. This tool is best used only for making a copy of a complete SSAS database from a development or a test server to a production server.

To synchronize in SSMS, you right-click the Databases folder in the Object Explorer for the SSAS database you want to synchronize, and then click Synchronize. This will start the Synchronize Database Wizard. The first page of the wizard is shown in Figure 13-7.

By configuring the dialog boxes in the wizard, you can specify the source and destination servers, SSAS databases, and other properties for synchronization. These properties include whether or not you want SSAS to compress the data being sent and how you want SSAS to synchronize the security settings across the servers. The choices for the latter are SkipMembership, CopyAll, or IgnoreSecurity. SkipMembership copies the security definitions but does not copy any membership information to the destination database.

Note When you are considering your SSAS cube deployment options, you could also use the SSAS Backup and Restore capabilites. We will discuss these features in more depth in the "Thinking About Disaster Recovery" section coming up next.

Figure 13-7. *You can generate the XMLA script to synchronize two SSAS databases by right-clicking the databases folder (which starts the Synchronize Database Wizard) in the SSAS tree in SSMS.*

Thinking About Disaster Recovery

You can perform an SSAS database backup or restore either by using an XMLA script or by using the GUI interface in SSMS.

To perform a backup of your SSAS database using the latter method, you connect to the database in SSMS, right-click the database name in Object Explorer that you want to back up, and then click Back Up. You'll then configure the dialog box shown in Figure 13-8. You can run the backup at this point, or you can generate the XMLA script by clicking the Script button at the top of the Backup Database dialog box.

Using this method, you are backing up all objects in the SSAS database, all cubes, dimensions, and data mining structures. To back up individual items using the GUI interface in SSMS, you should right-click the particular item in Object Explorer, and then script those particular items only.

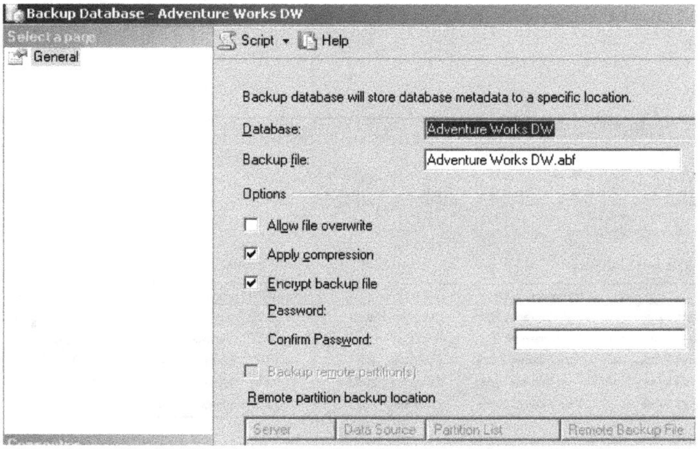

Figure 13-8. *You can generate a backup of your SSAS database in SSMS. If you choose to encrypt the backup, then you must supply a password in the Backup Database dialog box.*

To restore an SSAS database, you can use SSMS as well. Simply right-click the databases folder in the Object Explorer, and then click Restore. You'll then be able to configure the dialog box in Figure 13-9.

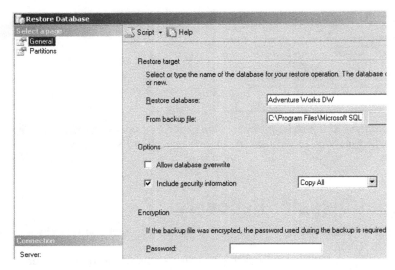

Figure 13-9. *The Restore Database dialog box allows you to configure several options for restoring your SSAS database from a backup. The options incorporate whether or not you want to include security information as part of the restore.*

As with the GUI SSAS backup, the GUI restore only allows you to restore an entire SSAS database (restoring all of its contained objects). If you wanted to have a more granular solution, that is, back up or restore only certain items (cubes, dimensions, and so on) within an SSAS database, then you use XMLA scripting rather than the GUI backup/restore.

You may also choose to restore to a location other than the original one. To do this, you'll configure the desired location on the Partitions property sheet of the Restore Database dialog box as shown in Figure 13-10.

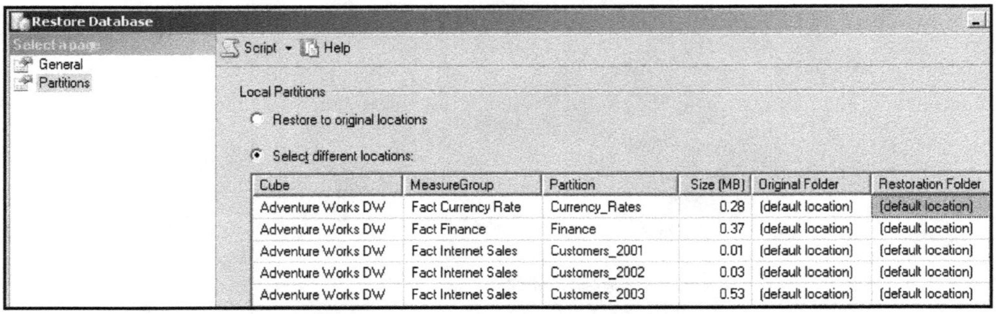

Cube	MeasureGroup	Partition	Size (MB)	Original Folder	Restoration Folder
Adventure Works DW	Fact Currency Rate	Currency_Rates	0.28	(default location)	(default location)
Adventure Works DW	Fact Finance	Finance	0.37	(default location)	(default location)
Adventure Works DW	Fact Internet Sales	Customers_2001	0.01	(default location)	(default location)
Adventure Works DW	Fact Internet Sales	Customers_2002	0.03	(default location)	(default location)
Adventure Works DW	Fact Internet Sales	Customers_2003	0.53	(default location)	(default location)

Figure 13-10. *The Partitions property sheet of the Restore Database dialog box allows you to restore your SSAS database to a location other than the original one by manually configuring the Restoration Folder value.*

If you choose to use an XMLA script to automate the process of backing up your SSAS database, you can schedule the backup as a job using SQL Server Agent. You simply add one (or more) job steps, enter SQL Server Analysis Services Command in the Type box, and then populate the Command box with the XMLA script as shown in Figure 13-11.

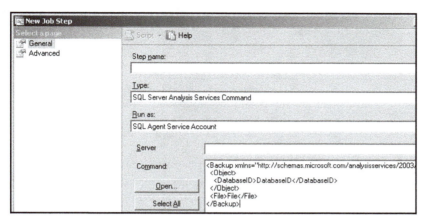

Figure 13-11. *You can use SQL Agent Jobs to schedule SSAS backups with XMLA scripts.*

Another consideration when planning your backup strategy is whether or not you've chosen to use HOLAP or ROLAP storage methods for your cube. If so, then you'll need to include a backup of the source star schema (relational) data along with your SSAS database backup solution because both HOLAP and ROLAP storage types retrieve (for both types) and store (for ROLAP only) information in that source RDMS structure as well. This type of backup can easily be done using regular SQL Server backup techniques, assuming your star schema is housed in a SQL Server database. If it is housed elsewhere, such as Oracle, DB2, and so on, then your SSAS backup solution (for SSAS databases that included HOLAP or ROLAP storage mode for cubes) must include appropriate backup for the particular star schema (RDMS) source data.

Considering Security

Security planning and implementation for SSAS databases (cubes and mining structures) begins with determining which staff members will be granted administrative privileges for the SSAS server. By default, local administrators on the server where SSAS is installed are granted full administrative rights to the SSAS server. If you want to add additional users or groups to the SSAS server administrators group using SSMS, you right-click the SSAS server instance name, select the Security property page, and then add the users or groups.

Note You cannot set permissions with more granularity by using the GUI at the level of Analysis Services itself; that is, either the user is or is not a server administrator.

Figure 13-12 shows the Security property page at the server level for SSAS in SSMS.

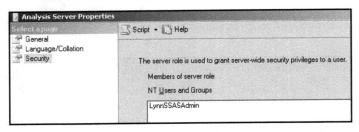

Figure 13-12. *When planning security, you can choose to add additional users or groups to the SSAS administrator role at the server level.*

Note You can set permissions more granularly for specific sections of cubes, such as measures or dimensional attributes, and you can use either BIDS or SSMS. To do so, you create custom security roles. We'll talk more about the process used to create these roles later in this section.

Another consideration when implementing security for your SSAS server is to determine which optional features may be needed for your particular BI solution. The new SQL Server 2005 Surface Area Configuration tool allows you to turn on selected features (that are disabled by default) by SSAS. These features are disabled by default because the general configuration approach Microsoft has taken for all products in the SQL Server 2005 suite is that the products should be "secure by design." Another way to understand this "off by default" approach is by thinking of the general security principle of "reducing the attack surface," which Microsoft has applied to the SSAS default configuration. One of the manifestations of this approach is to disable optional features by default.

Using the SQL Server 2005 Surface Area Configuration tool, you can enable four optional features for SSAS:

- *Ad Hoc Data Mining Queries*: This option allows ad hoc queries from external providers to data mining structures using the OPENROWSET statement.

- *Anonymous Connections*: This option allows unauthenticated connections to your SSAS instance.

- *Linked Objects*: This option allows you to permit links to and/or from your SSAS instance and remote objects.

- *User-Defined Functions*: This option allows loading of COM-based and .NET functions.

■**Caution** Enabling any of these advanced and optional features introduces a significant security risk into your solution. You should only do this after careful consideration of the potential negative impact of a security problem that could result from these features being made available.

The Analysis Services features view of the SQL Server Surface Area Configuration for Features is shown in Figure 13-13.

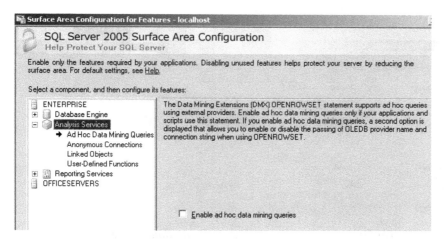

Figure 13-13. *The SQL Server 2005 Surface Area Configuration tool allows you to easily enable some advanced features that may be needed for your particular BI solution.*

Connection Strings

The next step in security planning for your BI solution is in planning the connection string information to the source star schema (or relational) databases. In BIDS, when you add one or more data sources to your SSAS solution, you have the following options for connecting to the data source:

- *Provider*: This setting determines the selected provider. Be sure to use the most efficient provider for your particular data source. For SQL Server 2005, it is the SQL Native client.

- *Authentication method*: This setting allows you to specify the authentication method and credentials. For SQL Server, your choices are Windows Authentication or SQL Server Authentication.

- *Isolation*: This setting allows you to specify whether the isolation level ReadCommitted or Snapshot will be used to access the data. ReadCommitted is the default setting.

- *Query Timeout*: This setting allows you to specify the timeout value (in seconds) for queries.

- *Maximum number of connections*: This setting allows you to specify the maximum number of connections. The default is 10.

- *Impersonation Information*: This setting allows you to specify what type of account will be used to connect to the data source. The default is to use the SSAS service account. You could also choose to use a specific username and password, use the credentials of the current user, or accept the default (which is the same as the setting use the credentials of the current user).

Figure 13-14 shows the dialog box in BIDS (Data Source Designer) where you configure the last four of these settings.

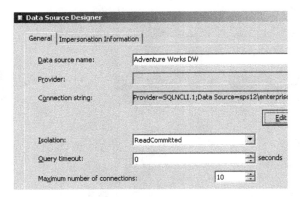

Figure 13-14. *To configure the connection properties for the data sources you are using in your SSAS solution, use the Data Source Designer dialog box. Note that you can take advantage of the new Snapshot Isolation level available in SQL Server 2005.*

After you've completed configuring your data source connection information, the next consideration in SSAS security planning is how you will implement security roles.

Security Roles

Security Roles in SSAS allow you to assign permissions (read, read/write, read schema, and so on) to various objects in your SSAS database. It is very important to plan carefully and to base your security roles on business requirements. You can assign permissions to all SSAS objects, that is, the entire cube, a dimension, attribute, measure, set, or even a single cell.

To begin to work with security roles, in the BIDS Solution Explorer, right-click the Roles folder, and then click New Role. The role designer interface will open as shown in Figure 13-15. The General tab allows you to set global permissions for the entire database.

On the next tab, Membership, you add the users and groups that you want to associate with this role. Following that, on the Data Sources tab, you specify the type of access you want to grant to this role for each data source associated with your project. Your options are None or Read. You may also specify on this tab that you want to allow the role to Read definition (of the data source).

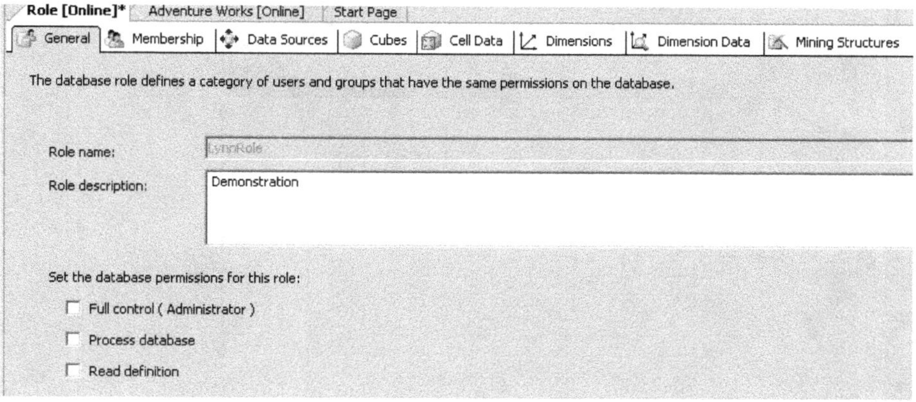

Figure 13-15. *The General tab of the roles designer allows you to set global permissions for your SSAS database.*

On the next tab, Cubes, you configure the type of access to each cube in your project. First you set the Access type by choosing None, Read, or Read/Write. Then you set the local cube/drillthrough type by choosing None, Drillthrough, or Drillthrough and local cube. Finally, you allow Process permission by checking the box. Figure 13-16 shows the Cubes tab in the role designer in BIDS.

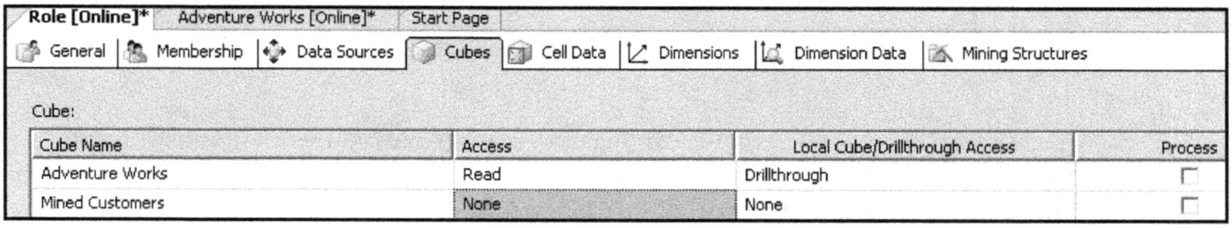

Figure 13-16. *On the Cubes tab of the role designer in BIDS, you configure the type of access for each cube in your project. This includes setting local cube and drillthrough settings.*

The next tab of the role designer, Cell Data, allows you to set specific permissions on defined subsets of the cube. These subsets are defined via MDX statements. On the following tab (which is named Dimension Data) of the role designer, you can set specific permissions for a complete dimension or for specific hierarchies, levels, or members of dimensions (see Figure 13-17).

To restrict the permissions to a particular subset of a dimension, you would use the Advanced subtab of the Dimension Data tab. You can specify member sets, and you can set a default member for this dimension for this role. You do this by writing MDX statements. A portion of the Advanced subtab is shown in Figure 13-18.

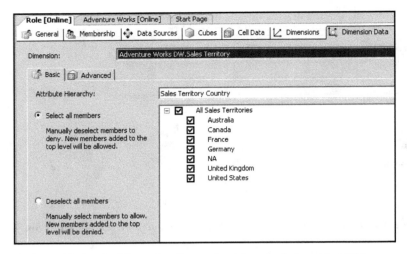

Figure 13-17. *On the Dimension Data tab of the role designer in BIDS, you can specify which members of a dimension are available for the role that you are designing.*

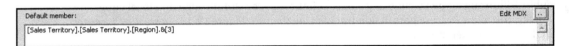

Figure 13-18. *On the Advanced subtab of the Dimension Data tab in role designer in BIDS, you can configure the default member for a particular dimension and role by writing a MDX statement.*

The last tab in the Role designer, Mining Structures, allows you to set permissions for mining structures and mining models. The configurable properties are shown in Figure 13-19. As with cubes, you also configure drillthrough permission here.

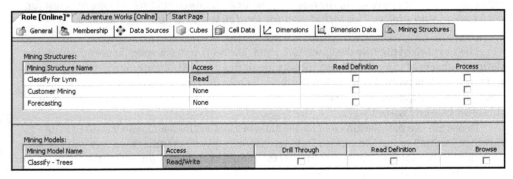

Figure 13-19. *On the Mining Structures tab in the role designer in BIDS, you can configure the permissions for mining structure and models. These permissions can include drillthrough.*

If your solution uses custom .NET assemblies, then you'll need to implement the appropriate .NET CAS (Code Access Security) permissions. Permission types for .NET assemblies were discussed in Chapter 12.

Other Security Planning Issues

Another consideration when planning security for your BI solution is determining whether (and possibly how) the client application(s) will flow end-user login credentials from the client software across the other tiers of your solution. Areas for you to review if you are, for example, using Microsoft client tools for SSAS, include connection string configuration approach for Excel pivot tables and/or data source connection information for SSRS.

One possible solution is to flow the end-user's Windows credentials all the way back to the SSAS cube. This is often done when business or regulatory requirements necessitate individual user access logging. Another type of credentialing that you may choose to configure is associating all connections with the SSAS (Windows or SQL) service account.

Tip If your project requirements include the need for you to capture login information to SSAS, then you can use SQL Server Profiler to capture a record of login activity on your SSAS database as long as you are using a unique Windows login for each user who is accessing your SSAS database (rather than validating credentials via a custom client-enforced mechanism, which usually results in SSAS access being granted to a single Windows login for all end users). To record login activity on Profiler, you configure a trace that captures login and logout events for the particular database that you are interested in monitoring.

Some third-party SSAS clients have specific limitations on the type of credentials that can be used. Remember to investigate the authentication mechanisms of your chosen client tools during the design phase of your BI solution.

Understanding Performance Tuning

You can improve the performance of your BI solution in a number of ways, including the following:

- *Aggregate intelligently*: Discussed in Chapter 7, you can use the Aggregation Design Wizard and the Usage-Based Optimization Wizard to tune the design of aggregations for the entire cube or for partitions.

- *Design efficiently*: Although it may seem like common sense to do this, nearly every cube design that I've been asked to evaluate included information that only a small number of users were interested in. In particular, you should be diligent about justifying the inclusion of a very large number of measures in any one fact table. The reason for this is that, of course, your fact tables are usually of most concern in terms of storage space (and resulting query overhead).

  Also, you should examine excessive attributes (more than 250) in one or more dimensions. This adds to dimension and cube processing time, takes up more storage space, and can be detrimental to usability of the cube due to the sheer complexity of information presented (as well as navigational complexity).

Another important consideration is the level of granularity of the fact tables; moving from days to hours, for example, exponentially increases the size of your fact table. This has similar consequences to overly large dimensions.

- *Optimize attributes*: To optimize your SSAS database, create attribute relationships within natural dimensional hierarchies. When you initially create your cube, the auto-build tool will attempt to detect natural hierarchies in the attribute data in each dimension.

If natural hierarchies are found, the tool will create hierarchies and associated attribute relationships; an example of this is shown in Figure 13-20. By validating that the tool has correctly associated attribute relationships with natural hierarchy levels (and by correcting or adding any missing values), you will improve query performance because SSAS will create aggregations and (internal) indexes to optimize navigation and query of those values. If you need to manually adjust these hierarchies and attribute relationships, you make changes in the BIDS dimension design area by dragging attributes from the tree view area in the dimension designer in BIDS to the Hierarchies and Levels area and then dropping those attributes on the appropriate <add attribute relationship> area.

If you make an adjustment that is not valid, that is, the underlying data does not actually have a a natural hierachy, then BIDS will display an error in the hierarchy (and level) where you've configured the information incorrectly. The error will be indicated by the presence of a red wavy line underneath the error (or errors).

Figure 13-20. *Adding attribute relationships to dimensions will improve query performance.*

Tip In MDX, attribute relationships are called member properties.

Another optimization technique is adjusting the `AttributeHierarchyOptimizedState` property value from the default value of `FullyOptimized` to the optional value of `NotOptimized` for attributes that few end users will browse in the cube. The default setting causes SSAS to build additional indexes for the attribute hierarchy during dimension or cube processing. This is done to improve query performance. The optional setting causes SSAS to not build any indexes for this attribute, which will result in faster dimension and cube processing times. End-user query performance for `NotOptimized` dimensional attributes will, of course, be slightly slower than for `FullyOptimized` attributes. Figure 13-21 shows the property sheet in the BIDS dimension designer interface where you adjust this setting.

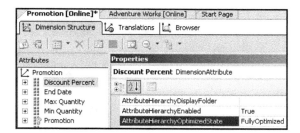

Figure 13-21. *You can adjust the optimization at the attribute level for a dimension to improve dimension and cube processing times.*

- *Retrieve data efficiently*: Another tuning technique is to use the most efficient means possible to retrieve data from the star schema source or DSV. The "cleaner" the DSV, the better the efficiency of the cube and dimension processing. Although you can easily add named calculations to the DSV, remember that processing these ad-hoc T-SQL statements will add to the processing overhead. It is preferred to prepare the data during the ETL portion of the project. A simple example is a name concatenation, such as FirstName + ' ' + LastName = (new) FullName column. Although you could easily create this new column by adding a NewNamed Calculation to the DSV, it is preferred to add this column via the ETL package that was designed to load the dimension source table.

- *Monitor intelligently*: Monitoring tools include Windows System monitor, the SSAS Query Log, and SQL Server Profiler. SSAS adds more than ten MSOLAP-specific objects to the Windows System monitor, and each of these new objects adds multiple counters. When planning for monitoring SSAS performance, you can also utilize many of the regular counters that are most important. Typical examples are monitoring usage of basic system resources, such as RAM, CPU, and disk utilization. You should plan to create baseline values for your particular solution and to regularly monitor to detect potential bottlenecks.

Tip You may want to check out Teo Lachev's blog for more information about SSAS Performance Monitoring and Tuning: `http://prologika.com/CS/blogs/blog/archive/2007/01/31/analysis-services-2005-performance-guide.aspx`.

SQL Server Profiler now allows you to do sophisticated monitoring of SSAS. For a list of all types of SSAS event that you can monitor, see the BOL topic "Analysis Services Event Classes." You also now have the ability to extract specific types of SSAS queries from Profiler traces. To do this, start a trace in Profiles and then click File ➤ Export ➤ Extract SQL Server Analysis Services Events ➤ Extract MDX Events (see Figure 13-22). You can use this capability to isolate specific problematic queries that have been generated by client tools.

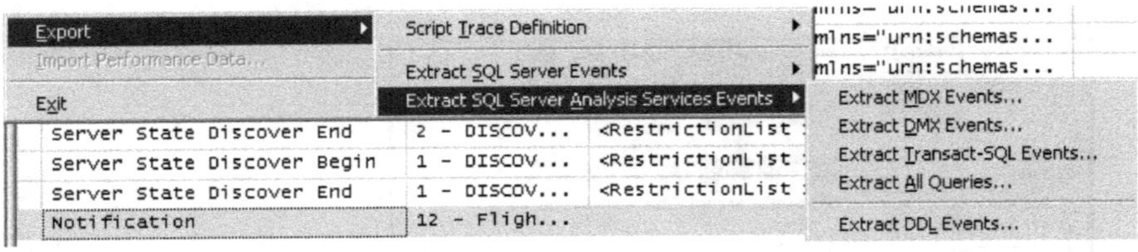

Figure 13-22. *Using Profiler, you can extract different types of SSAS queries from a trace.*

- *Query efficiently*: In Chapter 10, we discussed basic MDX. Like any query language, there are many known techniques to optimize MDX queries. A great reference to check out is *MDX Solutions: With Microsoft SQL Server Analysis Services* by George Spofford (Wiley, 2001).

If your solution includes data mining, then you may want to have more information about efficient DMX queries. Few resources on DMX are available as of the writing of this book, so your best bet is to use the MSDN documentation.

Tip For a detailed and interesting discussion of performance tuning for very large-scale enterprise environments, see the Microsoft whitepaper titled "Project REAL: Enterprise Class Hardware Tuning for Microsoft Analysis Server" at `http://www.microsoft.com/sql/solutions/bi/projectreal.mspx`.

Applying Scalability

There are at least four different types of methods to improve the scalability of your BI solution. The first is to add hardware to your SSAS server, which is called *scaling up*. Usually, processors or RAM are added. Also, you may consider using a 64-bit system that supports larger amounts of RAM. This is particularly important if your SSAS databases hold large amounts of information, and you want to improve cube processing times. If adequate memory is available, cube processing will be done entirely in memory and will be dramatically faster than the alternative of using a large amount of RAM on a 32-bit system. Although you can enable use of more than 3GB of RAM on a 32-bit system (see the following Tip), the way the OS accesses the additional RAM is not as efficient as a 64-bit system.

Tip If you are running your SSAS solution on a 32-bit system with 4GB of RAM, be sure to add the /3GB switch to your boot.ini file so that more than the default 2GB of RAM can be used by SSAS.

The second way to impact scalability for your solution is by using methods that employ *scaling out*. The Enterprise Edition of SSAS is required to implement this solution. Here you use remote partitions (placed on separate physical servers that each has SSAS on it) to "load balance" one or more cubes. Each partition can be processed using a different storage method—MOLAP, HOLAP, or ROLAP—and can use its own aggregation design.

The process used to create a remote partition is similar to creating a local partition. You can either use BIDS (on the cube design interface, in the Partitions tab, click New Partition) or SSMS (choose Object Explorer ➤ Cubes ➤ Cube Name ➤ Measure Groups ➤ Measure Group Name ➤ Partitions ➤ New Partition); either location will start the wizard. Figure 13-23 shows the wizard dialog box where you can optionally specify that the location of the partition be remote.

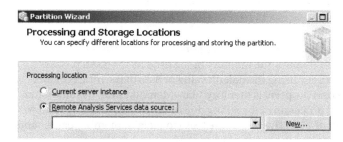

Figure 13-23. *The Partition Wizard allows you to specify that any particular partition you create will be stored on a remote SSAS server. This is a method of scaling out your SSAS solution.*

Tip Microsoft recommends a maximum size of 50GB or 20 million rows per partition (whether local or remote).

The third way to impact scalability is to adjust some of the SSAS server-level properties. To work with these settings, you use SSMS. In Object Explorer, you right-click the SSAS server name and then click Properties. You can work with either the basic or the advanced properties on the property sheet. A portion of this property sheet is shown in Figure 13-24.

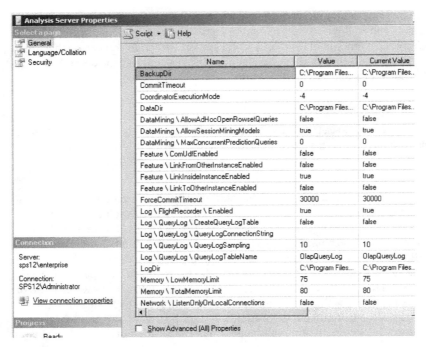

Figure 13-24. *The Analysis Server Properties sheet allows you to adjust many settings for your server. The default view shows only the basic settings; to view all settings, click the Show Advanced (All) Properties check box.*

Two properties available in this dialog box bear discussion. The first is Memory \ TotalMemoryLimit. You may want to monitor the memory being used by the SSAS process (msmdsvr.exe) to verify that it is actually using the default value or 80% of the total memory available on the machine. The second property is Memory \ LowMemoryLimit. In some situations (for example, SSAS scheduled processing jobs failing due to timeouts), you may want to reduce this value below the default of 75%. This will cause SSAS to reclaim memory earlier and will improve the reliability of processing jobs.

The fourth way to improve scalability is to make scalability changes in your client tools. This often involves load balancing, tuning the client software, or both. If you are using SSRS, for example, you could choose to configure some reports to run during nonpeak times (usually overnight) by scheduling them using the Snapshot feature.

Additionally, you could choose to implement caching for individual reports in SSRS. Both of these options can be set using the included Report Manager by changing properties associated with a particular report, or you could use SSRS scripts (written in VB.NET) or create an application that directly calls one or more of the Web methods in the SSRS Web Service. Figure 13-25 shows the Report Properties Execution page from the default SSRS Web site, which allows you to configure report caching or report snapshots.

If you are using the Enterprise Edition of SSRS, you can scale the processing of reports to multiple machines—initially one for the front-end (Web) processing and one for the back-end (database) processing. You could also add additional front-end servers to distribute the front-end processing load even more broadly if your business scenario warranted this.

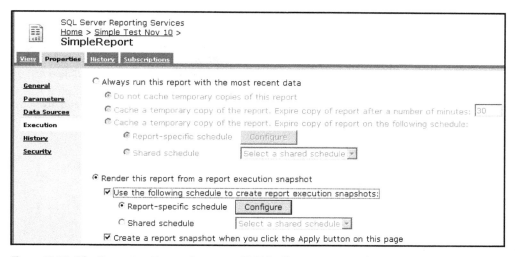

Figure 13-25. *The Execution Properties page of SSRS allows you to configure caching or snapshots for a particular report. This can improve scalability by reducing the load on your SSAS server.*

Using High Availability Clustering

New to the 2005 release of SSAS is support for installing this product into a Windows cluster. As with SQL Server failover clustering, this type of solution for increasing SSAS availability requires hardware and software that support Windows Clustering.

Failover clustering for SSAS is supported in both the Standard and Enterprise Editions. The Standard Edition supports only two-node clusters, and the Enterprise Edition supports as many nodes as the version of the operating system that it is running on supports; for example, for Windows Server 2003 Enterprise Edition, that is eight nodes.

In addition to supporting clustering, you may also choose to install multiple instances of SSAS on each node of a clustered environment. Be aware that the Standard Edition of SSAS does *not* support the clustering of multiple instances (that is, installed on the same physical server) of SSAS.

Another nice aspect of installing SSAS into a cluster is the ease of setup. You simply configure SQL Server setup (for SSAS) to join a cluster by selecting the Create an Analysis Services Failover Cluster check box during regular setup using the SQL Server source media.

Tip For more details about installing SSAS into a failover cluster, see the Microsoft Knowledge Base Article 910230 at http://support.microsoft.com/kb/910230.

Summary

We covered administrative tasks for your SSAS cubes, including the implications of working offline or online, uses of XMLA scripts, and implementation of backups and restores. We also discussed security roles, a high availability tool, and scalability techniques. We touched on health monitoring and performance tuning as well.

In the next (and last) chapter, we look forward, literally. We'll explore BI connectivity using the recently released Office 2007 and CTP release of Performance Point Server 2007 products. Our coverage for both products will be based on the Community Technology Preview (CTP) release current at the time of the writing, December 2006.

■ ■ ■

CHAPTER 14

Integration with Office 2007

This chapter covers the integration features for SSAS 2005 available in Office 2007 and other soon-to-be-released Microsoft products. We'll discuss the required service pack (SP2) for SQL Server 2005, Excel 2007, Microsoft Office SharePoint Server 2007 (otherwise known as MOSS), and Performance Point Server 2007.

Adding integration capabilities to SSAS is a focus for this release of Office 2007. At the time of this chapter's original writing, all products were in Community Technology Preview (CTP) release, and all information in this chapter is subject to change in the final release. The final release for Office 2007 occurred in December 2006 and January 2007. Performance Point Server is set to be released later in 2007. Given that backdrop, this is what we'll discuss in the chapter:

- Installing the SQL Server 2005 SP2

- Exploring Excel 2007, including updated pivot tables and charts, new support for SSAS data mining, and the new Excel service in available MOSS

- Integrating MOSS 2007 and SSAS, including Report Center (KPIs, reports, Excel Web, filters, dashboards), data connections, and MOSS KPIs vs. SSAS KPIs

- Exploring Performance Point Server 2007, including ProClarity integration, Business Scorecards, Business Modeler, Business Rules, and Microsoft Dynamics integration

SQL Server 2005 SP2

One prerequisite for using the new BI features (that relate to connecting to SSAS) in Office 2007 is to install SP2 for SQL Server 2005. In addition to a number of bug fixes and performance enhancements, this service pack installs features required for the integration between SSAS and Office 2007 to work. If you intend to use Office 2007 as a BI client, this service pack for both SQL Server 2005 *and* SSAS 2005 is a required installation. As of March 2007, this service pack is in final release and is available for download from `http://www.microsoft.com/downloads/details.aspx?familyid=D07219B2-1E23-49C8-8F0C-63FA18F26D3A&displaylang=en`.

Note A large number of significant enhancements are included in the service pack. For a comprehensive list of changes that SP2 makes to SQL Server 2005 and SSAS 2005 installations, see `http://download.microsoft.com/download/2/B/5/2B5E5D37-9B17-423D-BC8F-B11ECD4195B4/WhatsNewSQL2005SP2.htm`.

Exploring Excel 2007

We'll start our tour of enhanced BI support in Office 2007 applications with the Office 2007 application that has the most significant new or improved features—Excel 2007. You'll see that the depth and amount of changes are dramatic, which will result in many more of you choosing to use Excel, rather than a third party or custom client for your BI solution. It is a significant part of Microsoft's BI offering to provide you with an affordable (and powerful) end user client toolset. By offering such a rich feature set at such an attractive price, it is Microsoft's intent to make BI available to a larger percentage of your end user groups (rather than just a select few, which is often, for example, only the analyst community).

The first significant enhancement Microsoft has made in Excel is a concerted effort to improve the end user client SSAS experience by improving the pivot table interface. The primary focus is to make pivot tables (and charts) more intuitive to set up and use, so that more of your end users will be able to quickly become productive using pivot tables.

Before we explore pivot tables in Excel 2007, we need to step back to take a look at the new menu system. This menu redesign (which has been implemented consistently across the entire Office 2007 suite of products) is called the *ribbon*. The primary reason for the redesign was to improve usability.

Note The design of the ribbon was based on Microsoft's usability research. Interestingly, when Microsoft was preparing the specification for Office 2007, a very large percentage of the "new features" requested to be added to Office 2007 were actually already included in Office 2003. End users just couldn't easily find the existing features. This research is the primary driver of the ribbon menu redesign.

Figure 14-1 shows the first half of the Excel ribbon (menu) for the Data tab. You'll notice that this tab contains a group that allows you to Manage Connections to any data source to which you are making a connection. These connections would include connecting from Excel to SSAS.

Figure 14-1. *The first thing you will notice when working with Excel 2007 is the new ribbon that replaces the menu in Excel 2003. This figure shows the left half of the Data tab.*

Another type of ribbon in Excel gives your end users quicker access to the pivot table menu items. This type of menu is called a *contextual tabset,* and it appears in the ribbon when an end user selects any area of an active pivot table by clicking it. The right half of the contextual tabset for pivot tables is shown in Figure 14-2. You'll learn the specific procedure for creating a pivot table shortly.

Figure 14-2. *The contextual tab of the Excel PivotTable Tools ribbon gives your end users quicker access to the pivot table menu items and becomes available when end users click the pivot table design surface.*

The process for creating a pivot table or chart using SSAS source data is similar to that used in Excel 2003. All menus are now available on a tab (for creating the intitial connection to SSAS) or a contextual tab (for designing the pivot table) of the ribbon (which simplifies access to advanced features). Also, there is better support for some of the advanced SSAS features.

You can see another example of advanced SSAS feature support when you are using the Data Connection Wizard. After you specifiy the name of the SSAS server and database that you want to connect to, you can then (in the next dialog box) select from a list of not only SSAS cubes but also SSAS perspectives for that particular SSAS database (see Figure 14-3).

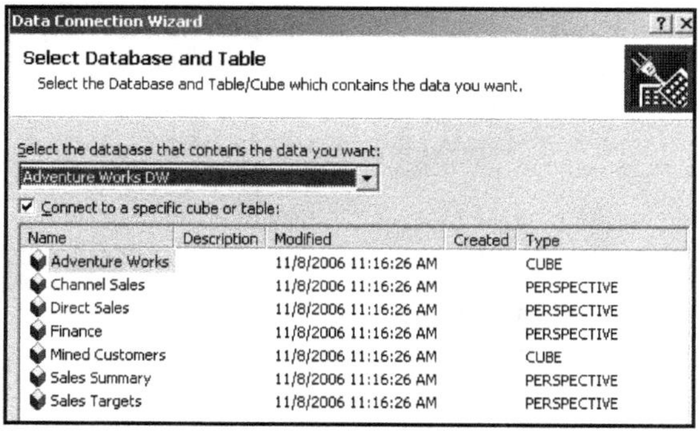

Name	Description	Modified	Created	Type
Adventure Works		11/8/2006 11:16:26 AM		CUBE
Channel Sales		11/8/2006 11:16:26 AM		PERSPECTIVE
Direct Sales		11/8/2006 11:16:26 AM		PERSPECTIVE
Finance		11/8/2006 11:16:26 AM		PERSPECTIVE
Mined Customers		11/8/2006 11:16:26 AM		CUBE
Sales Summary		11/8/2006 11:16:26 AM		PERSPECTIVE
Sales Targets		11/8/2006 11:16:26 AM		PERSPECTIVE

Data Connection Wizard

Select Database and Table
Select the Database and Table/Cube which contains the data you want.

Select the database that contains the data you want:
Adventure Works DW

☑ Connect to a specific cube or table:

Figure 14-3. *You may now associate your data connection with a specific cube or perspective from the selected SSAS database.*

Another welcome addition is the support for SSAS cube drillthrough. Also, you may set the maximum number of records that can be retrieved via drillthrough on the Connection Properties Usage tab.

After you've successfully connected to your SSAS instance, to quickly open the pivot table designer, you can simply click the Existing Connections icon on the Get External Data group of the Data tab. Next in the Existing Connections dialog box, click the AdventureWorks item in the Connections in this Workbook section, and then click Open as shown in Figure 14-4.

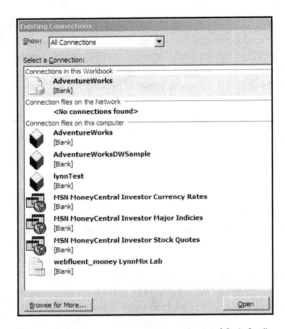

Figure 14-4. *One way to create a pivot table is by "opening" a connection to an SSAS database.*

You are then presented with an Import Data dialog box, which is set by default to Pivot-Table Report. You can configure Advanced properties of the connection by clicking the Properties button in the Import Data dialog box.

One of these advanced properties is the ability to use a specific single-sign-on (SSO) credential. To set this up, you click the Definition tab of the Connection Properties dialog box and then click the Authentication Settings button. Clicking this button opens the Excel Services Authentication Settings dialog box (see Figure 14-5). SSO is used in situations where Windows credentials are not part of your BI solution.

■**Note** Use of SSO in Excel 2007 data connections requires that the MOSS (Microsoft SharePoint Server) site administrator has configured a MOSS site to use an SSO database (where user names and passwords can be stored). SSO can be the most efficient when there are many users and when you cannot use Active Directory.

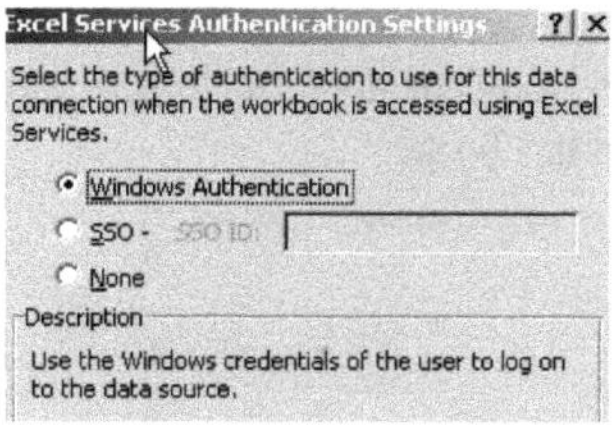

Figure 14-5. *Associating SSO credentials with a specific connection is a newly supported capability.*

Click OK to complete your connection configuration, and then Excel will open the pivot table design surface. If you have ever trained any end users in the use of pivot tables (or had to support any type of pivot table implementation) using previous versions of Excel, you'll be pleased to see that the pivot table interface has been redesigned. The previous designs, although adequate, were not really optimal in terms of intuitive usability, particularly for the initial pivot table setup.

The redesign of the pivot table work area has been thoughfully implemented, again, based on Microsoft's usability research. The work area is much more intuitive, including "hint" text on the design surface, as well as a much more intelligent PivotTable Field List. This list allows the user to drag and drop any field from the data source; for SSAS cubes, these fields will, of course, be measures, dimensions, and KPIs. The fields can either be dragged to the pivot table design surface or to the the new descriptive boxes (called *areas*) below the PivotTable Field List. Figure 14-6 shows the default (blank) pivot table design surface and the new PivotTable Field List work area.

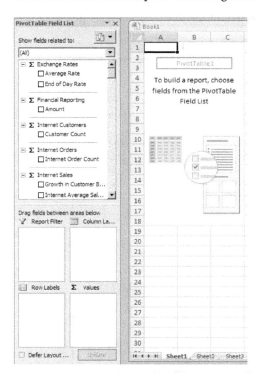

Figure 14-6. *The redesigned pivot table design surface and PivotTable Field List improve the design experience for end users.*

Note The default location for the PivotTable Field List is to the right of the workbook area. I've moved it to the left because it's easier to work with, and the screenshots will fit better in this book.

KPI Support

In addition to a more intuitive design area, you'll note that SSAS KPIs are displayed as part of the fields in the PivotTable Field List. If you drag KPIs onto the pivot table design area, you'll see also that the associated icons are displayed in the pivot table. Support for KPIs in Excel has been a highly requested feature, and you'll probably find yourself using KPIs in a number of business scenarios. Be sure to include planning for KPIs in the business requirements phase of your BI project.

Tip The support for KPIs in Excel 2007 includes the ability to display KPIs that have been created as part of an SSAS cube definition, and support for KPIs that have been created in Excel 2007 itself. It is preferred in a BI project to create KPIs on SSAS, rather than on the client. This results in a more consistent view of key metrics.

An example of the display of SSAS cube KPIs in an Excel 2007 workbook is shown in Figure 14-7.

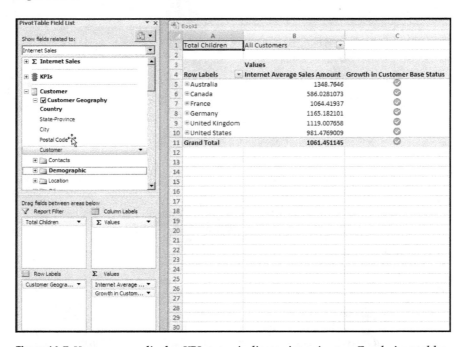

Figure 14-7. *You can now display KPI status indicator icons in your Excel pivot tables.*

You may also note the Report Filter area on the PivotTable Field List allows you to easily work with a large number of filter fields for your report. Also in Figure 14-7, we've set the field list to show fields related to the Internet Sales measure only. Because most SSAS 2005 OLAP cubes will now be built using multiple fact tables, this ability to filter available fields based on fact names will be welcomed by end users.

One of the important sets of general enhancements in Excel 2007 deals with better data visualization. Although these features are *not* specific to pivot tables or to BI, in other words, you can apply them to any worksheet, you will find them to be particularly useful when working with the large result sets that can be returned from SSAS cubes. Most of these data visualization features are found on the ribbon's Home tab by clicking the Conditional Formatting button.

One example of using these new data visualization features is that you can use the built-in data bars to give a visual clue to values in your pivot table. To do so, simply select the cells from the pivot table that you want to apply the conditional formatting to, click the Home tab, click the Conditional Formatting button to expose the Data Bars button, and then click the color scheme you want to apply (blue, green, red, and so on). You can also make your own custom scheme by clicking the More Rules button at the bottom of the supplied Data Bar Rules under the Conditional Formatting button on the Home tab of the ribbon. The result of applying this type of conditional formatting and using the Conditional Formatting button menu is shown in Figure 14-8.

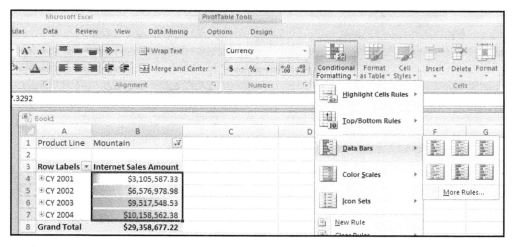

Figure 14-8. *Using Data Bars Conditional Formatting can improve the visualization of your pivot table data. They are simple to add via the new types of Conditional Formatting available on the Home tab of the Excel ribbon.*

Other types of data visualization tools included in Excel 2007 are the Color Scales and Icon Sets. All of these conditional formatting schemes can also be customized quite easily. Figure 14-9 shows the application of one of the default Icon Sets that Conditional Formatting schemes apply to the sample pivot table.

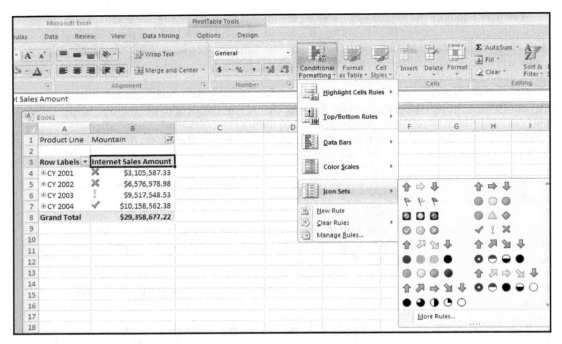

Figure 14-9. *You can quickly and easily apply built-in Icon Set Conditional Formatting to jazz up your pivot table. You can also customize the icons or rules quite easily.*

Another nice addition to pivot charts is the ability to easily add a trend line. To do this, create a column chart from your pivot table by clicking the Pivot Chart button on the ribbon. Then right-click any of the data bars in the chart, and click Create Trendline. The line is created, and you access the Format Trendline dialog box. A pivot chart with a trendline and the Format Trendline dialog box are shown in Figure 14-10.

As terrific as all of the cool new features are that we've seen in Excel so far, the biggest news is that Excel 2007 is a native data mining client for SSAS! End users can use all of the sophisticated data Mining Model Viewers that you've already seen in the BIDS and SSMS. Also, interestingly, you (or authorized end users) can perform administration, including mining structure creation from inside of Excel.

Figure 14-10. *To quickly create a trendline on your pivot chart, simply right-click any of the data bars, and then click Create Trendline. You will also have the ability to configure the properties of the trendline by using the Format Trendline dialog box.*

Configuring Excel 2007 as a Data Mining Client

One of the most exciting additions to Excel 2007 is the ability to work as a native client for SSAS data structures. We'll explore these features in depth in this section.

Caution The information presented in this section is based on the December 2006 CTP release of the Data Mining Add-ins for SQL Server 2005 and is subject to change for the final release. The final release occurred in March 2007.

After installing the prerequisite service pack on SQL Server 2005 (SP2), your next step in setting up Excel as a data mining client is to download the SQL Server 2005 DM (Data Mining) Add-ins for Office 2007. As of this writing, this download is in CTP release:

http://www.microsoft.com/downloads/details.aspx?familyid=7C76E8DF-8674-4C3B-A99B-55B17F3C4C51&displaylang=en.

> **Note** The Data Mining Add-ins add functionality to both Excel 2007 and Visio 2007. We'll only be reviewing the add-in functionality for Excel 2007 in this book.

After installing the downloaded files (per the included instructions), then you'll use either the Getting Started link or the Server Configuration Utility option located on the Start menu by choosing Start ➤ Programs ➤ Microsoft SQL Server 2005 DM Addins ➤ Getting Started (see Figure 14-11). You'll note that there is a link for Help and Documentation on this menu, but as of the CTP release, most of the help files are incomplete or missing.

Figure 14-11. *After installing SP2 for SQL Server, your next step in setting up Excel 2007 as a data mining client is to run the Getting Started Wizard from the Start menu.*

Assuming you intend to connect to an existing instance of SSAS using your administrative credentials (and you've selected that option on the wizard dialog box), you'll then click a link on the dialog box to open the Data Mining Add-in Configuration Wizard for Office 2007. This wizard contains a large amount of documentation on each page of its dialog boxes, making it easy to use. Figure 14-12 shows the first page of the wizard.

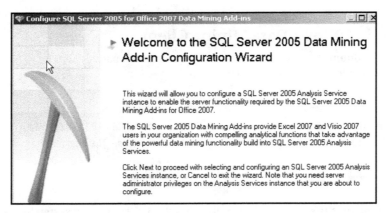

Figure 14-12. *The Getting Started Wizard contains a link that allows you to easily launch the SQL Server 2005 Data Mining Add-in Configuration Wizard.*

In the first step of the wizard, you specify the SSAS server name. In step two, you specify whether you want to allow the creation of temporary mining models as shown in Figure 14-13. If you choose to turn this option on, then a database called DMAddinsDB will be created (or you can specify that you want to use an existing database for this purpose). The reason to allow the creation of temporary mining models is documented on the dialog box: "Creating a new database for Office 2007 Data Mining Add-in users gives the flexibility to freely create temporary and permanent models while giving you the ability to manage the object permissions for these users without impacting other databases."

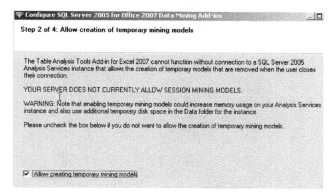

Figure 14-13. *When configuring Excel 2007 to work with SSAS data mining structures, you will choose whether or not you want to allow the creation of temporary mining models.*

In the last dialog box of the wizard, you grant add-in users appropriate permissions as shown in Figure 14-14. As with the other dialog boxes in this wizard, a full explanation of the implications of the task you are performing is given on the dialog box itself. You should, of course, implement security settings based on your business requirements. This usually includes, at a minimum, restricting the ability to create permanent models to the smallest possible subset of end users.

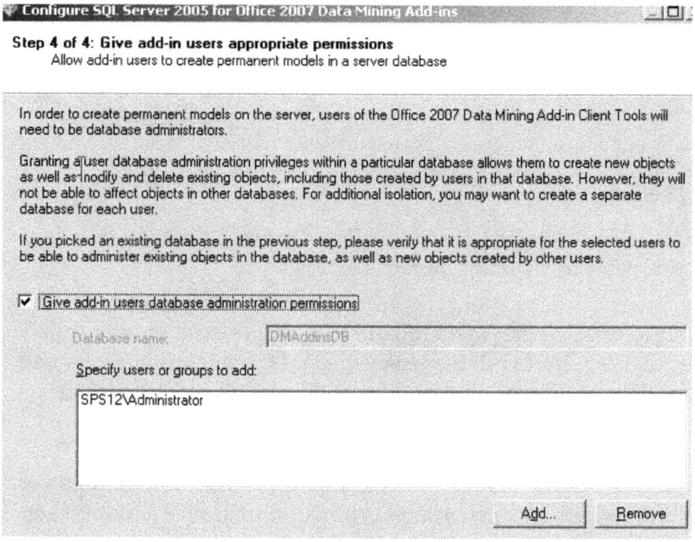

Figure 14-14. *In the last step of the wizard, you set user permissions for accessing data mining models.*

As the wizard completes, it presents you with a status dialog box, showing the success (or failure) of each of the required setup steps. If you have any failures showing up in this dialog box, then you can simply rerun the wizard. The most common causes for failure are incorrectly configured connection strings. This status dialog box is shown in Figure 14-15.

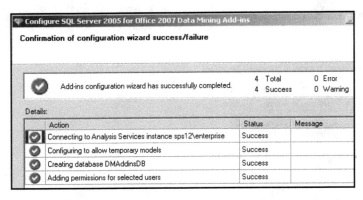

Figure 14-15. *After you've completed configuring the connection between Excel 2007 and the SSAS data mining capabilities, you'll be presented with a status dialog box to verify the status of all configuration steps.*

Using Excel 2007 as a Data Mining Client

The best way to start using Excel 2007 as a data mining client for existing SSAS data mining structures and models is to explore the various activities available on the Data Mining tab, which is added to Excel's ribbon when you install the Data Mining Add-ins. To start, we'll examine connecting to and browsing mining models. This section of the ribbon is shown in Figure 14-16.

Figure 14-16. *To begin to explore the data mining client capabilities of Excel 2007, use the ribbon tab groups called Model Usage, Management, and Connection.*

The Connection group of the ribbon allows you to add, edit, delete, test, or make current one or more connections to SSAS. In this CTP release, the DMTracer simply shows you the connection details information. In future releases, a "profiler-like" functionality likely will be added to this tool; that is, you'll be able to see the DMX queries generated by your activity in Excel.

Using the Manage Models button in the Management group, you can view metadata about data mining structures and models. You can also perform administrative actions, such as renaming, clearing, and processing the structure or model. The dialog box for this button in shown in Figure 14-17.

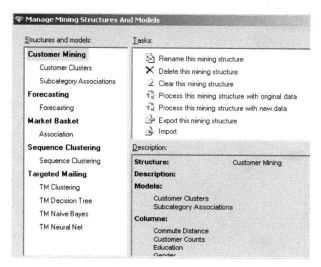

Figure 14-17. *Using the Manage Models button on the Management group of the Data Mining tab of the ribbon, you can perform administrative tasks on your mining structure and models.*

The Browse button on the Model Usage group allows you to view the mining models in the structures of the SSAS database to which you've connected using the sophisticated viewers that are availiable both in BIDS and SSMS. For example, if you want to view a model created using the Naïve Bayes algorithm, you'll be shown the Dependency Network Viewer, and so on. You'll be reminded that the type of viewer available depends on the type of mining model algorithm selected to build the original model. We discussed the viewers at length in Chapter 11.

When you click the Browse button, you'll be presented with a dialog box listing all of the mining models (arranged by algorithm type) associated with your particular mining structure. After you click a particular model to select it and then click Next, you'll be presented with the associated Mining Model Viewer or Viewers. In the Browse window, you can manipulate the mining model using the same techniques that you used in BIDS or SSMS. Figure 14-18 shows a sample Browse window in Excel. Note that you have the option to copy the information in the Browse window to Excel. The ability to Copy to Excel is only available from within Excel, that is, *not* from BIDS or SSMS.

If you choose to copy to Excel, the model will be rendered in a way that is "friendly" to Excel. The render method used by Excel varies depending on the type of Mining Viewer. Figure 14-19 shows the output of saving the model shown in Figure 14-18.

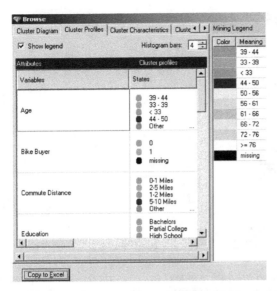

Figure 14-18. *After you select a mining model to browse, Excel 2007 will display the model viewer types associated with that particular algorithm. You also have the ability to copy the model's data to Excel.*

TM Clustering
Cluster Profiles

Variables	States	Population (All)	Cluster 1	Cluster 2	Cluster 4	Cluster 3
Size		18484	2718	2499	2232	2223
Age	39 - 44	3523	26 %	50 %	16 %	21 %
Age	33 - 39	3064	32 %	32 %	6 %	17 %
Age	< 33	3004	28 %	4 %	2 %	18 %
Age	44 - 50	2939	11 %	14 %	25 %	20 %
Age	50 - 56	2493	3 %	1 %	26 %	13 %
Age	56 - 61	1768	0 %	0 %	17 %	7 %
Age	61 - 66	1028	0 %	0 %	7 %	3 %
Age	66 - 72	498	0 %	0 %	2 %	1 %
Age	...	...	...	...	...	...
Bike Buyer	0	9352	54 %	41 %	64 %	32 %
Bike Buyer	1	9132	46 %	59 %	36 %	68 %
Commute Distance	0-1 Miles	6310	53 %	42 %	24 %	80 %
Commute Distance	2-5 Miles	3234	25 %	40 %	17 %	7 %
Commute Distance	1-2 Miles	3232	21 %	10 %	10 %	13 %
Commute Distance	5-10 Miles	3214	2 %	8 %	28 %	0 %
Commute Distance	10+ Miles	2494	0 %	0 %	21 %	0 %
Education	Bachelors	5356	0 %	44 %	31 %	62 %
Education	Partial College	5064	49 %	9 %	35 %	2 %
Education	High School	3294	30 %	0 %	22 %	0 %
Education	Graduate Degree	3189	0 %	47 %	10 %	36 %
Education	Partial High School	1581	21 %	0 %	2 %	0 %

Figure 14-19. *You have the option of copying the information from the Mining Model Viewer to Excel using the Copy to Excel button on the data mining Browse dialog box.*

Tip You really need to spend some time exploring the thoughtful design of the Copy to Excel feature. In the example shown here, the conditional formatting is applied automatically. This type of functionality is really incredibly powerful because it implements rich data visualization nearly instantly. Different mining model algorithms render in Excel differently, so have fun working with this feature set!

The Query button allows you to execute a DMX prediction query against a mining model. There are two modes in which to work: basic or advanced. As with many of the other Data Mining Wizard tools, the first page of this wizard provides a pretty good explanation of what you can accomplish by using it. You can better understand this functionality by remembering how the Mining Model Prediction section (from the mining model designer in BIDS) works; that is, you associate some external data with an existing model, mapping associated columns, and then use a DMX predictive query function to create new output based on these inputs. For example, you could use some competitor's data (that you've purchased) as external data to compare competitor's sales results with the results of an existing model that reflects your results for a particular business scenario. The first page of the Query Model Wizard is shown in Figure 14-20.

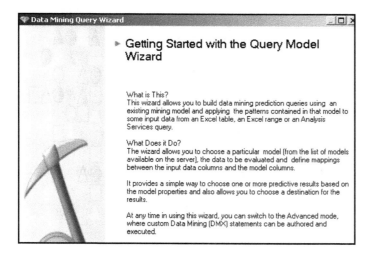

Figure 14-20. *The Query button invokes the Query Model Wizard. This tool is a wrapper around the functionality in the Mining Model Prediction section of the model builder in BIDS.*

The first step of this wizard is for you to select the source model. Here you are presented with the same dialog box that you worked with when using the Browse button. After you select the source mining model, you'll be asked to select the input data for comparision. As stated on the first page of the Query Model Wizard, you may choose from Excel tables, ranges or SSAS data sources for this data.

Also on this dialog box of the wizard, you have the option to move to the advanced view. If you do so, you'll have the ability to edit the query, add DMX templates, choose a new model, select input, map columns, or add output. This dialog box is shown in Figure 14-21.

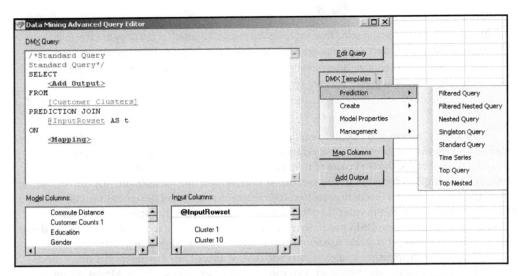

Figure 14-21. *Using the Advanced Query Editor windows allows you to modify the DMX query, input or output columns, and more.*

In the next step of the wizard, you can view (and possibly modify, if one or more columns wasn't relevant to your particular use of the data model) the column mappings of the source mining model and new data, and then you configure the Add Output dialog box to specify the type of prediction query you want to execute. The default selection values are as follows:

Predict: This function evaluates the numeric expression specified in Numeric_Expression in another data mining model.

PredictProbability: This function returns the probability for a specific value or state. It applies to a scalar column and returns a scalar value.

PredictSupport: This function returns the support value (that is, relevancy ranking) for a specific state.

You may also choose to display more values by selecting the Advanced button of the dialog box as shown in Figure 14-22.

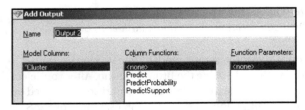

Figure 14-22. *As you continue to work with the Query Model Wizard, you will add output functions to your queries.*

Your final choice in the wizard is to determine where you want the output of the query placed. Your options are to Append to the input data, Create a new worksheet, or Place in an existing worksheet.

Using the Excel 2007 Data Preparation Group

This section of the Data Mining ribbon is primarily designed to allow Excel users to implement data mining techniques using Excel source data rather than SSAS data. Despite this limitation, the features are still worth exploring as your end users will probably find this functionality useful when they are performing data mining operations. Obviously, performing data mining operations on SSAS data provides the advantage of a centralized set of data to work with. There may be some situations, however, where data that is specific to a particular user (and stored in an Excel workbook) could be made more useful by performing data mining operations on it.

Explore Data, Clean Data, and Partition Data are the three buttons on the Data Preparation group of the Data Mining ribbon (see Figure 14-23).

Figure 14-23. *The Data Preparation group of the Data Mining ribbon contains the Explore Data, Clean Data, and Partition Data functions.*

The first two buttons (Explore Data and Clean Data) are designed to work with Excel data only. They use data mining concepts to allow you to view and clean your data by removing a specified number of outliers (or exception cases) and/or by relabeling (or renaming) specified column values. Performing one, or both, of these operations can improve the usability of a set of data by removing or minimizing exceptions or distractions.

To use the Explore Data function, you first select the table (worksheet) or data range in Excel, and then in the next page of the wizard, you select the column you want to generate a visualization for. The last page of the wizard produces a column chart by default; you may change this to a line chart by clicking that button on the dialog box. Figure 14-24 shows some sample output from the Explore Data button. The purpose of this view is to allow you to quickly visualize your data in a histogram format.

The Clean Data button, like Explore Data, is only designed to work with Excel data. There are two methods of data cleansing available: removing outliers and relabeling fields. We'll cover removing outliers first. *Outliers* are defined in data warehousing as exceptional cases, that is, those outside of a normal range. When you click the Clean Data button on the ribbon, the wizard is launched.

You perform the same setup steps as you did using the Explore Data Wizard, that is, select source data, and so on. The difference in this wizard is in the Outliers dialog box. Here you specify the threshold for outlier removal. This well-designed dialog box shows you a visual preview of the effect of removing a variable number of outliers (exceptional cases) as shown in Figure 14-25.

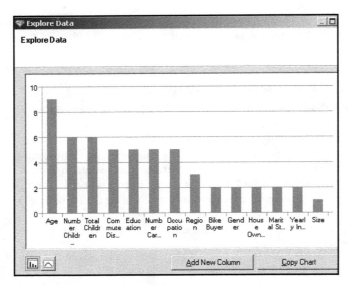

Figure 14-24. *The Explore Data button on the Data Mining toolbar allows you to quickly visualize Excel data using data mining concepts (in this case, a histogram).*

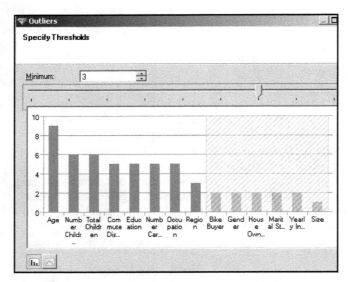

Figure 14-25. *The Clean Data button allows you to remove outliers based on the threshold you set. It is designed to work with Excel data.*

The Partition Data button, unlike the other two, can be used with Excel or SSAS data. The first dialog box of the Partition Data Wizard explains the functionality of this tool and is shown in Figure 14-26.

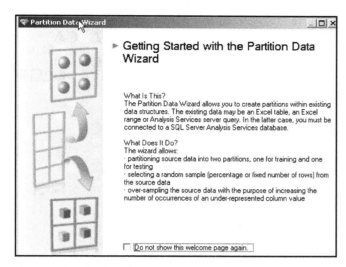

Figure 14-26. *The first dialog box of the Partition Data Wizard explains the wizard's functionality.*

The Partition Data Wizard allows you to sample your source data in one of three possible ways. For Excel data only, you can split your source data into two partitions so that you can use one set for data mining model training and the other setting for testing the validity of the mining model that you've created. You can also oversample columns from the source data to "balance" selected values in an underrepresented column to "smooth out" abnormalities in source data. If you are using SSAS data (or Excel) as a source for the Partition Data Wizard, then this wizard allows you to conduct random sampling. This technique is used to reduce the size of a data set that is used for input to a data mining model. The technique is also used to facilitate rapid prototyping because data mining models based on smaller sized data sets process more quickly.

In the second dialog box of this wizard, you are asked to select the Excel worksheet, data range, or the SSAS data source. The next choice in the wizard is dependant on your previous selection. If you've selected SSAS, then you'll use the visual query designer to create the SSAS data source. After you complete this step, then you'll be presented with the Select Sampling Type dialog box.

For SSAS queries, the only choice available is Random sampling. The output of this choice is well-documented on this dialog box as shown in Figure 14-27. As mentioned previously, the main purpose of this functionality is to reduce the size of an initial training sample. It is often used during the initial proof-of-concept or early rapid prototyping phases of an SSAS project to produce a small but structurally correct data source.

If you select Excel data as your source data for the Partition Data Wizard, then all sampling types are available via the wizard; that is, you can select the Split data into training an dtesting sets, Random sampling, or Oversampling to balance data distributions options.

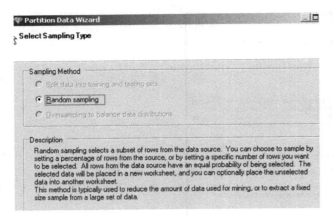

Figure 14-27. *If you select an SSAS query as your data source for the Partition Data Wizard, then your only available choice on the Select Sampling Type dialog box is Random sampling.*

Using the Excel 2007 Data Modeling Group

The next section of the Data Mining ribbon is the Data Modeling group. This group gives you access to all of the mining model algorithms available in SSAS. Here you can implement the algorithms using Excel as source data for your mining models. You can create temporary or permanent mining models using these buttons.

■**Note** You can create temporary mining models if, in the initial configuration of the Data Mining Add-ins for Office, you selected that option. Of course, any user who attempts to build permanent mining structures or models must have the appropriate permissions on the SSAS server.

Each button in this group is an "alias" for a particular SSAS data mining algorithm. If you want to create a structure or model using the mining algorithm names used in SSAS, then use the Advanced button on the ribbon as shown in Figure 14-28. The Accuracy Chart and Classification Matrix buttons will be covered in the next section; they are part of the Accuracy and Validation section of the ribbon.

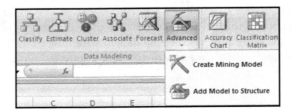

Figure 14-28. *The Data Modeling section of the Data Mining ribbon allows you to use the SSAS data mining algorithms with Excel data as source data. You can create temporary or permanent data mining structures or models using these buttons.*

You have four algorithm choices using the buttons on the ribbon. You can think of these as aliases for specific data mining algorithms available in SSAS. Here's the mapping:

- Excel *Classify* builds a Microsoft Decision Trees SSAS model (predicts any a single value of any type).

- Excel *Estimate* builds a Microsoft Decision Trees SSAS model (predicts any continuous—numeric or datetime—value).

- Excel *Cluster* builds a Microsoft Clustering SSAS model (creates groupings of related values).

- Excel *Associate* builds a Microsoft Association Rules SSAS model (creates groupings of related items per a configured value [3 by default] or market basket).

- Excel *Forecast* builds a Microsoft Time Series SSAS model (predicts a time-based value).

As with the other buttons on the ribbon, if you click any one of these buttons, then the first page of the respective wizards describes in nontechnical terms the functionality of the particular underlying algorithm.

If you (or your end users) prefer to use the SSAS data mining algorithm by original Microsoft name to create temporary or permanent mining models, then you can click the Advanced button on the ribbon, and then click Create Mining Model (or Add Model to Structure). This will launch a Mining Model Wizard that is similar, but not identical, to the one available in BIDS.

For example, one difference is on the dialog box where you select the particular algorithm. In the Excel version of the dialog box, there is a new Parameters button on the bottom left; clicking that button will allow you to configure the most common parameters for that particular algorithm. Interestingly, for some algorithms, more parameters appear to have been added to these dialog boxes than appear in the BIDS interface. Figure 14-29 shows the parameters available for the Naïve Bayes algorithm. In the BIDS data mining model interface, this particular algorithm has no parameters available in the Algorithm Parameters dialog box, whereas in the Excel version, there are four (that is, MAXIMUM_INPUT_ATTRIBUTES, and so on).

The level of integration between the Data Modeling section of the Data Mining ribbon and the native BIDS mining model functionality is really incredible. It brings the power of data mining to authorized Excel users. Because Excel is readily (and commonly) available, and because the Data Mining Add-ins appear to be a free addition, the possibilities for expanding data mining's reach into a tremendously broad section of end users is well within reach of most BI solutions. The point of BI projects is to make more information available in a more meaningful way to more users. Excel, as a general SSAS client, faciliates this. Its deep support for data mining simply increases the reach. This functionality is the most exciting point of BI integration between anything in Office 2007 and SSAS.

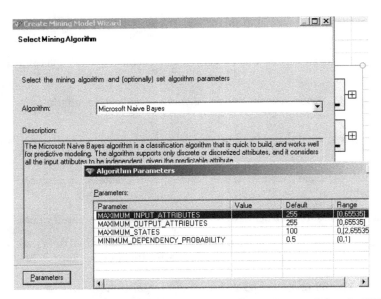

Figure 14-29. *The Advanced button allows you to create models using BIDS algorithm names. It includes more default parameters for some algorithms than the interface in BIDS does.*

Using the Excel 2007 Accuracy and Validation Group

After you've built your models, either in Excel or in BIDS, then you will probably want to evaluate their usefulness in answering the particular business questions they've been built to address. The Accuracy and Validation group of the ribbon gives you access to the Mining Accuracy Chart functionality in BIDS, which was covered in Chapter 11. The portion of the ribbon has three buttons: Accuracy Chart, Classification Matrix, and Profit Chart as shown in Figure 14-30.

Figure 14-30. *The Accuracy and Validation section of the Data Mining ribbon gives you access to the mining Accuracy Chart functionality in SSAS.*

As with most of the other buttons on the Data Mining ribbon, when you click the Accuracy Chart button, a wizard opens with the first dialog box documenting in detail exactly what this wizard does. To refresh your memory, the output here is a either a lift or a profit chart—both of which are designed to visually display effectiveness of a particular mining model. This is shown in Figure 14-31.

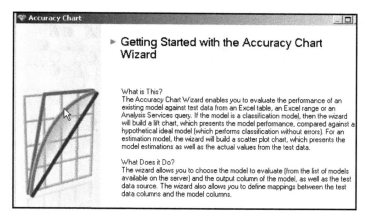

Figure 14-31. *The first dialog box of the Accuracy Chart on the Accuracy and Validation section of the Data Mining ribbon explains the functionality in plain English.*

The next step is to select a model to be used. If you attempt to validate a model that was built with an algorithm that isn't supported for this functionality, the dialog box will warn you.

For our example, we are using a model built with the Microsoft Sequence Clustering algorithm, which is supported for use with an Accuracy Chart.

In the next step of the wizard, you are asked to select the mining column and value to predict (see Figure 14-32). Next, you select the source data, which can be a worksheet, data range, or SSAS data source. In the step following that, you'll be asked to specify a relationship between the mining model column(s) and the table columns.

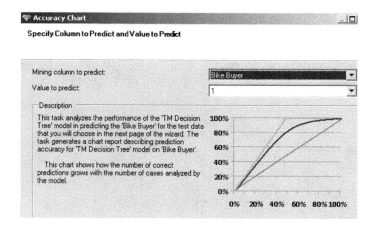

Figure 14-32. *In this key dialog box of the Accuracy Chart Wizard, you select the mining column to predict and the value.*

The output of the Accuracy Chart is a lift chart that is identical to using the mining Accuracy Chart functionality in BIDS.

The Classification Matrix button is used to allow you to see the number of correct and incorrect predictions made by your model in a spreadsheet format output. It too functions identically to features found in BIDS. As with the Accuracy Chart, when you click the Classification Matrix button, its wizard opens with a very descriptive dialog box. Configuration steps are similar to those performed when using the Accuracy Chart. The key dialog box is called Classification Matrix, in which you select the column to predict and specify options regarding the output (see Figure 14-33).

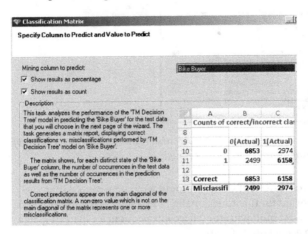

Figure 14-33. *The Classification Matrix dialog box allows you to configure the format of the output.*

The Profit Chart button allows you to quickly and easily build a profit chart. Again, the functionality is identical to the way profit charts work in BIDS as described in Chapter 11. The key dialog box of the wizard is the Specify Profit Chart Parameters dialog box shown in Figure 14-34.

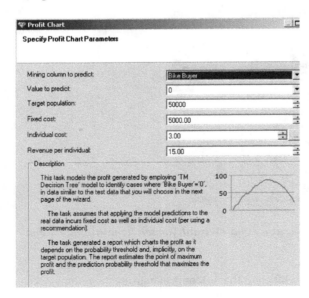

Figure 14-34. *The most important dialog box of the Profit Chart button on the Accuracy and Validation section of the Data Mining ribbon allows you to configure the parameters needed to produce the profit chart.*

Additions to the Final Release

During the writing of this book, the final version of the SQL Server 2005 Data Mining Add-ins for Office 2007 was released (March 2007). In addition to the features described in the preceding sections, that is, Excel 2007 integration via the Data Mining section of the ribbon, the final version of this toolset also includes data mining functionality that is directly applicable to Excel table data. You can access these features by using the new Analyze tab of the Table Tools section of the ribbon shown in Figure 14-35. Jamie MacLennan from Microsoft has recorded a Webcast on the use of this tool (as well as the rest of the tools in this toolset) at `http://msevents.microsoft.com/CUI/WebCastEventDetails.` `aspx?EventID=1032317015&EventCategory=4&culture=en-US&CountryCode=US`.

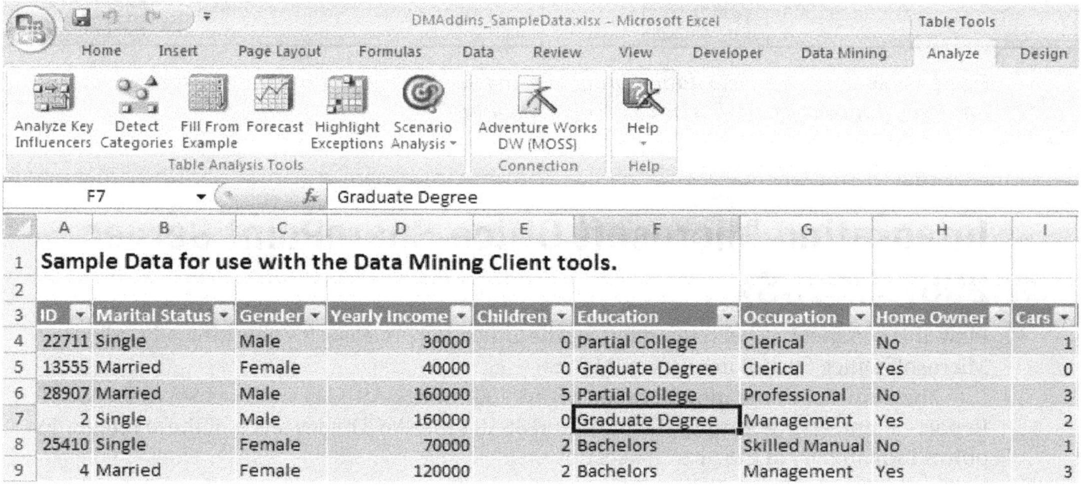

Figure 14-35. *The new Analyze section of the Table Tools area of the ribbon allows you to apply data mining functionality to Excel data.*

Another point of integration between SSAS and Office 2007 is the ability to create data-driven diagrams using Visio 2007. The SQL Server 2005 Data Mining Add-ins for Office 2007 include a Visio template that allows you to easily create Dependency Network, Cluster, or Decision Tree diagrams using SSAS mining model source data. You create these diagrams using wizards and can both customize the display and can annotate them as business needs dictate. A sample using the Decision Tree template is shown in Figure 14-36.

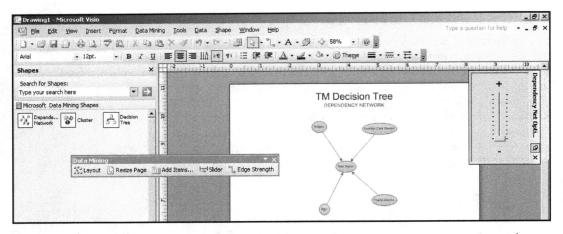

Figure 14-36. *Using the Visio data mining add-in templates, you can create, customize, and annotate data-driven diagrams based on SSAS data.*

Integrating Microsoft Office SharePoint Server 2007 (MOSS)

First, this product has been renamed for the Office 2007 release; it's now officially called Microsoft Office SharePoint Server (MOSS).

The points of integration between MOSS 2007 and SSAS 2005 are Excel Services, SSRS Report Center, and reporting Web parts and SSAS KPIs. We'll review each of these integration points individually in the next few sections.

Using Excel 2007 on the Web (Excel Services)

Excel Services is one of the new BI-focused features in MOSS. Excel Services allows users to publish Excel spreadsheets to a MOSS portal, where they can be accessed through a Web browser. Other than the fact that not all end users need to have Excel installed on their desktops, the advantages of using this new mode of working with Excel data are listed here:

- All of the calculations occur only on the Excel Web server.

- The overhead for processing the workbook calculations runs only on the server, rather than on each user's desktop.

- The business logic in the workbook is never exposed to any end user.

- There is only one copy of the workbook, and it is stored in a central, secure place, which results in better consistency of the data.

■**Note** Excel Services requires the Professional Pro, Enterprise, or Ultimate Editions of MOSS. MOSS is licensed as part of Office 2007. For feature comparison information, visit http://office.microsoft.com/ en-us/suites/FX101635841033.aspx.

One of the points of integration between MOSS and SSAS is the ability to display Excel workbooks created using SSAS cube data in a MOSS Web page. You'll select this client approach when you are building MOSS BI dashboards or general-purpose reporting Web pages.

Similar to the methods used to display report data in MOSS, this method also uses a particular set of Web parts. *Web parts* are specialized units that display content in a fashion specified in the design of the Web part (or configured by authorized end users at runtime). Many Web parts (including the ones that support Excel Services) are included with the default MOSS installation.

■**Tip** You can also develop your own custom Web parts. This process has been made significantly simpler with the inclusion of Web part framework items in the .NET Framework 2.0. These custom (templated) Web parts are part of the VS 2005 Toolbox.

To display an Excel workbook using the included MOSS Web part, you simply click Site Actions ➤ Edit Page on the page where you want to add the Web part, and then in the Web Part Zone of the editable page, click the Add a Web part link. In the Web Part Gallery dialog box that appears, scroll down until you locate the Excel Web Access Web part. Select it, and click Add. This Web part is shown in Figure 14-37.

Figure 14-37. *MOSS includes an Excel Web part by default.*

Although it's easy to add the Excel Web Access Web part to any page on your MOSS server, you will get the error shown in Figure 14-38 if you do not complete a couple of preliminary configuration steps prior to adding this Web part.

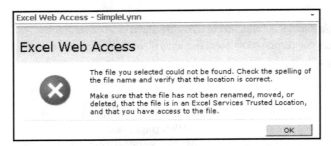

Figure 14-38. *Although you can easily add the Excel Web Access Web part to any MOSS page, you'll have to perform a couple of preliminary configuration steps or you'll see this error when trying to display a workbook using this Web part.*

To set a location as safe or trusted, you do the following:

1. Select the URL of a document library. Set the base type of this library to Excel spreadsheet. If you need to create a new library, navigate to the MOSS site in which you want to create the library, and click Site Actions ➤ Create ➤ Create Document Library. A sample document library configuration page is shown in Figure 14-39. Copy the URL to the clipboard after the library has been created.

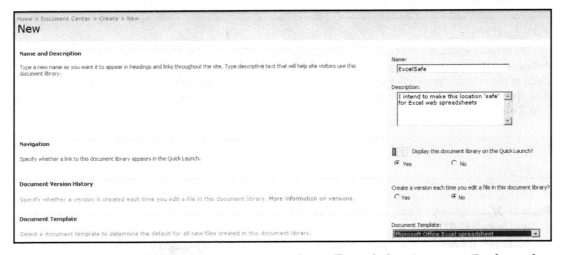

Figure 14-39. *The first step in creating a "trusted" (or safe) location to store Excel spreadsheets on MOSS is to create (or select an existing) document library location.*

2. Open the MOSS central administration Web site. Once there, click the Operations tab, and then click Services on Server. On this page, you'll need to verify that the Excel Calculation Service has been started. This service is not started by default. You should set the service to start by default using this page. Figure 14-40 shows this page with the service state shown as started.

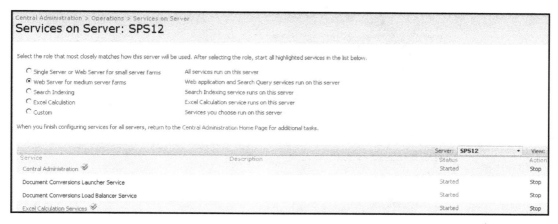

Figure 14-40. *You must verify that the Excel Calculation Service is turned on as part of the configuration steps to using this service.*

3. Configure the Excel Services Settings for the Shared Services Provider (SSP) for your MOSS installation. If you haven't created an SSP, you first must create one.

Note A Shared Services Provider (SSP) is a container for server-wide setting in MOSS. The settings it contains can be applied to multiple sites in your MOSS installation.

There are five configuration pages for you to work with, and each contains different types of configuration settings. This list of settings is in shown in Figure 14-41.

Figure 14-41. *There are five different pages available to configure Excel Services settings in MOSS.*

4. Click on the `Trusted File Locations` link, and then click the `Add trusted file location` on that page. Here you'll add the URL of the document library discussed earlier. This page contains many different configurable settings, including location, session, workbook properties, calculation behavior, external data, and user-defined function behavior. Figure 14-42 shows the location section of this page.

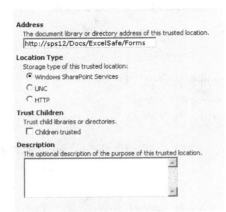

Figure 14-42. *Before MOSS will display an Excel workbook using the included Excel Web Access Web part, you must mark the saved location as "trusted" using this section of the Excel Services Add Trusted File Location configuration page.*

You must edit the default trust level for external data connection behavior for the workbooks available in this location if you intend to connect your Excel workbooks to SSAS cubes (or any other type of external data source). To make this change, you adjust the configuration settings in the External Connections section on the same page as shown in Figure 14-43.

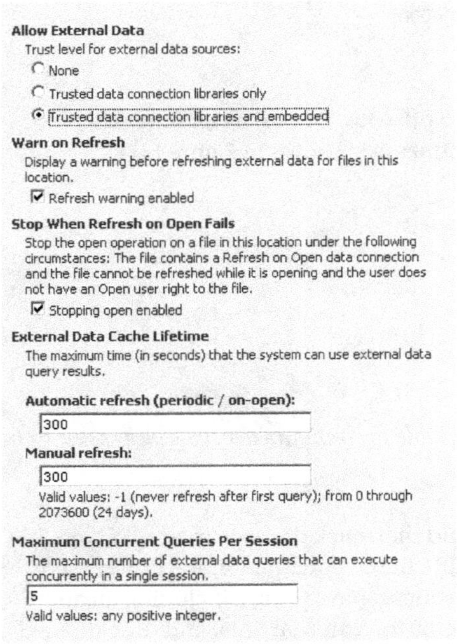

Allow External Data
Trust level for external data sources:
○ None
○ Trusted data connection libraries only
◉ Trusted data connection libraries and embedded

Warn on Refresh
Display a warning before refreshing external data for files in this location.
☑ Refresh warning enabled

Stop When Refresh on Open Fails
Stop the open operation on a file in this location under the following circumstances: The file contains a Refresh on Open data connection and the file cannot be refreshed while it is opening and the user does not have an Open user right to the file.
☑ Stopping open enabled

External Data Cache Lifetime
The maximum time (in seconds) that the system can use external data query results.

Automatic refresh (periodic / on-open):
300

Manual refresh:
300

Valid values: -1 (never refresh after first query); from 0 through 2073600 (24 days).

Maximum Concurrent Queries Per Session
The maximum number of external data queries that can execute concurrently in a single session.
5

Valid values: any positive integer.

Figure 14-43. *You will need to alter the default trust level for external data (which is set to None by default) when you are setting up a trusted location on MOSS for Excel workbooks if the data sources are external, such as an SSAS cube.*

You can now publish your workbook to the MOSS document library from Excel, and it will be displayed either in Excel (if you have Excel installed on your desktop) or in a browser. You can configure your workbook to default to displaying in a browser even if you have Excel installed on your desktop. You may want to enable this option if you are publishing content from Excel that other users will view in a browser. This will allow you to verify that the rendering is appropriate for your particular business requirements.

You select the publish destination during the publish process in Excel. To invoke the publish process from Excel, create your workbook, and then click the Office button ➤ Publish ➤ Excel Services as shown in Figure 14-44.

Figure 14-44. *After you've configured Excel Services in MOSS, you can publish your workbooks to the location marked as safe in MOSS using the Excel menus.*

When you select the Excel Services Options button while publishing, you are allowed to include particular worksheets from the workbook for inclusion. Also, you may configure parameters from named ranges in your particular workbook. These two dialog boxes are shown in Figure 14-45.

If you receive an error when you attempt to view the workbook in a browser, verify that the URL you entered on the safe location is correct. Your ouput should look very similar to "desktop Excel" by design. Figure 14-46 shows sample output.

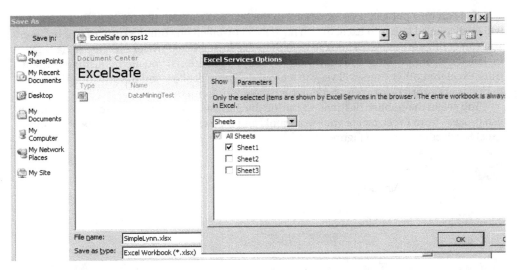

Figure 14-45. *When publishing to Excel Services by using the Excel Services Options button, you may select particular worksheets and configure parameters to be available for end users.*

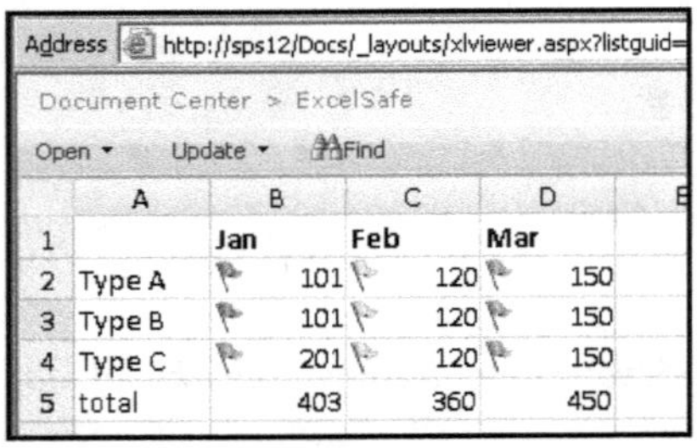

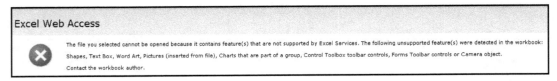

Figure 14-46. *Excel Services are designed to display your worksheet in a manner that is nearly identical to the desktop version of Excel.*

Although the Excel Services experience is nearly identical to the desktop Excel experience, it is not exactly identical. If you attempt to open a workbook that uses features which are not supported in the browser view, you will get a detailed error. Some of these unsupported features include Shapes, Word Art, and Pictures that have been inserted from a file. One example is shown in Figure 14-47.

Excel Web Access

❌ The file you selected cannot be opened because it contains feature(s) that are not supported by Excel Services. The following unsupported feature(s) were detected in the workbook: Shapes, Text Box, Word Art, Pictures (inserted from file), Charts that are part of a group, Control Toolbox toolbar controls, Forms Toolbar controls or Camera object.
Contact the workbook author.

Figure 14-47. *Excel Services has some limits of the types of information that can be displayed in a browser. Detailed error messages will be returned to you if you attempt to view workbooks with these content types in a browser.*

Tip The MOSS SDK topic "Unsupported Features in Excel Services" contains a complete list of features that are not supported when viewing workbooks in a browser.

To display a workbook using the Excel Services Web part on a particular MOSS Web page (for example, a dashboard), you simply navigate to that page and then edit the page to add the Web part as discussed earlier in this section. Next, you'll configure the Web part to display the particular workbook by entering the correct URL. The URL takes the form of the document library address plus the file name. After you've done this, then you can take advantage of the Excel Web Access Web part to place workbooks on any type of MOSS page. The sample shown here in Figure 14-48 is from the new Report Center, using a page of type dashboard. Note that the KPI Web part is displaying KPI information as well. (The KPI Web part is discussed later in this chapter.)

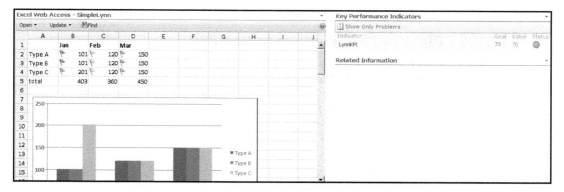

Figure 14-48. *Excel Services allows you to add your workbooks to MOSS pages using the Excel Web Access Web part. Using this, you can easily create dashboard pages.*

MOSS Data Connection Libraries

A *Data Connection Library* is a specific type of list available in MOSS. MOSS lists contain definitions related to allowable content and associated metadata. The Data Connection Library allows you to upload and store (and grant access selectively through permissions) data connections. These connections can be reused throughout the MOSS site. This is a starting point for working with SSAS databases information.

Storing data connections in the MOSS library allows for simpler access by end users and centralized administration for you. End users can actually use MOSS search and will be presented with links to any data connection with metadata that matches their search string. The search results in MOSS are security trimmed, meaning end users will only see the results that they have permissions to access. For administrators, centralized, shared data connection string values can be updated once rather than on each client machine.

To add a data connection to this library for reuse, you'll navigate to the Reports area of your site, then to the Data Connections page, and then click Upload to upload an existing data connection (or click New to create a new one). The result will look like the sample in Figure 14-49.

Figure 14-49. *In the MOSS Reports area, you can add data connections for reuse.*

Tip To make these data connections trusted by Excel Services, configure the SSP to Add trusted data connection library (location) using the MOSS administrative site.

MOSS KPIs (Key Performance Indicators)

MOSS allows you to display KPIs from four different sources: SSAS, MOSS lists, Excel, or manually entered values. A nice feature is the ability to combine KPIs from any source type in the same Web parts.

Figure 14-50 shows two of the four available Web parts in MOSS that allow you to display KPIs.

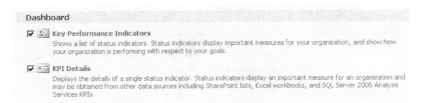

Figure 14-50. *MOSS includes two KPI Web parts by default.*

If you want to display KPIs that you've created as part of an SSAS cube, then you must upload a data connection to the SSAS database to the Data Connections Library as a first step. The next step is to put the page where the KPI Web part is displayed into edit mode, click the drop-down list on the KPI Web part, and then click Indicator from SQL Server 2005 Analysis Services. That will take you to the configuration page in MOSS as shown in Figure 14-51.

You must select any KPIs you want to display from SSAS databases one at a time. You can add as many KPIs as you want to a single KPI Web part. If the KPI has a nested value, end users will be able to drill down into the detail as shown in Figure 14-52.

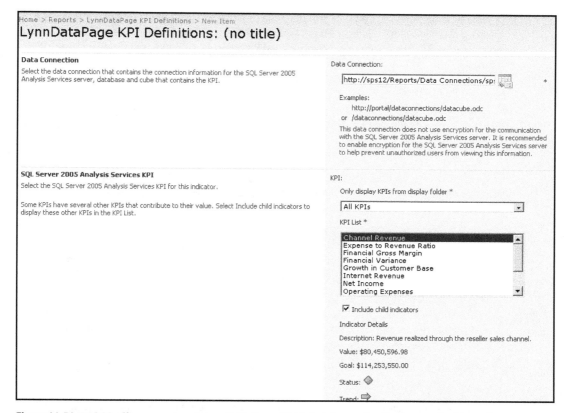

Figure 14-51. *MOSS allows you to retrieve KPIs from SSAS databases for display on dashboard pages.*

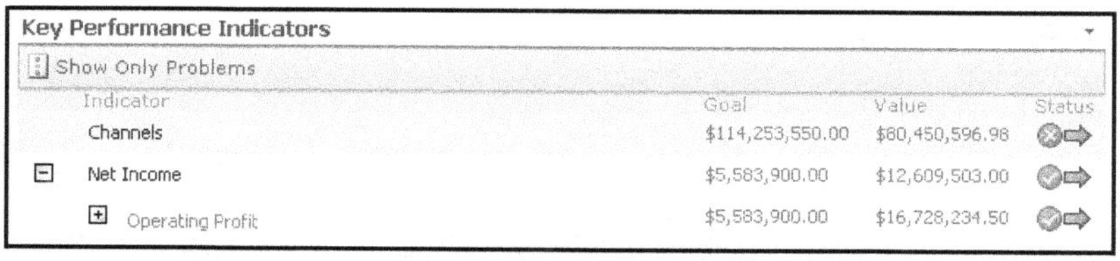

Key Performance Indicators			
Show Only Problems			
Indicator	Goal	Value	Status
Channels	$114,253,550.00	$80,450,596.98	
⊟ Net Income	$5,583,900.00	$12,609,503.00	
⊞ Operating Profit	$5,583,900.00	$16,728,234.50	

Figure 14-52. *MOSS displays SSAS KPIs, including drill-down paths, by default.*

Using the SSRS Report Center and Reporting Web Parts

MOSS includes a new section called Reports or Report Center. This is a centralized location designed to display many types of business data. In this group of MOSS pages, you'll find the Data Connections page, as well as a number of other pages related to displaying information about reports, such as a Reporting Calendar page.

The type of page that you will probably use most often is called a dashboard. This page type contains several BI-related Web parts, such as KPI and Excel Services viewers, by default, and you can easily pick from the other installed Web parts to further customize your particular dashboard.

If you want to display SSRS reports that you've created using SSAS cubes as a data source, then you'll need to download and install the SSRS Web part for MOSS. This Web part is called the ReportViewer, and it allows you to display any report available in SSRS. As of this writing, this download is available in CTP release.

Note To download the SSRS Web parts for MOSS (they are part of the SQL Server 2005 Feature Pack), visit http://www.microsoft.com/downloads/details.aspx?familyid=50B97994-8453-4998-8226-FA42EC403D17&displaylang=en.

When you download and install the SSRS Web parts, some additional functionality is made available to you, including the following features:

- The ability to synchronize the MOSS and SSRS (metadata) databases and a synchronization and configuration tool for SSRS and MOSS integration. This mode of operation is called SharePoint Integrated. In this mode, SSRS is now hosted within and running on top of MOSS, not IIS.

- The ability to use a new type of shared data source (.rsds file type) and to store this data source in a MOSS library.

- The ability to allow MOSS permissions to control access to SSRS operations and the ability to manage permissions using MOSS Web pages.

- The ability to deliver reports to MOSS libraries by implementing an included new delivery extension.

- The ability to add report models to a MOSS library and to use those models as sources in Report Builder.

Note The ReportExplorer Web part that was available for SPS 2003 will not be made available for MOSS because the Report Library in MOSS supersedes the previous functionality.

MOSS Business Data Catalog (BDC)

As part of your BI solution, you may need to directly connect to external data sources and to display and query that data in the MOSS environment. The Business Data Catalog (BDC) is a component that lets you expose data from your line of business systems through a MOSS portal as if it were native SharePoint data. The MOSS BDC allows you to establish these types of connections quickly and easily. Common targets for these types of connections to external data sources could include SAP, Siebel, and so on.

As with Excel Services, to work with the BDC, you must first configure it. You do this by accessing your MOSS administrative site, and then navigating to the particular SSP. Once there, you'll have five different pages to work with. Figure 14-53 shows this list.

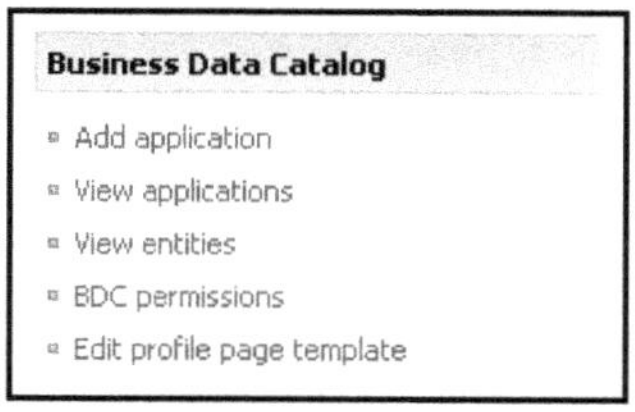

Business Data Catalog

- Add application
- View applications
- View entities
- BDC permissions
- Edit profile page template

Figure 14-53. *To use the BDC, you first configure it in the MOSS Web site, SSP area.*

The first step is to associate an Application Definition File (ADF) with this SSP. An ADF is a specialized type of XML file. You can also view the associated applications (and their contained entities) by using this interface.

Tip If you want to "try out" the BDC functionality, you can use a sample ADF available in the MOSS SDK. Be sure to set the connection string value to the correct server name before you deploy the sample to your MOSS server.

When you work with BDC information, you must also configure appropriate permissions. You do this in the same area that we've been working in already. The type of permissions you have to select from are shown in Figure 14-54.

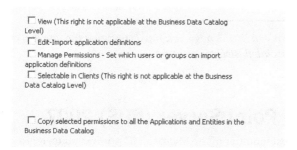

☐ View (This right is not applicable at the Business Data Catalog Level)

☐ Edit-Import application definitions

☐ Manage Permissions - Set which users or groups can import application definitions

☐ Selectable in Clients (This right is not applicable at the Business Data Catalog Level)

☐ Copy selected permissions to all the Applications and Entities in the Business Data Catalog

Figure 14-54. *To use the BDC, you must also configure appropriate permissions for BDC applications. You do this in the MOSS Web site, SSP area.*

Many included Web parts allow you to work with BDC data. The default installation of MOSS includes the following BDC Web parts: Business Data Actions, Business Data Item, Business Data Item Builder, Business Data List, and Business Data Related List (see Figure 14-55).

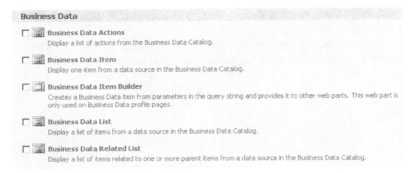

Figure 14-55. *MOSS includes five Business Data Web parts by default.*

Adding these Web parts after you've added one or more ADF files to the BDC allows you to view and take actions on the data. You can also configure SSO (single-sign-on) for connections to data using the BDC. Figure 14-56 shows these Web parts displayed on a MOSS dashboard page.

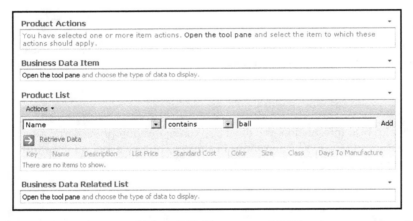

Figure 14-56. *After you add the BDC Web parts to a MOSS page, you must configure the particular data you want to see displayed from the associated BDC applications.*

Exploring Performance Point Server (PPS) 2007

Performance Point Server 2007 is the newest member of the Microsoft BI product suite. It is a new server product that integrates with MOSS and includes the functionality of both Business Scorecard Manager and ProClarity. Microsoft acquired ProClarity in 2006. ProClarity is a specialized OLAP client with many powerful features designed for use by analysts and power users. Two of the most interesting features of ProClarity are its support for direct MDX queries to your SSAS cubes and its visual Decomposition Tree. This graphical tree view allows users to see and understand the parts of data that make up the rolled-up results.

In early previews of PPS, Microsoft has demonstrated some interesting functionality, combining the powerful features of ProClarity with advanced features of SSAS. Particularly compelling is the integration of Decomposition Tree with SSAS's drillthrough feature. Drillthrough was enabled for authorized end users who clicked on a particular node of the visual tree.

PPS is more than ProClarity however. The vision for the product is to create an "all up" view of enterprise data using templated and easily configurable dashboards and scorecards. Microsoft is targeting this product toward fixing a common pain point for businesses, that is, the challenge of the wasted time within businesses as users attempt to standardize data and key business metrics.

Microsoft's plan for PPS is to accomplish the goal by allowing you to use PPS to create business-specific definitions for key metrics across the organization. You can use these metrics for analysis, reporting, planning, budgeting, and forecasting. A point of differentiation between the Report Center in MOSS and PPS is that PPS includes tools to help businesses look forward (or forecast), rather than just review past results.

This is implemented in PPS using the Business Modeler. The Business Modeler includes the ability for business managers to directly input business rules using language that they work with every day.

PPS also includes a high level of synchronization with other Microsoft products. Results can be delivered to MOSS, Outlook, or Excel 2007: `http://office.microsoft.com/en-us/performancepoint/FX101680481033.aspx`.

Summary

We covered the enhancements to Excel 2007, including pivot table and chart UI improvements. We then spent a good portion of this chapter reviewing Excel's data mining client functionality. Next we covered the integration between SSAS and MOSS. This included the new Report Center, reporting Web parts, KPI support, and data connection support. In the last section, you learned about Performance Point Server.

Caution At the time of this writing, the version of all of these products was CTP. By the time this book is published (April 2007), all of these products (with the exception of Performance Point Server) will be in final Release to Manufacturing (RTM) versions. There may be differences between the information discussed here and the final products.

Conclusion

We've come a long way, and you're ready to begin implementing BI solutions. I wish you the best of luck and much success. Although this is my first technical book, I'll end this with the same message that I've ended every technical class that I've taught over the past eight years—I truly enjoy working with technical professionals and love to hear from them. If you have questions, comments, or corrections about this book, please e-mail me at `Lynn@WebFluent.com`.

Index

GPSR Compliance
The European Union's (EU) General Product Safety Regulation (GPSR) is a set
of rules that requires consumer products to be safe and our obligations to
ensure this.

If you have any concerns about our products, you can contact us on

ProductSafety@springernature.com

In case Publisher is established outside the EU, the EU authorized
representative is:

Springer Nature Customer Service Center GmbH
Europaplatz 3
69115 Heidelberg, Germany